Biology Bias

Biology Bias

The Real Reasons Behind Our Decisions

Gill Merrill

BEP
BUSINESS EXPERT PRESS
Leader in applied, concise business books

First published in 2025 by
Business Expert Press, LLC
222 East 46th Street, New York, NY 10017
www.businessexpertpress.com

ISBN-13: 978-1-63742-806-1 (paperback)
ISBN-13: 978-1-63742-807-8 (e-book)

Business Expert Press Marketing Collection

First edition: 2025

10 9 8 7 6 5 4 3 2 1

EU SAFETY REPRESENTATIVE
Mare Nostrum Group B.V.
Mauritskade 21D
1091 GC Amsterdam
The Netherlands
gpsr@mare-nostrum.co.uk

To my parents, Helena and Juarez, who instilled in me the passion for lifelong learning and whose lives were tragically cut short by the Covid-19 pandemic in 2021. To all my family and friends, for always being there. To Keeley, for your unwavering love, support, and everlasting belief in me. And to Théo, the most precious gift of my life.

Description

Biology Bias gives a comprehensive understanding of the biological and psychological factors that influence our choices through the lenses of evolutionary psychology and consumer neuroscience.

Readers will gain valuable insights into the hidden impulses that shape their decisions and learn how to apply this knowledge to improve marketing and business strategies. It's a must-read for marketing practitioners looking to enhance their knowledge of consumer behavior, business leaders seeking a 360° perspective on human behavior to create more effective organizations, and educators and students interested in cutting-edge research in marketing and psychology.

Written by professor and researcher, **Gill Merrill**, this book uncovers cognitive, unconscious, and biological biases and forces that challenge and contradict rational thinking within the decision-making process.

Understanding the true drivers of consumer behavior is crucial to improving campaign performance. *Biology Bias* **offers readers the tools and knowledge they need to accurately interpret consumer reactions, develop high-performance campaigns, and have a competitive edge.**

Contents

Preface

Why do we make decisions that aren't always beneficial to ourselves or society? Why do we consume, vote for certain political candidates, or choose our romantic partners and friends? Are we simply following cultural norms, or do we exercise free will?

This book is for marketing practitioners familiar with current marketing approaches but who recognize that established theories and models often fall short in explaining consumer behavior. It aims to complement, not replace, existing marketing theories by proposing an integrated method to better understand consumers and develop more effective marketing strategies.

The book offers insights, practical knowledge, and a clear path to leverage *Evolutionary Marketing*. This cutting-edge discipline combines evolutionary principles with *Consumer Neuroscience*, using **biosensors** to study consumer motivation, preferences, behavior, and decision-making processes.

For business leaders in fields such as education, politics, human resources, and marketing, understanding human behavior from a 360° perspective is crucial for creating better societies and organizations. For marketing professionals, it means gaining and sustaining a competitive advantage, especially considering that 80 percent of all product launches fail, particularly in fast-moving consumer goods (FMCG). This high failure rate is partly due to surveys and focus groups not fully uncovering consumers' true preferences, often driven by unconscious and biological biases. The research in this book draws from *evolutionary biology, evolutionary psychology,* and *consumer neuroscience* to make this knowledge accessible and practical. By combining various theories, professionals can better interpret their target audiences' reactions and develop realistic, inclusive, high-performance campaigns, diverse teams, and a fairer society.

Acknowledgments

I would like to express my deepest gratitude to the following individuals who have been instrumental in my PhD journey: Dr. Michael Flavin, King's College London (UK): Your guidance and expertise have been invaluable throughout my research. Dr. Carmine Basile, Cranfield School of Management (UK): Thank you for your insightful feedback and continuous support. Prof. Dr. Svetlana Khapova, Organisational Behaviour and Leadership at Vrije Universiteit (NL): Your mentorship has profoundly shaped my academic and professional growth. Dr. Kobe Millet, Vrije Universiteit (NL): I am grateful for your encouragement and the knowledge you have shared with me and for introducing me to evolutionary biology and evolutionary psychology. Kiara Heide, iMotions (DK): Your technical support on biometrics and assistance has been crucial to my research. Prof. Dr. Marcel Bastiaansen, Tilburg School of Social and Behavioral Sciences (NL): Thank you for your valuable insights on consumer neuroscience. Dr. Ondrej Mitas, The Experience Lab at Breda University of Applied Sciences (NL): Your expertise and guidance have greatly contributed to my work. Theo van Iperen, Managing Partner, Giotto Management Consultants (NL): Thank you for believing in the application of my research into the business context. Dr. Edwin Weesie, Finance Economic Innovation, Utrecht University of Applied Sciences: I appreciate your constructive feedback and support. Prof. Dr. Samuele Murtinu, International Business and Entrepreneurship at the Utrecht University School of Economics: Your mentorship and advice have been and remain instrumental in my research.

PART 1

Consumer Neuroscience

CHAPTER 1

What Is Evolutionary Marketing?

Learning Objectives[1]—By reading this chapter, readers will be able to:
• Recognize some key developments within Marketing and Consumer Behavior in the 20th and 21st Centuries. • Define some of the main reasons that led advertisers to focus on consumers' affective and not only on cognitive needs. • Explain how hormones and innate biological impulses can affect human behavior. • Gain foundational knowledge of Evolutionary Psychology and its influence on Evolutionary Marketing. • Analyze if and why marketing practitioners would benefit from having a greater understanding and connection with the natural sciences.

The marketing discipline started in the early part of the 20th century as a by-product of the field of economic science. At that point, economics believed that price was the main determinant of demand levels for products and services. But as the 21st century has taught us, price may indeed play a role in influencing demand, but in many cases, it is not the core influencer of demand, even in the case of undifferentiated goods, that is, commodities such as fruit, vegetables, and so on. Nowadays, marketing professionals learn about the 11 Ps of marketing—*product, price, place, promotion, people, processes, physical evidence, personal relationships, packaging, positioning, and performance.* The marketing discipline took off when it realized that it appeals to consumers' *inner feelings* and *emotional needs,* not only their rationality.

In New York in the 1950s, advertisers began to create an emotional connection between consumers and a product or service, which were no longer sold based on need, following theories from "the father of Public Relations," and Sigmund Freud's nephew, Edward Bernays, who linked mass-produced goods with people's unconscious desires. Freud believed that people were led by dangerous instinctive drives and inner feelings of sexual and aggressive forces with origins in human's animal past. This knowledge helped advertisers promote their client's products by playing to people's irrational emotions, not based on factual information. How else can we explain the purchase of a $100K Hummer that only makes about 3.5 kilometers per liter when fuel prices never stop rising? Hummers were very popular through the noughties due to their oversized design and military background (particularly in celebrity-packed Hollywood), but were discontinued in 2010 by General Motors thanks to the global financial recession in 2008, which led fuel prices to skyrocket. Hummers made a comeback in 2022 as an all-electric sub brand of GMC, and some may not consider it a good buy due to the expensive price tag of $110K and the limited towing and payload capacities. Yet, this disadvantage did not stop Hummer's enthusiasts from paying a whopping $2.5 million in an auction in 2021 for the first 2022 Hummer EV pickup.

The Hummer advertisements are a typical example of a product positioned to appeal to men's inner drive for *dominance* using a paramilitary machismo in its copy. A 2008 study, conducted by the San Francisco-based research firm Quality Planning, which provides statistical information to insurance companies to enable them to determine rates, found that drivers of Hummer H2s and H3s received 4.63 times more traffic tickets than smaller vehicles. Some of the reasons speculated to have caused such behavior could have been because Hummer drivers allegedly feel like kings of the road because of their elevated driving position, which may cause them to violate the law.[2]

This internal need for dominance is mostly found in men (and showcased in sports events, business, the military, politics, gangs, jails, and other walks of life), supported by a growing body of evidence in both humans and animals suggesting that testosterone is a driver of such dominant behavior with a set of psychological and neurochemical processes that are modulated by testosterone and are relevant within social status hierarchies. Testosterone is the main sex hormone found in men and controls male physical features. Women also have testosterone in their bodies but in much smaller amounts than men. Testosterone is responsible for bringing about puberty and its physical changes, as well as the ability to produce sperm and offspring, and also present dominant behavior. Testosterone is a key influencer in such processes as it allows a low fearfulness, high-stress resilience, and a high motivation to acquire and maintain a high-status position, which requires the anticipation of social threats and aversive events to one's high status.

In human behavior, testosterone underlies the aspiration for, the defense and attainment of even higher social and economic status.[3] Basal testosterone could also play a role in acquiring leadership positions through the means of dominant and authoritarian behavior.[4]

From the perspective of evolutionary psychology (EP), conspicuous consumption also serves as a *costly signal* of one's display of wealth, thus demonstrating the individual's status within a social hierarchy.[5] With the growing research and evidence on the topic of hormonal influence on consumer behavior, marketers may continue to use well-established tools such as the VALS Survey[6] (Values and Lifestyles) and Hofstede's cultural dimensions[7] in combination with EP's theories, which may offer explanations of an individual's inner drives.

If marketers focused on Darwin's theories[8] and the connection between hormones and biological impulses on human behavior, their efforts would be more fruitful. Luckily, in recent years, we have witnessed a growing number of academic papers that investigate the links between consumption acts and their Darwinian roots[9]: survival, reproduction, kin selection, and reciprocal altruism. To understand, map out, and predict human behavior, marketing professionals need a discipline that is grounded in firm science, as in the case of evolutionary biology and EP, disciplines that the new and cutting-edge field of evolutionary marketing derives from.

Key Takeaways

1. **Evolution of Marketing**: Marketing originated from economic science in the early 20th century, initially focusing on price as the main determinant of demand.

2. **Shift in Focus**: Over time, marketing evolved to address consumers' emotional and irrational needs, influenced by theories from Edward Bernays and Sigmund Freud.

3. **The 11 Ps of Marketing**: Modern marketing encompasses a broader scope, including product, price, place, promotion, people, processes, physical evidence, personal relationships, packaging, positioning, and performance.

4. **Emotional Appeal**: Advertisers in the 1950s began creating emotional connections with consumers, moving beyond rational appeals to tap into unconscious desires.

5. **Testosterone and Dominance**: The text highlights the role of testosterone in driving dominant behavior, which marketers can leverage to appeal to consumers' inner drives for status and power.

6. **Conspicuous Consumption**: Evolutionary psychology (EP) suggests that conspicuous consumption serves as a costly signal of wealth and status within social hierarchies.

7. **Integration with Natural Sciences**: The chapter advocates for integrating evolutionary biology and psychology into marketing to better understand and predict consumer behavior.

CHAPTER 2

Why We Need Consumer Neuroscience

Learning Objectives[1]—By the end of this chapter, readers will be able to:
• Describe the theoretical background of neuromarketing and its evolution to consumer neuroscience.
• Identify the main neurophysiological tools used in consumer neuroscience research.
• Explain why traditional methods of consumer behavior research and segmentation approaches can lead to misconceptions and product failures.
• Determine some of the innate human behaviors derived from evolution and the evolutionary mismatch hypothesis.
• Expand the foundational knowledge of the biological and psychological drives of consumer behavior.

This chapter presents the theoretical background of consumer neuroscience and explains why traditional methods of consumer behavior research and segmentation approaches that only take personality and culture into account lead to misconceptions and product failures. The chapter also guides marketers and the foundational knowledge of the biological and psychological drives of consumer behavior.

For over a decade, *consumer neuroscience* has been used by a small percentage of innovative organizations of different sizes and industries to inform marketers on key aspects of consumer behavior and support strategic choices related to the consumer decision-making process, preference, interest, and motivation regarding new product development, pricing, branded materials, advertisement, and more. Although used interchangeably within the marketing literature, consumer neuroscience is focused on academic research between the neuroscience, psychology, and marketing disciplines with rigorous research methods that are used to inform theory, whereas the term *neuromarketing* refers to the specific use of neurophysiological tools[2] such as electrodermal activity (EDA), galvanic skin response (GSR), electroencephalography (EEG), eye tracking (ET; screen-based, glasses, virtual reality [VR] goggles), electrocardiogram (ECG/German spelling: Elektrokardiogramm—EKG), plethysmography (PPG), electromyography (EMG), facial electromyography (fEMG), facial expression analysis (FEA), functional magnetic resonance imaging (fMRI), and respiration line length (RLL).

In 2021, almost all Fortune 500 companies used focus groups as part of their overall marketing and branding strategy, as well as for public relations, image management, product development, and testing, leading to a whopping $4.6 billion (£3.27 billion), global spend in 2012 according to Esomar, a global market-research association.[3] Yet, in competitive industries such as fast-moving consumer goods (FMCG), between 80 and 85 percent of all products fail.[4] One of the reasons for product failures is that focus groups alone do not go far enough in uncovering consumer preferences, as exemplified in epic product launch failures such as the new Coke in 1985,[5] which, despite consumers' positive feedback for the new Cola flavor, still attracted brand boycotts, and even protests after the launch.

A counter-example of how why not to trust what consumers say in focus groups happened in 2008, when Frito-Lay (part of Pepsi-Co) approached NeuroFocus (part of Nielsen) market research agency to devise a plan to promote and sell its cheese-flavored snack, Cheetos.[6] Frito-Lay and NeuroFocus tested out a commercial that emphasized Cheetos's orange sticky dust in which a woman pranks another woman in a laundromat by putting Cheetos in her white clothes, highlighting the brand's mischievous positioning. When watching the advert, the focus group's participants said they did not like the prank and found it unkind as it broke social norms; however, electroencephalogram (EEG) tests conducted by NeuroFocus on participants demonstrated that their brain activity suggested women loved the advert and Frito-Lay decided to air it. In addition to enabling the commercial success of Cheetos, NeuroFocus later also earned the Grand Ogilvy Award[7] for advertising research given out by the Advertising Research Foundation. Had this advert been shown to a focus group a few decades before the advent of the field of neuromarketing, it would have most likely achieved a negative outcome.

Traditional theories, such as personality psychology and cultural studies, have been widely used by marketing professionals throughout the decades to create clusters in which the characteristics of customers could be combined for ease of understanding regarding customer preference, particularly when creating new products, segmenting the market, entering new foreign markets, and deciding whether to standardize or customize campaigns. Personality psychology (the widest division of psychology) encompasses well-known theories such as the theory of self-actualization[8] that aims at explaining human motivation via five core levels of needs (physiological needs, safety needs, love and belonging, esteem, and self-actualization); the search for status and intimacy[9]; innate instincts that motivate sex and aggression,[10] striving for superiority, and realizing their full potential.[11]

Being primarily concerned with individual differences, personality psychology has aimed at understanding the origins of human characteristics, the most important ways in which individuals differ, the psychological and physiological correlation between individualities, and the consequences of such divergence for life stages, social interactions, well-being, and psychopathology. Hence, personality psychology focuses mostly on the origins and causes of human diversity, which cannot be explained without theories of EP, which is a core theory behind consumer neuroscience as it measures the psychophysiological responses to stimuli and aims to understand the reasons why evolution would have favored such autonomic responses.[12]

Culture has also been used to explain individual differences and has been defined by Franz Boas (1858–1942),[13] as the arts, beliefs, transmitted behavior patterns, institutions, and other products of human thought and work, and that all ethnic groups are equipped with the same basic mental abilities, despite differences within each ethnic group. Yet, culture alone does not explain specific properties of the mind.[14]

However, as in the case of personality psychology, culture also cannot be used as a sole cause of individual differences either[15] because in recent years, behavioral genetic studies have found reliable evidence of heritability for personality dispositions.[16] On the other hand, EP has been primarily centered on species-typical psychological mechanisms and their raw material in which natural selection operates, and not as much on individual differences. This poses a challenge for evolutionary psychologists[17] considering that individual differences, especially the heritable types, are often ignored as they are perceived as of secondary importance to evolutionary psychologists by being thought to originate through non-selection forces such as random mutation, also seen as genetic "noise" or "junk."[18]

Influenced by theories from earlier centuries, marketing scholars' beliefs that behaviors are socially learned[19] and are shaped by culture and socialization, they follow the *blank slate theory*,[20] the *Skinnerian reinforcement*, and *Pavlovian's conditioning*, which still influence the *Standard Social Science Model* (*SSSM*) taught in the curriculum of some of the world's top business schools, most of which do not include EP in their curriculum.[21] Perhaps, this is because only 52 percent of the U.S. population[22] agree that *evolution is the best explanation for the origins of human life on earth*, compared with 98 percent of scientists.[23] Across religious groups, the highest acceptance percentages are Buddhists 81 percent, and the lowest are Jehovah's Witnesses 8 percent.[24]

The percentage of acceptance of the Darwinian evolutionary theory also varies greatly in the United States depending on the State, with Alabama, Mississippi, and Tennessee occupying the lowest positions at 18 percent, while Maine and Massachusetts take up the highest positions at 49 percent across all 50 U.S. states.[25] Political affiliation also plays a role, with 83 percent of liberal Democrats recognizing evolution, in comparison to only 34 percent of conservative Republicans.[26] In other developed nations, the recognition of the evolutionary concept stood at 71 percent in Russia, 72 percent in Australia, 73 percent in the United Kingdom, 74 percent in Taiwan, 75 percent in Italy, 77 percent in Canada and in the Netherlands, 81 percent in France and Germany, 82 percent in the Czech Republic, 85 percent in Sweden, 87 percent in Spain, and 88 percent in Japan.[27] Hence, the influence of EP within marketing has been limited and is still a nascent field with many opportunities to be explored as the basis of the use of consumer neuroscience research.

Across one hundred years, the marketing discipline has evolved from production, product, sales, marketing orientation, and mass customization to contemporary societal marketing. Throughout its evolution, marketing scholars developed a multitude of theories and two matrices to enable its development. Yet, the Darwinian framework of natural selection, which included variation, inheritance, and differential reproductive success,[28] has been disfavored within the marketing discipline, perhaps due to the simplicity of the theory of evolution, which may have caused misunderstandings[29] that led to the avoidance of it by the social sciences that prefer to use culture, socialization, learning, rationality, and consciousness, and, curiously, not evolutionary biology, to explain human behavior.[30] To bridge this gap between the natural sciences (biological) and the social sciences (behavior), let's first address some of the misconceptions of the Darwinian theory. The first misconception of the Darwinian theory was related to *genetic determinism* and the idea that behavior was exclusively determined by genes with hardly any influence from environmental factors. Yet, the evolutionary theory states that human behavior requires environmental input that in turn enables evolved adaptations.[31]

Another misconception is the notion that evolutionary theory entails that human behavior is immune to change.[32] There is also a perception that our current biology is based on an optimal design, yet evolutionary change happens over time and very slowly during thousands of generations based on the necessities of previous environments, which when compared to the present times, may lead to an evolutionary *mismatch*.[33] The *evolutionary mismatch hypothesis* argues that human psychological mechanisms are adaptations that emerge to process environmental inputs and then turn them into behavioral outputs that, on average, enhance the chances of survival or reproductive success.[34] The *mismatch hypothesis also* refers to the *adaptive lag* that happens if the environment that existed when a mechanism evolved changes more rapidly than the time necessary for the mechanism to adapt to the change.[35] This happens, for example, in our preference for sugar and fat, which is based on a previous situation of scarce food resources,[36] but that in today's more abundant environment can lead to heart attacks and type 2 diabetes.[37]

Another example of the needs that have arisen in our primal past is the need that tribes and villages had for protection from outside invaders. Ethnographic research has shown that across various cultures, from the Mehinaku tribe in the Brazilian Amazon rainforest to groups such as the Wappo, Dakota, Miwok, and Natick in North America to the Aka Pygmies in Africa, the term *big man* is assigned not only to the physical stature but also correlates with how societies rank tall men higher in the social order in respect to their physical attributes.[38] This is the case among humans and other animals. In ancestral times, a man's physical strength could mean the protection and prosperity of his family and tribe or village, yet today, in more peaceful and prosperous economies, a man's height and strength should not be a factor that influences his achievements, but sadly it still does.

Tall men are perceived as more desirable as mates than shorter or men of average height[39] because of the *adaptive problem* faced by women regarding resource acquisition and protection. Women of different cultures unconsciously consider tall men as having better genes that would contribute to the good health of children, and they are also associated with high income and status.[40]

Natural selection continues to exert its effect even in contemporary times, as in the case of Dutchmen who are currently the tallest people in the world and have grown 20 cm in height in the last 150 years, from about 165 cm (based on records of men in the military) to an average of 182.5 cm, as research shows that across decades (1935–1967), women favored taller men as they are perceived to offer better health and reproductive output.[41] Men's height also positively influences their careers at present as taller men have more chances of being hired, promoted, earning higher salaries, and commanding more status and authority,[42] regardless of whether their physical strength is needed or not for the position. Taller men also have an unfair advantage over shorter men as the former is more likely to be elected for political positions with research showing that during presidential elections in the 20th century, the taller of the two candidates won in 83 percent of the instances.[43]

Taller men themselves believe that they are more qualified to become leaders and show greater interest than shorter men in pursuing leadership positions,[44] which then becomes a vicious cycle as people already perceive

them as qualified leaders. Perhaps, this biological feature and its consequence in being unfairly selected as awareness of this mismatch helps us
avoid tall, yet incompetent male leaders[45] and increase our preference for
shorter, yet competent men and women.

A tall stature is also a biomarker of physical dominance[46] as demonstrated by evolutionary psychologists Ulrich Mueller and Allan Mazur,[47]
who assessed the facial dominance of 434 cadets of the highly competitive West Point Military Academy, and found that men with dominant-
looking faces (a prominent chin, heavy brow ridges, and a muscular
face) obtained higher ranks at the military academy, to the detriment of
colleagues who did not display the same facial dominance feature.

Other studies showed that the *Dark Triad Personalities* (i.e., psychopathy, narcissism, and Machiavellianism) predict social dominance and it
is correlated with psychopathy. Psychopathy is a human trait that has
evolved in the *genetic pool*, rather than being selected out of the gene
pool, suggesting that it offers survival and reproductive advantages.[48] It
is estimated that the prevalence of psychopathy (characterized by a lack
of empathy and conscience, disagreeableness, cruelty, and a parasitic lifestyle[49]) in the general adult population is only 4.5 percent.[50] Psychopathy is three to four times higher among men than women[51] and male
psychopaths make up between 15 and 25 percent of the males incarcer-
ated in North American prisons.[52] But *not all psychopaths are in prison,
some are in the boardroom.*[53] The so-called corporate psychopaths are
subclinical psychopaths based in an organizational setting[54] and are dark
and toxic leaders,[55] who demonstrate abusive, tyrannical, and destructive
behavior. They harass, ridicule, and degrade their employees, tell lies and
deceive others, blame others for their mistakes, and are key influencers in
a decrease in employee work performance,[56] and drive them to become
less committed and leave the organization.[57]

Sadly, research has suggested that psychopathy can become an advantage to individuals who display psychopathic traits,[58] as they are given
more opportunities to ascend to the top of their organizations,[59] as the
prevalence of psychopathic leaders in the corporate world ranges between
3 and 21 percent.[60] Corporate psychopaths tend to be bold, socially
dominant, fearless, risk-takers, and show low-stress reactivity,[61] qualities that are sought after in leaders, yet often coexist with psychopathic

tendencies.[62] This could be yet another *evolutionary mismatch* between what was perceived as good qualities of leaders in the remote past and what is required in the modern age, which might explain why organizations generally do not implement preinterview tests such as the Triarchic Psychopathy Measure[63] (TriPM) to protect employees from psychopathic leaders.

The same blind spot can be found within the consumer behavior and market research fields, as biological and evolutionary traits are often not considered as important for product development, advert creation, customer journey development, and many other opportunities to explore the potential of consumer neuroscience enabling marketing to become more of a science than an art. In the last decades, the marketing and consumer behavior disciplines became more of a science and have introduced data analytics tools to track the online presence and digital prints of consumers, created sophisticated sentiment analysis algorithms, developed personas and attribution models to best understand the perfect mix of online channels (e.g., online display, social media adverts, TV, podcasts, sponsorships, radio, events) focusing on the *online* actions of consumers (e.g., what they have searched for and which display advert they saw), and deciding which action the marketing team should take in response (e.g., which message consumers should see next, how much of the marketing budget should be invested in a paid search advert for specific customers, which emails to send them, which landing pages to give them); however, despite all this technology, return on marketing investments (ROMI) remains a challenge.[64]

New high-tech marketing tools are introduced every year, but consumer behavior also advances in response to marketing efforts. In recent decades, advertising evolved along with the internet and digitalization of commerce.[65] Traditional marketing campaigns switched to digital media channels (e.g., social media platforms) due to advantages such as the traceability of consumer engagement, learning about consumers' positive or negative reactions toward products and services through sentiment analysis tools, and the possibility of mass customization of content through personalized advertising,[66] which became a key part of marketing strategies.[67] Most marketing teams nowadays want to know everything there is to know about their target consumers and everything that their target audience has been exposed to online, which also explains the huge update in social media advertising, where it is possible to collect personal information regarding the consumers' interests, level of education, occupation, living arrangements, who their friends and communities are,[68] and much more. Personalized advertising has been preferential in marketing campaigns as they are perceived by companies as offering high customer value.[69]

Popular digital marketing tactics such as *retargeting* in which consumers are followed and presented with content related to products or services they have previously searched for or saw online but did not purchase[70] are made possible with customer information collected by *cookies* that save the consumers' browsing histories.[71] However, this level of personalization is increasingly perceived as an invasion of consumers' privacy, which in turn damages the value companies intended for this interaction.[72] Furthermore, consumers are outsmarting marketing teams and using online platforms to find pricing information, and later going to a physical store to obtain the best negotiation, try the product on, receive face-to-face service, and so on. With this in mind, organizations must aim to understand customers' *offline* behavior and what drives it in every stage of their lives, which may or may not become an online action, particularly when distrust is prevalent regarding how personal data is used by organizations, for example, who has access to it and for how long.[73] Hence, it is essential that organizations recognize the wholistic drivers of consumer behavior online and offline and how this behavior changes throughout their lives depending on which life phase they're in, based on the *fundamental motives* of human behavior,[74] which will be further explained in the upcoming chapters. With such knowledge, consumer behavior can be modeled without the need for online data to be collected.

Despite the ongoing global reach and financial success of online retailers such as the ecommerce giant Amazon, almost 90 percent of retail remains offline, in brick-and-mortar stores,[75] making it necessary for companies to base their decisions on offline and in situ behavior. In this way, by combining data about online and offline actions, organizations can reach the holy grail of marketing mix and attribution modeling.[76] Moreover, neuroscientific tools and methods can help consumer and marketing research understand why and how our biology shapes consumer behavior beyond the influence of personality and culture, a knowledge that will empower marketers to comprehend the *ultimate* drives behind consumer behavior that are shaped by the *fundamental motives* of *avoiding physical harm and disease, getting and keeping a mate, caring for family, obtaining status, and making friends.*[77]

These *fundamental motives* are activated in different cognitive and neural systems when cues of threats or opportunities associated with each motive arise.[78] In addition, steroid hormones also influence neural systems (internal bodily responses that help humans respond to the threats and opportunities posed by the *fundamental motives*) and consumer behavior is ingrained within this process.[79] Yet, this topic is hardly discussed or used by marketers in practice, perhaps due to the inaccessibility of this type of data, or due to a lack of understanding of these biological processes due to a lack of exposure to evolutionary biology or EP disciplines while obtaining their degrees. The last and probably the strongest argument against the Darwinian theories was its wrong association with Victorian-era capitalism: colonialism, classism, sexism, and racism.[80] However, it's necessary to differentiate the wrong associations with the value that these theories bring to the understanding of human behavior.

Sigmund Freud's theories that successfully influenced marketers and advertisers at the beginning of the 21st century, were based on Darwin's *theory of evolution* and explained from the psychoanalytical perspective of the *Id, Ego, and Superego.* These were the instinctual and life-preserving systems that included the need for air, food, water, shelter, fears of snakes, heights, and dangerous humans that served the function of survival. Freud also posed that the sexual instinct is another core human motivator. Furthermore, Freud's theories of sex and aggression influenced the branch of personality psychology,[1] along with Abraham Maslow's self-actualization, and Adler's theories that humans strive for superiority or status and intimacy.[81] However, many of Freud's theories became disfavored and discredited following empirical research decades later,[82] but perhaps his greatest contribution lies in drawing attention to the workings of the *unconscious.*

In *A General Introduction to Psychoanalysis,*[83] Freud suggested that unconscious disorders such as the *slip of the tongue,* and temporary memory loss in healthy people and his interpretation of dreams connected bodily and psychic functions. Freud addressed unconscious drives and disorders that the European Victorian society at the time found unpleasant and therefore branded them as *untrue*. Yet, Edward Bernays, Sigmund Freud's nephew and considered the "father of public relations," who emigrated with his family to the United States, used Freud's theories of the unconscious, first to support American politicians to understand human desires to control the masses in times of war,[84] and second by orchestrating the *engineering of consent*[85] in which corporations would understand individual and group behavior, their thoughts, and how they seek compensatory substitutes in products for desires that they have been obliged to suppress. Bernays taught politicians how to mold public opinion and advised brands not only to position a product for its intrinsic worth or usefulness but also to link products as symbols of something else, to a desire that consumers are ashamed to admit to themselves. He had also been influenced by Wilfred Trotter and his principles of herd instinct,[86] Graham Wallas's ideas of nature and nurture,[87] the father of modern journalism, Walter Lippmann who coined the term *stereotype*,[88] all principles that are still widely used in consumer segmentation, and Gustave Le Bon[89] for his studies on crowd psychology, its behavior, and its power of unity that menaces States and Sovereigns.

These theories were applied by Bernays and Madison Avenue's marketing agencies on advertisement campaigns as a stimulus to cause the desired reactions in individual consumers, and to exaggerate broad popular tendencies, rather than stimulate new ideas. Following the aftermath of World War II (WWII), the American economy experienced exponential growth and manufacturing had a primary focus on efficiency, mass production, and economies of scale. With consumer goods reaching most homes, there was an unsettling preoccupation from the American Government that consumers would simply stop buying once they had all they believed to be necessary. In the 1950s, the financial services firm, Lemann Brothers, became part of the movement that pushed American society into mass consumers. This was done with the support of Edward Bernays who also linked democracy and consumerism as two concepts that were inheritably intertwined, as per his "Democracity" exhibit at the 1939 New York World's Fair where he invited corporations to present the latest consumer products.

To address this national target, Bernays and other Viennese psychologists, such as Ernest Dichter, pioneered Freudian psychoanalytic techniques to uncover the consumers' unconscious demand for status, sexual attractiveness, and other motives[90] that they would be embarrassed to admit to themselves and others. Through psychoanalytic techniques such as free associations, Dichter created the first focus groups[91] at The Institute for Motivational Research Psychologists, where they did not ask consumers why they purchase products, but instead sought to "mine" their unconscious and understand their personalities, and self-image to unravel their real reasons for buying products, which the researchers believed to be rooted in their inner desires and feelings. Thanks to these techniques, companies such as Procter and Gamble, Chrysler, Esso/Exxon, and Mattel, Inc. (the toy company that launched the iconic Barbie doll) managed to tap into the unconscious motivations behind consumers buying behavior, which could be psychological, sexual, sociological, or a demand for recognition and status.

Another of Dichter's clients, the Betty Crocker company had a problem that it hoped "motivational research" or focus groups could help with as, although American housewives in the early 1950s liked the idea of a convenient cake mix, they weren't buying it. So Dichter and his team found that housewives felt guilty for not investing much time into making a cake from scratch and the solution was to require the addition of one egg to the cake mix, and from that point onward, the product became a success. Similar reports from different product categories such as dishwashers also faced a low consumer uptake even in 2021, as consumers from different ethnicities such as Brazil, India, China, Thailand, Romania, and Nigeria are examples of places with low penetration rates of dishwashers due to local gender norms of perceived female duties, and the wide availability of low wage maids who can perform these chores. Yet, instead of tackling long-held assumptions about the product and how it makes consumers *feel* (i.e., this product makes me feel guilty), dishwasher manufacturers including Bosch, Electrolux, and Whirlpool continued to advertise their dishwashers based on features and functionality such as color, internal space, finish, noise reduction, and energy efficiency, diagnostics and more, and not appealing as much to a consumer's need for cleanliness and hygiene. As successful as these manufacturers are, they still cannot stop their products from becoming mere commodities with this approach.

For these reasons, organizations, and marketing teams representing and aiming at creating unique brands must reconcile their relationship with life and natural sciences, and familiarize themselves with consumer neuroscience while also recognizing that, despite all sophisticated marketing tools and availability of data, human beings still have an animal essence and an animal mind, and as such, we are driven by our instincts more than by rationality. Instincts such as survival and procreation are two of the most latent drivers of behavior in our day-to-day lives, as much as we would like to pretend that we are not animals, and our consciousness and perception of the future do not make us less animal-like than other animals, it only makes us a different type of animal, but we remain instinctive beings.

Key Takeaways

1. **Importance of Consumer Neuroscience**: This chapter emphasizes the need for consumer neuroscience to address the limitations of traditional consumer behavior research methods that focus solely on personality and culture.

2. **Biological and Psychological Drives**: It provides foundational knowledge on the biological and psychological factors that drive consumer behavior.

3. **Innovative Applications**: Consumer neuroscience has been utilized by innovative organizations to inform strategic marketing decisions, enhancing understanding of consumer preferences, motivations, and decision-making processes.

4. **Neuromarketing Tools**: The chapter distinguishes between consumer neuroscience and neuromarketing, detailing various neurophysiological tools used to gather insights into consumer behavior.

5. **Limitations of Focus Groups**: Traditional focus groups often fail to uncover true consumer preferences, as demonstrated by historical product failures and successful neuromarketing case studies.

6. **Integration of Theories**: It highlights the integration of evolutionary psychology with consumer neuroscience to better explain

and predict consumer behavior, moving beyond the limitations of personality psychology and cultural studies.

7. **Political Influence on Evolution Acceptance**: Political affiliation significantly affects the acceptance of evolutionary theory, with higher recognition among liberal Democrats compared to conservative Republicans.

8. **Global Acceptance of Evolution**: Recognition of evolution varies across developed nations, with higher acceptance rates in countries such as Japan, Spain, and Sweden compared to the United States.

9. **EP in Marketing**: The influence of EP in marketing is still emerging, offering new opportunities for integrating consumer neuroscience research.

10. **Misconceptions of Darwinian Theory**: Common misconceptions about Darwinian theory, such as genetic determinism and the immutability of behavior, have hindered its acceptance in social sciences.

11. **Evolutionary Mismatch**: The concept of evolutionary mismatch explains how traits adapted for past environments can lead to maladaptive behaviors in modern contexts, such as preferences for sugar and fat.

12. **Height and Social Dominance**: Height is linked to social dominance and success, with taller individuals often perceived as more desirable and competent, influencing their social and professional opportunities.

13. **Psychopathy and Leadership**: Traits associated with psychopathy, such as dominance and lack of empathy, can sometimes provide advantages in leadership roles, despite their negative impact on organizational culture.

14. **Blind Spot in Marketing**: The fields of consumer behavior and market research often overlook biological and evolutionary traits, which could enhance product development, advertising, and customer journey development through consumer neuroscience.

15. **Evolution of Marketing**: Over the past decades, marketing has become more data-driven, utilizing tools such as data analytics, sentiment analysis, and attribution models to track and respond to online consumer behavior. Despite these advancements, achieving a high ROMI remains challenging.

16. **Digital Marketing**: The shift to digital media channels has allowed for better traceability of consumer engagement and personalized advertising. However, this personalization can sometimes be perceived as an invasion of privacy, potentially harming the intended value of the interaction.

17. **Consumer Behavior**: Consumers are increasingly savvy, using online platforms for research, but preferring to make purchases in physical stores. This highlights the need for organizations to understand both online and offline consumer behavior.

18. **Holistic Understanding**: It's crucial for organizations to recognize the holistic drivers of consumer behavior, which change throughout a person's life. This understanding can help model consumer behavior without relying solely on online data.

19. **Offline Retail**: Despite the success of online retailers, a significant portion of retail remains offline, necessitating decisions based on offline consumer behavior.

20. **Neuroscientific Insights**: Neuroscientific tools can help understand the biological underpinnings of consumer behavior, influenced by fundamental human motives such as avoiding harm, seeking mates, caring for family, obtaining status, and making friends.

21. **Historical Theories**: Theories from Freud and Darwin, despite their controversies and later discredited, have influenced marketing by highlighting unconscious drives and fundamental human motives.

22. **Privacy Concerns**: The collection of personal data for personalized advertising raises privacy concerns, which can damage consumer trust and the perceived value of marketing interactions.

23. **Integration of Data**: Combining online and offline data can help achieve a comprehensive understanding of consumer behavior, leading to more effective marketing strategies.

CHAPTER 3

Damasio and Descartes— Cognitive and Affective Decision Making

Learning Objectives—By reading this chapter, readers will be able to[1]:

- Distinguish between the rational thought theory[2] and the somatic marker hypothesis.[3]
- Come to see how recent studies within multiple domains show that cognition is subject to many types of biases.
- Connect the somatic marker hypothesis[4] to human behavior and attention.
- Explain the difference between emotions and feelings.
- Integrate cognitive and affective decision making in business-to-consumer (B2C) and business-to-business (B2B) marketing campaigns.

Cognition

Cartesian cognition and rational thought[5] is the belief that in the rational pursuit of knowledge and truth, one should doubt every belief derived from sensory reality. Yet, recent studies within cognitive sciences, behavior sciences, empirical psychology (heuristics and biases), neurobiology of emotions, evolutionary psychology, and computer science show that cognition is subject to many types of biases (see relevant chapter on Biases) and distortions. The *somatic marker hypothesis* proposed by neuroscientist Antonio Damasio[6] suggests that our feelings can, without words, through a cooperation between the brain and the body, decipher whether reality is conducive or not to our well-being from an evolutionary perspective, driving our attention to where it's needed the most, thus ensuring our survival, prosperity, and pleasure.[7]

I think, therefore I am (Je pense, donc je suis), the "first principle" of René Descartes's philosophy published in his 1637 *Discourse on the Method*,[8] argues that if an intelligent human being, someone able to form a thought, their existence was validated. Other sentient beings such as animals, for example, were considered by Descartes as "mechanisms," machines without minds or inner thoughts that operated automatically like watches. However, recent studies have shown that animals are not that different from us human apes. They too know who they are, they recognize their family, friends, and rivals. They compete for resources, a mate, and higher status within their group. They strive to survive through learned experiences, and they focus on having food, water, and shelter to raise their young, to ensure that their genes are passed on to the next generation. They communicate, love, play, sleep, get scared, build tools, devise strategies against predators, plan ahead of seasons, and much more. Increasing awareness that animals also experience emotions as humans is one of the motivating factors why 55 percent of vegans in the United Kingdom (about 600,000 people in 2018 and growing[9]) do not eat animal-based foods due to animal welfare concerns. Veganism is growing worldwide as societies are beginning to understand what Charles Darwin had already proposed in 1872 in his book *The Expression of the Emotions in Man and Animals*,[10] in which he argued that human and nonhuman animals demonstrate emotions through similar behaviors. In Darwin's view, emotions had an evolutionary history that could be traced across species and cultures, yet this was a very unpopular view during the Victorian Era in the United Kingdom, and it remains controversial in many parts of the world.

In his recent book, the Dutch biologist Frans de Waal describes the research conducted in a Netherlands zoo, which has led him to conclude that there are animal behaviors that express emotions that can be readable to outside observers that animals *feel*. In the book *Mama's Last Hug: Animal Emotions and What They Tell Us About Ourselves*,[11] de Waal observes that emotions and feelings should not be considered the same because emotions drive behavior (such as when we experience desire, anger, or fear) with accompanying facial and vocal expressions and have physical signs that allow them to be observed and therefore described, while feelings are internal subjective states known only to those who experience them.[12] Hence, the fact is not whether animals think, but whether human beings can tap into another animal's consciousness.

Descartes was not the only European philosopher to lead the West into erroneous ideas about the role of thinking and the role of emotions. The Greek philosopher Aristotle (384–322 BC) believed that women were irrational, weak (due to women's biology), passive, and imperfect for any activity other than those within the domestic sphere and those related to children bearers.[13] Unfortunately, this view still permeates many cultures and top corporations even in the world's most liberal countries to this date. For Aristotle, slavery was also a natural action as, in his view, human beings were divided into two types—slaves and nonslaves. But thankfully, despite the unfortunate lateness of this acknowledgment, people realized that slavery was made possible through racial attitudes, religious views, and military power (i.e., *dominance*), and not because slave traders had superior intelligence than those they enslaved. Thus, both Descartes and Aristotle might have suffered from an *in-group* and *gender bias*, which has been discovered (among at least 224 other biases) by renowned researchers in the 21st century.

Hence, just like artificial intelligence (AI), the way we think about cognition and affect is evolving with each passing decade as discoveries and technologies allow us to correct our past mistakes. AI is one of the most powerful technologies ever developed, and it's still undergoing multiple evolutions since its inception in the 1950s. The first generation of AI was *descriptive analytics*, which answers the question, *What happened?*, the second was *diagnostic analytics*, addressing such as *Why did it happen?*, the third and contemporary generation of AI is based on *predictive analytics*, which should answer the question: *Based on what has already happened, what could happen in the future?*[14] But what AI still lacks is one of the greatest strengths of human animals—*intuition* (i.e., the ability to simply know something without analytic reasoning), using the conscious and nonconscious parts of our minds, drawing from instincts, cognition, and experiences to draw quick conclusions and best case scenarios based on an *evolutionary algorithm*. In recent years, scientists found that intuition operates through the right side of our brain, the hippocampus, and through our guts (the digestive system that also has neurons). They also found that women's corpus callosum (the connective white matter that connects our left and right brain hemispheres) is thicker than men's, meaning that women have better and faster abilities to access both brain hemispheres, thus integrating emotions and gut feelings with the more logical left hemisphere into our decision making process.[15] Perhaps, this knowledge would have persuaded Aristotle and his peers to perceive women in a more positive light.

The predictive analytics of AI are helpful for data scientists and decision makers; however, it remains completely dependent on historical data, making data scientists helpless when faced with new and unknown scenarios. This is why it's necessary to create machines that can "think" on their own, particularly when facing unfamiliar situations, for them to be considered as possessing true "artificial intelligence." The new generation of AI will not only analyze the input data received from data scientists but also be able to express a "gut feeling" when something does not make sense, therefore mimicking human intuition. Hence, the third and current generation of AI is called "artificial intuition."

For the above-mentioned reasons, cognition and affective decision making should always be considered in combination when creating marketing campaigns to persuade consumers to behave in a certain way or to take a specific action. Campaigns aimed at persuading B2B customers, for instance, tend to be focused on cognition and rationality given that this type of customer usually buys through committees that include multiple decision makers involved in the process. However, the rational decision making process taught by business schools must be updated to encompass a more holistic view of human decision making as, like B2C audiences, B2B customers are also regular people, and as such, are influenced by the same emotions, feelings, and biases, and ethnocentrism as well as the physiological, mental, biological, and sociological process as highlighted in the following image. You cannot separate a person from a consumer. Both roles are intertwined.

Affect and Intuition

The quote by French philosopher, Blaise Pascal, "The heart has its reasons of which reason knows nothing"[16] is beginning to be more understood as

A Holistic View of Factor Influencing Buyer Behaviour

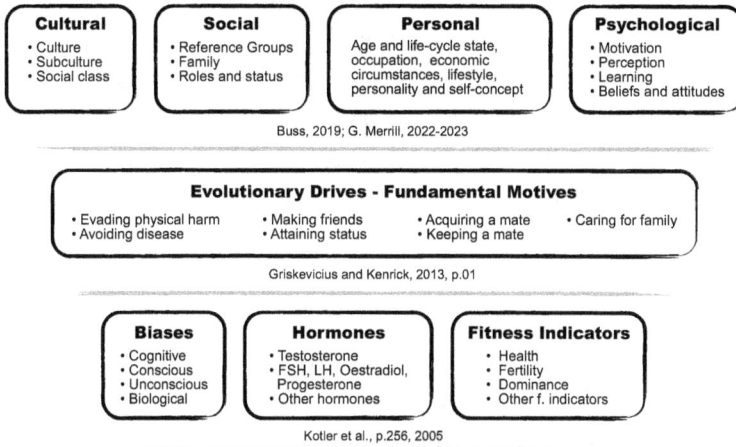

Cultural	Social	Personal	Psychological
• Culture • Subculture • Social class	• Reference Groups • Family • Roles and status	Age and life-cycle state, occupation, economic circumstances, lifestyle, personality and self-concept	• Motivation • Perception • Learning • Beliefs and attitudes

Buss, 2019; G. Merrill, 2022-2023

Evolutionary Drives - Fundamental Motives

• Evading physical harm • Avoiding disease	• Making friends • Attaining status	• Acquiring a mate • Keeping a mate	• Caring for family

Griskevicius and Kenrick, 2013, p.01

Biases	Hormones	Fitness Indicators
• Cognitive • Conscious • Unconscious • Biological	• Testosterone • FSH, LH, Oestradiol, Progesterone • Other hormones	• Health • Fertility • Dominance • Other f. indicators

Kotler et al., p.256, 2005

Figure 3.1 Factors influencing buyer behavior[17]

Illustrations by Roman, @ideahits.

scientists have found that there are neurons in the heart, hence its power over emotions is not only psychological but also physiological, connected by the vagus nerve that communicates emotions to the brain, a theory first developed by Charles Darwin's and further tested a century later.[18] Feeling-based choice, that is, consulting one's intuition or gut feelings when processing information during the decision making process[19] may lead to positive feelings as it's reinforced by the biological apparatus,[20] and may act as a reflection of the true self,[21] considered as the essence of the individual, where its real character and moral values reside.[22] Our feelings are believed to reflect our true selves and are also seen as stable[23] because we generally trust our reactions when using affect as information.[24]

Behavior

Business schools still teach theories such as the *theory of planned behavior (TPB)* introduced by the social psychologist Icek Ajzen in the 1980s,[25] which proposes that a person's decision to engage in certain behaviors (e.g., smoking, exercising) can be predicted based on the person's intention to engage in such behavior.[26] However, one major flaw with this theory is that it implies that human behavior is mostly based on reason, consciousness, and planning, and it does not consider the strong influence of emotions within the decision making process and its impact on behavior.

Contemporary humans are the descendants of successful ancestors who were able to control "the hostile forces of nature"[27] (e.g., extreme climate, harsh weather, food shortages, toxins, diseases, parasites, predators, and other hostile forces) as described by Charles Darwin. Hence, more relevant and timeless theories can be taken from the fields of EP and Evolutionary Biology. For instance, the "behavioral immune system," that is, adaptations that lead to unconscious behaviors and preferences enables humans to identify sources of biological danger posed by bacteria and viruses that could threaten human health. Evolutionary medicine (EM) or Darwinian Medicine became more popular since the 1990s[28] due to its value in understanding, preventing, and treating diseases,[29] as in the case of a more careful approach to prescribing antibiotics to reduce human resistance to bacteria[30] or the use of hormone replacement therapy in postmenopausal women.[31] In the same way, as humans have an evolved physiological immune system equipped to fight contagious diseases, the behavioral immune system focuses on preventing such infections from entering our bodies.[32] We do this automatically with the survival emotion of disgust,[33] which stops us from touching bad-smelling foods that look moldy or contaminated[34] and avoiding people who have poor hygiene, who look diseased or show broad wounds.[35] This is particularly the case of pregnant women who demonstrate a *"nesting behavior" and a tendency to* clean and organize their homes before their due date.[36]

Cognitive-Affective Processes

"Reason is the soul of all law" states the writings behind the Judge's bench in the United States Court of Appeals for the Tenth Circuit in the film *On the Basis of Sex*[37] based on true events about the life of Ruth Bader Ginsburg, the first Jewish woman and the second woman to serve as an associate justice of the Supreme Court of the United States, who fought for gender equality before the Law. But the irony is that reason (i.e., "consecutive logical thinking"[38]) was not the guiding principle of the Judges William Judson Holloway Jr., William Edward Doyle, and Fred Daugherty, but rather their emotions nurtured by cognitive, unconscious, and biological biases about the fixed gender roles that were the dominant thinking in the early 1970s. Yet, as best described in the film by Professor Freund, "Judges are bound by precedence, but they cannot ignore cultural change. A Court ought not to be affected by the day, but will be by the climate of the era."[39] Hence, reason also changes and evolves with what people are prepared to tolerate and uphold emotionally in any given era. The biological and instinctive drives of our ancestral past must always be fought in the present, as they do not evolve fast enough to catch up with the current environment in which in developed societies, equality between the genders, races, and people in general should be assured by the Law. Hence, inaccurate beliefs that human brains function "like a computer" must be debunked because brains, unlike computers, are subject to biases, emotional decision making, irrational problem-solving abilities, unreliable memory, and various visual illusions.[40] Our brains are in fact "survival machines," which have been enhanced by natural selection to enable our survival and reproduction.[41] Our inborn cognitive mechanisms and perceptual categories[42] are, therefore, information processing machines that curate the types of information that should be taken as input with the accompanied physiological activity to process it, and the behavioral outputs that it will produce,[43] which have been adapted to former environments.

Hormones and Decision Making

Since June 1905, when Professor Ernest Starling of University College London, UK, used the term *hormone* for the first time,[44] the focus on hormone-related research had spread across various fields such as epidemiology, molecular biology, and chemistry[45] and has enabled social change through advances in contraception and fertility (e.g., in vitro fertilization, IVF). And further exploration has facilitated the understanding of how hormones affect gender and racial differences in decision making.

In recent years, scholars have also put forward compelling findings that reveal how hormones shape the choices we make as decision makers and consumers.[46] Specifically, sex hormones such as estrogen and testosterone have an impact on both social and economic decisions. Socially, testosterone was found to increase the willingness to take risks,[47] also improving cognitive performance, coordination, and focus.[48] Financially, testosterone has influenced the male preference for sports cars (e.g., Porsches[49]), and wearable luxury goods, particularly when men were using a low-investment/short-term mating strategy.[50] Peak fertility, that is, when estrogen is high, it influences the female preference for sexy clothes[51] and appearance-related products.[52] Researchers and authors, including Griskevicius and Kenrick[53] and Saad,[54] have proposed that these physiological factors have their origins within the evolutionary drive that's been built to increase human *Darwinian fitness* and reproductive success.[55] So they suggest in fact that when we make a decision or choose a certain product, we do so subconsciously to increase our access to potential mates, resources, and social status.[56] Hence, possessing an understanding of how hormones affect decision making, professionals from the public and private sectors can create realistic and fairer policies and laws that take into account the multifaceted ways in which humans decide.

Key Takeaways

1. **Cartesian Cognition**: Descartes's philosophy emphasized doubting sensory reality in the pursuit of knowledge. However, modern studies show that cognition is influenced by biases and distortions.

2. **Somatic Marker Hypothesis**: Proposed by Antonio Damasio, this hypothesis suggests that our feelings, through brain–body cooperation, help us assess our well-being and guide our attention to ensure survival and prosperity.

3. **Animal Cognition and Emotions**: Contrary to Descartes's view of animals as mindless mechanisms, recent studies show that animals have complex behaviors and emotions similar to humans, influencing the rise of veganism due to animal welfare concerns.

4. **Evolutionary Perspective on Emotions**: Darwin proposed that emotions have an evolutionary history shared across species. This view, though controversial, is gaining acceptance.

5. **Frans de Waal's Research**: De Waal's work highlights that emotions drive observable behaviors in animals, while feelings are internal states. This distinction is crucial in understanding animal consciousness.

6. **Historical Biases**: Philosophers such as Descartes and Aristotle held biased views on cognition and emotions, influenced by gender and in-group biases. These biases have been challenged by modern research.

7. **Evolution of AI**: AI has evolved from descriptive to diagnostic to predictive analytics. However, AI lacks human intuition, which integrates instincts, cognition, and experiences for quick decision making.

8. **Intuition in Decision Making**: Intuition operates through the right brain, hippocampus, and gut. Women have a thicker corpus callosum, enabling better integration of emotions and logic in decision making.

9. **Artificial Intuition**: The next generation of AI aims to mimic human intuition, allowing machines to "think" and respond to unfamiliar situations, moving beyond reliance on historical data.

10. **Combination of Cognition and Affect**: Effective marketing campaigns should integrate both cognitive and affective decision making to persuade consumers. This is crucial for both B2B and B2C customers, as emotions and biases influence all human decisions.

11. **Holistic Decision Making**: The rational decision making process taught in business schools needs updating to include a more comprehensive view of human behavior, acknowledging the intertwined roles of cognition, emotions, and physiological processes.

12. **Affect and Intuition**: Emotions and intuition play significant roles in decision making. The heart, connected to the brain via the vagus nerve, influences emotions physiologically. Intuition, or gut feelings, often reflects our true selves and moral values.

13. **TPB**: While TPB suggests that behavior is based on intention, it overlooks the strong influence of emotions. EP and evolutionary

biology offer more relevant theories, such as the behavioral immune system, which helps humans avoid biological dangers.

14. **Cognitive-Affective Processes**: Human brains are not like computers; they are subject to biases, emotional decision making, and irrational problem solving. Our cognitive mechanisms are designed for survival and reproduction, shaped by natural selection.

15. **Hormones and Decision Making**: Hormones such as estrogen and testosterone significantly impact social and economic decisions. Testosterone increases risk-taking and influences preferences for luxury goods, while estrogen affects preferences during peak fertility.

16. **Evolutionary Drives**: Human behavior is influenced by evolutionary drives aimed at increasing Darwinian fitness and reproductive success. Understanding these drives can enhance marketing strategies.

17. **Cultural and Legal Evolution**: Reason and law evolve with cultural changes. Historical biases, such as those held by Descartes and Aristotle, must be challenged to ensure equality and fairness in modern societies.

PART 2

Human Universals and Biases

CHAPTER 4

The Traits We All Share and 225 Biases—Which Ones Do You Display?

Learning Objectives[1]—By reading this chapter, readers will be able to:

- Value the research conducted on the effect of biases on human behavior.
- Identify the connection between evolutionary drives and some of the biases we still see today.
- Understand others in terms of their innate behaviors and fundamental impulses.
- Be more interested in decision making and biases.
- Explain why it is necessary to decolonize AI.
- Decide to take the bias test and learn how to navigate it in contemporary life.
- Explain how mental adaptations in humans have evolved to the current *human universals*.[2]
- Contrast *human universals* with other established theories of personality and cultural stereotypes.
- Discern why the communist movement that influenced European writers in the 16th century did not succeed.
- Reflect on whether the *human universals* are present in your culture.
- Create, position, and promote products and services based on human universals.

Human universals are collections of psychological, cultural, societal, linguistic, and behavioral traits displayed by all cultures worldwide[3] and are the evidence of mental adaptations in the human species' evolutionary history.

These universal traits are helpful to the field of evolutionary marketing because they provide a more solid basis for which marketers can create, position, and promote their products and services than other models based on cultural stereotypes. Social structure and status differentiation, for example, are very important traits that drive the consumption of products that help an individual display these qualities, regardless of their nationality and background. To provide a specific example, let's consider the Communist movement that began to influence European writers in the 16th century, and gained strength by the mid-20th century in Europe's Eastern Bloc, and also in some Asian and South American nations, namely China, Cuba, Laos, and Vietnam.

The chapter "Bourgeois and Proletarians" *of* the classic book *The Communist Manifesto* by German philosophers Karl Marx and Friedrich Engels[4] starts by explaining that class struggles derived from the power conflicts between freeman and slave, patrician and plebeian, lord and serf, guild master and journeyman, or in other words—the oppressor and oppressed in opposite sides fighting for survival and dominance. The utopia of the founders of Communism, Marx and Engels, was that society would become more equal and fair once the State took control of private property and all resources, which would then belong to all citizens. Yet, over 174 years later, former countries of the Soviet Union (Russia, Ukraine, Georgia, Belorussia, Uzbekistan, Armenia, Azerbaijan, Kazakhstan, Kyrgyzstan, Moldova, Turkmenistan, Tajikistan, Latvia, Lithuania, and Estonia), Europe's Eastern Bloc (East Germany, Poland, Czechoslovakia, Hungary, Romania, Bulgaria, and Albania), China, and other Communist regimes collectively killed as many as 100 million people[5] under the leadership of authoritarian leaders such as Vladimir Lenin, Joseph Stalin, and Mao Zedong. Communist leaders had control to direct the production and distribution of virtually all the goods produced by these societies, leaving no incentive for people to strive for more in life. In these Communist countries, the concept of Democracy was not possible due to severe repression, violations of freedom of speech and religion, loss of property rights, and the criminalization of ordinary economic activity. While controlling every aspect of people's lives, the Communist regime underestimated a fundamental human instinct of *dominant behavior*, which is the innate motivation to accumulate assets and power and to achieve and maintain *high social status*, along with all the benefits that society gives to those who possess it.

We can learn from the misconceptions that the Communist leaders knew what motives humans had by comprehending first, the *ultimate functions* of human behavior, which are deep-seated and enduring.

Biases—A Theoretical Background

The quest to survive permeates human evolution. Living in a hostile environment filled with predators, disease, harsh weather, and scarce resources[6] meant that our ancestors had to develop tools and strategies to stay alive and care for kin who outlived them into the next generation. But to do that, humans often encountered human-to-human conflict along the way, and being part of the "right group" became crucial for survival. The first murder known to researchers dates back to 437,000 years ago,[7] which was then followed by countless other human deaths caused by deliberate homicides, war, or terrorism. Since then, many powerful rulers and Governments across the world have tried to curtail human conflict, starting with the Persian King Cyrus II (aka Cyrus The Great) in 539 BC who liberated slaves and gave people freedom of religious choice upon conquering the city of Babylon in Mesopotamia, present-day Iraq.[8] In 1215, in Europe, King John of England signed the Magna Carta (Latin for "The Great Charter"), which also made monarchs subject to the law and laid the foundations for fair trials.[9] Many other documents were drafted, namely the 1628 The Petition of Rights in England, 1776 The United States Declaration of Independence, 1787 The Constitution of the United States of America, 1789 The Declaration of the Rights of Man and the Citizen during the French Revolution, 1791 The U.S. Bill of Rights, 1863 The Emancipation Proclamation for the freedom of slaves in the United States, and the 1948 The European Convention of Human Rights.[10]

If almost all countries (194) in the world have signed the Universal Declaration of Human Rights, how is it possible that wars continue despite the availability of resources and the increase in wealth and modern technology? Why are there more slaves today than during the whole period of the slave trade? Why are there thousands of people dying of starvation every day? Are we wired not to uphold our human rights? This still happens because our present behaviors are the product of our animal biological and psychological instincts[11] that served us to protect ourselves, our families, and groups in ancient inhospitable environments, but that continue to drive our impulses in the present. This is, of course, an unpleasant realization, and as we have learned, "society thus brands what is unpleasant as untrue."[12]

While some instincts have been helpful for our self-protection (e.g., fear of snakes, heights, strange men), others are maladapted for the modern environment and the level of technological, social, political, and cultural sophistication our species has achieved in the last centuries since the Renaissance,[13] as it's the case of the human instinct to dominate others.[14] Many examples of dominant behavior come in many forms, even in developed societies in which civil rights are protected (e.g., in the Civil Rights movement in the United States since the 1950s),[15] the same rights are not upheld as the economic rights of citizens. But the irony is that it is not possible to have human rights without economic rights because, without them, people may make decisions that compromise their dignity and freedom,[16] thus leading them to end up, for instance, in multigenerational bonded labor or debt bondage[17] as is the case for almost 19 million people in India alone.[18] Despite being aware of such problems, the population becomes increasingly more desensitized, a phenomenon called *actor-observer bias* (i.e., attributing one's own actions to external causes while attributing other people's behaviors to internal causes). Dictionaries define biases as *an unreasoned and unfair distortion of judgment in favor of or against a person or thing*[19] or *the action of supporting or opposing a particular person or thing in an unfair way*,[20] which can be unconscious or instinctive.[21] This is the case of cognitive biases such as the *bandwagon effect* (i.e., our instinct to follow the herd,[22] or consciously learned biases as in the case of overt racism.[23] The *status-quo bias* (i.e., preferring detrimental existing arrangements at the expense of individual and collective best interests) is another important bias to mention, particularly when we see 860 million people around the world are still living with under $1.90 a day in 2022, and 263 million more thanks to the Covid-19 pandemic,[24] while global wealth increased by 9.8 percent in 2021 to $463.6 trillion[25] and the richest 1 percent owns 45.6 percent of the global wealth,[26] 2.6 percent more than in 2010.

If we take a bird's eye panoramic view of how ancient civilizations such as the Egyptian, Babylonic, Hellenic, and Mayan civilizations, or how the Roman Empire declined and vanished, historians, anthropologists, and sociologists refer to internal and external causes such as pandemics, foreign invasion, decline of social cohesion, socioeconomic complexity (bureaucracy) decay of creativity to problem-solve, rising inequality and oligarchy, an upsurge in violence, environmental catastrophes, and resource depletion.[27] While worries about the negative impact of human activity on nature have been of concern since at least the Roman Times, the environmental movement has increased in its strength and influence since the Industrial Revolution up to contemporary times,[28] thanks to efforts from nongovernmental organizations (NGOs) including World Wildlife Fund (WWF), Climate Foundation, and Greenpeace.[29] Environmental catastrophes receive significant media coverage and are the focus of organized protests by members of the public, led by prominent modern-day activists such as the Swedish climate campaigned Greta Thunberg, Time Magazine Person of the Year 2019,[30] who became famous for her School Strike for Climate movement[31] at 15 years old. Activists are becoming increasingly more creative with protests ranging from sticking themselves to the road with superglue in Berlin,[32] to throwing tomato soup at Vincent van Gogh's "Sunflowers" painting at the National Gallery in London.[33] Governments and organizations all over the world seem to be listening and are making efforts to reduce their carbon footprint, reduce waste, and the overall impact of their operations on natural resources. They are also influenced by the British author and entrepreneur John Elkington who coined the "Triple Bottom Line" concept of People, Planet, and Profit (aka, the 3Ps, TBL or 3BL) almost three decades ago and also created a sustainability framework that examines companies' environment, social, and economic impact.[34] After Elkington's TBL came, the United Nations (UN) created 17 Sustainable Development Goals (SDGs), which were agreed upon in 2015 by all 193 UN member states[35] and agreed on its influence on the business models of for-profit companies and start-ups around the world.[36] However, the same level of attention given to environmental problems does not seem to be given to other threats to societal collapse, such as social inequality. This is exemplified by a simple Google Trends research, which shows a disparity between the level of interest in search patterns between the

Interest over time   ⑨   ⬇ ⟨⟩ ⬍

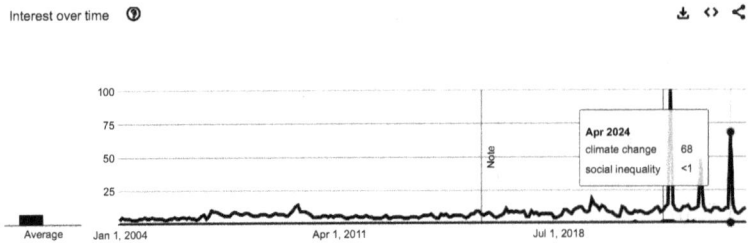

Figure 4.1 Google trends worldwide. Search on climate change versus social inequality from 2004 to 2024, December 23, 2024

topics of "climate change" and "social inequality," even though the former causes about 5 million deaths a year due to extreme hot or cold temperatures,[37] and the latter kills over 9 million people who die from hunger and associated causes, while 854 million people worldwide are undernourished.[38] Even though climate change and sustainability should be at the top of every Government and organization worldwide, why is there a disproportionate amount of attention toward climate-related issues and not as much on social inequalities that may cascade into environmental damages and deter the attainment of the UN's SDGs? The *salience bias* might be the answer because information that is more noticeable (more publicized) and is emotionally compelling (e.g., the images of deforestation, floods, and wildfires) triggers more action compared to statistics or images of the suffering outside one's group (i.e., *out-group bias*).

Biases in Practice

It's fair to say that 2020 was an unforgettable year in many ways. From the first quarter of the year, Governments installed strict lockdowns in an attempt to restrict the spread of the Covid-19 pandemic. By the beginning of April, 90 countries across the world were in lockdown, restricting the movement of nearly four billion people through curfews, confinements, and quarantines.[39] One month after the appalling killing of George Floyd, the 46-year-old African American man, in Minneapolis, Minnesota, on May 25, 2020, while he was under police custody, up to 26 million people across 550 cities in the United States led one of the biggest protests in history.

The murder of George Floyd sparked the global Black Lives Matter (BLM) movement with demonstrations in many capitals demanding justice for Floyd's death, a major reform within police departments, and more accountability from corporations about racially discriminatory policies. Sadly, this was not the first, nor the last time that a black person was killed by the police as statistics show that black people are nearly three times as likely as white people to be shot and killed by the police,[40] also accounting for 27 percent of the fatalities in 2021.[41] In reality, the names of 203 black victims of police killings in 2021 were published online,[42] yet, they did not ignite the same level of media attention and public commotion as the George Floyd case did the year prior. And two years earlier, Marielle Franco, a 38-year-old black, LGBTI, Brazilian Councilor, was shot dead along with her driver by members of the Rio de Janeiro Police in March 2018.[43] Ms. Franco was outspoken about the Police's fatal raids and denounced off-duty, paramilitary police known as "militias." Sadly, Ms. Franco's death did not reach the same level of protests as Mr. Floyd's, perhaps due to not happening in the world's first economy, and over four years later in 2022, the investigations have not yet revealed who ordered Ms. Franco's killing and why.[44]

So what could be the reasons that spark huge public outcry related to certain crimes but not others? One of the factors to consider is context. When the shocking video that displayed former police officer, Derek Chauvin kneeling on Floyd's neck for nearly 10 minutes while he was handcuffed and lying face down on the street and saying "I can't breathe," the United States was already in the third month of the global pandemic with most nonessential workers home-bound, removed from their professional, academic, and social life and filled with uncertainties and negative emotions ranging from frustration, anger, despair, helplessness, and sadness.[45] Floyd's unjust death in front of the camera in these circumstances accentuated the need for social connectedness, a shared sense of purpose, and empathy toward the BLM movement that has existed since 2013.[46] Second, the influence of American culture should also be taken into account as crimes committed in other countries tend not to reap the same repercussions as those committed in the United States. And third, compared to other black victims of fatal police brutality, Floyd's video humanized him, he wasn't just a distant concept or a statistic. To put it simply, "A single death is a tragedy, a million deaths is a statistic," a quote attributed to Joseph Stalin, the former Premier of the Soviet Union in the

1940s.[47] One of the explanations for this phenomenon is that our brains have a narrow scope of empathy, which is not distributed equally; hence, we do not feel compassion for all victims as some become only statistics in our view. This is another bias, the *identifiable victim effect*. From an evolutionary standpoint, we have reasons to react to threatening events that involve specific individuals, rather than vague groups unknown to us. The amygdala, a small part of our brains located in the limbic system, or reptilian brain, is a system that appeared in the first mammals and is involved in the processing and regulation of emotions, the creation and retention of memories, sexual arousal, and learning[48] and is a crucial component of our body's response to stress. The amygdala regulates emotions and is triggered by stress and fear, thus releasing hormones such as cortisol as part of the fight-or-flight reaction to threats that include fearful stimuli including faces, images, and other cues.[49] This biological response to fear highlights that we are not purely rational thinkers, and the *identifiable victim effect* is acutely linked with our emotions, or affect heuristic. This explains why knowing the number of hundreds or thousands of black people (or people from any race) who were killed by the police in a given year does not move us to take action as much as one vivid image or video that triggers our amygdala.

The public outcry on the streets and social media over George Floyd's case also flared budget cuts for police departments, dismissals, resignations, and the removal of statues and monuments considered to be of slave traders and owners. And as 64 percent of consumers stated that they would reward companies who engage in brand activism,[50] it's unsurprising that as many as 950 brands including Mercedes-Benz and Apple joined tens of millions of posts against racism and inequality that still exist in all settings from the streets to boardrooms. Chief executive officers (CEOs) of major corporations voiced their support to the BLM movement, and other large companies, such as Nike, pledged to donate 40 million U.S. dollars to support black communities in the United States.[51] Yet, it was also one of the many companies accused of hypocrisy as they did not engage in the change they wished to promote on social media channels with an all-white leadership team, despite widely promoting its products through African American athletes and spokespeople.[52] In fact, in 2021, there were over 38,000 CEOs employed in the United States. In

2019, over 68 percent were men, and just over 31 percent were women. Eighty-one percent of the CEOs were white men (a mere 2 percent drop since 2010), 7 percent were Hispanic or Latino, almost 7 percent were Asian, and only 3 percent comprised Black or African American.[53] Most CEOs were 52 years old.[54] Historically, only 19 out of 1,800 CEOs of the Fortune 500 list[55] were black (out of which only two were women). This data leads to an environment that cultivates *in-group bias*, the act of favoring members of one's in-group over out-group members, as well as favoritism within the evaluation of others, and the allocation of resources among other benefits.

Humans have a built-in *in-group bias*, plus at least 225 other cognitive, memory, unconscious, and biological biases including gender, race, age, and other biases that guide our decisions and consumers and citizens daily.

All the instances of injustices mentioned before are of course not exclusive to the United States. Considering the racial issue, the U.S.'s South American neighbor Brazil, for instance, is a country that still struggles with its colonized past in which the Portuguese became the first Europeans to engage in African slave trading in the 15th century[56] and only abolished slavery as late as 1888, despite the outlaw of slavery in 1807 by Great Britain (Portugal's oldest ally since 1386). The release of millions of slaves into "freedom" without education, assets, or land gave rise to the "favelas," shanty towns or slums, home to 27 million people in 2020,[57] the equivalent to the whole population of Portugal and The Netherlands combined,[58] another country that commissioned slave trade and ruled Brazil from 1637 to 1644.[59] The legacy of slavery is inequality, which remains a huge problem as 79 percent of victims killed by the Brazilian police in 2020 were black, while they make up just over 56 percent of the total population.[62] The middle class in Brazil still prides itself on not having to cook or clean in their homes as the country has the highest number of domestic workers in the world[63] with over 7 million people employed in the sector (second to India which has over 4 million domestic workers). Ninety-seven percent are women and the vast majority are of African and Indigenous descent.[64] They are denied their basic rights such as working long hours and earning low wages while also facing physical and sexual abuse[65] as only 28 percent of these workers have a labor contract that grants them workers' rights.[66]

49 Types of Biases

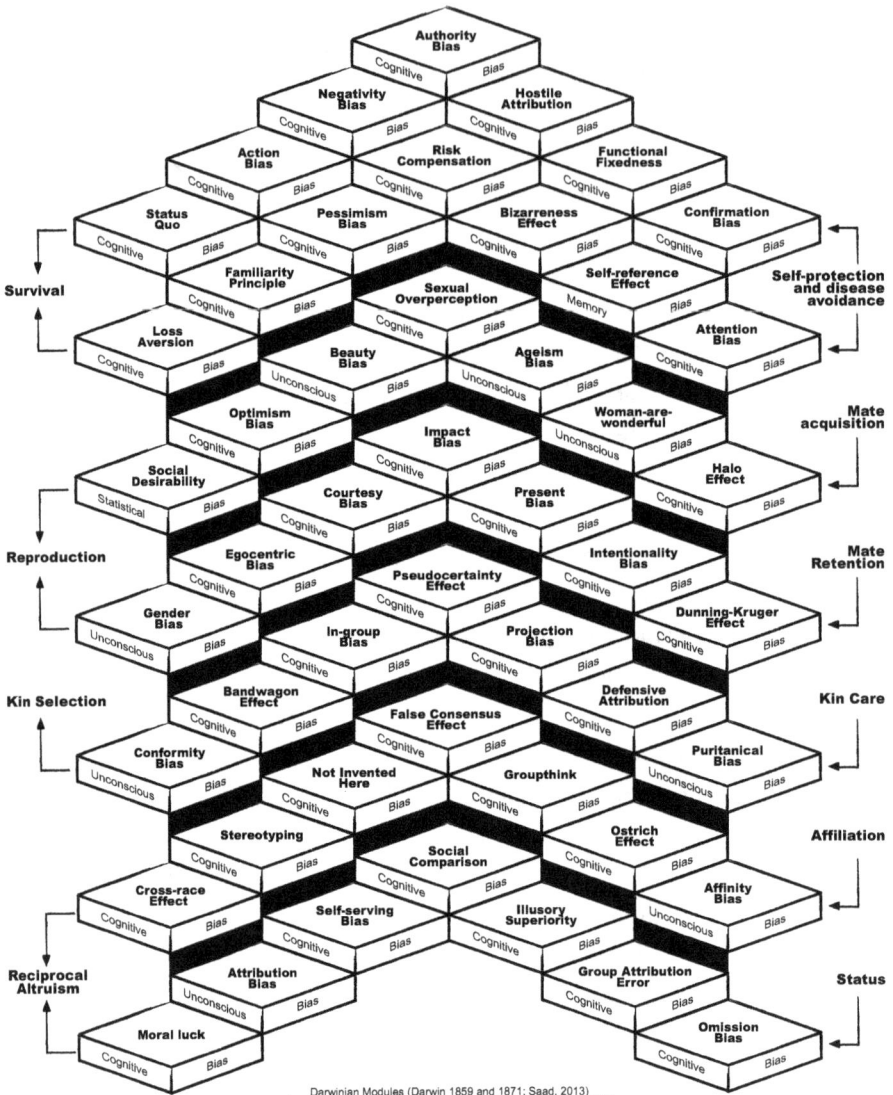

Darwinian Modules (Darwin 1859 and 1871; Saad, 2013)
Fundamental Motives of Behavior (Kenrick and Griskevicius, 2013)

Figure 4.2 A sample of 49 out of 225 biases. From cognitive, memory, unconscious, and biological biases plotted against the Darwinian modules of evolutionary drives[60] and fundamental motives[61]

In the Appendix section, you will find the full list of 225 biases and their equivalent effect Illustrations by Roman, @ideahits.

Children are particularly vulnerable to working without payment and having their movement restricted.[67] The middle and upper classes in Brazil, India, and beyond are subject to the *status quo* bias, that is, preferring that things stay relatively the same. But Brazil gives us only one of the many examples of the legacy of slavery as modern slavery remains and has increased in numbers. During almost four centuries of the transatlantic slave trade, about 13 million Africans were taken as slaves to the Americas,[68] but the global population explosion and the drastic decrease in the price of slaves from the past average cost of $40,000 per slave to a mere $100 in the last decade, made people even more disposable than in former times.[69] Particularly within developing countries such as India and China, the massive population increase in the last few centuries has helped to increase the population of modern slaves to a colossal number of 50 million people,[70] which amounts to almost the whole population of South Korea[71] or Colombia.[72]

As we have seen, biases can be summarized as behaving in a prejudicial or unfair way toward an individual or a group, or a type of belief, as well as a systematic error when it comes to science and engineering. Biases can be instinctive or learned. Biases can be pervasive, affecting every area of our lives, from the person we marry, to whom we hire or fire, the investments we make or not, who we vote for or avoid, the experts we listen to (or not), and even serious mistakes we commit that can cost us our lives and the lives of others. Our biases lead us to cause accidents, misjudge, discriminate, hate, segregate, and commit some of the worst crimes against human rights. But we must have the courage to look squarely into some of the darkest, morally repugnant facets of human behavior. Although this is an incredibly difficult task, when we begin to *explain* (not *justify*) the worst of human behavior, we begin to outgrow the worst of our human tendencies, which is achieved only when we first and foremost understand them and their origins.

Daniel Kahneman's and Amos Tversky's Prospect Theory[73] and the Heuristics and Biases approach[74] exemplified how people commit systematic deviations from rationality and judgment errors due to cognitive biases. With at least 225 biases ranging from cognitive, memory, beliefs, decision making, social, biological, and behavioral biases that cloud our decision making process under uncertainty, our intuition is perceived as recognition. Our thinking becomes a bodily process, with the fast, automatic, emotional *System 1* being guided by the ease of retrieval of information, availability, and affect, while the slow, conscious, and effortful *System 2* relies on logic for decision making or a lack of it.[75] Thanks to availability heuristics, the process of judging, and the fluency or ease of information retrieval, people make decisions and choices based on how they *feel*, based on the experiencing self's memories of pain and pleasure.[76] But we can go deeper than cognition and examine how our biology may direct us toward biases for reasons that might have served us in the distant past to protect us from harm or enhance our chances of passing on our genes to the next generation.

As seen in previous chapters, EP explains how the human brain has deep-seated impulses to ensure the survival of humankind. Our instincts continue to push us to avoid physical harm and disease; to acquire status to attract the respect and fondness of peers and help us attract and keep a mate; to make friends as we're social animals; and to care for family so we can live through them for generations to come.[77] In recent years, studies suggested that such *fundamental motives* are interlinked for the attainment of one another. In this context, it's worth remembering that hormones influence our decision-making process and shape our behavior whether in a social or economic setting. Acting as messengers, hormones travel from one organ to another through our bloodstreams and bodily fluids to modify and control our bodily functions, emotions, and moods.

Starting from the viewpoint that we have primal motives to act the way that we do for reasons that may have served us well in the past, we can also realize that the behavior that might have given us an advantage in the animal kingdom thousands of years ago is no longer necessary in the 21st century, which brings us again to the *mismatch theory* (i.e., the evolutionary mismatch that happens when the environment that our organism is adapted to changes faster than our biology, as the latter is based on a much slower process of change and adaptation).

To further exemplify how biases that originated in primal times still affect us today, let's consider *gender bias or false priors*. The necessity to hunt large-game animals to share among family and neighbors 2 million years ago could be an explanation for the *sexual division of labor*. The argument is that men possess more upper-body strength than women and their ability to throw projectiles at long distances accurately made them better hunters, while women were tasked with food-gathering activities, which enabled them to take children with them.[78] Fast-forwarding to the 21st century we see that women made up 54 percent of tertiary students (universities, trade schools, and colleges) in Europe[79] and 59.5 percent of college students in the United States in 2020 to 2021.[80]

Country	Media Net Wealth (.000€)		Media Net Wealth (.000€)		Ratio Women vs. Men	
	Men	Women	Men	Women	Median Net Wealth	Median Net Wealth
Euro area	137.4	84.8	263.9	191.4	0.62	0.73
Austria	110.4	59.6	324.1	218.2	0.54	0.67
Belgium	241.7	177.7	382.3	288.2	0.74	0.75
Germany	66.8	37.0	207.5	182.3	0.55	0.88
Spain	205.4	158.5	344.0	237.4	0.77	0.69
France	146.2	71.8	272.3	173.0	0.49	0.64
Greece	110.2	97.6	173.8	129.9	0.89	0.75
Italy	202.4	142.3	318.1	221.8	0.70	0.70
Luxembourg	446.6	358.9	767.2	626.1	0.80	0.82
Netherlands	145.5	40.6	208.1	105.1	0.28	0.51
Poland	69.1	52.9	114.4	81.3	0.76	0.71
Slovakia	62.3	60.4	84.0	76.1	0.97	0.91

Figure 4.3 Net wealth levels by gender in thousands of euros, European Commission[81]

This dataset was collected between 2010 and 2011 and contains information on wealth, income, and sociodemographic characteristics of over 62,000 households from 15 countries of the Euro Area12 Source: Sierminska, E., and A. Girshina. 2017. "Wealth and Gender in Europe," 39. Publications Office of the EU.

Despite being qualified, women make up only 39 percent of global employment, but they account for 54 percent of overall job losses.[82] In Europe, women account for only one in three national parliamentarians; they make up only 30 percent of boardroom members; in large companies, women represent less than 1 in 10 board presidents or CEOs; and women's median net wealth is 62 percent than that of men.[83] The situation is also poor in the United States as only 8.2 percent of women are CEOs of Fortune 500 companies.[84] If women want to create a start-up instead of becoming the CEO of a large corporation, there's more bad news as only 2.3 percent of venture capital goes to women-led start-ups.[85] If some of these gender disparities were reduced, $13 trillion could be added to the global GDP in 2030[86] or $20 trillion by 2050.[87]

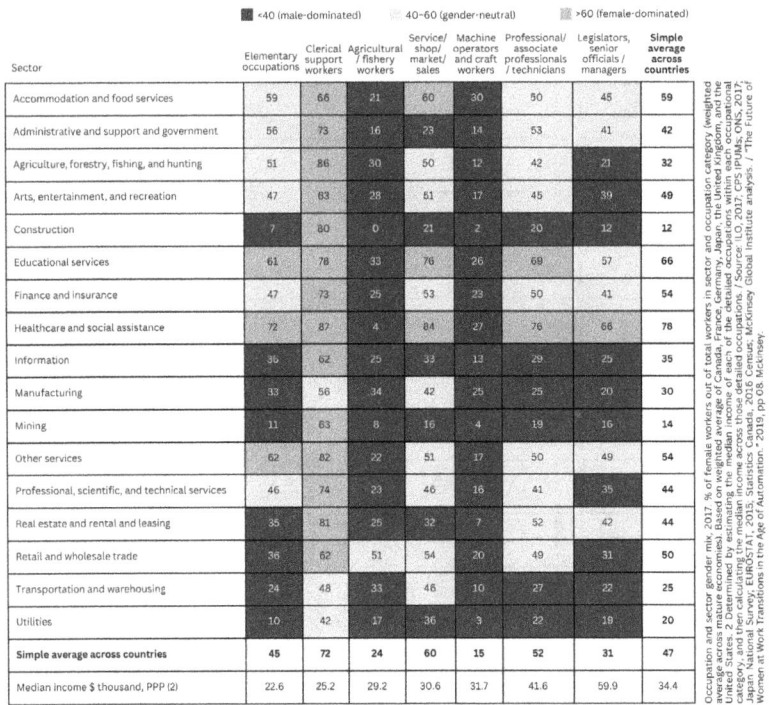

Legend	
■ <40 (male-dominated) 40–60 (gender-neutral) ▨ >60 (female-dominated)	

Sector	Elementary occupations	Clerical support workers	Agricultural / fishery workers	Service/ shop/ market/ sales	Machine operators and craft workers	Professional/ associate professionals / technicians	Legislators, senior officials / managers	Simple average across countries
Accommodation and food services	59	66	21	60	30	50	45	59
Administrative and support and government	56	73	16	23	14	53	41	42
Agriculture, forestry, fishing, and hunting	51	86	30	50	12	42	21	32
Arts, entertainment, and recreation	47	63	28	61	17	45	39	49
Construction	7	80	0	21	2	20	12	12
Educational services	61	78	33	76	26	69	57	66
Finance and insurance	47	73	25	53	23	50	41	54
Healthcare and social assistance	72	87	4	84	27	76	66	78
Information	36	62	25	33	13	29	25	35
Manufacturing	33	56	34	42	25	25	20	30
Mining	11	63	8	16	4	19	16	14
Other services	62	82	22	51	17	50	49	54
Professional, scientific, and technical services	46	74	23	46	16	41	35	44
Real estate and rental and leasing	35	81	25	32	7	52	42	44
Retail and wholesale trade	36	62	51	54	20	49	31	50
Transportation and warehousing	24	48	33	48	10	27	22	25
Utilities	10	42	17	36	3	22	19	20
Simple average across countries	45	72	24	60	15	52	31	47
Median income $ thousand, PPP (2)	22.6	25.2	29.2	30.6	31.7	41.6	59.9	34.4

Occupation and sector gender mix, 2017. % of female workers out of total workers in sector and occupation category (weighted average across mature economies). Based on weighted average of Canada, France, Germany, Japan, the United Kingdom, and the United States. 2. Determined by estimating the median income of each of the detailed occupations within each occupational category, and then calculating the median income across those detailed occupations. / Source: ILO, 2017; CPS IPUMs; ONS, 2017; Japan National Survey; EUROSTAT, 2015; Statistics Canada, 2016 Census. McKinsey Global Institute analysis. / "The Future of Women at Work Transitions in the Age of Automation." 2019, pp 68. McKinsey.

Figure 4.4 Gender and industry presence, the future of women at work, McKinsey Global Institute[88]

Women still disproportionately occupy gender-stereotypical professions that focus on caring for others such as service workers (shop and market sales workers), clerical support, and health care and social assistance even in mature economies.[89]

Let's take a closer look at many other types of biases and systematic errors we commit in our society, professional, and personal lives, some of their evolutionary origins, and the consequences throughout history.

Table 4.1 How evolutionary drives affect the biases that we still see today

Evolutionary Psychology Principle	21st-Century Bias Type	21st-Century Mismatch Effect
Fixed action patterns: An innate behavioral sequence in response to a stimulus	*Action bias:* The human propensity to favor action over inaction	Humanity's failure to prevent wars through diplomacy has resulted in at least 137 major conflicts from the Trojan War to the ongoing Arab–Israeli conflict
Respect for authority: Restraining from one's urges in favor of those in a dominant position	*Authority bias association fallacy:* Blindly accepting advice from an authoritative person	The acceptance of Apartheid in South Africa and Namibia from 1948 until the 1990s, racial segregation in the United States from 1526 until the Civil Rights Act of 1964, and antisemitism from the 1st-century BCE, peaking during the Holocaust in WWII (1941–1945) when nearly 6 million European Jews were killed in Nazi concentration camps
Human attention: Selective memory focuses on noticing, storing, and retrieving information crucial for solving adaptive problems[90]	*Availability heuristic:* The process of judging with ease of retrieval of information	Media coverage extends economic cycles,[91] often being negative, which influences consumers' future economic expectations[92]
Ecological dominance/ social competition (EDSC) hypothesis: Large social groups address challenges such as forming alliances, punishing cheaters, detecting deception, and managing complex hierarchies[93]	*Availability cascade bias:* When a viewpoint gains relevance in public discourse, it becomes more available in people's minds, making them more likely to believe and spread it	The Nazi party used propaganda to promote German pride and anti-Semitism, blaming Jews and Communists for postwar economic issues. They targeted young, economically disadvantaged Germans, reflecting and exaggerating popular tendencies

(Continued)

Table 4.1 (Continued)

Evolutionary Psychology Principle	21st-Century Bias Type	21st-Century Mismatch Effect
Hyperactive agency detection device (HADD): An evolutionary device believed to cause the rise of Gods and spiritual beliefs, attributing meaning and intentions to inanimate agents such as the sun, wind, waves, and fire[94]	*Agent detection bias*: The tendency to assume a sentient agent intervened in situations, even without proof	From the Middle Stone Age (300,000 to 30,000 years ago) to the 21st century, humans developed religions, leading to religious wars, country separations (e.g., Netherlands and Belgium, India and Pakistan), and mass suicides by cults such as The People's Temple in 1978
Error management theory (EMT): Under uncertainty, humans favor "adaptive biases" to minimize costly errors[95]	*Ambiguity effect bias*: A cognitive bias where humans avoid ambiguity and dislike uncertainty	People prefer fixed-rate mortgages over variable ones due to uncertainty. In the United Kingdom, long-term fixed-rate mortgages have made up half of new lending since 2016, despite low interest rates at 0.25% that year[96]

Possible Evolutionary Psychology Principle	21st-Century Bias Type	21st-Century Mismatch Effect
Group living and cooperative alliances: Group living is essential for human evolution; without cohesion in tribes, animal packs, or teams, nothing could be accomplished	*Bandwagon effect Groupthink*: The tendency to follow others' behaviors or styles	Economic bubbles, from the 1640 Tulip Mania to the 2008 property crash, have shown crowd psychology traits such as impulsiveness, credulity, avoidance of uncertainty, servility to authority, and extreme morality[97]
Beauty as a fitness indicator: Contrary to cultural theories, infants and toddlers show a natural preference for attractive faces and dolls.[98] Evolutionary theory suggests beauty signals youth and health, such as clear skin and symmetry, which are universally attractive.[99] Studies also link beauty to a better immune system[100]	*Beauty bias*: Using a person's physical appearance as a judgment of their character of competency	Studies show beautiful people are more likely to be hired,[101] earn higher salaries, and receive better evaluations.[102] They also have a 20% advantage in politics[103] and are perceived as more likable and trustworthy[104]

Possible Evolutionary Psychology Principle	21st-Century Bias Type	21st-Century Mismatch Effect
Adaptation: Adaptations have a prerequisite that genes should be self-centered	*Bias blind spot/ Egocentric bias:* Perceiving oneself as less biased than other people	Over 88% of chartered plane crashes are due to human factors, often from captain and first officer disagreements. Pilot loss of control is the leading cause of crashes, and even commercial pilots sometimes ignore cockpit warnings, leading to serious accidents[105]
Adaptive memory: Remembering survival and mating-related topics. *Instinctual system:* Life-preserving and sexual instincts, acting without prior knowledge or anticipation. Includes needs such as air, water, food, shelter, and fears such as snakes, spiders, heights, and dangerous animals	*Bizarreness effect bias:* Humans tend to remember bizarre content better than common information	Throughout history and across cultures, the media highlight unusual events, mainly covering: death, assault, robbery, suicide, harm to offspring, rape, infidelity, reputation, heroism, destitute families, and acts of defiance[106]
In-group cohesion: Humans have evolved to favor in-group members and show hostility toward out-groups in response to threats from hostile groups	*Cross-race effect bias:* Humans more easily recognize faces from their racial group than other races, known as *the other-race effect*	*The other-race effect has impacted criminal justice, as seen in the mistaken shooting of Jean Charles de Menezes in 2005. The National Registry of Exonerations recorded 2,944 wrongful convictions in the United States from 1989 to 2021. Machine learning algorithms have shown bias[107] due to training on biased data, leading to discrimination.[108]* However, early exposure to diverse races can prevent the other-race effect, and older individuals can mitigate it through education, according to psychologist Gizelle Anzures[109]
Deceiving down: Acting submissively to appear nonthreatening and avoid retaliation from dominant individuals[110]	*Conformity bias:* Imitating peers to gain acceptance rather than using personal judgment	In 2019, smoking caused over 8 million deaths, including 1.2 million from second-hand smoke.[111] Despite the known risks, the number of smokers reached 1.1 billion, with 155 million aged 15 to 24.[112] Most smokers start between 14 and 25, an age marked by risk-taking and peer pressure. The prefrontal cortex, crucial for decision making, isn't fully developed until around 25[113]

(Continued)

Table 4.1 (Continued)

Possible Evolutionary Psychology Principle	21st-Century Bias Type	21st-Century Mismatch Effect
Sexual selection theory: Choosing mates with traits that offer survival and reproductive benefits. Dependability and emotional stability are highly valued traits, indicating reliable resource provision over time[114]	*Consistency bias:* The human tendency to align actions with past commitments and self-image. Once a stand is taken, people feel compelled to act consistently with that commitment[115]	A study found that 53% of participants preferred to die immediately with a good reputation rather than live to 90 and be falsely remembered as pedophiles[116]
Social attachment and affiliation: *Social attachment* involves deep emotional bonds with a few significant others, providing support during stress from infancy to adulthood. *Social affiliation* is about engaging in positive interactions and forming connections, driven by social motivation. Both are crucial for psychological and physical health, stress management, and a sense of belonging	*Courtesy bias Conformity bias:* Being polite to others at the expense of honesty	In 2021, nearly all Fortune 500 companies spent around $4.6 billion (£3.27 billion) on focus group market research for marketing, branding, PR, image management, and product development.[117] However, 80%–85% of new products still fail in competitive industries like fast-moving consumer goods[118]
The sexual division of labor: Men, with their greater upper-body strength and projectile accuracy, became hunters, while women gathered food, often taking children along[119]	*Gender bias or false priors:* Gender bias involves assuming that women are less capable of high-ranking, intellectually demanding jobs and defaulting to male when gender is unspecified	Reducing gender roles, leadership gaps[120] and income disparities for women could add $20 trillion to the global GDP by 2050.[121] In India, where 90% of women are not in the workforce, closing the gender gap could boost the economy by $6 trillion by 2050[122]

Possible Evolutionary Psychology Principle	21st-Century Bias Type	21st-Century Mismatch Effect
Sexual strategies theory/ Human mating: Women have evolved to prefer men who can protect them and their children, making traits such as size, bravery, masculine body type, and athletic ability attractive. Throughout history, societies have attributed power, prestige, and resources to tall and strong men[123]	*Halo effect association fallacy bias:* Perceiving a single trait, whether good (halo) or bad (horn), as more important than other traits such as behaviors, actions, or beliefs[124]	Tall men are more likely to be hired, promoted, and elected.[125] They earn higher salaries and have more status and authority.[126] Physically strong men also attain higher positions, even if strength isn't needed.[127] In the 20th century, the taller presidential candidate won 83% of the time. Taller referees in European football have more status[128] The *halo effect* can also be disguised beneath people with psychopathic traits. Psychopaths can be charming and engaging, masking traits such as lack of empathy, manipulativeness, and recklessness.[129] About 1% of the population are psychopaths, with 15% of the prison population and 90.8% of serial killers being men. Up to 12% of CEOs may have psychopathic traits.[130] In 2021, 94% of CEOs of the largest publicly listed corporations appointed globally were men[131]
Human attention: Selective memory focuses on noticing, storing, and retrieving information crucial for solving adaptive problems[132]	*Hot–cold empathy gap bias:* A cognitive bias where people underestimate the impact of visceral drives (such as hunger, thirst, pain, and emotions) on their attitudes and decisions. This bias makes it hard to predict behavior in different emotional states. The cold-to-hot empathy gap is the reverse, where people in a calm state struggle to imagine themselves in a heightened emotional state	In the past, getting a bank loan often depended on impressing the bank manager, who would assess personal and financial details. Decisions could be influenced by biases such as gender or ethnicity. Today, automated systems use data and mathematical models to make lending decisions, reducing human bias[133]

(Continued)

Table 4.1 (Continued)

Possible Evolutionary Psychology Principle	21st-Century Bias Type	21st-Century Mismatch Effect
Aggression and warfare: Aggression and warfare have been common throughout human history, mainly driven by men targeting other men, though women also suffer as a result	*Hostile attribution bias/Attribution bias:* Assuming others have hostile intentions	The excessive use of force at times by the Police is a leading cause of death for young men of color in the United States. African American, Native American, and Latino men face higher risks than white men, with black men having a 1 in 1,000 chance of being killed by police. Women's risk is about 1 in 33,000, peaking between ages 20 and 35[134]
Social anxiety: Loss of status, ostracism from a group	*Ingroup bias—Not invented here:* In-group favoritism is the tendency to favor members of one's group over those in other groups, affecting evaluations and resource allocation	Tribal Conflict in Africa: Africa, with over 50 countries and 3,000 tribes, has seen tribalism collapse governments and trigger wars. For example, General Idi Amin's regime in Uganda (1971–1979) resulted in the massacre of about 300,000 civilians from the Acholi and Lango tribes. Tribes of the Amazon: In Amazonian tribal societies, violent conflict over jealousy, revenge, honor, and territory accounted for 30% of deaths before European contact, according to anthropologist Robert Walker[135]
Neophobia is the fear of new things, often causing anxiety about new places and foods.[136] It affects both humans and rats, leading to feelings of anxiety and fear of dying when encountering new experiences.[137] This fear is part of the behavioral immune system, which helps avoid diseases transmitted by viruses and bacteria	*Mere exposure effect:* Developing a preference for familiar things	The mere exposure effect is widely used in advertising, as familiarity with a product or brand can increase consumer preference.[138] In 2020, advertisers spent about $59.22 billion on paid search ads[139]. Major investors included Alphabet, Amazon, Microsoft, Walmart, Nike, Apple, and Facebook,[140] which were among the world's most valuable brands that year[141]

Possible Evolutionary Psychology Principle	21st-Century Bias Type	21st-Century Mismatch Effect
Emotional responses are evolutionary brain reactions to experiences,[142] especially strong emotions such as fear, anger, sadness, or happiness.[143] They can be triggered by direct environmental stimuli or indirectly by memories and thoughts, causing mental and physiological changes such as hunger, pain, love, and gratitude.[144] These responses help identify threats and opportunities for optimal functioning[145]	*Mood-congruent memory bias:* The tendency to remember experiences that match your current mood	Divorce rates are decreasing from the previous 50 percent rate.[146] Common reasons for divorce include lack of commitment (75%), infidelity (59%), and too much conflict and arguing (57.7%).[147] Conflicts can be driven by stress and negative moods, which may indicate problems.[148] Mood-congruent memory bias leads people to remember events that match their current emotions, such as recalling past arguments during a fight[149]
Fear of strange men: The evolutionary fear of strange men stems from our ancestors' need for survival. Unfamiliar men posed threats to safety and resources, so avoiding them increased survival chances. This caution has been passed down, influencing our modern reactions to strangers	*Negativity bias or negativity effect:* The tendency to focus more on negative experiences than positive ones. Negative events often impact our thoughts, emotions, and behaviors more strongly than positive events of the same intensity. This bias likely evolved to help our ancestors quickly recognize and respond to threats	Bad news is 22% more likely to be published than good news.[150] Since the 1970s, news from over 130 countries has been predominantly negative.[151] We are 30% more likely to pay attention to bad news, such as wars or disasters.[152] For example, the Russian newspaper, *The City Reporter*, lost two-thirds of its readership after publishing only good news for one day.[153] This is due to our brains being wired to react more strongly to negative news,[154] which triggers negative emotions and changes our behavior to avoid harm,[155,156, 157] and overall negative affect[158]

(Continued)

Table 4.1 (Continued)

Possible Evolutionary Psychology Principle	21st-Century Bias Type	21st-Century Mismatch Effect
Evolution has shaped our brains to save energy and ensure survival. According to psychologist Daniel Kahneman,[159] we have two thinking systems: one that is fast, intuitive, and emotion-driven, and another that is slow, deliberative, and rational.[160] Therefore, focusing on trivial topics is less mentally demanding and more enjoyable for the brain	*Parkinson's law of triviality, or bikeshedding*: The tendency to prioritize trivial issues over more important ones	*Since the 1969 moon landing,[161] the United States has led space spending, investing over $41 billion annually. Other countries such as China, Russia, and members of the European Union also invest significantly.[162] Private companies such as Elon Musk's SpaceX have raised $1.5 billion[163] to colonize Mars by 2060.[164] Meanwhile, 1.7 billion people lack safe sanitation, causing deadly diseases,[165] as one in three schools lacks proper toilets.[166,167]* *Football is the world's most popular sport, with 3.5 billion fans.[168] In 2021, Cristiano Ronaldo earned $125 million, while UK nurses received a 1% pay rise, bringing their average salary to £35,000 ($43,900)[169] while helping the United Kingdom fight the Covid-19 pandemic[170,171]*
Error management theory (EMT): This suggests that psychological systems and biases evolved to minimize costly errors affecting fitness, survival, and gene dissemination.[172] Evolutionary biology posits that men face higher costs than women if they miss mating opportunities due to fewer women being willing to mate compared to men[173]	*Sexual overperception bias/Sexual under-perception bias*: Men are more likely than women to misinterpret a woman's smile, eye contact, or gestures as sexual interest	Studies show that sexual overperception bias occurs even in highly gender-equal countries such as Norway, indicating it's not solely due to social roles.[174,175] This bias can lead to sexual harassment, assault, and rape, forms of coercion and patriarchal control over women. Globally, nearly one in three women have experienced physical or sexual violence, excluding harassment.[176,177] In the United States, over 135,000 rapes were reported in 2017, with less than 1% of perpetrators convicted.[178,179] Most crimes go unreported, and many survivors suffer from physical and mental health issues.[180] High-profile cases have fueled the #MeToo movement, highlighting the prevalence of sexual harassment and assault[181,182,183, 184]

What People and Organizations Can Do to Avoid or Diminish the Effects of Biases on Their Decision-Making Process

On September 1, 1939, the Nazi German Party invaded Poland culminating in the declaration of war by Britain and France, and two days later, the start of the Second World War. It was considered the most destructive human conflict in history, and a period that led to a decline in democratic values in Europe.[185] In the same year, British mathematician, cryptanalyst, and often considered the father of modern computer science,[186] Dr. Alan Turing began crucial work at a Bletchley Park mansion in Buckinghamshire to help British Intelligence crack the "Enigma" code, an enciphering machine used by the German armed forces to send secure messages to their troops and allies.[187] Yet, despite Turing's remarkable key role in saving lives in the United Kingdom by cracking the German enigma code, he was convicted for "homosexual activity" that was still illegal in Britain in 1952 and was sentenced to "chemical castration"[188] by the very Government he helped years prior. The irony in this tragic story is that Turing enabled the United Kingdom to win the war against the German Nazis, yet the British Government at the time acted against homosexuals (luckily later changed to become one of the most inclusive countries for LGBTQIA+ communities in the world[189]), in the same way as the German Nazis, who created a cult of masculinity in which its leaders (namely Heinrich Himmler), developed a plan to exterminate homosexuals in concentration camps along with Jews and other minorities.[190]

It was not until 1967 that England and Wales passed the Sexual Offenses Act Bill,[191] but it did not extend to Scotland until 1980 nor to Northern Ireland until 1982.[192] Homosexuality was also classified by the American Psychiatric Association (APA) as a "sociopathic personality disturbance" and a "sexual deviation," and it was not until 1973 that the APA de-pathologized "homosexuality" from the second edition of its *Diagnostic and Statistical Manual*.[193] But dismally in 2020, 69 countries (and UN member States) continued to criminalize homosexuality,[194] while other nations still consider it a mental disorder,[195] despite not having any scientific basis for such belief, only cultural or religious biases. Contemporary scientists and researchers continuously find that homosexuality is common across the animal kingdom, as it's observed in over 1,000 species and theorized to offer an evolutionary advantage through coparenting and support toward raising relatives' offspring. This discovery by evolutionary biologists clarifies the "Darwin's paradox,"[196] which posed that sexual behavior had to be reproductive. In the case of Britain, the unfairness toward Alan Turing was corrected through a royal pardon by Queen Elizabeth II (the same year that the Same Sex Couples Act 2013 was passed in the British Parliament,[197] and later added the codebreaker to the 50-pound banknote in 2021,[198] thus recognizing how much the nation owed to the genius).

As we've seen thus far, being part of the herd is important to human and nonhuman animals alike as it gives the members of the herd protection from predators and a share of resources among other benefits. So the instinct to survive, to procreate, and to be part of the group drives a whole range of behaviors, even if those behaviors are unfair toward members of minority groups as in the case of the Nazi German Party's hate toward Jews and other groups. Research shows that homosexuals make up approximately 10 percent of the population[199] and are a perfect example of how majority groups can be perceived as a threat to larger groups due to the "deviation" from the standard behavior of the majority, who, as it perceives such menace, find ways to change it or eliminate it. This resulted in the *tyranny of the majority*,[200] a problem that concerned ancient Greek political thinkers, French political scientist Alexis de Tocqueville, and British philosopher John Stuart Mill, who advocated the dangers of ochlocracy, or a Government by mob rule.

Another example of disease misclassification based on a minority group is autism. Autism spectrum disorder (ASD) affects only 1 percent of the world's population[201] and includes positive characteristics such as attention to detail, deep focus, excellent long-term memory and recall, creativity, novel approaches, in-depth knowledge, tenacity and resilience, fearlessness, and the ability to being brutally honest.[202] Thus, these behaviors should be considered superpowers and not a disease as they enabled geniuses such as Michelangelo, Mozart, Charles Darwin, Albert Einstein, Thomas Jefferson, Isaac Newton, Emily Dickinson, Nikola Tesla, Alan Turing, Steve Jobs, Bill Gates, and so many more to enable human progress and create what regular or neurotypicals could not even imagine.[203] However, research conducted by British clinical psychologist and professor of developmental psychopathology at the University of Cambridge, Sir Simon Philip Baron-Cohen, shows that the majority of autistic adults are unemployed

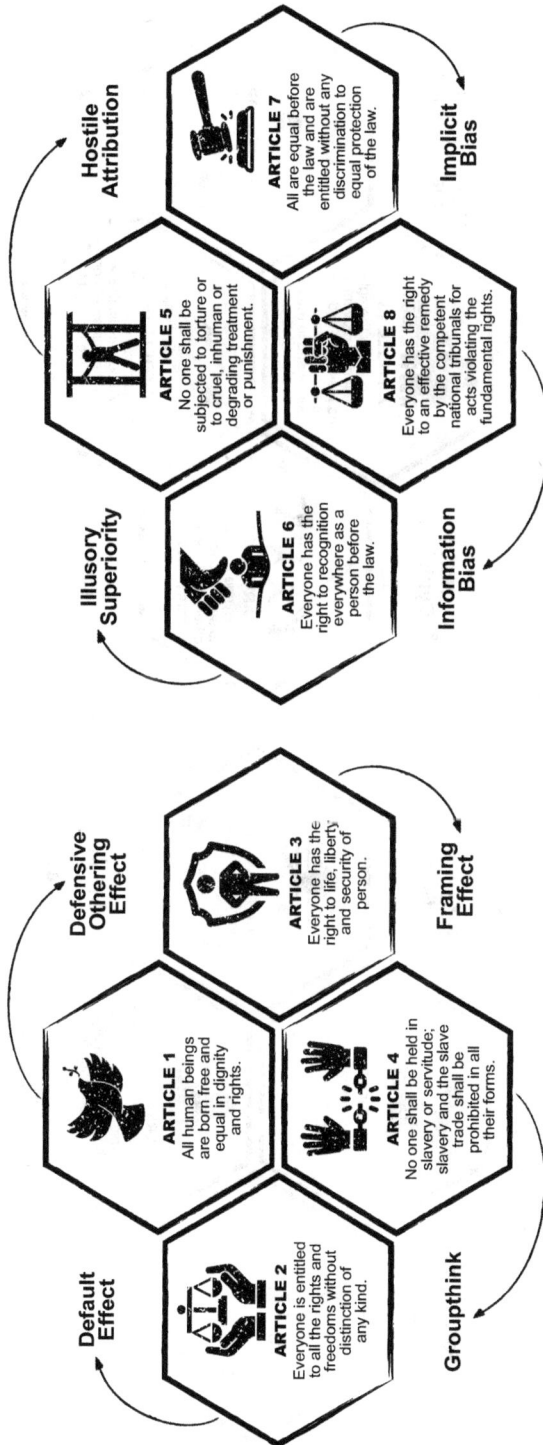

Figure 4.5 How biases are obstacles to achieving human rights

Source: Adapted from the United Nations' Universal Declaration of Human Rights, 1948.[204] A full explanation of each bias (and a full list of 225 biases) is provided at the end of this book. Illustrations by Roman, @ideahits.

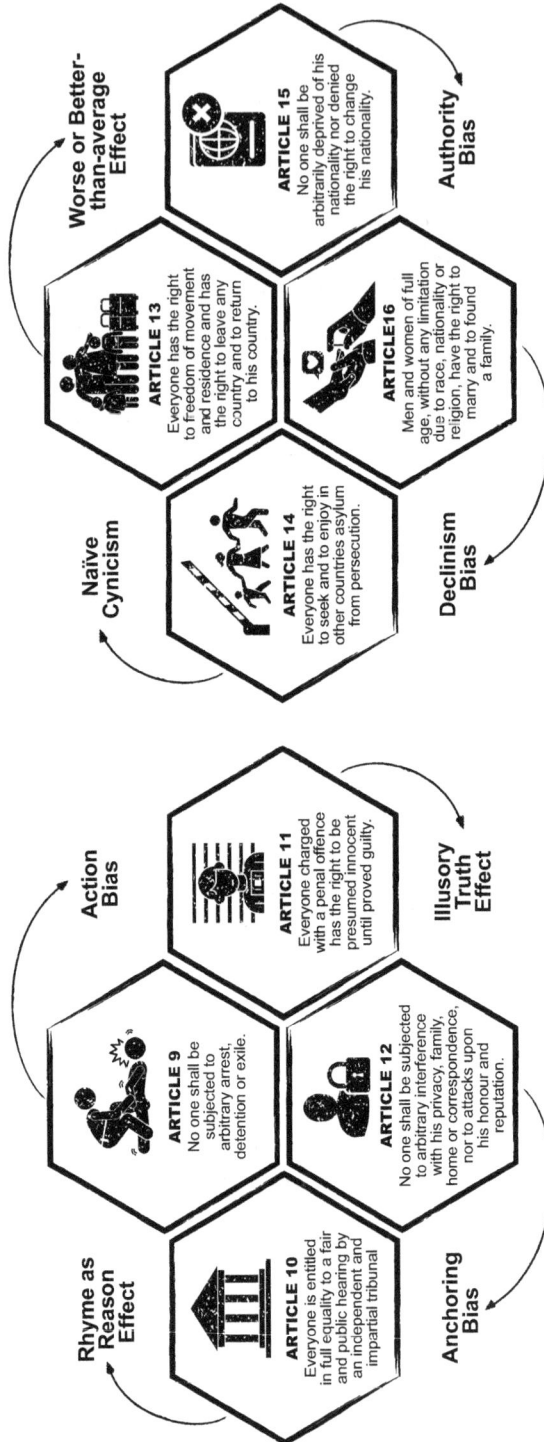

Figure 4.5 (Continued)

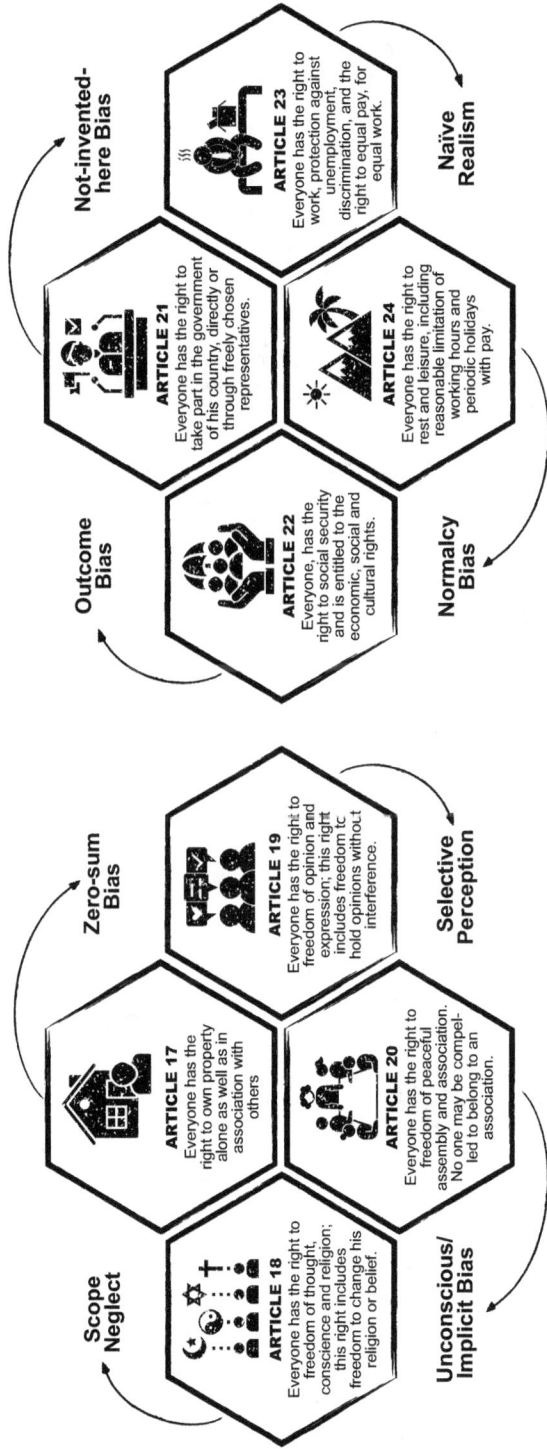

ARTICLE 23
Everyone has the right to work, protection against unemployment, discrimination, and the right to equal pay, for equal work.

ARTICLE 21
Everyone has the right to take part in the government of his country, directly or through freely chosen representatives.

ARTICLE 24
Everyone has the right to rest and leisure, including reasonable limitation of working hours and periodic holidays with pay.

ARTICLE 22
Everyone, has the right to social security and is entitled to the economic, social and cultural rights.

Not-invented-here Bias

Naïve Realism

Outcome Bias

Normalcy Bias

ARTICLE 19
Everyone has the right to freedom of opinion and expression; this right includes freedom to hold opinions without interference.

ARTICLE 17
Everyone has the right to own property alone as well as in association with others

ARTICLE 20
Everyone has the right to freedom of peaceful assembly and association. No one may be compelled to belong to an association.

ARTICLE 18
Everyone has the right to freedom of thought, conscience and religion; this right includes freedom to change his religion or belief.

Zero-sum Bias

Selective Perception

Scope Neglect

Unconscious/ Implicit Bias

Figure 4.5 (Continued)

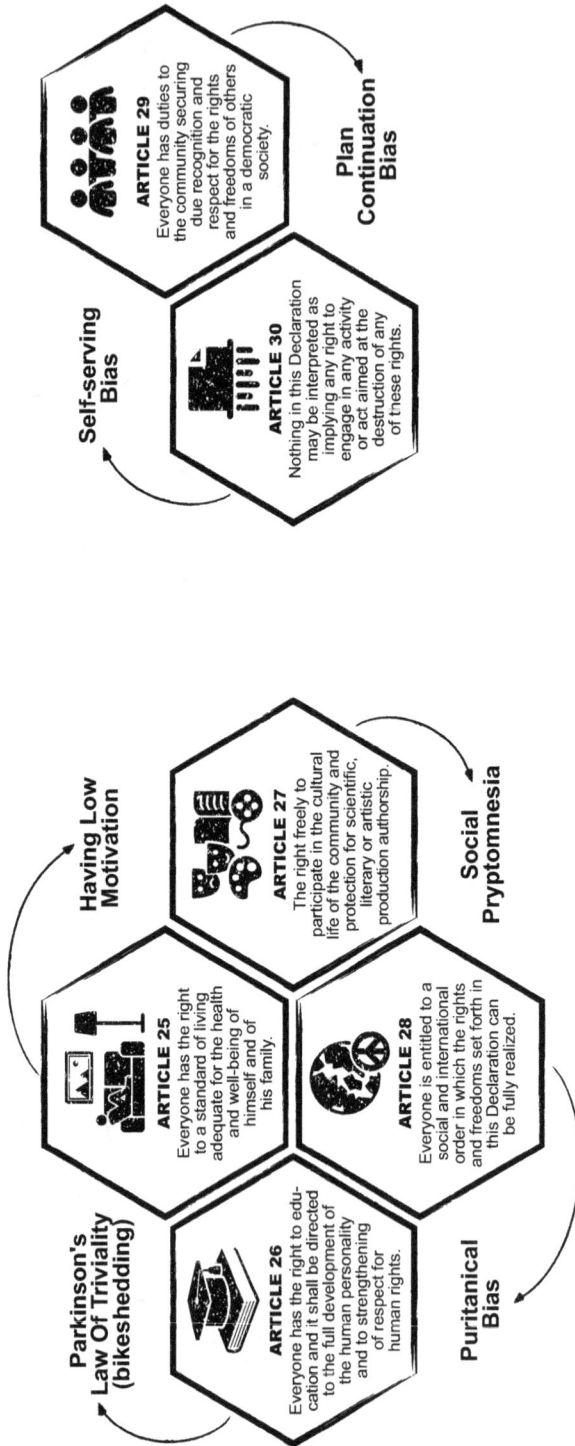

Figure 4.5 (Continued)

and suffer from poor mental health (e.g., with depression and anxiety) as a result of how society treats them (e.g., exclusion and lack of support). And in a world where 21 percent of company CEOs exhibit psychopathic traits[205] that include charm, deceit, manipulation, and lying,[206] being brutally honest and socially awkward as an autistic leader would not be suitable in such a highly political and deceptive environment.

As we have seen thus far, to truly uphold Human Rights, it is first necessary to identify and isolate the root of the problems that stop us from achieving our most fundamental rights in the first place. To do that, we must first acknowledge our animal status and the evolutionary needs we have and how some of them continue to push us to behave in the most inhumane ways toward each other through the biases we display as per the following examples.

Now taking into account the UN's SDGs as another example of how biases deter the progress of equality, wasn't the USD 463.6 trillion global wealth achieved in 2021[207] enough to meet the UN's first goal, "no poverty?" What about SDG number 5, "gender equality" in many developed economies such as the U.S. women make up 59.5 percent of all university students,[208] yet only 8 percent of CEOs are women.[209] By analyzing and addressing the reasons behind the lack of accomplishment of the UN's SDGs, we stand more chance to reach them in the first place as in the following example.

Be Black-and-White About Biases and Walk the Talk

Considering the examples given, biases can be found everywhere and be displayed by anyone because it's simply part of the human experience and decision-making process. But as we progress into more inclusive and fairer societies, what can we do to spot the biases in our thinking and stop them in their tracks? This can happen in several ways and the effects may vary depending on which "hat" or role we are wearing at any given moment. As consumers, we can be more scrupulous in how we select brands and the products we buy. Nowadays, it is quick and easy to research companies, their values, their operations, business models, and if the board of directors is aligned with the brand promise the company makes on its website, annual reports, and social media channels. Companies that promote themselves as fair, yet are set up in ways that do not pay taxes and mistreat employees and the environment are very clear signs of corporate hypocrisy

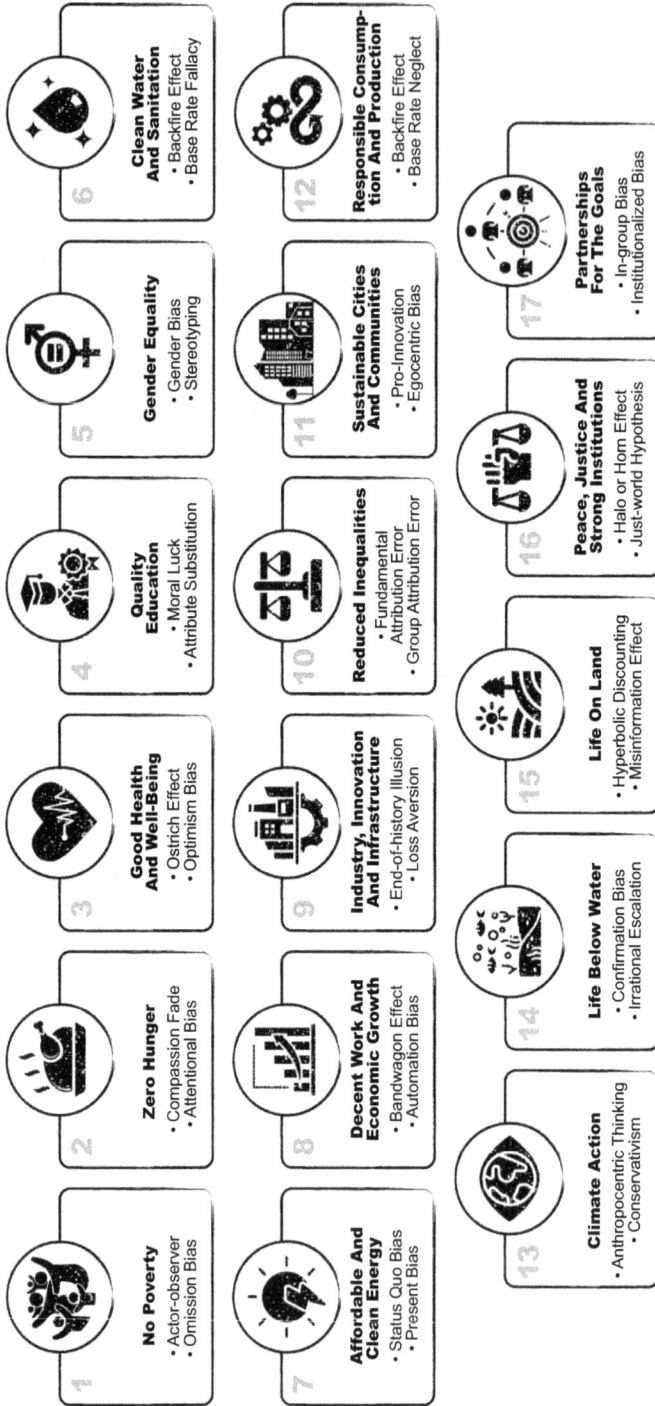

Figure 4.6 Biases and the UN's SDGs

Source: Adapted from the United Nations Sustainable Development Goals[20] by adding some of the biases that help prevent the implementation of each goal. A full explanation of each bias is provided at the end of this book. Illustrations by Roman, @ideahits.

that consumers can find out about, take action through consumer vengeance, and hold these corporations accountable. Are these companies positioned as diverse and inclusive, but the top management is made of a single gender and ethnic background? You will soon find these inconsistencies and purchase products and services from companies that truly live their brand values, vision, and mission statements. For online businesses with a "freemium" business model such as social media companies in which our data is the product (e.g., Twitter, Facebook, Instagram), the difference can be made by boycotting them. Some consumers voice their distrust toward these platforms, but a more effective approach is to leave the platforms completely as it is only via mass evacuation of users that their shares will plummet and an effect can be made to make them listen.

Companies are increasingly engaging in "brand activism" and joining established social movement campaigns to better resonate their values with their target audience, but some of these efforts lack sincerity as their marketing campaigns are far removed from how the company is run in reality. They can, for instance, take steps to close the gender, racial, age, social, and economic gaps during the recruitment process. How is it possible that the CEO-to-worker pay ratio is only increasing, despite recessions, pandemics, and inflation? In the past 20 years, CEOs of the Standard and Poor's 500 (or S&P 500) companies in the United States earned an average of $18.3 million in compensation in 2021, which is *324 times* the median worker's salary pay, an increase from 2020's pay ratio of 299-to-1 and 2019's ratio of 264-to-1.[211] The "greedflation" is allowing for incredible salary discrepancies as in the case of companies such as Amazon where the median salary in 2021 stood at $32,855.00, while CEO Andy Jassy received a whopping $212.7 million in total compensation and the highest CEO-to-worker pay ratio of all S&P 500 companies at 6,474-to-1 ratio.[212] What about recruiting employees from mostly Ivy League schools and universities when it is possible to be creative and innovative without a university degree as is the case of billionaires Bill Gates, Richard Branson, Mark Zuckerberg, Steve Jobs, Ralph Lauren, and many others?[213]

Does your organization select employees (or not) based on their gender, age, and appearance? During the interview process, do you evaluate candidates based on their clothes, appearance, tone of voice, eye

Pre-Interview Screening

Develop a job and skills, not a personality-based pre-screening test to best match candidates with the job and considering neurodiverse talents.

Competence-based Test

Send an online link and or request applicants to perform a test at a local library or university where no one from your organisation is present for a nonjudgemental assessment of results.

Fair Interviewing

The first part of the interview should be performed by a diverse external group with a job-focused, not an appearance/socially/racial/age personality-focused criteria.

Final Interview & Hiring

In this phase, the two parties meet for the first time and candidates also have an opportunity to interview the hiring party to align personal values to avoid arbitrary power asymmetry. Background checks are also performed by diverse external groups.

Job Description

Ensuring that the job description is not done by a single group (i.g. white, heterosexual men) and that the wording is not gender, age or ethnic-based.

Job Advertising

Include a wide range of medias and ways to submit the application of candidates and creating a generic advert that appeals to people of all backgrounds with the required skills.

Receiving Applications

Invest in software that remove applicants personal details and e-mail or advise them not to submit photos, name, age, marital status, nationality, school/university.

Evaluating Applications

Put together a diverse team that can objectively evaluate each application based on what the job requires and invite the best CV /Resume to complete an online screening.

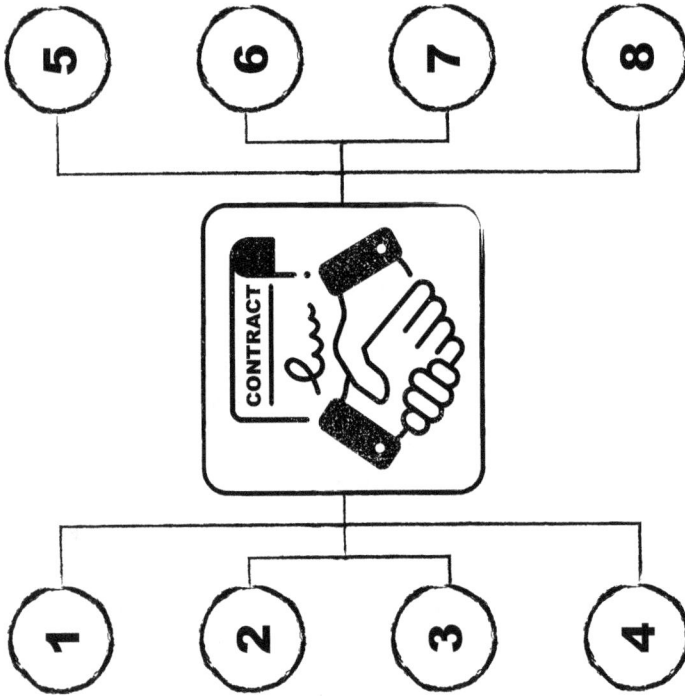

Figure 4.7 Creating a nonbiased recruitment process

Illustrations by Roman, @ideahits.

contact, and handshake? But what if the candidates are autistic, or from a neuro-diverse group, which do not behave in the same way as neurotypicals, but still has an amazing and unique intellectual capacity? If your company accepts employee referrals for vacancies, isn't it encouraging in-group bias and jeopardizing meritocracy (i.e., my network is my net worth type of scenario) by hiring people based on their privilege (of knowing someone who works there)? How about asking employees about their previous salary, which perpetuates low salaries for women and other groups[214] instead of paying them for what the role brings in value to the business? As employees and collaborators, particularly if you are environmentally focused, vegetarian, or vegan, and care for animal welfare, would you want to share your talents with organizations that do not uphold human rights?

Redistributing Investments Worldwide to Remove Geographical Biases

Another important aspect of biases that create inequality comes from the start-up world as in 2021 venture capitalists (VCs) invested over $675 billion in new ventures worldwide (doubling the 2020 investments), and almost half of this amount went to start-ups based in the United States,[215] making it an unequal distribution of wealth. But what is even more disconcerting is the investment percentage received by black female founders, which stood at a mere 0.34 percent of the total venture capital invested in 2021, while 77.1 percent of capital went to white start-up founders (regardless of education or gender), followed by Asians who received 17.7 percent, Middle Easterners received 2.8 percent, and Latinos 1.8 percent.[216] Furthermore, 90 percent of VCs graduated at some of the world's top universities such as Stanford or Harvard and 70 percent of start-ups that successfully raised venture capital had a white male cofounder who also went to Stanford or Harvard.[217] Considering the average annual cost of $70,000 to attend Harvard University and $74,570 to attend Stanford University,[218] having these brand names on the résumé of a student from a family whose salary stands at an average of $51,168 in the United States[219] seems far-fetched, hence the status quo bias is maintained (although effort has been made by Harvard and Stanford to offer financial aid to students in need).

What Else You Can Do About Biases?

How biased are you, your family, your school, your community, your workplace, your local and national Governments, and the brands you buy or help promote? Besides the consumer behavior and marketing applications of the research on biases, the social aspect of this research can and should be considered by all brands and organizations that place a focus on diversity, inclusion, fairness, and social justice in the 21st century. To do so, it is important to start from a ground-level belief that, contrary to what is promoted by governments and religious groups across the world who preach that human beings are born equal, in practice this is not the case as certain groups are of course more privileged than others and inequality permeates most countries. This is certainly a daunting realization, but one that can help people focus on what needs to change to truly offer equality for all. But how can this happen if only small groups control virtually the majority of the wealth and have a vested interest in maintaining the status quo? To make an impact, the first area to be addressed is the education system. To begin with, schools can enroll students by taking into account that there are at least nine different types of intelligence (not only the stereotypical "academic" type), and through this assessment, schools consider "intelligence" in a broader context and thus adapt to students' needs, rather than continue to place "square pegs in round holes" that do not fit them. Schools can also encourage debate and teach about biases that we exhibit and those shown by others and how to tackle them. The education system can enable the next generations to critically evaluate the past and the mistakes of our ancestors, often driven by the necessities of harsh environmental and economic conditions, most of which are unknown to developed nations nowadays. The stereotypes about cultures other than one's own that are presented to children and teenagers will be perpetuated if not challenged.

Take cultural heritage, for instance, supported by technology such as virtual and augmented reality, books, paintings, and sculptures can be brought to life by not merely stating facts such as the year of completion and information about the author or the artist, but by providing context into which biases influenced the views of that generation and why it is no longer accepted to support these views. Antisemitism in Europe, for instance, was widespread up to WWII in the 1940s, particularly in Germany, the home of the Nazi Party. Yet, unfavorable views of Jews decreased after the fall of the Berlin Wall in 1989. In 2019, 88 percent of the population on the West side of the former Berlin Wall had a favorable view of Jews (this view was 51 percent in 1991), compared with 81 percent of people on the East side (59 percent in 1991 had this view), according to the Pew Research Center.[220] The same goes for the belief of Europeans who used the Christian religion to justify slavery from the 15th to the 19th centuries.[221] With knowledge of historical facts, combined with awareness of biases that were most prominent in different regions of the world in specific eras, scholars and researchers can create clusters of biases and tag keywords that show biased and prejudicial views in cultural heritage, therefore allowing for a contemporary view of equality among races and genders. This is one of the ways that AI and machine learning can be decolonized and be rid of built-in biases based on the perceptions of nondiverse groups of developers.[222] The same principle applies to other areas including policy making, the justice system, safety and security, voting, recruitment, investment, and more.

Individuals can take a DNA test and learn about their own ancestry, contact their cousins and other family members from around the world, and try to understand them. They can also take a bias test. We can also aim to try to separate the person from their opinion (e.g., agreeing or disagreeing with someone based on who they are, how they look through the *beauty bias*, their social-economic status under the influence of the *halo* or *horn effects*).

Companies can encourage employees to take bias tests and train them accordingly. As 75 percent of office workers have directly experienced or witnessed some form of misconduct (i.e., bullying, sexual harassment, and discrimination) during their careers, and considering that workplace misconduct cost U.S. companies $20.5 billion alone in 2020,[223] it just makes business sense to tackle this huge problem. Politicians can review their tactics and stop the *othering* bias and the blame game, particularly when it comes to difficult and controversial topics (e.g., holding a gun license, immigration, abortion rights, gay and transgender rights) and be more collaborative and less disruptive with other parties to achieve what is ultimately best for the overall population. Scientists and

What to Consider In a Fairer Decision-making Process

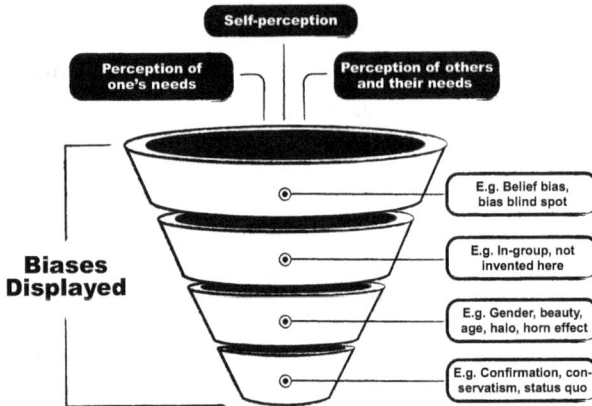

Self-perception

Perception of one's needs

Perception of others and their needs

Biases Displayed

E.g. Belief bias, bias blind spot

E.g. In-group, not invented here

E.g. Gender, beauty, age, halo, horn effect

E.g. Confirmation, con-servatism, status quo

Figure 4.8 **A fairer decision-making process**

Illustrations by Roman, @ideahits.

researchers should also assess their own biases before researching to avoid the *observer-expectancy effect* (aka *Rosenthal effect*) in which researchers can influence how participants react to surveys, experiments, or events as they pick up cues on the researchers' body language, intonation, and facial expressions. Researchers are also prone to the *illusory correlation* bias that leads to a misinterpreting of relationships between variables, thus creating invalid conclusions of correlations.

Finally, all of us need to acknowledge the dualistic nature of biases similar to the Chinese yin and yang philosophy that depicts antagonistic, yet interconnected forces. Our evolution enabled certain biases to exist as they offer a benefit to our survival (e.g., *in-group bias*), reproduction (e.g., *beauty bias*), another aspect of our well-being or the welfare of our family and close groups, but they tend not to conform to the realities of modern and developed societies in which they no longer serve an evo-lutionary purpose. Following a decision-making process that recognizes such natural flaws in our thinking can allow us to create an equal society.

Key Takeaways

1. **Human Universals**: These are psychological, cultural, societal, lin-guistic, and behavioral traits shared by all cultures, reflecting mental

adaptations in human evolutionary history. They provide a solid foundation for evolutionary marketing, avoiding cultural stereotypes.

2. **Social Structure and Status**: Traits such as social structure and status differentiation drive consumption of products that display these qualities, regardless of nationality or background.

3. **Communist Movement**: The Communist utopia envisioned by Marx and Engels aimed for equality by state control of resources. However, it led to severe repression and millions of deaths under authoritarian regimes, highlighting the fundamental human instinct for dominance and high social status.

4. **Survival and Conflict**: Human evolution involves developing tools and strategies for survival in hostile environments. Being part of the "right group" was crucial for survival, leading to human-to-human conflicts.

5. **Historical Efforts for Peace**: Throughout history, rulers and governments have tried to curtail human conflict, with significant milestones such as the Magna Carta, the U.S. Declaration of Independence, and the European Convention on Human Rights.

6. **Biases**: Human biases are deeply rooted in our evolutionary past, influencing our behavior and decision-making processes. Understanding these biases is crucial for creating effective marketing strategies.

7. **Persistence of Conflict**: Despite the Universal Declaration of Human Rights, wars and conflicts persist due to deep-seated biological and psychological instincts that drive human behavior, rooted in ancient survival mechanisms.

8. **Modern Maladaptations**: Some instincts, like the drive to dominate others, are maladapted to the modern world, leading to issues such as economic inequality and the violation of human rights.

9. **Economic Rights and Human Rights**: True human rights cannot exist without economic rights. Economic deprivation forces people into compromising situations, such as bonded labor, highlighting the interconnectedness of civil and economic rights.

10. **Desensitization and Biases**: People often become desensitized to widespread issues such as poverty and inequality, influenced by biases such as the actor-observer bias, bandwagon effect, and status-quo bias.

11. **Historical Declines**: The decline of ancient civilizations often resulted from a combination of internal and external factors, including pandemics, social cohesion decline, and resource depletion, which are still relevant today.

12. **Environmental Concerns**: Environmental issues have been a concern since ancient times, but the modern environmental movement has gained strength, driven by NGOs and activists like Greta Thunberg, pushing for significant changes to reduce human impact on nature.

13. **Activism and Change**: Creative and high-profile protests by environmental activists have raised awareness and pressured governments and organizations to take action on environmental issues.

14. **TBL**: John Elkington's concept of People, Planet, and Profit (TBL) emphasizes the environmental, social, and economic impacts of companies, influencing global business models.

15. **SDGs**: The UN's 17 SDGs, agreed upon by 193 member states in 2015, aim to address global challenges, including poverty, inequality, and climate change.

16. **Disparity in Attention**: Despite the severe impacts of social inequality, climate change receives more public attention, possibly due to salience bias, where more noticeable and emotionally compelling issues trigger greater action.

17. **Biases in Practice**: The Covid-19 pandemic and the murder of George Floyd in 2020 highlighted how context and media coverage can influence public outcry and activism, with significant protests and movements like BLM gaining momentum.

18. **Racial Inequality**: Statistics show that black people are disproportionately affected by police violence, but not all cases receive the same level of attention, influenced by factors such as media coverage and cultural context.

19. **Empathy and Context**: The context of events, such as the pandemic during George Floyd's death, can amplify public empathy and response. American cultural influence also plays a role in the global reaction to such events.

20. **Narrow Scope of Empathy**: Human empathy is often limited and not equally distributed, leading to varying levels of compassion and action for different victims and issues.

21. **Historical Context of Bias**: The story of Alan Turing highlights how biases and discriminatory laws can lead to unjust treatment, even of those who have made significant contributions to society.

22. **Legal Progress and Remaining Challenges**: While some countries have made progress in LGBTQIA+ rights, many still criminalize homosexuality or consider it a mental disorder, reflecting deep-seated cultural and religious biases.

23. **Evolutionary Perspective**: Homosexuality is common in the animal kingdom and may offer evolutionary advantages, challenging the notion that sexual behavior must be reproductive.

24. **Group Dynamics and Bias**: The instinct to be part of a group can lead to unfair treatment of minority groups, as seen in historical and contemporary examples of discrimination.

25. **Autism and Misclassification**: ASD includes many positive traits that should be valued, but societal biases often lead to exclusion and poor mental health outcomes for autistic individuals.

26. **Psychopathic Traits in Leadership**: A significant percentage of company CEOs exhibit psychopathic traits, which contrasts sharply with the honesty and directness often found in autistic individuals, highlighting a bias in leadership preferences.

27. **Addressing Biases**: To uphold human rights, it is crucial to identify and address the root causes of biases, acknowledging our evolutionary instincts and how they influence behavior.

CHAPTER 5

We Are All Hormonal

Learning Objectives—By reading this chapter, readers will be able to:

- Gain more knowledge about how hormones can affect human biology and behavior.
- Differentiate the types of sex hormones that are present in men and women and the effects.
- Ascertain which hormones affect decision making and how they function.
- Explain how the pleiotropy theory of senescence[1] influences a range of behaviors.
- Devise a marketing plan including male and female hormones and their related behaviors.

Source: Adapted from *Creating Significant Learning* Experiences[2] Taxonomy of Significant Learning Experiences.[3]

The research on decision making by Israeli-American psychologist, economist, and Nobel prize winner, Daniel Kahneman describes the terms System 1 (i.e., the intuitive) and System 2 (i.e., analytical thinking) styles, respectively. In *Thinking, Fast and Slow*,[4] Kahneman describes the two systems in depth. *System 1* is the fast, automatic, intuitive, and mostly unconscious thinking style, whereas *System 2* is slow, deliberate, analytical, conscious, and most importantly, it is effortful. And we can expand on Kahneman's studies by considering the influence of hormones on decision making. So let's examine what triggers love, hate, maternal bonding, or dominant behavior. Is it produced by our personalities, our upbringing, or by our instincts? Or is it by a combination of all of them? Since the first scientific experiment on hormones of domesticated roosters in 1849, conducted by the German scientist, physiologist, and zoologist

Dr. Arnold Berthold,[5] it has been demonstrated that hormones such as testosterone influence a range of behaviors in human and nonhuman animals. In his experiment, Dr. Berthold removed the roosters' testicles and after that, the cockerel stopped chasing hens in the backyard.[6] After that, Dr. Berthold castrated two more roosters and implanted a testicle from each one into the other's abdomen, and *voilà*, the birds returned to their normal hen chasing and aggressive behavior, thus enabling Dr. Berthold's novel understanding of how hormones impact the body's control systems.[7] Subsequently, the role of the endocrine system and the secretions of our internal organs (i.e., hormones) have led to further discoveries related to weight gain and loss, hair growth or the lack of it, height, fertility, aging, mood, and a wide range of consequences related to hormones. Further research in the past century has led to the development of the birth control pill[8]; hormone replacement therapy to reduce the effects of menopause in women[9]; and testosterone therapy to boost men's memory and bone density, and remedy anemia.[10]

The effects of oxytocin, the so-called love hormone, were found to go beyond the maternal–child bonding as researchers learned that oxytocin works as both a hormone and a neurotransmitter. It is also associated with long-term mating and other social behaviors that foster trust, love, friendship, family bonds, economic transactions, and even political networks.[11] For instance, an experiment organized by the economist Ernst Fehr of the University of Zurich and his colleagues showed that men who inhaled a nasal spray spiked with oxytocin were willing to give more money to partners in a risky investment game when compared to men who sniffed a spray that did not contain oxytocin.[12] However, despite all these varied discoveries that affect the male and female genders, hormones are still mostly associated with women and the menstrual cycle.

This is best exemplified in the words of James E. King who was the president of the American Association of Obstetricians, Gynecologists, and Abdominal Surgeons[13] when he addressed the audience in his inaugural presidential speech in 1939 stating:

The fear or surprise that her first menstruation may cause depends upon how well she has been prepared to expect it. From this moment it would appear that she, like Mother Eve, had eaten of the fruit of the Tree of Knowledge and had thereby become sex conscious. With the complex physical phenomena that result from the secretion of the temporary glands with that of the permanent glands concerned in menstruation, it is not surprising that there also may be associated with certain mental reactions during the menstrual cycle. Women so frequently experience mental depression at those times, that slight degrees may be regarded as normal. Other types of mental disturbances may also be seen. One that is relatively common is varying degrees of unreasonableness. Women who may be lovable and sweet-tempered at other times, during menstruation become termagants. She has been the enigma of all ages, a creature swayed by moods and impulses. Neither the imagination of the poet nor the wisdom of the philosopher has solved her. But the solution is now at hand; it lies in those complex and potent chemicals, the secretions of the endocrine glands. As one contemplates the changes which have taken place in a woman's estate in the past one hundred years, and considers the economic importance which today she often assumes in supporting a husband and home, one may well wonder what her position will be in the next one hundred years. Will she, as some timid souls fear, mentally and physically dominate and enslave us as we in the past enslaved her? Probably not; so long as she is controlled by her reproductive glands, she will remain basically the same loveable and gracious homemaker.[14]

Slavery indeed was tackled quicker than sexism as full voting rights were extended in 1870 to African Americans under the Fourteenth and Fifteenth Amendments to the American Constitution.[15] The same rights were only granted to women in 1920, following the ratification of the Nineteenth Amendment.[16] The United States elected its first African American president in 2008,[17] while, as of 2025, the United States has still never had a female president.[18] Perhaps, King's misogynistic thinking that only women, not men, had their physiological and biological behavior influenced by hormones had its origins over 2,000 years earlier in writings from antiquity as the ancient Greeks including grand historical figures such as the philosopher Plato (c. 428–347 BC)[19] and the physician Hippocrates (c. 460– 375 BC),[20] who believed that the uterus was the "origin of all disease" and described it as an illness called *hysterike pnix* (i.e., *the suffocation of the womb*) that caused women's *erratic and unreliable behavior.*[21] One of the prescribed treatments for *hysterike pnix* in those days was to keep women pregnant all the time.[22]

Various references in the Bible refer to the uncleanliness of the menstrual cycle, such as the passage of Leviticus 15:19,[23] which states that "when a woman has a discharge of blood that is a menstrual discharge from her body, she shall be in her impurity for seven days, and whoever touches her shall be unclean until the evening."[24] Some 1,600 years later in the American estate of Massachusetts, New England, the infamous Salem Witch Trials occurred almost regularly between 1638 and 1725 where 78 percent of the people accused and executed for alleged witchcraft were women.[25] The accusation for "crimes" committed ranged from being too poor (i.e., perceived as a sign of a bad character); stepping outside the prescribed roles as wives, mothers, and homemakers; having too many children meant that the woman may have made a pact with the devil, and too few children was also suspicious; not being gentle or grateful; being unpleasant, showing a forcible speech and domineering ways; being confident and determined; or expressing their opinions and standing their ground.[26] The deeply held beliefs of the Puritan community in those days recalled the Biblical sinful apple eaten by Eve and the view that women were more likely than men to be tempted by the devil.

William Shakespeare reinforced this view in literature decades earlier with the characters of the three witches (i.e., Weird Sisters or Wayward Sisters), which led to the downfall of Macbeth. The play Macbeth is believed to have been first performed in the English course in 1606, three years after James VI and I ascended to the English throne following the death of his cousin Elizabeth I, who did not leave direct heirs.[27] Historians state that James VI and I became troubled by the subject of witchcraft following the execution of his mother, Mary Queen of Scots, in 1587. Upon their return from Denmark, James VI and I and his new wife, Anne, faced a violent storm while sailing back to England; he blamed it on evil spells and ordered a barbarous witch hunt, which was only ordered to stop 130 years later.[28] Fast-forwarding to 2016, the misogynist insult of "witchcraft" and "witch hunts" remain in many walks of life, as well as in politics as presidential candidate Hillary Clinton was often depicted on social media in a stereotypical witch costume, wearing a black hat, riding a broom, and green skin.[29] Clinton followed in the footsteps of over 200 other female candidates who had sought the U.S. presidency at one time or another,[30] yet were not elected, perhaps due to biases explained in Part 2, Chapter 4, *225 Biases—Which Ones Do You Display?*

The first of such women was Victoria Woodhull, the first female broker of Wall Street and the first woman who ran in the U.S. presidential elections in 1872, 50 years before the ratification of the 19th Amendment, which allowed women the right to vote. Her candidacy was dismissed even by the suffragist leaders for having "indecent" ideas and moral judgment such as "free love" (e.g., the ability for men and women to get married, divorced, and remarry if they wished); universal suffrage, an eight-hour workday; the abolition of the death penalty and slavery.[31] But the ceiling started to crack, and as of January 20, 2021, the United States elected its first woman, and its first woman of color as vice president, Kamala Harris alongside President Joe Biden, who defeated the incumbent president, Donald Trump, and vice president, Mike Pence, in the 2020 election.

In recent years, studies have found possible associations between moral judgment, hormones, and decision-making theories are expanding from the traditional rationalist logic[32] to approaches such as the social intuitionist model,[33] which states that moral judgment, the result of quick, automatic evaluations (i.e., intuitions); and the dual-process theory,[34] defined as a process model of moral judgment where alternative modes of processing are associated with different moral outputs, one called the *automatic processing* with *deontological judgment* (e.g., an action is morally based on the intent of the act and the actor's adherence to moral principles), and *controlled processing* with *utilitarian judgment* (e.g., choosing whether to sacrifice one life to save the lives of a greater number of people). Both theories do not only highlight the role of reason but also the importance of emotions within the moral judgment process influenced by personal, biological, and social variables, thanks to discoveries from the field of neuroscience.[35] Hormones function similarly to neurotransmitters and also influence behavior, keeping our bodies working normally, and affecting how our moods, emotions, and stresses are triggered. Hormones matter in the context of decision making as recent studies suggest that hormones such as testosterone and estrogen shape a wide range of behaviors both in social and economic decision making as drivers to achieve resources, social status, and prospective mating partners.[36] With that, differences have been found in how hormones affect the physical development and the behavior of men and women because both genders have been facing different *adaptive challenges* and opportunities throughout evolution.

The first challenge faced by men and women alike is addressed by the *senescence theory*,[37] which states that the human body has an innate deterioration process that leads to the decline in fitness components such as fertility in old age and life expectancy[38] and that the function of *natural selection* declines greatly as old age increases. This occurs because some organisms have a limited amount of resources, namely, time, energy, and nutrients, and therefore require trade-offs to be made between the allocation of bodily maintenance, growth, and reproduction.[39] The *pleiotropy theory of senescence*[40] observed that a gene is able to have two or more opposing effects, which is exemplified by the mortality-enhancing circumstances found in both men and women once their peak fertility years have passed. In women, the onset of menopause may also lead to serious diseases such as weight gain, hypertension, and cardiovascular diseases, thus potentially causing the death of women not long after she reaches the end of the child-bearing phase of her life.[41] In the case of men, testosterone (e.g., which enables men to outcompete other men in procreating and also achieving social status), if found in too much quantity in men's bodies, it poses a negative effect with an increased risk of prostate cancer.[42] Moreover, the fertility window of women[43] starts at puberty (i.e., from the late teens) and ends with the arrival of menopause (i.e., usually by 45 years old). Women are already born with all the eggs they are going to have in their lifetime and by age 37, 90 percent of eggs are gone.[44] Men, by contrast, start to produce sperm during puberty and will continue to produce it throughout their lifetime; however, the quality of the sperm declines with old age,[45] and by the time a man is 40 years old, he and his partner are 30 percent less likely to conceive,[46] and at age 45, it can take five times longer for him to enable his partner to conceive than if he was 25 years old or younger.[47]

The *pleiotropy theory of senescence* also clarifies why our organs decay in old age and why men tend to die on average approximately seven years younger than women[48] due to the men's reproductive variability compared to women. Men can produce as many children as women are willing and able to carry, or not produce a single child in their lifetime, whereas women generally can produce about a maximum of 12 children in their lifetimes.[49] Men's potential reproductive success compared to women thus becomes a trade-off with decreased survival.[50] Other animals such as the giant tortoise can live over 150 years, whales over two centuries, and the freshwater mussel celebrates 280 birthdays[51]; other water-based animals like the *Turritopsis dohrnii* also called "immortal jellyfish" and the invertebrate *Hydra* can self-regenerate, do not show signs of aging and die only when eaten by other fish or causes other than aging, or diseases.[52] Both the *Turritopsis dohrnii* and *Hydra* are considered to be immortal because they are mostly made up of *stem cells* that are the "engine" of regeneration and self-renewal with the ability to duplicate or clone themselves.[53]

These stem cells are being used in regenerative medicine in an attempt to interrupt or even reverse chronic diseases, repair or replace tissues or organs that were damaged by congenital defects, diseases, and traumas.[54] There are three types of these special stem cells: embryonic, which are pluripotent (i.e., they can increase all types of cells that comprise the human body), umbilical cord (i.e., mesenchymal or MSC), and adult stem cells that are multipotent, which means that they can develop into more than one type of cell; however, they are more limited than pluripotent cells.[55] Hormones affect the biology of stem cells in the ovary, intestine, hematopoietic system, and the mammary gland because hormones control all stages of stem cells' life, from their creation, expansion, maintenance, and differentiation.[56] Keeping the umbilical cord fluid (which is filled with stem cells) in cord blood banks is very popular among celebrities who hope to use these stem cells to treat anything from cancer, anemia, immune system disorders, and even other conditions such as Alzheimer's, diabetes, heart failure, and spinal cord damage.[57] This is the human attempt to increase the human body's ability to recover and cheat old age and death beyond the current range between 120 and 150 years old[58] in a dream-like goal to be like the biblical character Methuselah who was said to have lived to 969 years old.[59] Technology giants such as the technology conglomerate holding, Alphabet (Google's parent company), invest heavily in life extension technologies and drug-producing companies

such as the California-based Calico Life Sciences, led by molecular biologist Dr. Cynthia Kenyon whose remarkable research on *Caenorhabditis
elegans* hermaphrodites found that mutations in the gene *daf*-2 can enable
them to live over twice as long, and therefore discovering that the rate of
aging can be manipulated biologically.[60]

Various hormones act in distinct ways in men and women to create the corresponding physical and behavioral attributes necessary to
conceive. Given the *adaptive challenge* that women face in having a limited window of opportunity to reproduce, men became sensitive to the
observable qualities displayed by women, which correspond to cues of
fertility or their *reproductive value* such as women's youth and physical
attractiveness, which explains why men of all cultures and throughout
history developed a preference to mate with young as instead of with
older and postmenopausal women.[61] Behaviorally, men spend more
money on engagement rings when they date younger rather than on older
brides-to-be, and the brides become younger and younger each time men
remarry.[62] Hence, a man's predilection for younger women leads women
to withhold information about their age on different occasions, as in the
case of dating sites when looking for new mates.[63] A study related to a dating service in Germany found that as men's income increases, they tend
to look for younger partners.[64] Men married to younger women were
found to display more effort in *mate retention*[65] by hiding their partners
from social occasions, showing possessiveness, emotional manipulation,
threats, and even physical violence.[66] When marrying younger women,
men would therefore increase their chances of paternity through continuous or exclusive sexual access to a woman, and with reproductive success,
men's genes would also continue into the next generation, thus justifying
their paternal investment and protection.[67] Hence, theories show that it is
not the beauty of youth itself that men seek in women, but their fertility
or reproductive value,[68] which these physical observable qualities present
about a woman's health.[69]

New studies continue to support "the lipstick effect" theory as women
seek to boost beauty, particularly during economic recession.[70] The
beauty industry has been targeting mostly women for millennia with
varied products that accentuate their facial and bodily features to allure
men. From the Ancient Egyptians who used makeup to enhance their

eyes and cosmetics to paint their faces, to the Ancient Greeks, Romans, and Israelites who adopted skin-care products, hairstyles, jewelry, fashion, fragrances, and plastic cosmetic surgery to today's multitrillion-dollar beauty industry worldwide.[71] The search for beauty and the retention of youth continues to lead women to spend money on makeup (e.g., lipstick and mascara) that promises to make women's faces more feminine and attractive,[72] and many do not stop there and take further steps in the pursuit of beauty by undergoing plastic surgery such as breast augmentation, liposuction, and rhinoplasty and comprise 86.3 percent of the 10,129,528 plastic surgeries performed worldwide.[73] Beauty enhancements serve the evolutionary purposes of *acquiring* and *retaining a mate*, *to* signal wealth and *social status* among other benefits such as increasing one's self-confidence and self-esteem.[74]

Women's menstrual cycle has been associated with hormonal shifts that have been shown to influence a variety of physiological and attitude changes and also influence consumer behavior. Multiple studies suggested that during the fertile phase of the menstrual cycle (i.e., approximately days 8 to 15), women choose sexier clothing, engage in greater beautification behavior,[75] prefer products that improve social standing to outcompete rivals,[76] and are more interested in attending social gatherings. In this phase, women also become more attracted to socially dominant, masculine, tall, and muscular men as they command fear, respect, and genetic quality. Studies have shown women's preferences for men with a more symmetrical and masculine-looking face, featuring longer and broader lower jaws, heavy brow ridges, pronounced cheekbones, and a prominent chin, and men with a deep voice as it shows sexual maturity and also implicitly demonstrate high levels of testosterone, which is unconsciously perceived as a sign of good health.[77]

In addition, food-related desires, consumption, and purchasing behavior increase at the luteal phase (i.e., approximately days 21 to 28[78]). Furthermore, higher levels of estrogen in women (i.e., the ovarian hormone) have been correlated with fertility and facial femininity,[79] which in turn is associated with increased health and disease resistance.[80] Progesterone hormones regulate the menstrual cycle and are responsible for the maintenance of pregnancy.[81] A spike in progesterone levels is linked to the luteal phase (i.e., a phase that begins after ovulation and finishes on the first day of the period) and was also associated with an increase in caloric intake.[82] Studies have shown that men found women more attractive when progesterone levels were low, which is the follicular (i.e., fertile) phase of the ovulatory cycle, and also when estradiol levels were high compared to progesterone levels, a period that coincides with high conception risk.[83] During the menstrual cycle, increased estradiol levels cause the maturation and release of the egg, as well as the thickening of the uterus lining to allow a fertilized egg to implant.[84] It is estimated that, for most women, the menstrual cycle is about 28 days and is divided into four phases in which the two core feminine sex hormones estrogen and progesterone stream, thus creating diverging levels of energy[85]:

- **Period phase:** The first day of a menstrual period in which estrogen and progesterone hormone levels are at their lowest level but rise gradually
- **Follicular phase:** The week after a period finishes, estrogen levels start to rise rapidly in preparation for ovulation
- **Luteal phase:** The time of ovulation, roughly 14 days ahead of the next period (for the majority of women), estrogen levels increase
- **Premenstrual phase:** The week ahead of the next period, estrogen and progesterone levels fall and some of the symptoms may include mood swings, fatigue, and bloating

Although men do not have a menstrual cycle or go through menopause, they too, like women, are physically influenced by sex hormones such as testosterone, which is responsible for the maintenance of masculine physical characteristics and behaviors.[86] Often called "male menopause," andropause is classed as the number of symptoms that men experience after 30 years old and it is attributed to the gradual decrease in testosterone levels at the rate of about 2 percent per year.[87] In this phase, men can also experience[88]:

- Mood swings and irritability
- Loss of muscle mass and experience a reduced ability to exercise

Before

1. Constant fatigue
2. Increased risk of Alzhemer's Disease
3. Depression
4. Excess fat tissue
5. Risk of low libido and Erectile Dysfunction (ED)
6. Exposure to osteoporosis

After

1. Sharper mind
2. More muscle mass
3. Healthier heart
4. More confidence
5. Boost in energy
6. Healthy libido and strong erections
7. Robust bones

Figure 5.1 Hormone replacement therapy—offered by clinics around the world to reduce the effects of aging in men and women

Source: Illustrations by Roman, @ideahits.

- A large belly and or gynecomastia (i.e., "man boobs")
  develops
- A lack of energy and enthusiasm
- Difficulty sleeping (i.e., insomnia)
- Increased tiredness
- Poor concentration and short-term memory
- Loss of libido and erectile dysfunction as a result of stress
- Depression and anxiety

The "male menopause" or andropause has also been associated with late-onset hypogonadism (i.e., when the testes produce few or no hormones), which can also present from birth later causing symptoms such as small testes and delayed puberty.[89] The testes (i.e., testicles) make testosterone and the physical changes that turn a boy into a man during puberty with changes such as the growth of the penis and testes, the production of facial, pubic, and bodily hair, the deepening of the voice, the building muscles and strong bones and an increase in height. Men need normal amounts of this hormone to make sperm and be able to have children.[90]

Studies continue to correlate testosterone with male-related behaviors such as dominance, competitiveness, aggression, and a willingness to achieve and maintain status.[91] In popular culture in many countries, the link between men's bravery and the testosterone from his testes that enables him to act in a virile, "manly" way equates to the saying that a man "does not have the balls" or the "cojones"; in other words, he is an emasculated coward who lacks the courage to make a decision, as described by former U.S. vice presidential candidate Sarah Palin as she stated that the then President Barack Obama did not have the "cojones to secure the nation's borders and fix its immigration system," while she backed the decision of the Arizona Governor Jan Brewer to fight the Federal Government in court over Arizona's new and controversial immigration law.[92]

The topic of "cojones" or the lack of it has been a topic of interest and has been featured in famous paintings as in the case of *The Mutilation of Uranus by Saturn* by the Renaissance artist Giorgio Vasari,[93] which depicts the mythical episode in which Saturn, the Roman agricultural deity (or Cronus in ancient Greece) castrates his father Uranus (representing heaven in Greek mythology and Caelus in the Roman version).[94] In literature, eunuchs (i.e., men whose sexual organs have been removed) have been referenced for thousands of years, from the Bible references several Eunuchs by name (e.g., Shaashgaz, the King's eunuch who was in charge of the concubines, Esther 2:14[95]; Hegai, the king's eunuch who was in charge of the harem, Esther 2:15[96]) to the Cumming Manuscript Collection of the New York Academy of Medicine Library, which contains over 1,200 references and documents on the early history of human castration from before the time of Aristotle in the 4th-century BC.[97] Male castrations have been performed throughout history by many cultures including Egyptian, Chinese, European, Byzantine, Indian, and the Ottoman Empire for a variety of reasons such as to punish and obtain revenge, to demonstrate one's religious fanaticism, to protect women, to enable eunuchs' trade as in the case of China's Forbidden City, or for a therapeutical function.[98] In more contemporary times, men were castrated for racial or eugenics reasons, or simply to obtain soprano voices and sustain a strong falsetto, as in the case of renowned Italian 20th-century *castrato* singer, or "angel of Rome" Alessandro Moreschi or Carlo Broschi, known by his stage name Farinelli, who was considered in the 18th century as one of the greatest singers in opera history.[99] The *castrati* (i.e., castrated in Italian) singers were the "answer"[100] that the Catholic Church found for the Bible's quote, which says that "women should remain silent in the churches. They are not allowed to speak, but must be in submission, as the law says," Corinthians 14:34.[101] For this reason, female singers were banned from singing on any stage in Rome, due to the decree by Pope Sixtus V from 1588 to 1798, leading many poor Italian families to castrate their young boys in an attempt to support their young son's singing careers at the Church.[102]

The decriminalization of homosexuality[103] and the legalization of same-sex marriages[104] in many countries in the 21st century have made a significant difference in the lives of the LGBTQ+ community who have also benefited from hormone treatment in gender reassignments (i.e., gender-affirmation) procedures or surgeries to improve their mental health and quality of life.[105] Clinics nowadays offer feminizing hormone therapy for male-to-female gender congruence in which patients take estrogen (e.g., as a pill, an injection, cream, gel, spray, or patch) to decrease testosterone production and thus activate feminization. Within weeks to a few months, *feminizing hormone therapy*[106] begins to produce changes in the body and in the psychological state of the patient, such as a decline in libido and automatic erections (one to three months after starting treatment), the redistribution of body fat (from three to six months after the treatment commencement), a decrease in muscle mass (from three to six months), and a reduction in facial and body hair growth (within 6 to 12 months). Other effects include testicular atrophy (from three to six months), and the development of breasts (which takes place from three to six months after the beginning of the treatment).[107] On the other hand, female-to-male transitions, or *masculinizing hormone therapy* involve taking testosterone, which suppresses the menstrual cycle, while also decreasing the production of estrogen from the ovaries to match the patient's gender identity.[108] The changes produced will cease the menstrual cycle (from two to six months after the start of the treatment), the growth of facial and body hair and body fat redistribution (three to six months), the increase of muscle mass and strength (within 6 to 12 months after treatment), the deepening of the voice (from 3 to 12 months), and clitoral enlargement and vaginal atrophy (which begins between 3 and 12 months after treatment[109]).

The first openly transgender Olympic athletes competed in Tokyo in 2021, but since 2004 the International Olympic Committee has authorized transgender athletes to take part in the Olympics, as long as they transitioned four years before competing (at the earliest) and can demonstrate that they had lower levels of testosterone for 12 months before competing,[110] as high testosterone levels are considered to provide a competitive edge to transgender athletes[111] and "an unfair competitive advantage" that can give them 12 percent leverage in running tests, even after two years of taking hormones to suppress their testosterone, as recent studies found.[112]

Testosterone is also present in women but in much smaller amounts than in men. Hence, saying that someone does something "like a girl" implies that a male way of doing something is correct, better, stronger, and so on. This was best exemplified in the 2014 Always:#LikeaGirl advert[113] created by the maker of feminine period products, Always owned by Procter and Gamble. The #LikeaGirl advert became a huge success and evolved into an empowering movement led by Always to help girls keep their confidence through puberty and enable them to tackle limiting beliefs found in many societies about what it means to be a girl. Yet, these physiological and psychological differences between men and women originate in the adaptive challenges that each faced throughout evolution. Our environment today still has evolved mechanisms from hunter-gatherer societies from the past, which are no longer advantageous in peaceful and prosperous societies,[114] and being aware of what they are and how they operate, can enable us to address them accordingly as in the case of unconscious and cognitive biases discussed in Chapter 4. The evolutionary process, best described by Charles Darwin, tells us that "as more individuals are produced than can survive, there must in every case be a struggle for existence, either one individual or another of the same species, or with the individuals of distinct species, or with the physical conditions of life."[115] Hence, fighting the "hostile forces of nature," or *adaptive problems* such as severe weather, diseases, food shortages, parasites, predators, and hostile conflicts with members of the same species helped enable the mechanisms that facilitate survival, which is still imprinted within the human biology and psychology today.[116] Each new generation has tried to solve these adaptive challenges with new strategies and tools thought to be suitable for that period. Consequently, we have developed a sense of what foods are safe to eat compared to food that might be poisonous (e.g., our ingrained disgust for contaminated food, infectious animals and insects, gaping wounds, and poor hygiene).[117] We have also learned which were the right animals to hunt and which animals to fear and avoid (e.g., our innate fear of snakes and spiders and our ability as children and adults alike to locate these animals significantly faster than other harmless ones.[118] And finally, we have mastered whom to obey or fight with (e.g., fear of strange men and authoritative or higher status others[119]) to increase our chances of survival.

Although the "men-hunter" and the "female-gatherer" theory is being debunked by new research that shows that in 13 out of 179 societies surveyed, women also participated in big-game hunting activities[120] Researchers confirmed that women did not hunt often[121] due to conflicting demands between the provision of child care and hunting. Recent research confirmed this hypothesis and found that although women are capable of hunting big game, pregnant, lactating, and those with dependents did not hunt often unless child care was available or a rich hunting ground was near the camp or village.[122] This necessity to care for children helped shape risk preferences between the genders. Men were more likely to hunt alone or in small groups and targeted big game that required the muscular strength needed in fast-paced, long-distance travel, to launch projectile weapons, and fearlessness to face the risks of failure.[123] Women, by contrast, preferred to hunt in groups and targeted smaller and easier-to-capture prey near camps or villages, usually accompanied by dogs.[124] Women also developed logistical, ritualistic, and crafting skills to manufacture clothing, weaponry, and transportation equipment to support hunters in their endeavors.[125] Furthermore, women's smaller physiques meant that their strategic abilities were developed to locate, surround, and drive the game to the killing location in the safest way.[126] In addition to gender-specific risk tolerance, there are also discrepancies between fears and phobias exhibited by men and women. Charles Darwin summarized the role of fear as inherently independent from having experienced the threatening events that lead to it when he wrote: "May we not suspect that the fears of children, which are quite independent of experience, are the inherited effects of real dangers ... during ancient savage times?"[127] This matters because humans developed an *attention bias* toward ancestral dangers and evolved visual, olfactory, auditory, and other senses to spot such dangers.[128] Accordingly, we are way more likely to develop fears of dangers that existed in ancestral times, such as fear of poisonous animals that we do not often find in larger cities, than the threats that we find widely available in our current environment such as cars, cigarettes, guns, and other dangers that are more likely to harm our health and well-being.[129] The evolutionary psychological basis of specific fears promotes our survival function and guides our intuition in avoiding dangers such as by freezing (i.e., becoming more vigilant), fleeing (i.e., running away from the threat), fighting (i.e., directly attacking the source of the threat), submission (i.e., appeasing a member of one's species to prevent attack), fright (i.e., turning muscularly immobile, e.g., "playing dead"), faint (i.e., losing one's consciousness to signal to an attacker that one is not a threat).[130] The physiological reactions to predictable threats in both men and women[131] are underpinned by hormones such as *epinephrine*, also known as *adrenaline* (both a neurotransmitter and a hormone), which gives us a kind of tunnel vision, an enhanced focus to acting as it propels the bodily reactions related to the fight-or-flight response. This hormone becomes active in the blood receptors to sustain blood clotting on wounds, and it operates on the liver to release glucose and create energy so that muscles can be ready to fight or flight.[132]

Although men and women may experience the same physiological reactions to fear, the types of fear they experience tend to differ based on specific adaptive challenges they continue to face that are particular to their physiology. Men, for instance, are more likely than women to fear sexual infidelity due to the adaptive problem of *parental uncertainty* when they were required to leave their homes on hunting trips,[133] and to this day, male sexual jealousy is a cross-cultural and universal phenomenon.[134] In the United States, 93 percent of the 10,018 female killings were related to a current or former male romantic partner, according to the data collected between 2003 and 2014 in 18 states by the Centers for Disease Control and Prevention.[135] Hence, it's more likely that women could die through the hands of their partners than through the hands of strangers. Out of these homicides, 12 percent were associated with male jealousy.[136] Most female victims were under the age of 40, and 15 percent of them were pregnant at the time of the crime.[137] Fatal crimes against male victims through intimate female partners stood between 5 and 7 percent of the victims.[138]

Women are more likely than men to not only develop fears of snakes and spiders but also any event that poses the threat that they might get injured as in the case of robbery, assault, rape, burglary, and car accidents,[139] and developing vigilant strategies continues to favor women who are also committed to protecting their offspring. Studies have also shown that women exhibit greater physiological distress at the thought of *emotional infidelity* from their male partner (i.e., suffering more if their partner loves another woman as opposed to having a short sexual encounter with such a woman), yet the opposite is true for men.[140] One of the evolutionary explanations is that if a man leaves and does not invest time and resources into offspring, both the women and the children would face greater survival challenges, particularly during ancient times.[141]

A growing number of research has shown that testosterone levels in men have been positively associated with high-risk behaviors (e.g., impulsive decision making, aggression, violence, irresponsible sexual behavior, and drug abuse).[142] In the United States, between 1975 and 2019, road

Aldosterone
Controls blood pressure with the water reabsorption in the kidney and the increase of salt.

Cortisol
Released in stressful situations, it increases blood pressure, glucose, heart rate, respiration and muscle tension.

Estradiol
It's increase during the menstrual cycle matures and releases the egg, thickens the uterus lining to allow a fertilized egg to implant.

Glucagon
Produced in the pancreas, it stabilizes sugar levels, it breaks down stored glucose for energy.

Insulin
Pancreas cells release insulin after a meal that transports glucose from the bloodstream into the body's tissues to be used for energy.

Oxytocin
A.K.A. "love hormone", it increases with physical contact with others. It's also released during childbirth and supports lactation.

Prolactin
It increases during pregnancy as the pituitary gland increases production after childbirth to produce lactation and breastfeeding.

Adrenaline
Released by the body in moments of extreme emotions when a fight or flight response is needed.

Dehydroepi- androsterone (DHEA)
Produced in the ovaries and adrenal gland, it creates female and male sex hormones, acne, body odor and pubic hair.

Estriol
Stimulates the production of cortisol.

Glucagon-Like Peptide 1
It regulates appetite through hormone production in the gut after a meal.

Leptin
It controls appetite and food intake, it enables the brain to regulate how much energy the body burns daily.

Parathyroid Hormone (PTH)
Produced in the parathyroid glands, it helps bone vitality and balances calcium and phosphorus levels.

Serotonin
It increases and maintains mood, digestion, sleep, wound healing, bone health, blood clotting, nausea, and libido.

Adrenocorticotropic (ACTH)
Stimulates the production of cortisol.

Dihydrotestosterone
It stimulates the development of male characteristics.

Follicle Stimulating Hormone (FSH)
It controls women's estradiol hormone blend, menstrual cycle and egg production. It controls sperm production in men.

Growth Hormone
It boosts growth, muscle mass and bone development. It protects tissues from breaking down thus avoiding injury.

Luteinizing Hormone (LH)
It controls the production of estrogen in women and testosterone in men.

Peptide YY (PYY)
It's produced in the small intestine, and its released into the bloodstream after a meal to decrease appetite.

Testosterone
It masculinizes physical features, muse voice, bone density, muscle strength, sex drive and risk-taking.

Anti-Müllerian Hormone (AMH)
Acting within the female fertility and reproductive development.

Estrogen / Oestrogen
A female sex hormone produced in the ovaries. It controls female physical features, reproduction and the menstrual cycle.

Ghrelin
It's made by the stomach and arouse appetite to prepare the body for food. Might be linked to weight loss.

Human Chorionic Gonadotropin (HCG)
It triggers the corpus luteum to produce progesterone to maintain pregnancy.

Melatonin
A hormone that regulates sleep and wake patterns.

Progesterone
Following the ovulation its levels rise to prepare the uterus for embryo implantation. But if there's no pregnancy, its levels drop releasing the period.

Thyroid Hormones
The hormones secreted by the thyroid determines the body's energy levels, weight, skin, hair and nail growth, temperature and mood imbalance.

Figure 5.2 A table of core hormones

Source: Adapted from the U.S. Department of Health and Human Services National Institutes of Health, 2016, and the Endocrine Society, 2022.[152] Illustrations by Roman, @ideahits.

traffic collisions caused twice as many male fatalities as female fatalities.[143] Data from 2019 also showed that 71 percent of all motor vehicle crash fatalities were males. Car insurance providers have taken notice of behavioral gender differences when driving and charged less on premiums for female drivers compared to their male counterparts. To avoid discrimination against male drivers, 7 out of the 50 U.S. states prohibit the use of gender as a pricing factor from auto insurance companies (i.e., California, Hawaii, Massachusetts, Michigan, Montana, North Carolina, and Pennsylvania[144]).

Women's *premenstrual syndrome* (PMS) is a well-researched phenomenon as it affects about 90 percent of women of reproductive age[145] negatively influencing their mood and behavior, with symptoms such as irritability, tearfulness, tension, depression, and mood swings, as well as somatic symptoms such as breast tenderness[146] and bloating.[147] Like women, men also experience hormonal shifts with testosterone levels changing throughout the day, peaking between 4 and 8 a.m., and falling to their lowest levels approximately 12 hours later.[148] Studies found that testosterone levels can also fluctuate around the year, and also the seasonal highs and lows in different parts of the world. These daily and seasonal variations can change by as much as 19 percent.[149] During these fluctuations in testosterone, men experience a range of symptoms including hypersensitivity, anger, anxiety, low self-esteem, depression, fatigue, confusion, and low libido.[150] Men's "PMS" equivalent was coined in 2001 as "IMS" or *irritable male syndrome* by Dr. Gerald Lincoln, who conducted research at the Medical Research Council in Edinburgh, Scotland, and found that low levels of testosterone in animals made them more agitated, irritable, fearful and aggressive, and fighting with other males.[151]

Since then, other empirical research has found that, out of the 6,000 men between the ages of 10 and 75 years old, who answered the *Irritable Male Syndrome Questionnaire* developed by psychotherapist Dr. Jed Diamond, 21 percent said they are depressed often or almost always; 40 percent of the men are rarely sexually satisfied; 40 percent are irritable often or almost always; 46 percent said they are often or almost always stressed; 46 percent feel sorry for themselves or pathetic; 50 percent are annoyed often or almost always; 50 percent engage in sexual fantasies through flirtations, pornography, or emotional intrigue; 51 percent have sleep problems; 51 percent feel self-critical (i.e., focusing on failures), gloomy, negative, or hopeless often or almost always; and 57 percent reported feeling impatient often or almost always.[153] IMS has also been used to describe the behavior of middle-aged men with attitudes considered as part of a midlife crisis, such as ending long-standing relationships and starting new ones with younger women or buying a sports car or a motorbike to feel younger.

Key Takeaways

1. **Kahneman's Decision-Making Systems**: Daniel Kahneman's research describes two thinking styles: System 1 (intuitive, fast, and unconscious) and System 2 (analytical, slow, and conscious).

2. **Hormonal Influence**: Hormones significantly impact behaviors in both humans and animals. Historical experiments, such as those by Dr. Arnold Berthold, demonstrated how hormones like testosterone influence behavior.

3. **Oxytocin's Role**: Known as the "love hormone," oxytocin affects not only maternal–child bonding but also social behaviors, trust, and economic transactions.

4. **Gender Bias in Hormonal Research**: Hormones are often associated with women and the menstrual cycle, reflecting historical biases. Misogynistic views have long influenced perceptions of women's behavior.

5. **Historical Misconceptions**: Ancient beliefs, such as those from Greek philosophers and Biblical references, have perpetuated misconceptions about women's health and behavior.

6. **Sexism versus Racism**: While slavery was abolished earlier, sexism persisted longer, with women gaining voting rights much later than African Americans in the United States.

7. **Cultural and Historical Biases**: Literature and historical events, such as the Salem Witch Trials and Shakespeare's works, have reinforced negative stereotypes about women.

8. **Hormones and Behavior**: Hormones function like neurotransmitters, influencing moods, emotions, and stress responses, highlighting their broad impact on human behavior.

9. **Hormonal Influence on Decision Making**: Hormones such as testosterone and estrogen significantly shape social and economic behaviors, influencing decisions related to resources, social status, and mating.

10. **Gender Differences**: Hormones affect men and women differently due to distinct adaptive challenges faced throughout evolution. These differences impact physical development and behavior.

11. **Senescence Theory**: This theory explains the innate deterioration process in the human body, leading to a decline in fertility and life expectancy with age. It highlights the trade-offs between bodily maintenance, growth, and reproduction.

12. **Pleiotropy Theory of Senescence**: This theory suggests that genes can have multiple effects, some beneficial and some harmful, which explains why certain traits that enhance reproductive success can also lead to increased mortality in old age.

13. **Fertility Windows**: Women's fertility starts at puberty and ends with menopause, while men produce sperm throughout their lives, though sperm quality declines with age.

14. **Men's Reproductive Variability**: Men can potentially father many children, but this reproductive success comes with a trade-off of decreased survival, leading to a shorter average lifespan compared to women.

15. **Regenerative Medicine**: Stem cells, which can self-renew and regenerate, are being used in regenerative medicine to treat chronic diseases and repair damaged tissues.

16. **Menstrual Cycle and Behavior**: Hormonal shifts during the menstrual cycle influence women's behavior, including preferences for clothing, social activities, and attraction to certain male traits.

17. **Andropause**: Men experience a gradual decrease in testosterone levels after age 30, leading to symptoms such as mood swings, loss of muscle mass, and decreased libido, often referred to as "male menopause."

18. **Cultural Perceptions of Testosterone**: In many cultures, testosterone is linked to traits such as dominance, competitiveness, and bravery, influencing societal views on masculinity.

CHAPTER 6

Biomarkers of Behavior and Bioanalytics

<table>
<tr><td>

Learning Objectives—By reading this chapter, readers will be able to:

- Explain what biomarkers are and why they are important to marketing professionals.
- Create new possibilities of combining online and offline customer behavioral data from biomarkers.
- Explore research possibilities within marketing and the fields of bioinformatics, genomics, and *bioanalytics*.
- Become aware of how biomarkers can offer new insights about consumer behavior.
- Develop an appreciation for focusing on the factors that unite and harmonize people, rather than on what divides them.

</td></tr>
</table>

Source: Adapted from *Creating Significant Learning Experiences*[1] and Taxonomy of Significant Learning Experiences.[2]

Biomarkers (i.e., biological markers) are measurable characteristics of our bodies and are used by physicians, scientists, and epidemiologists to detect regular biological processes or pathologies developed by the body.[3] It is also used to evaluate therapeutic interventions and in response to drug development. Most of us are accustomed to undergoing physiological checks through clinical assessment (e.g., blood pressure, blood insulin, cholesterol levels, and heart rate variability, among others); imaging (e.g., X-ray, CT scans, MRI scans, Ultrasound[4]), and in more recent years, big data and DNA profiles are being used in personalized medicine as *predictive biomarkers*.[5] These DNA profiles, made by personal genomics and biotechnology companies such as the California-based 23andMe, reveal not only ancestry composition but also genetic predispositions to diseases as well as physiological (e.g., skin pigmentation, finger ratio, eye color), and even behavioral traits such as fear of heights, motion sickness, wake-up time, preference for sweet versus salty foods, and more.[6] Other studies established multiple correlations between physiological systems such as heart rate synchronicity between mothers and infants using the "coordination of visual-affective social signals" during their social contact,[7] and the same synchronicity happens with older couples.[8]

Sex hormones such as testosterone (mostly produced in men) and estrogen (largely originated in women) are biomarkers that signal one's overall health and physical traits[9] such as masculine faces,[10] a deep voice, muscle mass, facial and body hair[11] in men and facial femininity,[12] and increased deposits of fat in the buttocks, hips, and upper thighs in women.[13] These biomarkers also influence social attitudes triggered in men by high circulating testosterone levels, including dominance, aggression, antisocial behavior,[14] displaying a short-term mating strategy,[15] rebellion[16] risk-taking in business,[17] decreased mate bonding,[18] shallow generosity,[19] and low parental investment.[20] Researchers showed that behavioral differences emerge early in life as girls become more concerned with fairness than boys, are more proficient at reading people's facial expressions, talk more about their emotions and feelings, and show more empathy for others' distress.[21] Such behavioral differences stem from gender-specific reproductive strategies as women need superior communication skills for negotiating alliances, social hierarchies, and childbearing.[22]

From a consumer perspective, men with high testosterone levels exhibit a preference for products that show their equally high status in society.[23] They desire more masculine products[24] and are more willing to spend more on courtship-related goods to potential mates.[25] Female consumers with an increase in estrogen levels have been associated with a decrease in calorie intake during the late luteal phase[26] and appearance-enhancing products.[27]

Research conducted in the past two decades has demonstrated that digit ratios, particularly the 2D:4D ratio (2D relates to the second or index finger and 4D is the fourth or ring finger and the ratio is calculated by dividing the length of each finger), have considered 2D:4D as a proxy biomarker for the amount of androgen that a fetus was exposed to while in the womb. Strictly speaking, if a fetus had more exposure to testosterone, it is likely to exhibit a lower (masculine) digit ratio, while a higher estrogen exposure will show higher (feminine) ratios.[28] Interestingly, 2D:4D has been associated with a whole range of behaviors from cognitive abilities to academic performance, diverse personality traits, eating disorders, numerical competence, depression, and even autism.[29]

In the era of big data, AI, genomics, and bioinformatics, marketers have an extraordinary opportunity to capitalize on the many possibilities offered through the combination of these technologies and biomarker research. This is even more imperative in an age where the need for consumer privacy is becoming pervasive, yet companies still strive for brand differentiation and having an enhanced knowledge of consumer needs and preferences, as well as being able to recognize why, when, where, and how to make such products and services available without having to mine consumer data. One of the biggest challenges for marketers is to incorporate online and offline customer behavior into a seamless customer journey, for instance, creating dashboards based on cutting-edge *bioanalytics* can lead to novel types of customer insights that go beyond tactics, such as retargeting, which many consumers find disturbing and invasive.

In the past, marketing and consumer behavior fields have focused on oversimplified individual differences, ethnicity, race, gender, age, religion, sexual orientation, political affiliation, or cultural stereotypes and clichés to represent target consumers in segmentation campaigns (e.g., Germans are efficient[30]; the French don't work hard[31]; the British don't like confrontation[32]; Americans are misinformed about the rest of the world[33]; all the Japanese are polite[34]; Brazilian women are hypersexual[35]). While stereotypes tend to arise from past behavior in certain areas of society, as is the case with renowned German efficiency, which has its origins in the virtues of the former Prussian Empire (Preussische Tugenden) that promoted diligence, punctuality, frugality, and a sense of duty to create an efficient state, which was later embraced by the Nazi Party.[36] But this stereotype does not prevail among the whole population. Thus, assumptions based on stereotypes and generalizations are particularly problematic when taking into account the drastic shifts that the world underwent in the 21st century (i.e., mass migration, globalization, demographic, political, economic, cultural, and religious changes).

Stereotypes are, of course, used as they offer a mental short-cut that enables us to make snap judgments about certain groups in new situations, but they can also be damaging as it's based on "othering," a type of bias in which individuals are defined and labeled as being outside of one's group,[37] thus making us ignorant of the similarities between individuals,[38] regardless of the perceived differences. Hence, the theories this book presents are based on ground-breaking, peer-reviewed research regarding the characteristics that unite us, not ones that divide us. The most well-known and valuable brands, such as Apple, Coca-Cola, Disney, Nike, Louis Vuitton, Mercedes-Benz, and McDonald's,[39] thrive all over the world positioning themselves in ways that target consumers at the *universal level*, in other words, based on the utmost deep-seated needs of the human experience (e.g., avoiding disease, the need for status, finding and keeping a mate).

Table 6.1 Biomarkers

Biomarker Type	Application	Associated Health and Behavioral Outcomes
2D:4D	Prenatal androgen exposure, indicated by digit ratios, has been linked to various traits and conditions, including numerical and spatial skills, handedness, cognitive abilities, academic performance, sperm counts, personality traits, and the prevalence of obesity, migraines, eating disorders, depression, myopia, and autism[40]	Prenatal testosterone exposure significantly influences brain organization and future behaviors.[41] It inhibits the growth of the index finger relative to the other fingers, making the digit ratio (2D:4D) a rough estimate of this exposure.[42] Low digit ratios indicate high prenatal testosterone exposure, while high digit ratios indicate low exposure[43]
Body mass index (BMI)	Indicator of energy balance	Cardiovascular disease (CVD), diabetes, stroke, mortality, certain cancers, osteoarthritis
Cortisol	Steroid hormone indicates physiological stress response	CVD, poor cognitive functioning, fractures, functional disability, mortality

Biomarker Type	Application	Associated health and behavioral outcomes
Diastolic blood pressure (DBP)	Index of cardiovascular activity: lowest pressure in an artery when the heart is resting	Sudden cardiac death (SCD), stroke, Coronary heart disease (CHD), mortality
Electrocardiogram (EKG)	Measurement of electrical impulses in the heart	Cardiovascular risk, stroke, mortality
Fasting glucose	Measures the amount of sugar in the blood; an indicator of diabetes	Diabetes, CHD, mortality, poor cognitive function
High-density lipoprotein (HDL) cholesterol	Protective cholesterol	Lower atherosclerotic CVD
Low-density lipoprotein (LDL)	Transports cholesterol from the liver to be incorporated into cell membrane tissues	CHD, atherosclerosis, stroke, peripheral vascular disease
Menstrual cycle	Fertility and reproduction	Associated hormonal shifts have been shown to influence consumer behavior
Resting pulse rate	Indicator of heart functioning and measure of overall fitness	CHD, mortality
Systolic blood pressure (SBP)	Index of cardiovascular activity: maximum pressure in an artery when the heart is pumping blood throughout the body	Sudden cardiac death (SCD), stroke, CHD, mortality
T-cells	White blood cells that protect against pathogens and tumors	Cancer, mortality, atherosclerosis, Alzheimer's disease
Total cholesterol	Aids in the synthesis of bile acids and steroid hormones	In middle age: CHD and all-cause mortality. In older ages: U-shaped relation to death
Testosterone	Masculinization, fertility, and reproduction	Aggression and risk-taking
Triglycerides	Fat substance stored for energy use	Heart attack, CHD, coronary artery disease, pancreatitis
Waist-to-hip ratio	Indicators of abdominal obesity	Hypertension, CHD, noninsulin-dependent diabetes, and stroke

Please note that this is not an exhaustive list of biomarkers but only a few examples given.

Key Takeaways

1. **Biomarkers:** Biomarkers are measurable characteristics used to detect biological processes or pathologies. They are crucial in clinical assessments, imaging, and personalized medicine, revealing genetic predispositions and behavioral traits.

2. **Hormonal Influence:** Hormones like testosterone and estrogen signal overall health and influence physical traits and behaviors. Testosterone is linked to dominance and risk-taking in men, while estrogen affects women's reproductive strategies and social behaviors.

3. **Gender-Specific Behaviors:** Behavioral differences between genders emerge early, influenced by reproductive strategies. Women tend to have superior communication skills for social negotiations, while men often display behaviors linked to high testosterone levels.

4. **Consumer Preferences:** Hormonal levels influence consumer behavior. Men with high testosterone prefer status-signaling products, while women with increased estrogen levels show preferences for appearance-enhancing products.

5. **Digit Ratios:** The 2D:4D digit ratio is a biomarker indicating prenatal androgen exposure, associated with various behaviors and traits, including cognitive abilities and personality.

6. **Big Data and Bioanalytics:** The integration of big data, AI, genomics, and bioinformatics offers marketers new opportunities to understand consumer needs without relying on invasive data mining, enhancing customer journey insights.

7. **Challenges of Stereotypes:** Traditional marketing often relies on stereotypes, which can be damaging and oversimplified. Modern marketing should focus on universal human characteristics rather than cultural clichés.

8. **Universal Marketing:** Successful global brands target deep-seated human needs, such as avoiding disease and achieving status, rather than relying on stereotypes.

CHAPTER 7

Fitness Indicators and Their Corresponding Products

Learning Objectives—By reading this chapter, readers will be able to:
<ul><li>Analyze why the "classical fitness" theory[1] matters and its evolution.</li><li>Explain what fitness indicators are and why they are helpful for the marketing discipline.</li><li>Distinguish between the gender-specific types of fitness indicators and their behavioral effects.</li><li>Review the peer-reviewed research about fitness indicators and corresponding products.</li><li>Create marketing plans and data dashboards including relevant fitness indicators.</li></ul>

Source: Adapted from *Creating Significant Learning Experiences*[2] and Taxonomy of Significant Learning Experiences.[3]

Fitness Indicators

Throughout history, human and nonhuman animals have been making huge sacrifices (including sacrificing their own lives) to safeguard the lives and the futures of their children. This was evident during the Holocaust years (1933 to 1945), when the German Nazi regime targeted Jews for death, and children in particular, as only 6 to 11 percent of prewar European-Jewish children survived compared to 33 percent of Jewish adults.[4] This was the case for the courageous Anne Frank, who died at the young age of 16 years old (along with her sister Margot, age 18/19) of typhus at Bergen-Belsen concentration camp in Germany after being captured from their secret annex in their Amsterdam home. To ensure the survival of their children, Jewish parents sent their children away to be hidden with Christian families or religious institutions, hoping they would pass as "Aryan," while other children hid in cramped spaces such as closets, attics, cellars, or even sewers. Parents' instinct to protect their children at their own expense is because children carry copies of their parent's genes within them and thus can offer parents the opportunity to "live through them" should they too produce children, thus providing parents with a "fitness currency"[5] into the future under the "classical fitness" theory.[6]

The concept of *fitness indicators* is one of the most important theories to be grasped and used by marketing and consumer behavior professionals, as it offers the possibility to understand not only the physical but also the psychological traits that consumers strive to display through the products and services they buy. Fitness indicators can be classed as *physical fitness* (e.g., cardiovascular/respiratory endurance, heart rate [HR], blood pressure, stamina, strength, flexibility, power, coordination, agility, balance, accuracy, body mass index [BMI]),[7] *reproductive fitness* (e.g., physical attractiveness and the ability to reproduce),[8] *cognitive fitness* (e.g., intelligence, creativity), *personality fitness* (sense of humor, conscientiousness, agreeableness, etc.), and *affect fitness* (attachment style, dominance, etc.). The sixth indicator is *fake fitness*, which displays the evolved human ability (unlike nonhuman animals) to create a new fitness indicator to attract and keep a mate, intimidate and deter rivals, kin care, obtain status, and other evolutionary benefits through cultural, rather than genetic means (i.e., credentials, job titles, status, luxury products).

Hence, this chapter focuses on discussing the multiple facets of the *biological and nonbiological virtues* that consumers aim to broadcast to the world through the products and services they consume to attract love, respect, and support from family members, mates, friends, and allies, and thus increase their chances of survival and reproduction. As consumers rely more on their emotions than their rationality when making purchases,[9] understanding the evolutionary origins and functions behind each purchase will enable them to "push the right buttons" when researching, creating, positioning, and launching their products and services. Let's first examine the "fixed" (although it could change due to plastic surgery or other external interventions) *fitness indicators* and how they affect consumers' *mate value* scores (i.e., one's overall desirability to members of the opposite and also the same sex).[10] From an evolutionary biology and psychology viewpoint, the physical and psychological attributes that our prehistoric ancestors evolved over the past few million years served the purpose of fitness indicators for survival and for reproductive reasons (i.e., to attract high-quality sexual partners[11]). In the following table, we'll examine some of these physical and cognitive attributes displayed by men and women alike, and how they may affect consumer behavior.

When marketers start the product development process, instead of focusing on what the competitors are doing, they should focus on the types of fitness indicators that target customers may want to purchase and display throughout the different phases of their lives and create them. Their research for new products should also center around helping consumers meet the fitness indicators they require with the fake fitness indicators that their products and services can offer. By understanding the human preference for the so-called, good genes, good health, and good social intelligence, for instance, the *fake fitness* indicators will enable consumers to act and present themselves in a way that enables them to reap the benefits of the status, social and sexual benefits of such indicators

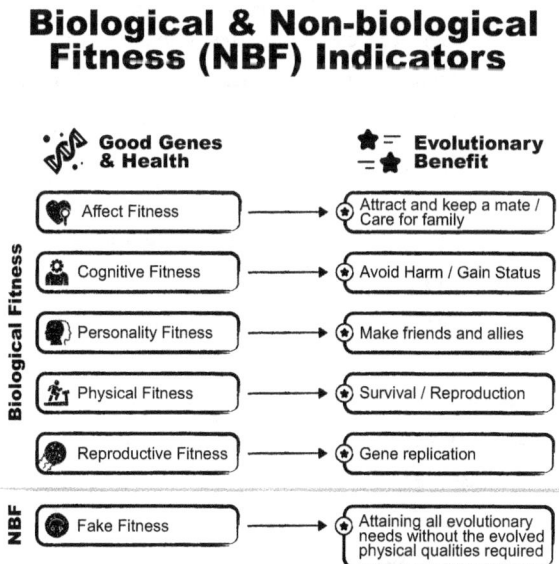

Biological & Non-biological Fitness (NBF) Indicators

Figure 7.1 Biological and nonbiological fitness indicators (based on multiple evolutionary psychology and evolutionary biology theories[12])

Illustrations by Roman, @ideahits.

that encourage social interest and attraction, but without possessing them in the physical form through their bodies.[13] This is certainly the case with cosmetics that enhance feminine beauty and convey the notion of youth and fertility,[14] the sought-after degree from a prestigious university, or a Ferrari that transmits the perception of abundant resources that are attractive to potential mates. However, consumers don't always need to make changes to their appearance or acquire expensive items to gain notoriety and high status among their groups. Being perceived as kind, generous, and "green" (i.e., caring for the environment) at the cost to oneself, can also help consumers achieve the desired status.[15] Even seemingly creative human creations such as art, music, and language are said by researchers to have evolved in both genders based on the same motivation to attract high-quality sexual partners.[16]

Key Takeaways

1. **Parental Sacrifice**: Throughout history, parents have made significant sacrifices to ensure the survival of their children, driven by the instinct to protect their genetic legacy.

2. **Fitness Indicators**: These are traits that signal an individual's health, reproductive potential, and social status. They include physical fitness, reproductive fitness, cognitive fitness, personality fitness, affect fitness, and fake fitness (cultural indicators such as job titles and luxury products).

3. **Consumer Behavior**: Understanding fitness indicators helps marketers create products that appeal to consumers' desires to display these traits. Consumers often rely on emotions rather than rationality when making purchases.

4. **Fixed Fitness Indicators**: Physical and psychological attributes evolved for survival and reproduction. These indicators affect mate value and consumer behavior.

5. **Product Development**: Marketers should focus on the fitness indicators that target customers want to display and create products that help them achieve these indicators.

6. **Fake Fitness Indicators**: Products and services can provide cultural indicators of fitness, such as cosmetics for beauty, prestigious degrees, or luxury cars, which signal status and attract social interest.

7. **Alternative Status Signals**: Consumers can also achieve high status by being perceived as kind, generous, and environmentally conscious, without needing expensive items.

8. **Evolutionary Motivation**: Creative human activities such as art, music, and language may have evolved to attract high-quality sexual partners, driven by the same motivations as other fitness indicators.

PART 3

Evolutionary Marketing
in Practice

CHAPTER 8

An In-Depth Understanding of Customers—B2C, B2B, and B2G

Learning Objectives—By reading this chapter, readers will be able to:

- Challenge existing views of differences between B2B, B2C, and business-to-government (B2G) customers and their preferences.
- Recognize the challenges and opportunities within the different types of customer groups.
- Expand the knowledge of customer and consumer decision-making processes and their motivations.
- Gain knowledge from case studies and solutions to specific marketing challenges within the buyer's process.
- Improve marketing campaigns with the knowledge gained in this chapter.

Source: Adapted from *Creating Significant Learning Experiences*[1] and Taxonomy of Significant Learning Experiences.[2]

In an increasingly competitive environment, marketers strive to create differentiated brands and solve four fundamental problems: 1. All customers differ; 2. All customers change; 3. All competitors react; 4. All resources are limited,[3] and these challenges apply to target audiences within B2C, B2B, and B2G. Marketing lectures at some of the world's top business schools teach future business managers that purchasing decisions are an organized set of processes starting with a consumer or a customer recognizing that they have a problem that needs to be solved, searching for information about a possible solution for the problem, evaluating alternatives, deciding to purchase a product or service, which is followed by a postpurchase behavior assessment.[4] This process happens under the influence of the marketing mix (product, place and time, price, promotion, process, physical environment, people, productivity, and quality) as well as the sociocultural impact (personal influence, reference groups, family and religious influence, social class, culture, and subculture), situational forces (physical and surroundings, purchases task, temporal effects, and antecedent states), and psychological influences (motivation, personality, perception, learning, values, beliefs and attitudes, and lifestyle). While these are all important factors to consider throughout the buying process, a major influence of decision making is not considered: the human biological drives and needs when selecting a product or service. Whether you're targeting B2C, B2B, or B2G customers, the same needs and drives will apply as, regardless of their buying status (i.e., sole decision makers or through a buying committee), they are all still human and are influenced by the same homeostasis as described in "Part 3: Evolutionary Marketing in Practice, Chapter 11 Quantify and Operationalize Emotions" of this book. Yet, it's most common to find information throughout the web and established courses about the differences between the B2C buyer's journey, which some authors claim should be based on creating an emotional connection, inducing an impulsive action, and a more rational and factual approach when it comes to B2B/B2G customers.[5] However, the same person who buys an Apple computer, phone, or watch is likely to compare the experience received from this brand with a proposition from a B2B offer. Even though B2B/B2G may have a different buying system through a tender and committee, they still have fears and personal motivations such as the need for self-promotion and status, which your product or service can offer them. Cutting-edge studies from the past decade have gone beyond the standard marketing theories about what drives consumption and developed new methodologies for assessing consumers' motivations based on their biological composition. One study conducted by Jaakko Aspara and Bram Van Den Bergh[6] in Finland showed that the characteristics and behaviors of consumers are influenced by sex hormones[7] as is the case of male consumers with a more masculine digit ratio (i.e., that had higher prenatal testosterone exposure) tend to prefer products with

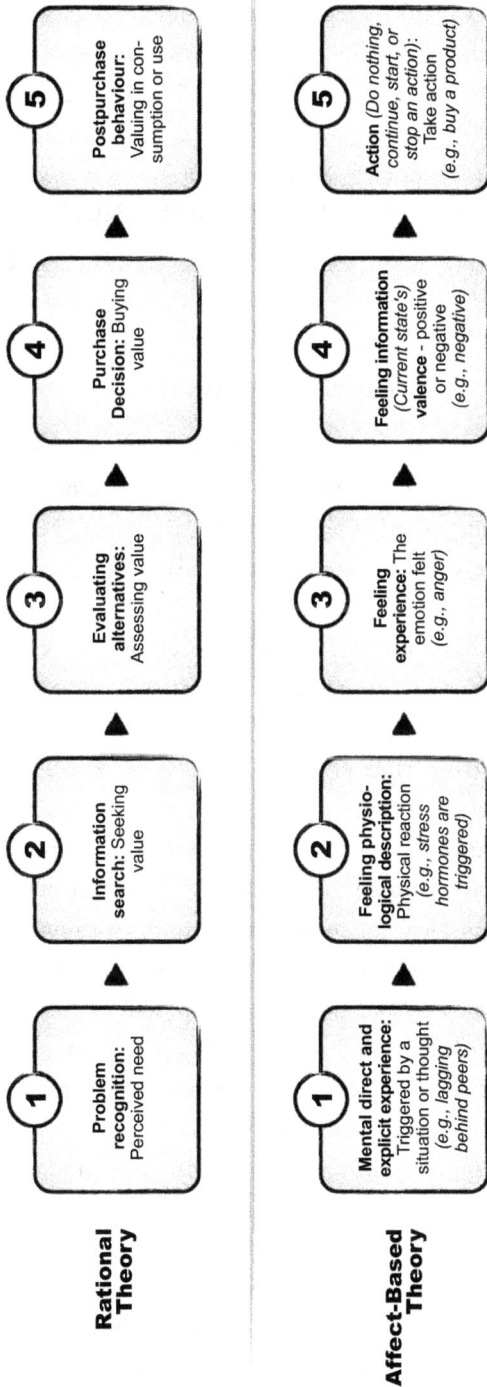

Rational Theory

1. **Problem recognition:** Perceived need
2. **Information search:** Seeking value
3. **Evaluating alternatives:** Assessing value
4. **Purchase Decision:** Buying value
5. **Postpurchase behaviour:** Valuing in consumption or use

Affect-Based Theory

1. **Mental direct and explicit experience:** Triggered by a situation or thought *(e.g., lagging behind peers)*
2. **Feeling physiological description:** Physical reaction *(e.g., stress hormones are triggered)*
3. **Feeling experience:** The emotion felt *(e.g., anger)*
4. **Feeling information** *(Current state's)* valence - positive or negative *(e.g., negative)*
5. **Action** *(Do nothing, continue, start, or stop an action):* Take action *(e.g., buy a product)*

Figure 8.1 Consumer decision-making process—a rational and feeling-as-information approach

Source: Adapted from Damasio and Damasio, 2016, and Mukherji, 2017.[11]

a masculine image, while other studies found that testosterone plays a significant role in a man's search for and maintenance of social status.[8] In women, hormonal shifts throughout the ovulation period have many effects that range from an unconscious search for appearance-enhancing products[9] to a predilection for physically attractive and charismatic men.[10] Equipped with this knowledge, new customer journeys that encompass all neurobiological motivations should be used for B2C, B2B, and B2G target groups to increase the success rate of marketing campaigns as per the following example.

Key Takeaways

1. **Fundamental Marketing Challenges**: Marketers face four key challenges: customer diversity, customer change, competitor reactions, and limited resources. These apply across B2C, B2B, and B2G markets.

2. **Buying Process**: The buying process involves recognizing a problem, searching for solutions, evaluating alternatives, making a purchase, and postpurchase assessment. This process is influenced by the marketing mix, sociocultural factors, situational forces, and psychological influences.

3. **Biological Drives**: Human biological drives and needs significantly influence decision making across B2C, B2B, and B2G markets. These drives are often overlooked in traditional marketing theories.

4. **Emotional and Rational Approaches**: While B2C marketing often focuses on emotional connections and impulsive actions, B2B/B2G marketing is seen as more rational and factual. However, all buyers are influenced by personal motivations and status needs.

5. **Hormonal Influence**: Studies show that sex hormones influence consumer behavior. For example, men with higher prenatal testosterone exposure prefer masculine products, and testosterone impacts social status pursuits. Women's hormonal shifts during ovulation affect their preferences for appearance-enhancing products and attractive men.

6. **Unified Customer Experience**: The same individual may have different roles as a consumer in B2C and B2B/B2G contexts, comparing experiences across these roles. Marketers should consider this overlap in their strategies.

CHAPTER 9

In the Future There Will Be a Lab in Every Company

Learning Objectives—By reading this chapter, readers will be able to:
• Learn from case studies and some of the most cutting-edge consumer neuroscience at large organizations.   • Focus on your consumers' and customers' biological, affective, and cognitive experiences.   • Redesign marketing strategies to capitalize on biodata.   • Find opportunities to create a mini lab in your organization.   • Create a project plan to deploy consumer neuroscience to create a competitive edge in your industry.

Source: Adapted from *Creating Significant Learning Experiences*[1] and Taxonomy of Significant Learning Experiences.[2]

Neuromarketing, also known as consumer neuroscience, started as a marketing fad in the 1990s,[3] but in recent years, thanks to results achieved by NeuroFocus and other firms such as Emotient Inc. (a California-based start-up that uses AI technology to analyze facial expressions and read people's emotions, the kind of data that is now in growing use by advertising agencies that was acquired by Apple in 2016) who published some ground-breaking studies of the brain to predict consumer decision making and behavior, and an immense value for marketers and their firms.

Consumer neuroscience measures vital physiological functions such as heartbeat, blood pressure, respiration rate, neural signals, and reflexes (e.g., face expression, pupil dilation, and gaze fixation) to gain genuine, nonverbal insights into customers' emotional valence (negative or positive), their responses related to preferences, motivations, and decisions. Some of its research methods include fMRI, EEG, functional near-infrared spectroscopy (fNIRS), ECG, ET, and GSR to allow for real-time measurements of brain and bodily activity when exposed to marketing stimuli.

In 2004, researchers at Emory University placed subjects in an fMRI machine to evaluate their preference for Coca-Cola and Pepsi. When the drinks were unidentified, a consistent neural response was noted; however, when subjects could see the brand, their limbic structures, the areas of the brain associated with unconscious processing, memories, and emotions, had an enhanced activity, showing that awareness of the brand changed how the brain perceived each beverage, highlighting the intangible meaning and value of brands in the subject's mind. In 2008, a research team led by Hilke Plassmann from INSEAD, scanned the brains of test subjects while they tasted three wines with different prices. Although the wine in question was the same, the subject's brains perceived each wine differently with their neural signatures indicating a preference for the most expensive wine.

These findings highlight the need for a deeper understanding of mental and bodily functions to increase the ROMI, as what consumers say and what they prefer can often be different.

In another academic study, fMRI reported that when consumers see prices, it may change their psychological calculation of value.[4] For example, when the price was displayed before consumers' exposure to the product, the neural data was different from data collected after the discovery of the product, thus pointing toward the existence of two separate mental calculations of value. When the price came first, the calculation was set to evaluate if the product was worth the price, and when the product came first the calculation was based on whether consumers liked the product or not.[5]

Despite these encouraging results, fMRI and EEG are costly equipment, usually out of reach of the average marketing department as fMRI machines typically cost about $5 million, and EEG costs about $20,000, both requiring specialized training and high overhead. But as neuroscience continues to advance and equipment costs decline rapidly, brain activity tracking and biomarkers (abbreviation for biological markers) are

Table 9.1 Biosensors and their applications

Technology	Applications	Benefits	Setup Time	Ease of Use	Average Cost
ECG (Electrocardiography) To record heart rate to understand consumers' arousal through heart rate (HR), heart rate variability (HRV) and interbeat interval (IBI)	Response to marketing messages, reactions in autonomous vehicles, packaging testing, reactions to virtual environments	Understanding the physiological arousal and psychological state (emotional regulation) of consumers	Medium	Medium	Medium
EEG (Electroencephalography) It logs the electrical activity of the brain via electrodes placed on top of the scalp. Recording the electrical activity as brain waves, it highlights how neurons communicate with each other through electrical impulses and its link with cognitive processes, including approach or avoidance, alertness and drowsiness, and more	Predicting preference for music streaming, evaluating emotional responses to virtual reality (VR) environments	Analyzing how alert, engaged, motivated, distracted, drowsy, or frustrated a consumer is and how difficult it is to perform a given task	Medium	Medium	Medium
EMG (Electromyography) It records muscle contractions and responses via bursts of electric activity on the skin	To be used when consumers are confronted with decision options (product choice, price)	Validating how different muscles react to stimuli and the intensity of an emotion	Medium	Medium	Low

(Continued)

Table 9.1 (Continued)

Technology	Applications	Benefits	Setup Time	Ease of Use	Average Cost
ET (Eye Tracking) A projection of light from infrared cameras is directed toward the consumer's pupils, thus making reflections in the pupil and the cornea, and the center corneal reflections (PCCR) inform the movement and direction of the eyes	Testing videos, images, web content, VR environments, shopping experience at the store	Identifying where the focus is or is not as well as stressful or arousing stimuli or thoughts	Low	High	Medium (low with desktop versions)
FEA (Facial Expression Analysis) Emotions expressed on the face are captured by automated computer algorithms that record facial expressions live through a webcam or a recorded video	Persona identification, product optimization, customer targeting, market segmentation	Obtaining unbiased and unconscious responses to a product, service, and/ or advert and its valence (positive/negative/neutral)	Low	High	Low
fEMG (Facial electromyography) It measures the electrical activity displayed by muscle contraction via electrodes placed on top of the skin. It can replace a webcam-based FEA	Identifying emotional responses toward advertisements	Validating the truthfulness of affective facial expressions	Medium	Medium	Low

Technology	Applications	Benefits	Setup Time	Ease of Use	Average Cost
Technology	Applications	Benefits	Setup Time	Ease of Use	Average Cost
GSR (Galvanic skin response) or EDA (Electrodermal activity) Electrodes are placed on sensitive parts of the body where sweat glands are located and skin conductance is reported	Product unboxing, footfall analysis, advert analysis	Measuring the intensity of emotions (emotional arousal)	Low	High	Medium
PPG (Photoplethysmography) An LED light is placed on arteries (fingertips or earlobes), which measures the increases in pulse pressures as the heart contracts	Comparable to ECG but with dry optical sensors placed on the capillary tissue, fingertip, or ear lobe	Similar to ECG but easier and quicker to set up and less inconvenient for participants	Low	High	Low
Respiration It records the strength of chest movements during respiration with the use of a transducer belt and an amplifier placed in the thorax or abdomen	Evaluating customer journeys, surveys, written pieces	Studying the level of attention given to a task and if negative emotions are aroused	Low	High	Low

(Continued)

Table 9.1 (Continued)

Technology	Applications	Benefits	Setup Time	Ease of Use	Average Cost
Surveys Easily set up on various platforms online and offline	To measure message and product recall, brand attraction, and attitudes	Being able to compare responses with biometric data to analyze autonomous versus cognitive and rational reactions	Low	High	Low
Voice Analysis	To quantify prosody (the patterns of intonation and stress in a language) usually applied in linguistic and clinical research, pitch (fundamental frequency), which might indicate impromptu high pitch surges, loudness scores, and speaking rate	Measuring expressions of disgust or surprise, pauses and hesitations, normal, monotonous or lively speaking, and valence (positive or negative) vocal expression	Medium	Medium	Medium

Source: Harrel, 2019; Farnsworth, 2020; Smith et al., 2011; Wilson, 2018.[6]

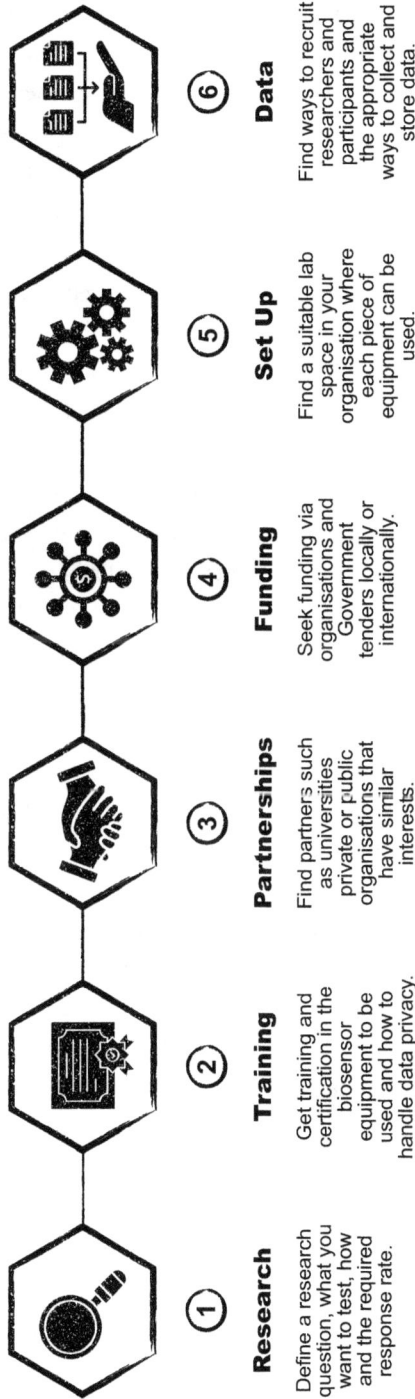

Research ①
Define a research question, what you want to test, how and the required response rate.

Training ②
Get training and certification in the biosensor equipment to be used and how to handle data privacy.

Partnerships ③
Find partners such as universities private or public organisations that have similar interests.

Funding ④
Seek funding via organisations and Government tenders locally or internationally.

Set Up ⑤
Find a suitable lab space in your organisation where each piece of equipment can be used.

Data ⑥
Find ways to recruit researchers and participants and the appropriate ways to collect and store data.

Figure 9.1 The process of creating a research laboratory

Illustrations by Roman, @ideahis.

likely to become more popular with marketers working for organizations of all sizes. At large companies such as IKEA, high-resolution EEG headsets and eye trackers have been used to test consumers' neurophysiological reactions to the new business models,[7] Google applied consumer neuroscience to best understand the part of the brain that makes decisions and applied it to its search engine optimization (SEO), and PayPal used an EEG to interpret brain signals and found out that consumers care more about convenience and speed than security and reliability.[8] If you don't yet know how to apply consumer neuroscience, the following table will help you and your organization identify good opportunities.

Thanks to an increase in interest from varied fields including psychology, marketing, design, consumer behavior, and customer experience combined with a decrease in the cost of technology, it's easier than ever for small- and medium-sized organizations to set up their research lab with relatively low initial and ongoing costs. The following timeline provides an overview of what is required.

Key Takeaways

1. **Evolution of Neuromarketing**: Initially a marketing fad in the 1990s, neuromarketing has gained credibility and value through the work of firms such as NeuroFocus and Emotient Inc., which use AI to analyze facial expressions and emotions.

2. **Consumer Neuroscience Methods**: This field measures physiological functions such as heartbeat, blood pressure, neural signals, and reflexes to gain insights into customer emotions and decision making. Methods include fMRI, EEG, fNIRS, ECG, eye tracking, and GSR.

3. **Brand Perception Studies**: Research at Emory University and INSEAD demonstrated that brand awareness and price perception can alter brain activity, highlighting the intangible value of brands and the psychological impact of pricing.

4. **Importance of Understanding Mental Functions**: These studies underscore the need for marketers to understand mental and bodily functions to improve ROMI, as consumer preferences may differ from their stated choices.

5. **Cost of Neuromarketing Tools**: While fMRI and EEG equipment are expensive and require specialized training, advancements in neuroscience and decreasing costs are making these tools more accessible to marketers.

6. **Applications in Large Companies**: Companies such as IKEA, Google, and PayPal have successfully used consumer neuroscience to test reactions to business models, understand decision making, and prioritize consumer preferences.

7. **Future Accessibility**: With growing interest and decreasing technology costs, it is becoming easier for small- and medium-sized organizations to set up their research labs, making neuromarketing tools more widely available.

CHAPTER 10

Quantify and Operationalize Emotions

Learning Objectives—By reading this chapter, readers will be able to:
• Expand their expertise about feelings and emotions, and how to work with them in practical ways.
• Develop an understanding of homeostasis and why it matters for the marketing discipline.
• Increase the possibilities of measuring customers' emotions beyond Net Promoter Scores (NPS) and A/B tests.
• Become familiar with homeostasis and its importance to understanding customers.
• Create new types of sentiment analysis, differentiated and highly targeted products.

Source: Adapted from *Creating Significant Learning Experiences*[1] and Taxonomy of Significant Learning Experiences.[2]

Our minds' focus is to create meaning about everything we do, see, feel, experience, and think, and what we think is felt by our bodies. From our first conscious thoughts, our brains recognize patterns and trigger certain reactions according to the most memorable experiences from our formative years. The way our parents bond with us in early childhood and teenage years leads to the development of patterns of attachment, which will guide our thoughts, feelings, and expectations of our parents and others that surround us later in life. The English psychotherapist John Bowlby (1907–1990) was the pioneer of attachment theory—the study of how children form an emotional bond with their parents and how they will manage their future relationships as adults. An avoidant attachment style, for example, may lead someone to act coldly and push them away because their capacity to trust others was already damaged in childhood. Someone who has a secure attachment style, on the other hand, experienced a stable and consistent upbringing from their parents where a healthy and strong bond has been developed between parents and children, which in adulthood will represent a self-confident person who can form successful relationships. But how does attachment and so many other theories from psychology influence consumer behavior, the products and services that we buy or not buy? Marketers need Bowlby, Freud, and Darwin to help them answer this and so many other questions on how to understand and influence consumer behavior from a root-cause-analysis perspective, rather than only focus on the surface behavior. When we ask ourselves: "how do I feel about this?" we're using the valence of our feelings to figure out our preferences and attitudes toward something, a person, or a situation, that is, if we feel good, we believe it is because we like something or someone and the opposite is also true about our intuitive interpretation, appraisals, beliefs, and thoughts enabled by our feelings' judgments. Feeling-as-information[3] affects our judgments and decisions through our moods, emotions, and affective reactions. Over 88 percent of all chartered plane crashes are attributed to human factors and many airplane crashes happened due to disagreements between captains and first officers, such as the Air Florida Flight 90 crash in 1982. The copilot tried to warn the pilot three times about the presence of ice on the airplane's wings and low speeds, yet the pilot continued to ignore this information, causing the plane to crash only two miles from the White House.[4] In the United States alone, it's estimated that at least 250,000 people die each year as a result of miscommunication between doctors and nurses, making it the third cause of death on the list of deadliest conditions behind heart disease and cancer.[5] If these well-trained professionals can still be affected in their daily professional performance by their emotions, what about our day-to-day decisions as regular people?

Gender, Age, and Other Differences When Consuming

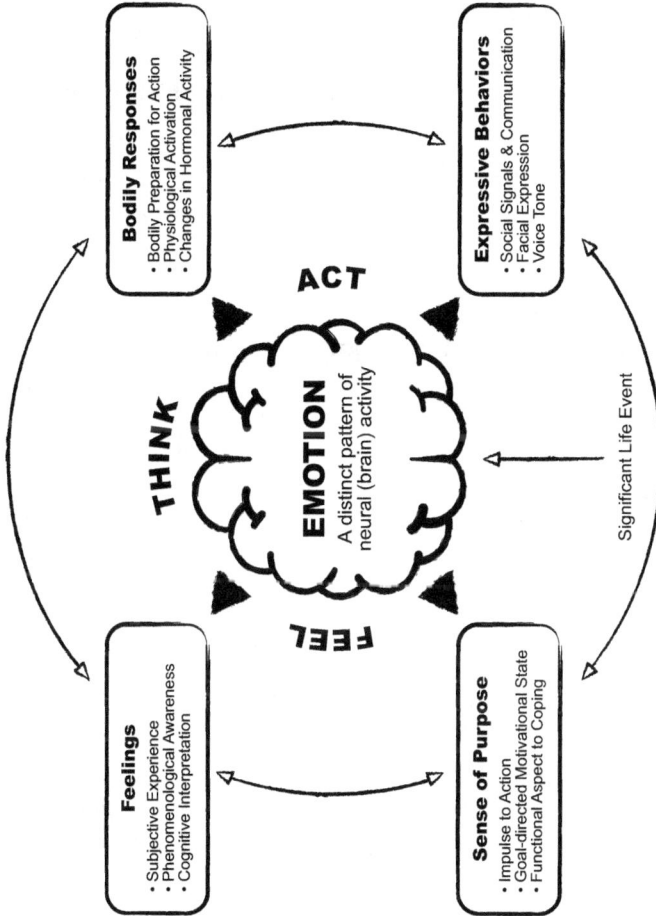

Figure 10.1 Four components of emotions

Source: Adapted from Understanding Motivation and Emotion.[6] Illustrations by Roman, @ideahits.

The Contribution of Evolutionary Psychology

EP focuses on unraveling the complex functions and components of the human mind and brain. One of the main questions that EP aims to answer is how exterior inputs influence the brain and the output it produces in the form of behavior. Recent scientific and technological developments enabled EP researchers to create a unified theoretical framework of the mind, which includes findings from disparate disciplines such as emotion, memory, cognition, biology, brain imaging, culture, religion, medicine, ethics, and others.[7] This advancement meant that nowadays we have a more wholesome approach to measuring, quantifying, and operationalizing emotions, which are essentially what makes us human.

Homeostasis—The Root of Mental Experiences

Since the inception of the homeostasis theory by the French physiologist, Clause Bernard, who described how bodily functions are maintained through a series of coordinated chemistries in the metabolism and nervous system,[8] the Portuguese-American neuroscientist, Antonio Damasio, presented a new hypothesis about *homeostatic feelings*, for example, hunger, thirst, illness, some types of pain, well-being, pleasure, and desire that trigger the physiological apparatus as well as the *mental experiences* of human beings, which allows them to sense the internal state, it's in through the emotions experienced at a given time, as in the case of fear when one is about to drown.[9]

The function of such *feeling experience* is to inform us in a very quick way, whether we're in a state of pleasure or danger, and through the understanding of its strength (weak or strong) and its *valence* (positive or negative) we are compelled to take action.[10] Even what we know as *rationality*, Damasio argues, is the repeated deployment of *homeostatic feelings* across long periods of evolutionary history including social cooperation, in-group and out-group behavior, individual and a group's sense of identity derived from past social experiences, and the demonstration of *social emotions* such as altruism, compassion, gratitude, indignation, and geographical aspects.[11] Geographic conditions, as in the case of *climate*, influence the pace of life (e.g., hotter countries tend to have a slower pace

1. Mental direct and explicit experience: Ex. Limited air into the lungs under water

2. Feeling physiological description (heart acceleration, difficulty breathing)

3. Feeling experience: The emotion of fear is experienced with a state of anxiety

4. Feeling information (Current state): The valence of a feeling (positive or negative) creates an action (i.e., Does it contribute to well-being or is it against it?) to do nothing, continue, start, or stop an action)

5. Automatic regulation of internal body functions and motor reaction: Ex. Attempting to swim, gaining access to air and calling for help.

Figure 10.2 How homeostasis drives behavior

Source: Adapted from Damasio and Damasio,[12] 2016. Illustrations by Roman, @ideahits.

of life and vice versa) and population size as larger cities have faster tempos.[13] Hence, by following a purely *homo economicus (or "economic man")* theory that humans are rational beings that are led by rational judgments in their decision making,[14] led by the "invisible hand" of the market[15] instead of by irrational decision making, marketers risk not meeting the needs of their target consumers at their peril.

Quantifying Homeostasis

Since the publication of Darwin's *The Expression of the Emotions in Man and Animals* in 1872, several researchers and authors attempted to expand on Darwin's work that laid the foundations of how we perceive emotions and feelings in humans and nonhuman animals. Psychologist Robert Plutchik developed a psycho-evolutionary theory of basic emotions and a wheel of emotions[16]; psychologist and professor Paul Eckman focuses on the role that emotions play in facial expressions,[17] cultural historian and author Tiffany Watt Smith has appraised 154 emotions and feelings based on cultures from around the world[18] among other researchers whose theories still inform our understanding of emotions and feelings today.

For marketers, it is crucial to grasp how your brand image and message, product, and even company culture make consumers feel by considering the following table. The goal of companies is to develop emotion-focused systems that can identify the facial (i.e., facial expressions) and biological (i.e., hormone levels, temperature) to influence the right emotions to be triggered in a given moment of the customer journey and go beyond simple NPS measurements and A/B testing. By expanding on the following six basic emotions and including as many emotions as possible in your customer journey, you will be able to perceive how each touch point and interaction between the company and the customer might be pulling them in or pushing them in the opposite direction of your wish.

Biosensors—Measuring Internal Experiences

Our emotions are exhibited physiologically with different levels of arousal when triggered by internal or external stimuli[22] (Strack 1988). Emotional

Table 10.1 *Stimulus, emotions, cognition, valence, response, and need*

Stimulus	Emotion	Evolutionary Cognition	Valence	Response	Need
Restrictive	Anger	You're an enemy	Negative	Aggression (verbal/physical)	Destruction
Appalling/Ugly	Disgust	Risk of contamination	Negative	Sickness/rejection/avoidance/dehumanization	Cleanliness/safety
Risk	Fear	Facing death, danger, and loss	Negative	Fight, flight, hesitation, worry, withdrawal	Protection
Beauty (persons, objects)	Happiness/Joy	Attract/retain	Positive	Admiration, attraction, desire, engagement, indulgence	Status, reproduction
Loss (of a person or valued object)	Sadness	Solitude	Negative	Seeking isolation and later help, shame, rumination	Recovery/reintegration
A new person or object	Surprise	Curiosity	Positive or Negative	Alertness, amusement, alarm, panic	Familiarization

Source: Adapted from Plutchik's wheel of emotions,[19] Paul Ekman's basic emotions,[20] and the Humane—Human-Machine Interaction Network on Emotion project by Prof. Dr. Elisabeth André.[21]

behavior research taps into our minds using biosensors to interpret our facial expressions with computer-based FEA software that codes muscle movement when we laugh, cry, and express a range of emotions. With over 40 autonomous muscles, our faces are very different from other parts of our bodies, as each muscle in our face can be triggered independently and it's highly specialized in sharing information for a social context, communicating emotions nonverbally with a brain-to-muscle and muscle-to-brain connection.

The brainstem controls involuntary and unconscious expressions, while the motor cortex is responsible for conscious and intentional facial expressions. Hence, we can distinguish a fake smile from a genuine one. The same regions in the brainstem that trigger our facial expressions also control our emotional processing and regulation. Functional imaging studies (FMRI) have identified the right and left amygdala (in the brainstem) are responsible for emotional arousal, and it's activated when faced with threats or sexually appealing visual or auditory stimuli. The amygdala regulates the discharge of cortisol and other stress hormones into the bloodstream, controlling heart rate, respiration, skin conductance, and changes in facial expressions and posture. In the presence of strong external stimuli, we express certain emotions in unconscious and involuntary ways through an increase in heart rate or skin conductance in a "fight-or-flight" way preparing for a physical attack, while our facial expressions may include frowning and baring teeth. Facial expressions can also be triggered by thoughts, memories, and mentalizations in experiments.

Human emotions can be classified because there are seven specific facial shapes (also linked with their relevant physiological and cognitive processes) that are universally associated with certain emotions[23] regardless of cultural background, irrespective of gender, or age. These are namely joy, sadness, surprise, anger, fear, disgust, and contempt. Thanks to affective neuroscience and biosensor engineering, emotion analytics has been made possible for consumer behavior researchers and marketers, as products, services, content, and tangible and intangible stimuli that can elicit emotional arousal can be tested against consumer/customer preferences without the need of surveys or focus groups (or it can be used in combination to correlate responses between implicit and explicit attitudes).

Biometric sensors can be used to reveal aspects of human emotions, behavior, and cognition, and are powerful tools when used in combination to analyze the relationships between cognition, emotional arousal, valence, attention, and motivation.

ET is used to monitor our eye movements and attention. It also tracks the dilation of the pupil, which indicates stimulus changes, stressful situations, arousing thoughts or stimuli, and brightness in the room. GSR/EDA, indicates the amount of sweat secretion from sweat glands. Sweating, or skin conductance, is controlled unconsciously when exposed to an emotionally triggering stimulus and can be perceived in our hands, feet,

Table 10.2 Biosensors and their application within marketing and consumer behavior

Biosensor	Why Use It	How It Works
Electrodermal Activity (EDA)/Galvanic Skin Response (GSR)	To assess emotional intensity through the skin conductivity or response to demonstrated emotional arousal or stress in response to a stimulus. To track emotional responses such as fear, joy, and other strong emotions	Controlled by the autonomic nervous system, which manages many bodily processes that influence cognitive and emotional behaviors, skin conductance provides insights into emotional responses due to increases in activity in the eccrine sweat gland and it can be captured on hands or feet
Electroencephalography (EEG)	To uncover cognitive processes, gain insights into visual processing, executive functioning, memory encoding, and language, and learn about consumer levels of alertness, engagement, motivation, if a required task is perceived as easy or difficult, and more	The electrical activity in the brain is recorded as a sequence of brain waves, which shows how the neurons in the brain communicate through electrical impulses. The underlying cognitive processes inform researchers if consumers are in an approachable or avoidant state, if they are alert or lethargic, attentive or relaxed
Eye Tracking (screen-based, glasses, VR goggles)	To record the position of the eyes in real-time when stimuli are presented and determine visual attention in a given moment. Used to identify which items or scenes attract attention and which elements are ignored	A light from an infrared camera is aimed at the consumers' pupils, which produces reflections in the pupil and the cornea (also known as pupil center corneal reflections, PCCR) and informs researchers about the movement and the direction of the eyes
Electrocardiogram (ECG/ German spelling, (elektrokardiogramm—EKG) Plethysmography (PPG)	The brain sets the rhythm of the heart based on what the body needs at a particular time and this heart–brain activity can change how we feel. EEG is used to show physiological arousal and psychological state through heart rate activity via measurements of heart rate variability, which correspond to psychological or physiological calmness or stress	ECG transcribes the electrical movement generated by heart muscle depolarizations (meaning that a negative adjustment happens in the electric charge leading to the contraction of the heart muscles, which is then picked up by the ECG as an indirect signal of heart muscle contraction), which proliferate as pulsating electrical waves against the skin

Biosensor	Why Use It	How It Works
Electromyography (EMG) Facial Electromyography (fEMG)	EMG is useful to examine the associations between emotions and behavioral events through muscular movements and activities	EMG records muscle movement by tracking the outbreaks of electrical activity created when a muscle contracts
Facial Expression Analysis (FEA)	As in the case of EMG, FEA shows affective states through the emotional expressions people display on their faces, which are some of the most robust displays of our emotions	Current FEA software uses computer vision techniques to detect seven emotions: joy, sadness, fear, anger, disgust, contempt, and surprise[24] and provide information on engagement level and emotional valence toward a stimulus
Functional Magnetic Resonance Imaging (fMRI)	fMRI measures unconscious emotions and reactions that consumers express when presented with adverts. This information helps align the goal of a specific campaign and the effective response that it elicits in consumers	An fMRI scanner detects shifts in blood oxygenation and changes in blood flow that arise in response to neural activity. When neuronal activity increases, there is also an increased demand for oxygen and the local response is an expansion in blood flow to regions of increased neural activity[25]
Respiration line length (RLL)	A person's level of stress and emotional arousal have been found to correspond with the respiration rate. Respiration rate has also been correlated with heart rate variability as such processes are controlled by the same system. This data provides insights into sustained attention, the display of negative emotions such as fear, cognitive overload, and even deceptive behavior[26]	It's possible to infer cognitive processes from respiration using the RLL procedure by analyzing respiratory tracings[27] against stimuli over some time. While we breathe, our lungs allow the carbon dioxide in our blood to disseminate externally, and it is then removed from the body while we breathe out. This process is called respiration, and it is documented as respiratory rate

and forehead. With EEG, you can measure brain activity associated with unconscious emotional processes, cognitive behavior, and perception to gain valuable insights into levels of cognitive workload, frustration, motivation, and engagement, among other responses. EEG shows the parts of the brain that are active when exposed to stimuli such as a product, video, and so on, and when performing required tasks. EMG sensors monitor the electric energy generated by the face, hands, or fingers, and it's used to measure muscular responses to stimuli. An ECG tracks heart rate, or pulse, to obtain information about respondents' anxiety and stress levels (arousal), which can be measured against changes in their physiological state related to their actions and decisions.

Traditionally, biomarkers have been mostly used within clinical assessments to monitor normal health states and to predict health states to plan for pharmacological responses or therapeutic interventions. There is a wide range of biomarkers used to assess the health or the disease state of a person, and each biological system has its biomarker—for example, the cardiovascular, metabolic, immune system. Please note that the following table is an illustrative, not a comprehensive list of biosensors and applications.

How Emotions Drive Behavior—
A Brand Loyalty Case

Since the introduction of "tokens of gratitude" in 1793 in the United States by merchants such as the Grand Union Tea Company and the Babbit Company,[28] loyalty programs became widespread in companies of all sizes and industries in the 21st century. Yet, research conducted by French consultancy Capgemini in 2015 showed that 90 percent of consumers have a negative image of loyalty programs, while 54 percent of loyalty memberships become inactive, and 28 percent of consumers abandon loyalty programs without redeeming any points earned.[29] Instead, the research concluded that customer loyalty is mostly driven by emotions triggered by brand values and behavior related to honesty, trust, integrity, and belonging. With this information, it is possible to create loyalty programs that focus on emotions rather than rational aspects such as price, promotions, convenience, or same-day delivery as, in developed economies, these benefits tend to be perceived as a given.

Emotions-Focused Technology

Imagine this scenario, you are sleeping and while you sleep you move in ways that are perceived by your pillow and mattress as unusual and a report is sent to your smart watch in the morning with tips to improve your sleeping patterns. You wake up and as you're about to make your coffee, your coffee machine reads your facial expression and asks if you would benefit from a stronger coffee brew than usual. As you speak to your virtual assistant, it detects through your voice pitch and command that you're feeling stressed and recommends mindfulness products that you can try at that moment to help improve how you're feeling. As you enter your car to go to work, it detects that you're fatigued and distracted and sends you a message on your screen followed by a voice message on the radio, which alerts you of how many accidents are caused a year by drowsiness while driving and advises you to stop for a quick break as a safety measure. As you enter the office and join a meeting, your smart watch detects that you are sitting down and that your heart rate is way higher than your regular resting heart rate across multiple measurements, so alerts you to take a break and recommends breathing exercises to help reduce stress and a possible heart attack. After work, you go to the shopping mall to cheer yourself up with some retail therapy, and while passing by a pharmacy, a personalized notice board tells you that you might be on your menstrual cycle, and are therefore more susceptible to overspending on appearance-enhancing products and treating yourself to chocolate, so it offers you the latest promotions of painkillers and period pads. Some people may find these ideas as an invasion of privacy, while others will see them as examples of how technology can capitalize on emotions to improve the lives of consumers.

Key Takeaways

1. **Attachment Theory:** John Bowlby's attachment theory explains how early childhood bonds with parents shape future relationships and behaviors. Secure attachment leads to self-confidence and successful relationships, while avoidant attachment can result in trust issues.

2. **Emotions and Consumer Behavior:** Emotions play a crucial role in consumer behavior. Marketers need to understand the root causes of consumer emotions, influenced by psychological theories from Bowlby, Freud, and Darwin.

3. **Feeling-as-Information:** Our feelings guide our judgments and decisions. Positive or negative emotions influence our preferences and attitudes toward people, products, and situations.

4. **Impact of Miscommunication:** Emotions can significantly affect professional performance, as seen in cases of miscommunication leading to plane crashes and medical errors.

5. **Evolutionary Psychology:** This field studies how external inputs influence brain functions and behavior. It integrates findings from various disciplines to understand and quantify emotions.

6. **Homeostasis Theory:** Proposed by Clause Bernard and expanded by Antonio Damasio, this theory explains how bodily functions and mental experiences are maintained through coordinated physiological processes, influencing our emotions and actions.

7. **Geographic and Social Influences:** Geographic conditions and social experiences shape our emotions and behaviors. For example, climate affects the pace of life, and population size influences social interactions.

8. **Quantifying Emotions:** Researchers such as Robert Plutchik and Paul Ekman have developed theories and tools to measure and understand emotions. Marketers can use these insights to create emotion-focused systems that enhance customer experiences.

9. **Biosensors:** These tools measure physiological responses to emotions, helping researchers and marketers understand how internal and external stimuli affect emotional behavior.

10. **Facial Muscles and Emotions:** Our faces have over 40 autonomous muscles that can independently communicate emotions nonverbally. The brainstem controls involuntary expressions, while the motor cortex handles conscious expressions.

11. **Amygdala's Role:** The amygdala in the brainstem is crucial for emotional arousal, regulating stress hormones, and controlling heart rate, respiration, and facial expressions in response to stimuli.

12. **Universal Emotions:** There are seven universally recognized facial expressions linked to specific emotions: joy, sadness, surprise, anger, fear, disgust, and contempt.

13. **Emotion Analytics:** Advances in affective neuroscience and biosensor engineering allow researchers to measure emotional responses to stimuli without relying solely on surveys or focus groups.

14. **Biometric Sensors:** Tools such as ET, GSR/EDA, EEG, EMG, and ECG provide insights into emotional arousal, cognitive workload, stress levels, and other physiological responses.

15. **Clinical Use of Biomarkers:** Traditionally used in clinical settings to monitor health, biomarkers are now being applied in consumer research to understand emotional and behavioral responses.

16. **Brand Loyalty and Emotions:** Customer loyalty is driven more by emotions related to brand values and behavior (honesty, trust, integrity) than by rational factors such as price or convenience.

17. **Emotion-Focused Technology:** Emerging technologies can detect and respond to consumers' emotional states, offering personalized recommendations and improving overall consumer experience.

CHAPTER 11

Contemporary Segmentation, Targeting, and Positioning

Learning Objectives—By reading this chapter, readers will be able to:
<ul><li>Learn from the successes and pitfalls of other organizations.</li><li>Challenge traditional ways of segmenting, targeting, and positioning products and services.</li><li>Consider new and innovative ways of segmenting, targeting, and positioning.</li><li>Have a holistic view of consumers and customers.</li><li>Identify opportunities to combine biological and affective-cognitive customer data into marketing analytics.</li></ul>

Source: Adapted from *Creating Significant Learning Experiences*[1] and Taxonomy of Significant Learning Experiences.[2]

Traditional Segmentation Methods

Businesses and not-for-profit organizations invest a considerable amount of time researching the portions of a population that are most open to their branding communications and advertising efforts. Successful campaigns are imperative to retain a company's market position and a marketer's job in the long term. Traditionally, this segmentation has been executed according to demographics such as age, generation cohort (from Depression Cohort born between 1912 and 1921 up to the Generation Alpha, those born after 2010), gender, level of education, income, family size, and life cycle, as well as the geographic segmentation of nations, states, regions, or cities, which was made easier to perform with digital marketing tools in the 21st century. However, marketers realized that demographics and geographic segmentation don't always work because people from the same demographic segment may exhibit very different preferences, and people from different demographic segments may exhibit very similar preferences. Following the demographics and geographic segmentation approach, King Charles III and singer Ozzy Osbourne (both male, born in 1948, raised in the United Kingdom, married twice, live in a castle, and are wealthy and famous) could be part of the same target cohort for a particular product or service, but this information certainly does nothing to determine their needs and preferences. Another example is Apple, which has cool brand positioning to attract innovators and disruptors, yet it attracts all generations and people from all walks of life to queue for hours in front of its stores to buy the latest products. To solve this dilemma, marketers and advertising agencies found a solution by adding psychographic segmentation, using theories such as Abraham Maslow's Theory of Human Motivation from 1943 where eight basic and higher order human universal needs are described. They also adopted the values personality lifestyle (VALS Survey developed in 1978 by social scientist and consumer futurist Arnold Mitchell who took the work of sociologist David Riesman and psychologist Abraham Maslow as a basis), which includes an individual's self-orientation and primary motivations of ideals, achievement, and self-expression. However, Maslow's hierarchy of needs received criticism in academia for the methodology used and the lack of consideration of needs across cultures, availability of resources in a given locality, geopolitical characteristics, and individual differences. Maslow's hierarchy of needs failed to include the difference between the social and intellectual needs of people raised in collectivist (valuing acceptance and community) versus individualistic (more self-centered, focused on their self-actualization, valuing freedom and individuality). The VALS Survey was also considered to be flawed in the sense that it did not predict consumer choice and purchases and it's also not a good tool for international market entry. If a person lives in a stable environment, their values tend to also be quite stable, while the opposite is also true. In 1992, Max-Neef expanded Maslow's hierarchy of needs and identified nine fundamental needs that we all have: subsistence, protection, affection, understanding, participation, leisure, creation, identity, and freedom, which was linked to a model of consumer behavior joining the nine types of universal needs mentioned to the four types of existential categories: being, having, doing, and interacting.[3] This was another generic model utilized for segmentation, but that did not offer more in-depth information on cultural differences. Geert Hofstede aimed at bridging this gap with the *Cultural Dimensions Theory* developed between 1967 and 2010, by adding the opposing cultural values of masculinity–femininity (task-orientation versus person-orientation), individualism–collectivism; uncertainty avoidance; power distance (the strength of social hierarchy), long-term orientation, and indulgence versus self-restraint. Hofstede's theory was also criticized due to sampling discrepancies as interviews were conducted mostly with male sales and engineering personnel (working at IBM's global offices), and only had a few women and social minorities participating,[4] hence not representative of the characteristics of whole nations. In 2012, the social psychologist and cross-cultural researcher, Shalom H. Schwartz, developed the *Theory of Basic Human Values*, which included seven types of values for comparing different cultures: conservatism, harmony, egalitarianism, intellectual autonomy, affective autonomy, mastery, and hierarchy. Schwartz's survey asked respondents from all inhabited continents to rate the importance of 56 single values considered as their life's guiding principles. Although considered to be useful for international marketing campaigns, the methodology of the *Theory of Basic Human Values* was said to have its limitations due to the lengthy completion time and the respondent's tendency to select high-scores, thus putting into question the validity of the results.

These theories offer a generalized and stereotypical view of populations and do not take into account changes in personal preferences due to globalization, the advent of the internet and social media, migration, and social, political, economic, cultural, and racial integrations.

Behavioral Segmentation

Behaviorists such as Burrhus F. Skinner and James B. Watson considered that human behavior could be studied with the same precision applied in the physical sciences, also ignoring the mind and brain processes, namely perception, selective attention, and memory. But in the 1960s, George Miller, Ulric Neisser, Herbert Simon, and other founders of cognitive psychology could already convince the scientific community of the limitations of behaviorism. These cognitive psychologists expanded on evidence from Gestalt psychology, European neurology, and work by the British psychologist Frederic Bartlett, to demonstrate that our worldview is based on our biological apparatus for perceiving it, and this perception is a constructive process that not only depends on the information ingrained in a stimulus but likewise on the mental process of the perceiver (Milner et al. 1998). As the majority of mental processes are still largely inaccessible to experimental analysis, cognitive neuroscience emerged from the disciplines of psychology (i.e., methods for analyzing behavior), cognition, and systems neurobiology (i.e., studying the structure and function of neuronal circuits of the sensory and motor systems of the brain).

Analytics Segmentation

In 1987, the world's richest man was Japanese Taikichiro Mori, the owner of the property development firm Mori Building Company. Fast-forward to 2021, Jeff Bezos, founder of the ecommerce giant Amazon (founded in 1994) occupies the top of Forbes magazine's list of richest people in the world. Technology is the industry that takes 6 out of 10 spots on the same list, which includes other billionaires who founded companies created under 50 years ago such as Microsoft (founded in 1975), Oracle (founded in 1977), Google (founded in 1988), and Facebook (founded in 2004), and obtained their wealth from software and the extensive use of data. In 2017, the British magazine, *The Economist*, declared that "The world's most valuable resource is no longer oil, but data," which is "mined" by technological giants such as Alphabet (Google's parent company), Apple, Facebook, Microsoft, and Amazon, and takes half of all dollars spent online in the United States. Amazon has been blamed for the closure of several thousands of stores in the United Kingdom alone (which has been accelerated by the Covid-19 pandemic with an average of 50 shops closing their doors each day) and also for the changes in consumer shopping habits (PwC 2021). Companies acquired by Amazon, from various industries from Whole Foods to Metro-Goldwyn-Mayer Studios (MGM) all have one thing in common: Valuable data that provides an insight into consumers' buying habits and patterns. And, of course, the more data a company has about a person, the easier it is to understand and influence them to take an action or make a purchase. For this reason, Amazon continues to use data to decide which products should be recommended to customers based on their previous purchases and search behavior patterns. Amazon uses data analytics and machine learning as a key part of its recommendation system with 35 percent of its consumer purchases linked with its recommendation system.[5]

Hence, the new digital battlefield is won by companies with the most valuable consumer data and the best algorithms to process and predict human behavior. Every year, new technological developments and marketing tools are launched; however, customer behaviors are evolving as well. Consumption now happens online, in virtual environments, and offline. Companies need to understand what stimulus their customers are exposed to online and offline, but the challenge for companies lies in obtaining offline information, especially for those companies operating primarily online. This "dataism" is being made even harder by data protection laws in Europe General Data Protection Regulation (GDPR), the California Consumer Privacy Act 2018 (CCPA), the *Lei Geral de Proteção de Dados Pessoais* (LGPD) in Brazil, and others around the world.

Data-driven decision making that use analytical tools such as *cluster analysis* (e.g., to understand the characteristics of consumers and create segmented markets); *factor analysis* (e.g., to reduce variables into fewer dimensions and simplify the data and underlying beliefs of consumers); *discriminant analysis* (e.g., for a definition of relationships between consumer characteristics and their group membership used for customer targeting); *customer lifetime value* (e.g., handling historical transaction data to predict future revenue generated by individual customers and inform customer acquisition and retention strategies); *recency, frequency, and monetary* value (RFM, e.g., using historical data to predict consumer response to new offers); *perceptual map* (e.g., measuring similarities and dissimilarities between brands or products to create a visual representation of market structure and best understand the competition); *conjoint analysis* (e.g., to interpret consumer preferences of different versions of products used to inform features in new product development and pricing); *social network analysis* (e.g., sensing interactions between consumers to identify influencers, information diffusion patterns); *linear regression* (e.g., to examine how company performance is related to many variables such as the marketing mix, consumer characteristics); and *logistic regression* (e.g., to predict consumer choice with binary variables) can be used to identify variables about consumers. With this information, it will be possible to treat consumers distinctly and to develop a multidimensional score that predicts behavior and therefore use it for microtargeting, thus addressing individual needs. It would also be possible to incorporate the analytical approach with psychology principles to devise a plan and create a message based on people's emotions, biological changes (e.g., influenced by hormones), cultural tastes, ethics, social behavior, and belief systems.

Biological Segmentation

We have learned that humans evolved to behave in ways that would give us an advantage in surviving the threats posed by our environment, and our psychological processes, motivation, and behavior continue to influence us in the same ways that enabled our ancestors' survival, development, and reproduction, the *ultimate functions* of behavior. Yet, if we ask consumers why they buy a certain product, they are likely to respond with a *proximate reason* for buying the product such as mentioning the features of an expensive product, but without expressing the *ultimate function* of the product that caused them to buy it (e.g., an expensive sports car or a handbag), namely, the *high status*, which is attached to the brand.[6]

The *pleiotropic theory of senescence*[7] refers to the deterioration of all bodily mechanisms during the aging process. *Senescence theory* states that natural selection decreases with aging. Some examples are fertility levels and the immune system of a woman in her 20s versus those of a woman in her 50s.[8] In men, for instance, high testosterone levels early in life enable their success in competing with other men for resources, status, and mates, but later in life these high levels may hurt their health through an increase in the risk of prostate cancer.[9]

Humans have various inbred motives that help the optimum survival of our species: A*voiding physical harm and disease, obtaining status, acquiring and keeping a mate, making friends, and caring for family.*[10] These *fundamental motives* can be intertwined for the attainment of one another, such as in the case of obtaining status and acquiring and retaining a mate because (in heterosexual relationships in particular) men and women behave in a way that is aligned with the preference of the opposite gender. For instance, studies have found that women prefer men who demonstrate high social status because it's perceived as a reliable sign of the control of resources, which could offer better opportunities to be enjoyed by their children.[11] Men who are high in status, power, and resources are considered to be also high in mate value by women. High social dominance in men is perceived by women as a predictor of future elevation in status, which is a trait valued by women.[12] Women, on the other hand, unconsciously demonstrate their health, youth, and slim waists because these are perceived by men to be biological markers of fertility (e.g., even congenitally blind men from birth prefer lower WHRs).[13] In the fields of psychology, business, marketing, and advertising, it's often assumed that humans have stable preferences based on our personalities, which are traits that define how we think, feel, and behave after our teenage years have passed. It's still believed that our personalities and preferences remain the same throughout our lives and advertisers develop their campaigns matching specific consumer segments. However, a growing amount of evidence leads to the conclusion that we do not have only one, but multiple *subselves*, each with its distinctive traits, needs, and wants dependent on a given situation, location, activity, and who's accompanying us at a time. This means that products and services may be appealing or not appealing to a particular consumer group depending on which self is in charge at that time solving evolutionary problems (i.e., avoiding physical harm, attracting a mate, taking care of children, or doing business).

Many films such as Girl, Interrupted,[14] American Psycho,[15] and Split,[16] portray characters with mental illnesses like borderline personality disorder, which may cause people to suffer serious symptoms such as depression, anger, and anxiety, and experience difficulty regulating their emotions or recovering from intense mood shifts. It is estimated that one in five people in the United Kingdom[17] and 9.1 percent or almost 30 million people in the United States have a prevalence of any personality disorder,[18] yet, having various *subselves* may be more common than we think from the lenses of the *fundamental motives*. Managing our evolutionary challenges (i.e., *self-protection, disease avoidance, affiliation, status-seeking, mate-acquisition, mate-retention, and kin-care*) means that each of our evolutionary needs also evokes matching subselves, which come to the surface in each life phase, from childhood to old age.

The reader might be asking themselves how to segment consumers to accommodate the *Seven Selves*[19] within us? The answer is by first understanding the needs of each of our *subselves*, and second, at which point in our lives they may surface. Traditional market segmentation usually follows a geographic, demographic, psychographic, and behavioral approach underpinned by *Maslow's Hierarchy of Needs*,[20] yet, an evolutionary model is more helpful in capturing the *fundamental motives* of our *Seven Subselves*, which are more reliable.

Table 11.1 Fundamental motives, subselves, products, and services selected

Evolutionary Human Need	Age or Period It May Appear	Kinds of Products and Services Selected (By the Person or Someone Related to the Person of That Age Period)
Kin-Care	After the first child is born	Baby and toddler clothes, diapers, baby bottles, prams, toys, vitamins, medicine, day care, babysitters, doctor visits, health insurance, school tuition, books, and so on.
Mate Retention	Youth to later years	Expensive wedding parties and honeymoons, Valentine's Day dinners, gifts for birthdays, Christmas, anniversaries, and other special days, therapy sessions, and so on.
Mate Acquisition	Teenage years (through the flow of hormones)	Attractive clothing, hair treatments, gym memberships, going out to bars, concerts, churches, and other public spaces, dating apps, sports, artistic and charitable endeavors, lingerie, romantic restaurants, drinks, trips and gifts, and other products to make people more desirable
Status	From seven to eight years old (respect-seeking and giving)	Expensive cars, houses, restaurants, clothes, jewelry, yachts, first-class tickets, platinum credit cards, personal jets, exclusive schools, universities, holidays and restaurants, private members clubs, a good credit rating, or with blatant benevolence such as "being green" and charitable donations

Evolutionary Human Need	Age or Period it May Appear	Kinds of Products and Services Selected (By the person or someone related to the person of that age period).
Affiliation	Three to five years old (wanting to be liked, seeking and keeping new friends)	Facebook, WhatsApp, Instagram, LinkedIn (and other social media platforms), merchandise from former universities, societies, sports and religious groups, etc.
Disease Avoidance	Toddler years (avoiding new foods)	Health insurance, cleaning products, sanitary wipes, alcogel, vaccines, medicine, vitamins, organic foods, etc.
Self-Protection	Age one (fear of strangers starts)	Motion sensors, cameras, guns, burglar alarms, monitoring service, security guards and dogs, locks, life and travel insurances, self-defense lessons, bullet-proof cars, 4x4s, others

Source: Adapted from A Hierarchy of Evolved Human Needs.[21]

The needs of our *Seven Subselves* make us act in an unpredictable and inconsistent way for the purpose of dealing with a specific ancestral problem. Our *Subselves* can also be primed (i.e., exposing one to a stimulus, which then influences how a person responds to another stimulus) for one or more of the evolutionary human needs and some of these needs may have conflicting goals, making us behave like hypocrites.

For instance, every month, millions of women around the world go through the ovulatory cycle, which regulates fertility, and previous consumer research studies have found that the menstrual cycle influences women's choices in clothing, food, beauty products,[22] the amount of money spent on products, and a preference for positional goods that help improve their social standing relative to other women but not compared with men.[23] During the menstrual cycle, women experience an increased desire for men who are physically attractive, charismatic, and adventurous, yet unreliable.[24]

Marketers and advertisers might be wondering how to use this information in their campaigns as they are generally unable to determine women's ovulatory cycles, but they can create a 28-cycle (e.g., the average cycle is 28 days, but it can also last from 21 to 35 days) forecast model to send targeted and timely messages that reiterates evolutionary needs such as mate acquisition and retention that triggers female competition when they are most open to such messages. Another study showed similar effects on men as those who smelled t-shirts worn by ovulating women later exhibited a surge in their testosterone levels compared to men who smelled t-shirts worn by nonovulating women, or t-shirts with a control scent.[25]

As we have seen, testosterone is a masculinizing hormone that has long-term effects on the brain, the body, and behavior[26] and some of the positive associations between circulating testosterone include dominant, aggressive, antisocial behaviors,[27] and cheating predisposition,[28] hence a surge in testosterone could also mean a behavior change. Recent empirical evidence makes a connection between *mate acquisition* motives and men's motivations to acquire wealth and expensive products after being physically close to women.[29] Moreover, the experience of driving a Porsche Carrera has led to an increase in testosterone, while testosterone decreased in men who drove a dilapidated car in a public space.[30]

Other studies showed that men spent more on expensive products in the presence of a physically dominant male shop assistant, particularly when these male customers were short in stature or had lower levels of testosterone, thus demonstrating that when opposed by physically dominant men, customers are more likely to signal status through the purchase of an expensive product and also preferring larger logos.[31]

Hormonal Segmentation, Targeting, and Positioning

The study of hormones and their application within the fields of marketing and consumer behavior is in its infancy; however, such understanding can lead to a deeper level of awareness about *why* humans consume. In previous paragraphs, I showed how hormones impact physical attributes and psychological behavior, and now I'll discuss the practical implications for the practical application. The link between hormones and behavior is not a biological "cause-and-effect" system, it is rather a bidirectional exchange that relies on intrinsic individual differences and propensity for certain behaviors, social context, and other factors.[32]

Hormones Of The Adrenal Gland

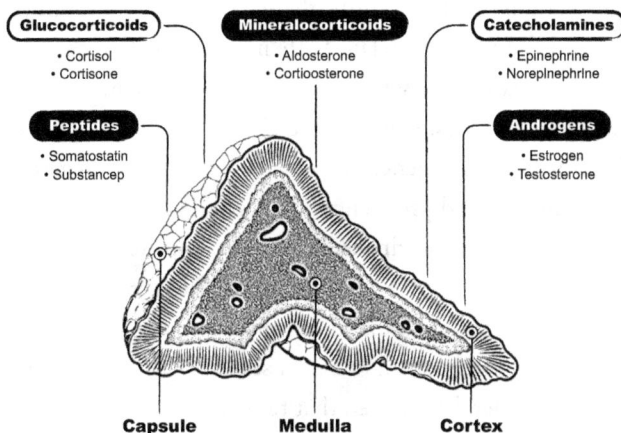

Glucocorticoids	Mineralocorticoids	Catecholamines
• Cortisol • Cortisone	• Aldosterone • Cortioosterone	• Epinephrine • Norepinephrine

Peptides	Androgens
• Somatostatin • Substancep	• Estrogen • Testosterone

Capsule   Medulla   Cortex

Figure 11.1 Hormones of the adrenal gland

Illustrations by Roman, @ideahits.

Hence, steroid hormones influence various neural systems and increase the likelihood of certain consumer behaviors[33] that are grounded within the human *fundamental motives (i.e., avoiding physical harm and disease, getting and keeping a mate, caring for family, obtaining status, and making friends,*[34] mentioned in "Biological Segmentation" of this chapter).

1. **Market Research**

Dr. Glenn Wilson, one of the UK's best-known and most cited psychologists, is a pioneer in the field of evolutionary theories of sex differences, sexual attraction, and love, and he's also known for being the first to hypothesize in the 1980s that 2D:4D ratio (i.e., the ratio between the index and the ring finger, which is calculated by dividing the length of the index finger of a given hand by the length of the ring finger of the same hand), could explain gender differences and other traits.[35] In 1998, another British psychologist, John Manning, professor at Swansea University, discovered that 2D:4D ratios were determined by prenatal exposure to testosterone established in utero.[36] The second digit is usually shorter in both men and women, while the difference in length of the two digits is higher in men than in women (i.e., in men, digit 2 is shorter than digit 4, but in women, digit 2 is the same length or longer than digit 4) and more importantly, the second-to-fourth-digit (2D:4D) ratio was found to correlate with many sexually dimorphic (i.e., where the sexes of the same species exhibit different characteristics) behavioral and physiological conditions.[37] In the past two decades, 2D:4D research has generated very fruitful insights regarding consumer behavior and preferences. Bailey and Hurd[38] found that men with more masculine finger ratios (i.e., smaller, more masculine digit ratios and higher levels of prenatal testosterone) are perceived as being more masculine and dominant by female observers, and they also tend to perform better in several physical sports.[39] Aspara and Van den Bergh[40] showed that testosterone exposure to the fetus in the womb is a significant predictor of future consumer preference for masculine products.[41] Moskowitz and colleagues demonstrated that men with smaller 2D:4D ratios were more agreeable toward women than other men.[42] Sorokowski and colleagues investigated the seminomadic people of Namibia and learned that women and men with more masculine 2D:4D got married younger.[43] Wlodarski, Manning, and Dunbar[44] suggested that 2D:4D small-ratio men are more likely to be promiscuous (i.e., to cheat[45]). A low 2D:4D (i.e., high prenatal testosterone) has been found by Manning and Hill[46] to correlate with high performance in sport and athletics. Prenatal hormones have also been associated with men's sexual orientation.[47] Richard A. Lippa discovered in a sample of over 2,000 research participants, that heterosexual men displayed a significantly lower (more masculine) 2D:4D ratio than homosexual (i.e., gay) men and the results were consistent across ethnic groups, while results for heterosexual and lesbian women did not show significant differences in 2D:4D ratios, after ethnicity was taken into account.[48] Lower 2D:4D men were found to be more risk-seeking than women across five domains (e.g., the financial, social, recreational, ethical, and health domains) as observed by Eric Stenstrom and colleagues.[49] Prenatal testosterone (PT) also affects smoking and alcohol consumption, as John Manning and Bernhard Fink[50] revealed that a high intake of nicotine was related to a high

MASCULINE (LOW)
2D:4D RATIO

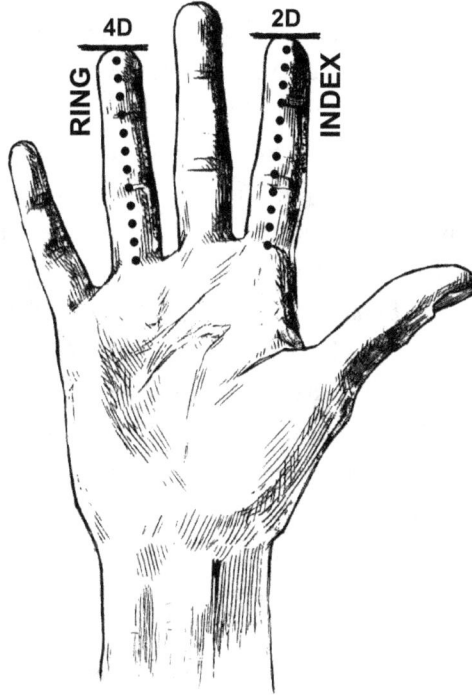

Figure 11.2 Men's masculine 2D:4D ratio

Research has found that men's masculine (low) 2D:4D (i.e., high prenatal testosterone) correlates with high performance in sports and athletics, risk-seeking, and competitive behavior (e.g., financial, social, recreational, ethical, and health) among other traits. To measure your digit ratio, take your right hand (as studies have found that the right hand, R2D:4D, is related to prenatal androgen exposure (PAE),[51] make sure that your fingers are straight, focus on the index and the ring finger. On the crease of each finger that is closer to the palm of your hand, mark the middle of the line with a pen, then measure it from the mark you've made to the tip of your finger. Contrast the index finger against the ring finger. Do you have a low (masculine, with more prenatal testosterone), whereby your index finger is lower than your ring finger, or a feminine (less prenatal testosterone) 2D:4D ratio?
Illustrations by Roman, @ideahits.

2D:4D, while a high intake of alcohol was related to a low 2D:4D (independent of gender, age, height, education, and individual choices regarding nicotine or alcohol intake). Many other studies have shown a correlation between 2D:4D and a variety of behavioral and physical traits such as the risk of obesity,[52] heart disease,[53] prostate cancer,[54] and even penis length.[55]

Recruiting participants for individual interviews, focus groups, or product testing and measuring their digit ratio could offer interesting possibilities to marketing researchers in answering a multitude of questions about consumers.

2. Product Development

In a letter to shareholders in 2018, Jeff Bezos, former CEO and current executive chairman of Amazon, stated that *"as a company grows,* everything *needs to scale, including the size of your failed experiments."*[56] However, if your organization does not have Amazon's $480 billion annual turnover,[57] and the possibility of depleting shareholders or your investment with failed product launches is a major concern for your business, you are likely to execute it with care. Research has shown that 75 percent of packaged goods and retail products, for instance, fall short of earning $7.5 million in the first year of launch, while the benchmark for a highly successful launch should be at least $50 million in large organizations.[58] In the United States, consumers tend to buy the same 150 items regularly, which constitutes 85 percent of consumers' household needs.[59] In other research, 62 percent of male and female consumers said that they prefer to buy brands they already trust, and 54 percent of male and 61 percent of female consumers prefer brands with a "made in the U.S.A." label, valuing quality and consistency over innovation.[60] Hence, finding a space in consumers' minds and enticing them to try out new products is becoming increasingly challenging, especially for certain product categories more than others.

It took 27 years for smartphones to become almost omnipresent, from a modest 30,000 users in 1994 to 1 billion in 2012, and finally reaching a record 3.95 billion users, or almost half the world's population by June 2021.[61] Since Apple's first use of the phrase "there's an app for that" in adverts in 2009, smartphone users could choose between 3.3 million apps on Google Play and 2.1 million apps on Apple's iOS. So another expression became popular, "app fatigue" as users become more selective about which apps they use, as research shows that, on average, people delete apps 5.8 days after the last use, and in the case of entertainment apps, that drops to deletions happening after only half a day.[62]

While product failures can be attributed to a variety of reasons, experts have proposed that not finding the commercial viability for the product or service, not ensuring sufficient product testing, not appropriately educating consumers about the product or service's benefits, a lack of adequate preparation for product launches, and a company's inability to sustain fast growth are some of the major reasons of product failure.[63] As such, marketers must consider the why, how, and when to collect feedback from target consumers about new products, and which weight to attribute to their opinion from the initial stages until the postlaunch evaluation and commercialization phase, as well as the biases of the product development and launch teams (as per part 2, Chapter 4 "225 Biases—Which Ones Do You Display?") to minimize costly product failures.

Considering the shifts in mood and behavior that both men and women experience during their respective hormonal variations (as described in the chapter "We Are All Hormonal"), marketers and consumer behavior researchers should also consider how these shifts may impact the opinions of customers during the product development phase so that brands can ascertain how *real* the perceptions of target consumers are about the product.

Cycle syncing, for instance, is a (menstrual) *cycle mapping* or simply *a* method of adjusting many aspects of a woman's life (e.g., energy management, sleep patterns, exercise, appetite, nutrition, fertility, mood, sex drive, giving up bad habits) according to the phases of the menstrual cycle to correct hormonal asymmetries and therefore reduce hormonal symptoms.[64] And despite privacy concerns about the use of cycle syncing apps, particularly following the ban on abortions in 12 American estates when Roe versus Wade was overturned. (In 1973, the U.S. Supreme Court had authorized abortions after the court case brought by Norma McCorvey, who was addressed by the legal pseudonym "Jane Roe" who wanted an abortion,[65] almost one-third of American women still use period tracker apps such as Flo and Clue, which have 55 million users combined.[66]) Prominent athletes like the British Olympic gold medalist, Dame Jessica Ennis-Hill, have spoken about the benefits of tailoring a woman's diet and exercise around their menstrual cycle to build more lean muscle, become stronger, optimize their overall performance as an athlete, and improve their quality of life. Dame Jessica Ennis-Hill and physiologist Dr. Emma Ross jointly developed the period-tracking app, Jennis, as a result.[67]

Even though the discussion of menstrual cycles remains taboo among women and men, marketers would benefit from the knowledge of how periods affect a variety of women's moods and behavior, which vary from having a negative body image to being successful at quitting cigarettes.[68] This information is of importance, particularly during the product development and testing phases in which the opinion of consumers informs the next phase of investment into the product, segmentation, targeting, positioning, and the overall marketing mix.

3. Branding

Brand trust is a multidimensional construct related to hormonal, affective, and cognitive mechanisms that may enhance brand loyalty behavior via consumer confidence and reduce the perceived brand risk.[69] Despite the popular thinking that hormones affect our decision-making abilities mostly during puberty in our teenage years,[70] or throughout a woman's menopausal phase,[71] our hormones continue to affect our behavior and decision-making processes throughout our lives. Relationship marketing researchers have stressed that brand trust is an essential element of brand loyalty[72] and that trust (i.e., acting without calculating immediate benefits and costs[73]) is particularly relevant to consumers in uncertain or risky situations.[74] Hence, brands serve the purpose of reducing customers' perceived uncertainty in an environment where consumers feel vulnerable.[75] Aligned with this idea is our built-in *social self-preservation system*, which audits the environment not only to identify possible threats to one's physical *survival* but also to determine risks to one's social *status* and self-esteem.[76] Such basic threats to one's survival evoke the release of cortisol (i.e., a stress hormone related to elevated levels of stress and lower psychological well-being,[77] from the hypothalamic–pituitary–adrenocortical (HPA) network and provide an adaptive purpose to increase the bioavailability of energy in *fight or flight*, responses that are generally followed by symptoms of anxiety and sweating, among other physiological responses in survival-relevant behaviors.[78] Consumers or buyers can experience high levels of cortisol throughout the buying process in response to a possible change that a product or service may offer, or when one's goals are interfered with or threatened.[79] Research has suggested that high levels of cortisol decrease testosterone (i.e., a hormone associated with dominant, competitive, and aggressive behavior,[80] so it's therefore important to discern which hormones are being triggered via the interaction between consumers and the brand).

Oxytocin (i.e., the "love hormone"), which is responsible for fortifying relationship bonding, has a dual role in producing or reducing anxiety, depending on the social context. This is because, in times of social defeat or trauma, oxytocin targets the *lateral septum,* the

The Hypothalamic Pituitary Adrenocortical (HPA) Network

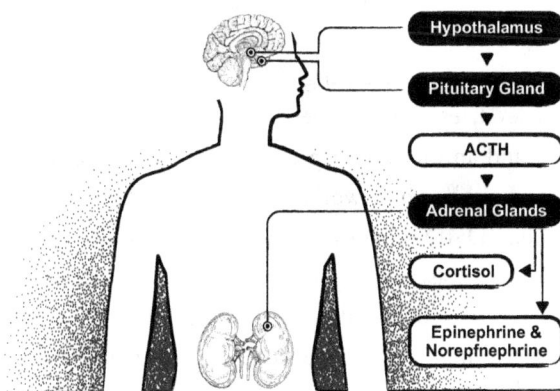

Figure 11.3 The hypothalamic–pituitary–adrenocortical (HPA) network

Illustrations by Roman, @ideahits.

brain region that mediates the fear-enhancing effects of the oxyto-cin receptor (i.e., Oxtr), thus heightening feelings of social isolation, solitude, and suffering.[81] For this reason, the interaction between cortisol and oxytocin matters because oxytocin affects the degree of trust we feel toward others, with higher levels increasing trust, an essential component within the consumer/customer-brand relation-ship.[82] Furthermore, an increase in cortisol might alter the preference of consumers away from *status-enhancing* products to products that offer comfort and safety,[83] while the high levels of oxytocin and vaso-pressin are linked with the willingness to buy products that enhance caring for spouses or children.[84] Considering these effects, the effects that a brand will have on consumers depend on situational factors that elicit specific hormones and their corresponding behavior.

4. **Pricing Products and Services**

Estrogen (aka oestrogen) is an ovarian hormone correlated with fer-tility, facial femininity, and a low waist–to–hip ratio (WHR), all fea-tures that men have universally been considering as physical cues to women's fertility since ancestral times.[85] Estrogen is also associated with female mood disruptions during premenstrual syndrome, pre-menstrual dysphoric disorder, and postpartum depression.[86] Studies showed that women in the fertile phase (i.e., high in estrogen) of their cycle are more likely than nonfertile (i.e., low in estrogen) to insult other (perceived) female rivals' physical appearance,[87] therefore engaging in intrasexual competition for good *mates* through their physical attractiveness during this time of critical reproduction.[88] At peak level, estrogen influences the reduction in women's food intake,[89] and an increase in preference for sexier clothing and fash-ion accessories[90] while women with particularly feminized digit ratios (i.e., 2D:4D, high estrogen-to-testosterone ratio) who partic-ipated in an intrasexual competitive situation recorded materialistic traits.[91] Hence, understanding how your product or service relates to enhancing women's intrasexual competitiveness might support your pricing strategy.

5. **Product Positioning**

As discussed in the chapter "We Are All Hormonal," it's known that in humans and many other species, testosterone fluctuates in males based on outcome-dependent changes in social status, with circulating testosterone levels increasing in winners of competitions and decreasing in losers of the same competitions.[92] Positional goods such as a sports car, a boat, or an expensive motorbike are positional goods because they constitute an observable sign of status and hierarchy in society (e.g., when compared to utilitarian items such as health or life insurance), and by possessing a sports car, for instance, men communicate their social standing to potential *mates*.[93] As a result, men's endocrinological responses, especially their testosterone levels, have been shown to increase (and decrease) when driving an expensive sports car (compared to an old family sedan vehicle). The location of the drive (a busy or deserted area) and who's observing men in their sports cars also influenced men's hormones.[94] While men flash luxury products to attract mates, women on the other hand use pricey products (e.g., designer handbags, clothes, and shoes) to express their identity, boost their self-esteem, and signal their status. But when in a committed relationship, women might showcase these products to obstruct other female rivals perceived as threats to their romantic relationships, and to show their partner is exclusively dedicated to them.[95]

With this knowledge, it's essential to craft brand and product positioning in a way that evokes the desired hormone-related behavior.

6. **Distribution Channels**

Dopamine is a hormone and neurotransmitter called a *chemical messenger* because our bodies produce it and our nervous system uses it to send messages between nerve cells. It also plays an important role (along with another hormone, serotonin, which is related to emotions, metabolism, and digestion) in how we feel pleasure, and how we find things interesting.[96] Dopamine increases in fast and high amounts during drug misuse or addition because it satisfies our natural reward system, which sets new pleasure thresholds in each subsequent drug use (e.g., that's why addicts need to consume higher amounts of drugs to get the same "high," which explains the emotional lows when addicts are sober), as drug use decreases the body's ability to produce dopamine naturally.[97] It is related to other addictions such as our attachment to mobile phones, social media, or video games.[98] Brands can also incentivize dopamine production in consumers through rewards and loyalty programs. However, dopamine highs are ephemeral and hard to maintain, especially in long sales cycles (e.g., in B2B sales). Studies found that dopamine is released in *anticipation* of a reward, not when the reward itself is received;[99] this is why dopamine-inducing strategies must be well managed to delay customers' gratification throughout the shopping/buying experience across the distribution channels.[100]

7. Advertisement and Promotion

In the last decade, customer or buyer personas (i.e., fictional and generalized depictions of ideal target customers and clients) became ubiquitous in marketing and customer service teams to best understand the wants, needs, wishes, goals, and pain points of their target audience.[101] It is commendable that companies incorporate such tactics in their marketing campaigns, using customer demographics (i.e., gender identity, age, location, profession, income), psychographics (e.g., customers' attitudes and interests, generalized personality traits, introverted versus extroverted, sociability, self-confidence), values (e.g., social, cultural, religious, political), lifestyle (e.g., based on broad cultural trends), behavior (e.g., emotional and social factors, online and offline information of searching and buying habits, frequency patterns, trends) data to understand and categorize buyers' perspectives, and challenges to tailor product development, services, content, and channels to suit the specific needs of different groups.[102] While collecting and using all of this customer data is better than developing marketing campaigns without any data with which to create advertisements and promotional tools, these types of data are only the tip of the iceberg when trying to create communication pieces that resonate with customers across all cultures and backgrounds. Marketers also rely on generalized customer data found on social media platforms (which are subject to the *social desirability bias*) and search engine platforms, as well as interviews with buyer personas, thus making the assumptions made by marketers rooted in superficial information of how customers want to be perceived, not necessarily on how they truly are, and what they are looking for in a product and service. After all, which consumers would admit that their proenvironmental behavior is based on their underlying need for social *status* among their peer group as studies have suggested?[103] Or what (liberal) parents would express their bias to invest more in daughters than in their sons during poor economic conditions to improve the *reproductive value* of girls[104] as some studies showed? As people/customers are often unaware of their motivations that originate at a subconscious level, the answers provided by consumers/customers about their challenges, pain points as well as the gains they expect from the product or service could be misjudged and misplaced by marketing teams and businesses.

8. **Customer Experience**

As the famous quote by Carl W. Buehner in 1971[105] (wrongly attributed to the renowned poet and writer, Maya Angelou in 2003) says "People will forget what you said, people will forget what you did, but people will never forget how you made them feel," and this happens because customers evaluate their present feelings as sources of information.[106] Positive feelings such as liking, satisfaction, and well-being, or negative feelings such as disliking, dissatisfaction, or frustration are interpreted by customers as actual evidence that a company is reliable or not and that it cares about them as customers or not.[107] Hence, crafting a pleasant customer experience in B2C, B2B, or B2G marketing is essential to generate trust, an indispensable bond to keep customers coming back to your business and advocating it to others. This means that the promise that a brand makes through its communication and advertising should be carried through every single customer touchpoint. Furthermore, there must be a differentiation between how your brand is positioned and how it intends to make your customers feel. The experience provided by fast-moving consumer goods brands such as Nestlé or Procter and Gamble, which may focus on offering reliability, trust, convenience, and a wide selection of products (that have been adapted to the local countries in which they operate in), is vastly different from the experience provided by French and Italian luxury brands such as Louis Vuitton or Ferrari. This is because true luxury brands should not respond to rising demand from clients to keep their exclusivity, making it difficult for clients to buy their products, making them wait for products, and using advertisement pieces that were developed with the intent of creating and increasing desire. The job of the sales teams of such luxury brands is based on advising and educating the target audience regarding the value of the brand, not on selling it.[108] Once the brand positioning has been defined, the relevant customer experience can be crafted to encompass how customers should *feel* in each interaction (i.e., based on an understanding of which hormones will be triggered in each interaction). As we have seen in previous chapters, cortisol will be produced in stress-inducing situations and make customers more sensitive to risk and less likely to accept a change. Situations that enable the release of oxytocin, on the other hand, will create a feeling of trust, closeness, excitement, openness to change, and positivity toward your brand. This is possible in brand–customer interactions such as rewarding customers on special occasions, sending customers a gift at home, inviting them to exclusive events (particularly in the case of B2B clients), and so on.

9. **Storytelling**

In 2018, over 90 percent of inmates in prisons around the world were males,[109] and men are also the majority of victims accounting for almost 80 percent of all homicides worldwide.[110] Studies found that inmates who committed crimes related to sex, violence, and rule breaching in prison had higher levels of testosterone than those who undertook crimes linked with drugs, burglary, and theft.[111]

Figure 11.4 Testosterone, masculine behaviors, and dominance

Studies have correlated testosterone with masculine behaviors including dominance, competitiveness, aggression, and a willingness to achieve and maintain status
Illustrations by Roman, @ideahits.

Psychologists have also placed a spotlight on socialization and the different roles it plays in men and women, with men being rewarded by society for aggression and violence in different walks of life, while women are taught to have more feminine traits such as kindness and empathy.[112] Brands such as Gillette have tried to influence a more positive masculine role model with the controversial advert by Gillette titled "We Believe: The Best Men Can Be"[113] against "toxic masculinity," yet the brand suffered from *consumer vengeance* as sales remained flat following the launch of the advert in 2019.[114] This is one of the many examples that teaches brands to craft messages to their target audience in a way that inspires positive social change, yet without alienating them at the same time. This is, of course, not an easy task, and knowing our audience's emotional and biological reactions to our storytelling efforts is crucial to achieving commercial success.

10. **Sales Teams**

A study showed that when men's social status was threatened by wealth displays of other men in the presence of a woman, their testosterone levels increased, suggesting that there are evolved mechanisms for men's responses to intrasexual competition.[115] Similar field studies focusing on intrasexual competition of consumers in a retail environment have demonstrated that male customers spend more money and purchase more expensive products than their female counterparts in the presence of a physically dominant male employee, which was coined as the "The Abercrombie and Fitch Effect."[116]

Other research found that men in a committed (monogamous) relationship had 21 percent lower testosterone levels than single men, while another found that men in long-term relationships (longer than 12 months) had considerably lower testosterone levels than single men or men in newly formed relationships (less than 12 months), and married men with children had even lower levels of testosterone.[117] Evolutionists explain that this happens because once men have been successful at attracting a mate and conceiving, testosterone has served some of its core purposes (i.e., attracting, keeping a mate, and procreating[118]). However, research has demonstrated that by simply interacting with attractive women, or by being in their presence, men's testosterone levels increase and so does their behavioral risk-taking.[119] Could this be the reason why almost 44 percent of casino game dealers in the United States are women?[120] Other field experiments involving skateboarders found that in the presence of attractive women, skateboarders increased their risk-taking behavior and were involved in more crashes, while their testosterone levels also increased in the process.[121]

The consequence of this knowledge of how men's testosterone levels affect their behavior are as follows:

- The first is related to understanding how your brand message might impact men's moods and behavior, and contrast it with the brand positioning and objectives to ensure they match.
- Recognizing that the traditional demographic segmentation based on gender, age, marital, and parental status may not be as effective as traditionally thought, because of the intricate ways in which testosterone might enable or curtail a desired action, and with this insight conduct field- and lab-based experiments, which include testosterone testing, such as saliva samples that remove the need for blood samples and provide valuable learnings regarding consumer individual differences and social behavior.[122]
- The whole marketing mix should be aligned by including sales teams that can attract the desired target audience and instigate the desired behavioral outcomes.

Table 11.2 *Using hormones and neurotransmitters in marketing campaign planning*

Hormone	What Consumers Should Feel	What Consumers Should Think	What Consumers Should Do
Adrenaline (Epinephrine)	Heightened senses, increased energy	A boost in their ability to focus on a task required by the brand.	Better notice their surroundings and an increased willingness to act in making a purchase (e.g., Black Friday promotions or perceiving the scarcity of a desired product).

Hormone	What Consumers Should Feel	What Consumers Should Think	What Consumers Should Do
Cortisol	A motivation to take an action ("fight") or remain in the same position ("retreat")	I am stressed because a change is needed, or I am stressed and need to stay with this brand.	Try a new product or service, or remain with a current provider (because a change is risky).
Dopamine	Rewarded and recognized by the brand	That the brand appreciates them as customers	Commit to a purchase, recommend the brand to others, and post about the brand on social media
Estrogen or Estrogen (estrone (E1), estradiol/ oestradiol (E2), and estriol (E3)	Sexier More confident about their physical appearance and attractiveness	Products and services can help her improve her confidence and attractiveness compared to other women	Consider how she can benefit from the product or service
Oxytocin	Excitement, closeness, warmth	I trust this brand.	Take a step toward the change that a brand offers
Testosterone	Empowered High in status Dominant	The product/service enables him to embody and achieve certain benefits that the luxury (conspicuous) brand entails, such as prestige, class superiority, and endurance	Take a chance with the product/service, be daring to try. Differentiate oneself from others in the pack

Key Takeaways

1. **Traditional Segmentation**: Historically, segmentation has been based on demographics (age, gender, income, etc.) and geographic factors (nations, regions, cities). However, these methods often fail to capture the diverse preferences within demographic groups.

2. **Limitations of Demographics**: People from the same demographic segment can have very different preferences, and people from different segments can have similar preferences. For example, King Charles III and Ozzy Osbourne share many demographic traits but have vastly different needs and preferences.

3. **Psychographic Segmentation**: To address the limitations of demographic segmentation, marketers use psychographic segmentation, which considers psychological traits, values, and lifestyles. Theories such as Maslow's hierarchy of needs and the VALS survey are used, though they have their own criticisms and limitations.

4. **Cultural Dimensions Theory**: Geert Hofstede's theory adds cultural values to segmentation, such as individualism versus collectivism and power distance. However, it has been criticized for sampling biases and not being fully representative.

5. **Behavioral Segmentation**: This approach focuses on studying human behavior with precision, considering perception, attention, and memory. Cognitive psychology and neuroscience have contributed to understanding how behavior is influenced by mental processes.

6. **Analytics Segmentation**: The rise of technology and data analytics has transformed segmentation. Companies such as Amazon and Google use extensive data to understand consumer behavior, making data the most valuable resource in modern marketing.

7. **Impact of Technology**: The extensive use of data by tech giants has reshaped consumer habits and led to the closure of many physical stores, especially accelerated by the Covid-19 pandemic.

8. **Value of Data**: Companies acquired by Amazon, such as Whole Foods and MGM, provide valuable consumer data. Amazon uses this data to understand and influence consumer behavior, with 35 percent of purchases linked to its recommendation system.

9. **Digital Battlefield**: The competition is won by companies with the most valuable data and the best algorithms to predict human behavior. Customer behaviors evolve, and companies need to understand both online and offline stimuli.

10. **Data Protection Laws**: Regulations such as GDPR, CCPA, and LGPD make data collection challenging, especially for companies operating primarily online.

11. **Analytical Tools**: Tools such as cluster analysis, factor analysis, discriminant analysis, customer lifetime value, RFM, perceptual maps, conjoint analysis, social network analysis, linear regression, and

logistic regression help in understanding consumer behavior and predicting future actions.

12. **Biological Segmentation**: Human behavior is influenced by evolutionary motives such as avoiding harm, obtaining status, acquiring mates, making friends, and caring for family. These motives drive consumer preferences and purchasing decisions.

13. **Pleiotropic Theory of Senescence**: This theory explains the deterioration of bodily mechanisms with age, affecting fertility and health. High testosterone levels in men, for example, can lead to health risks later in life.

14. **Fundamental Motives**: Men and women have evolved behaviors aligned with the preferences of the opposite gender. High social status in men and indicators of fertility in women are valued traits.

15. **Multiple Subselves**: Humans have multiple subselves with different traits, needs, and wants depending on the situation. This means consumer preferences can change based on the context and evolutionary challenges being addressed.

16. **Mental Health Representation**: Films such as "Girl, Interrupted" and "American Psycho" depict mental illnesses, highlighting the complexity of human behavior and the prevalence of personality disorders.

17. **Understanding Subselves**: To segment consumers effectively, it's essential to understand the needs of each of our *Seven Subselves* and when they surface in our lives. Traditional segmentation methods (geographic, demographic, psychographic, and behavioral) are less effective than an evolutionary model that captures fundamental motives.

18. **Influence of Menstrual Cycle**: Women's choices in clothing, food, beauty products, and spending habits are influenced by their menstrual cycle. Marketers can use a 28-day forecast model to send targeted messages that align with evolutionary needs such as mate acquisition and retention.

19. **Testosterone's Impact**: Testosterone influences male behavior, including dominance, aggression, and status-seeking. Men exposed to ovulating women or driving luxury cars experience increased testosterone levels, affecting their purchasing decisions.

20. **Hormonal Segmentation**: Understanding the link between hormones and behavior can lead to deeper insights into consumer behavior. Hormones influence neural systems and increase the likelihood of behaviors grounded in fundamental human motives.

21. **Market Research**: Studies on the 2D:4D digit ratio (index to ring finger length) reveal correlations with gender differences, physical traits, and behaviors. Men with more masculine digit ratios tend to prefer masculine products and exhibit dominant behaviors.

22. **Practical Applications**: Hormonal influences on behavior are not straightforward cause-and-effect, but involve a bidirectional exchange influenced by individual differences, social context, and other factors.

23. **Behavioral Insights**: Research shows that men with lower 2D:4D ratios are more risk-seeking, agreeable toward women, and perform better in sports. These insights can inform targeted marketing strategies.

24. **Consumer Preferences**: Hormonal segmentation can help marketers understand why consumers prefer certain products, such as expensive items that signal status or appearance-enhancing products during specific phases of the menstrual cycle.

CHAPTER 12

A Summary of the Control System, the Brain

Learning Objectives—By reading this chapter, readers will be able to:

- Learn how different parts of the brain, such as the prefrontal cortex and amygdala, influence decision making.
- By combining all the knowledge gained in this and previous chapters, readers will increase their effectiveness in understanding consumer preferences and improve marketing and communication strategies.
- With the Appendix, readers recognize common cognitive biases (e.g., anchoring, confirmation bias) that affect consumer behavior and understand how marketers can leverage these biases to influence purchasing decisions.

The human brain weighs roughly 1.4 kg (approximately 2 percent of an adult's body weight), consumes 20 percent of the body's energy, and is the core organ of the central nervous system (CNS). There are roughly 85 billion neurons in the human brain with cells that handle the majority of communication in the brain. Billions of other cells also transport a range of functions to support, nurture, and facilitate neural signaling. Neurons are made of a cell body and one or more axons that all end at synapses. Synapses create gateways of inhibitory activity between neurons. Synaptic transmission generates the release of neurotransmitters (such as dopamine, epinephrine, acetylcholine).

The cerebellum is divided into two hemispheres and contributes to the regulation of movements, balance, and posture. It takes input from the sensory systems of the spinal cord and other brain areas and consolidates these inputs to calibrate motor movements. The cortex (cerebrum)

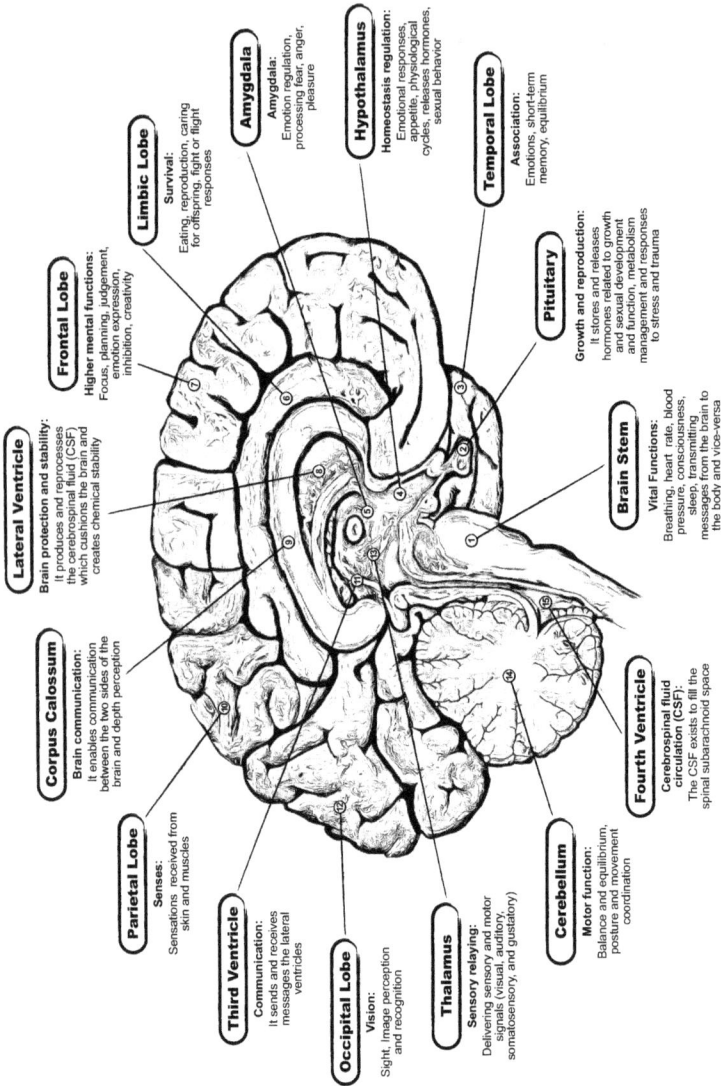

Figure 12.1 Areas and brain behavior[1]

Illustrations by Roman, @ideahits.

is the largest part of our brain (located in the frontal part) and is made of gray matter with between 14 and 16 billion neurons, and it is responsible for higher brain functions including conscious thought, personality processing sensory information, language, sensory processing, and movement. The brain stem (also called the reptilian brain) is the oldest part of the brain (in the lower part), encompassing the midbrain, medulla, and pons, controlling autonomic body processes (breathing, heartbeat, bladder function, and equilibrium). The limbic system (the emotional brain) is an evolutionarily old structure, which includes the thalamus, hypothalamus, and amygdala.

The occipital lobe is the visual processing center of the brain, motion perception, and color differentiation. The temporal lobe processes sensory input, using language, visual memories, and emotional association. The temporal cortex is engaged in long-term memory. The Wernicke's area (in the left temporal cortex) is part of your comprehension of spoken and written language. The parietal lobe combines information from peripheral origins with internal sensory feedback from skeletal muscles, head, eyes, limbs, and so on. It fuses different information sources into a consistent image of how our bodies relate to the environment, and how people and objects spatially relate to us. Tasks related to eye–hand coordination need the parietal cortex. The frontal lobe controls our conscious thoughts, and decisions, and the voluntary movement of our eyes and limbs. It accommodates most of the dopamine-sensitive neurons (responsible for cognitive processes associated with attention, reward, planning, motivation, and short-term memory).

Final Considerations

The research conducted by the author and presented in this short book is intended to highlight the core topics of how humans operate and what makes us tick within the realms of ethics, social interactions, and consumption. It was meant as an introduction to topics that are complex and require a thorough study of their implications. As a woman within the Autism Spectrum (Aspergers), understanding human motivations and the subtle meaning behind unspoken words, gestures, and facial expressions has become my lifelong passion, and I hope I have managed to spark

Brain Regions and Some of its Core Functions

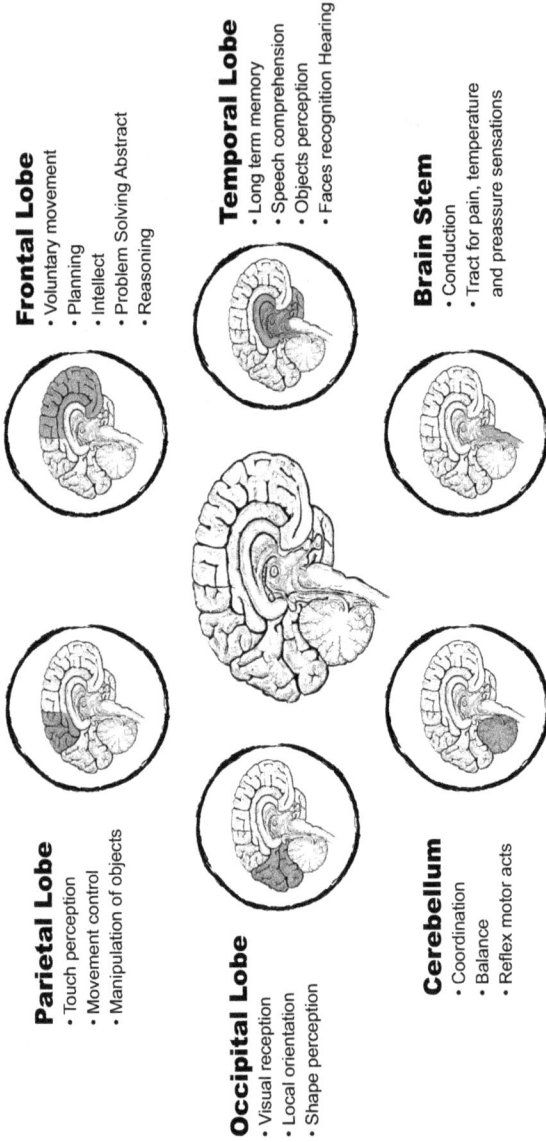

Parietal Lobe
· Touch perception
· Movement control
· Manipulation of objects

Occipital Lobe
· Visual reception
· Local orientation
· Shape perception

Frontal Lobe
· Voluntary movement
· Planning
· Intellect
· Problem Solving Abstract
· Reasoning

Temporal Lobe
· Long term memory
· Speech comprehension
· Objects perception
· Faces recognition Hearing

Cerebellum
· Coordination
· Balance
· Reflex motor acts

Brain Stem
· Conduction
· Tract for pain, temperature and preassure sensations

Figure 12.2 Brain regions and their core functions

Illustrations by Roman, @ideahits.

curiosity in my readers toward the topics presented and encouraged you to also become researchers of human decision making.

Key Takeaways

1. **Brain Overview:** The human brain weighs about 1.4 kg, consumes 20 percent of the body's energy, and is the core organ of the CNS. It contains roughly 85 billion neurons responsible for communication and various other cells that support neural signaling.

2. **Neurons and Synapses:** Neurons consist of a cell body and axons ending at synapses, which facilitate inhibitory activity between neurons. Synaptic transmission releases neurotransmitters such as dopamine and acetylcholine.

3. **Brain Regions and Functions:**
   - **Cerebellum:** Regulates movements, balance, and posture.
   - **Cortex (Cerebrum):** Responsible for higher brain functions such as conscious thought, personality, sensory processing, and movement.
   - **Brain Stem:** Controls autonomic body processes such as breathing and heartbeat.
   - **Limbic System:** Includes the thalamus, hypothalamus, and amygdala and is involved in emotional processing.

4. **Lobes of the Brain:**
   - **Occipital Lobe:** Visual processing center.
   - **Temporal Lobe:** Processes sensory input, language, and emotional association.
   - **Parietal Lobe:** Integrates sensory information and coordinates eye–hand movements.
   - **Frontal Lobe:** Controls conscious thoughts, decisions, and voluntary movements.

5. **Final Considerations:** The research aims to highlight how humans operate within ethics, social interactions, and consumption. The author, who is on the Autism Spectrum, emphasizes the importance of understanding human motivations and encourages readers to explore human decision making further.

Appendix

Table A.1 Bias dictionary

No.	Bias	Definition
1	Action[1]	The propensity to favor action over inaction
2	Actor–observer[2]	Attributing one's actions to external causes while attributing other people's behaviors to internal causes
3	Additive[3]	Solving problems through addition, even when subtraction is a better approach
4	Affinity	Having a preference for people who have a similar appearance, beliefs, and backgrounds to our own while avoiding and disliking people who are different from ourselves[4]
5	Agent detection[5]	The human tendency to conclude that a sentient or intelligent agent intervened in situations for a purpose, even if there is no proof that it might have been the case
6	Altruism	Women prefer kind and altruistic men as long-term partners[6]; men increase in spending on luxurious products when motivated by romantic reasons.[7] Men in a committed relationship tend to display higher agreeableness and thoughtfulness to women, children, and animals and are more concerned with family values, social justice, and the environment[8]
7	Ambiguity effect[9]	Avoiding options that are ambiguous (with incomplete or missing information)
8	Anchoring or focalism[10]	Relying too much on preexisting information or the first piece of information received when making decisions
9	Anticorporate[11]	Believing that large corporations tend to be dishonest[12]
10	Anthropocentric thinking[13]	The philosophical viewpoint of many Western religions and philosophies is that human beings are the central or most significant entities in the world
11	Anthropomorphism or Personification[14]	To instill a real or imagined behavior of non-human agents with human-like characteristics, motivations, intentions, or emotions

(Continued)

Table A.1 (Continued)

No.	Bias	Definition
12	Attention or Attentional[15]	Paying attention to some things while simultaneously ignoring others
13	Attractiveness	Women consider men's physical attractiveness when they're in a long-term mating strategy,[16] while men view women's physical attractiveness as essential and nonphysical qualities as nonessential[17]
14	Attribute substitution[18]	Using various techniques to reduce the effort of making decisions (particularly in complex situations)
15	Authority[19]	Attributing greater accuracy to the opinion of an authority figure even beyond the authority's field of knowledge
16	Automation[20]	The human tendency to choose alternatives that offer the least cognitive effort by overrelying on automated aids and decision support systems, thus assuming that things will not be very different in the future
17	Availability cascade[21]	Expressing opinions based on what (perceived) more knowledgeable people have said about a topic
18	Availability heuristic[22]	The tendency to prioritize infrequent events based on the events' recency and vividness (e.g., plane crashes can make people afraid of flying)
19	Backfire effect[23]	When someone believes even more strongly in an erroneous fact, despite receiving an evidence-based correction of the misconception believed
20	Bandwagon effect[24]	When people think or act a certain way if they believe that others are doing the same
21	Base rate fallacy or Base rate neglect[25]	People's tendency to erroneously judge the likelihood of a situation by not taking into account all relevant data
22	Beauty	People considered beautiful are more likely to be hired, and receive a higher salary and better performance evaluations as the "beauty premium."[26] Male or female good-looking politicians have a 20 percent advantage compared to less attractive rivals.[27] Beautiful people are also perceived to be more likable, and trustworthy,[28] among other positive qualities. Heroes in films tend to be good-looking while villains are usually bad-looking

No.	Bias	Definition
23	Belief[29]	Overrelying on preexisting beliefs and knowledge when evaluating the conclusions of an argument
24	Ben Franklin effect[30]	Beginning to like someone (who you were indifferent to or disliked) more after you do that person a favor
25	Berkson's paradox (collider bias)[31]	A bias that occurs in research when two variables seem negatively correlated in sample data, yet are positively correlated in the overall population
26	Bias blind spot[32]	Perceiving oneself as less biased than other people, or identifying more biases in others than in oneself
27	Bizarreness effect[33]	The tendency to remember bizarre material more than common material
28	Body mass index (BMI)	A general preference for people who display physical fitness and who are not overweight
29	Cheerleader effect[34]	The illusion that individuals look better while they are in a group, as opposed to when they are by themselves
30	Choice-supportive[35]	People's tendency to defend their decisions or later perceive their choices as better than they are simply because they have made them
31	Clustering illusion[36]	A tendency to underpredict the amount of variability likely to appear (due to chance) in a small sample of random or semirandom data
32	Common source/method[37]	When scholars use the same data source (e.g., a survey), to measure both independent and dependent variables simultaneously
33	Compassion fade[38]/ Identifiable victim effect	Showing less compassion for people in trouble as the number of victims increases (i.e., *psychic numbing*, indifference in the face of mass suffering)[39]
34	Confirmation[40]	Processing information by searching for, or interpreting, material that is consistent with one's preexisting beliefs
35	Congruence[41]	A tendency to overrely on testing an initial hypothesis (the most congruent one) while neglecting to test alternative hypotheses
36	Conjunction fallacy[42]	Judging that a conjunction of two events happening in conjunction is more likely to occur than one of those events happening alone
37	Conservatism[43] (belief revision)	Clinging to prior views or forecasts at the expense of acknowledging new information

(Continued)

Table A.1 (Continued)

No.	Bias	Definition
38	Consistency[44]	Judging one's behavior in a given situation by their general self-image, even if one's actual behavior, current or previous behavior is/was different
39	Context effect[45]	Being influenced by environmental factors through one's perception of a stimulus (e.g., in-context memory is easier to retrieve than out-of-context memory, remembering work-related topics is harder at home and vice versa)
40	Contrast effect[46]	When our perception of something becomes distorted when we compare it to something else, thus enhancing the differences between them
41	Courtesy[47]	People's tendency to respond to questions in a socially acceptable, polite, or positive manner at the expense of the truth of how they think or feel
42	Cross-race effect (Other-race effect or own-race bias)[48]	Being better at recognizing the faces of one's race, rather than those of a different race
43	Cryptomnesia[49]	Thinking that a memory or an idea is one's original creation, yet it is an unconscious plagiarism of someone else's memory or idea
44	Curse of knowledge[50]	Thinking that others possess the same knowledge as one's own, and communicating with others assuming that they have the background and knowledge to understand what is being discussed
45	Diclinism[51]	Perceiving the past more positively than the present or future and thinking that things have only become/will get worse
46	Decoy effect[52]	When faced with the choice between two options, the addition of a third (and less attractive) option, the decoy, influences people's perception of the original two choices
47	Default effect[53]	People's tendency to remain with the default option
48	Defensive attribution hypothesis[54]	When confronted with a situation in which there might be blame, one may attempt to reduce one's responsibility
49	Defensive othering effect[55]	The process in which an individual or groups align themselves with the dominant culture and hegemonic identities, and attribute negative characteristics to other individuals or groups
50	Denomination effect[56]	An irrational behavior where consumers are less likely to spend larger currency denominations/bills than their same value in smaller denominations/bills

No.	Bias	Definition
51	Disgust	Humans display the emotion of disgust automatically as it's a key component of the *behavioral immune system*, thought to be an adaptation that serves as a defense mechanism against microbial attack, protecting people from the risk of disease.[57] Women incur a higher risk than men of contracting diseases from sexual activity and develop stronger disgust reactions than men to protect themselves against those hazards.[58] Men's ancestral hunting responsibilities exposed them to blood, wounds, and dead bodies, which could explain why men tend to show less disgust sensitivity than women[59]
52	Disposition effect[60]	In loss-aversion behavior, people will tend to be reluctant to sell assets that have diminished in value, yet are more likely to sell assets that have increased in value
53	Distinction[61]	Overpredicting how small increments in value will impact one's overall happiness/well-being/another improvement (once the choice has been made) when contrasting two options (joint evaluations)
54	Double discrimination and intersectionality	When a woman of color faces double biases for being a woman and a person of color. The same happens to women who face biases for being women and for being LGBTQIA+, leading to compounded discrimination. People (women and men) with two or more minority identities (e.g., religious belief, being an immigrant, being very young/old, or having a nonstandard background or disability) are made to feel like they don't belong anywhere[62]
55	Dominance	Displaying dominant behavior—physically, behaviorally, and through one's appearance. Men with physical signs of dominance, that is, prominent chin, heavy brow ridges, a muscular face,[63] an imposing stature, athleticism and upper-body musculature, a larger number of sexual partners on average,[64] and enjoy more reproductive success[65] than men with less, or who lack these markers of dominance. Men also show their dominance through conspicuous consumption (e.g., buying luxury goods),[66] resource display, talking about their professional success, flashing money, driving expensive cars, and bragging about their accomplishments[67]

(Continued)

Table A.1 (Continued)

No.	Bias	Definition
56	Dread aversion[68]	People's propensity to be dread-averse as they anticipate displeasure and losses from future negative outcomes and this outweighs possible future pleasures or gains to be experienced
57	Dunning–Kruger effect[69]	According to the psychologists and researchers David Dunning and Justin Kruger, the effect represents people's cognitive deficiencies in thinking that they are more skilled in a given domain than they are
58	Duration neglect[70]	A phenomenon in which the duration of affective experiences has a small impact on how a person evaluates a particular memory[71]
59	Egocentric[72]	Overrelying on one's point of view or experiences, while underestimating the perspective of others
60	End-of-history illusion[73]	People's tendency to believe that they have changed in the past but will not experience much more growth and change in the future
61	Endowment effect[74]	A *loss aversion* behavior in which people place a greater value on items that are owned by themselves and a lower value on items owned by others[75]
62	Exaggerated expectation	The tendency to amplify possible outcomes exaggeratedly
63	Experimenter's or Expectation[76]	A propensity that researchers have to concede their expectations of a certain research or experiment outcome to influence their interpretations of the findings
64	Extrinsic incentives[77]	Attributing the motives of other individuals to external incentives and the opposite toward themselves
65	Facial femininity	Women with feminine facial features are more likely to experience upward social mobility[78] while less feminine-looking women, or as they age,[79] tend to use cosmetic enhancements to disguise this physiological change through facial contrast[80]
66	Fading affect[81]	Remembering more positive information and recalling more positive emotions and experiences and forgetting negative ones faster
67	False consensus effect[82]	Perceiving one's own beliefs, behaviors, and attitudes as more normal, common, and typical than is the case

No.	Bias	Definition
68	False memory[83]	Having a false memory about a past event due to misinterpretations or fabrications of new memories
69	False uniqueness[84]	People tend to think that they are better than the average person in different domains
70	Fears and phobias	The survival function of fears induces people to deal with the source of dangers through behavioral responses to acute threats by: *freezing, fleeing, fighting, submitting*, or becoming *frightened*, or *fainting* to prevent an attack.[85] Men and women express their fears differently due to evolutionary reasons and this sex discrepancy originates in infancy.[86] These sex differences may lead to disparate levels of risk tolerance[87]
71	Forer effect or Barnum effect[88]	Believing that generic information can apply specifically to oneself
72	Form function attribution[89]	Placing one's expectations of an object's form and appearance, and deduces certain responses from it based on assumptions, not truth or experience (e.g., as in the case of a robot's functionality)
73	Framing effect[90]	Deciding between different options depends on whether the options are presented positively or negatively
74	Frequency illusion or Baader–Meinhof phenomenon[91]	The tendency to notice something for the first time and after that, believe that its frequency of occurrence has increased
75	Fundamental attribution error[92]	Attributing an occurrence to someone's personality or character, while attributing such circumstance on one's case to an external factor
76	Functional fixedness[93]	Being unable to use an object to solve a different type of problem that it has been originally planned to solve
77	Gambler's fallacy[94]	Assuming that the following event will resemble a previous random event (whether lucky or unlucky)
78	Gender[95]	Giving a differentiated treatment based on a person's real or perceived gender identity
79	Generation effect (Self-generation effect)[96]	Remembering content more if it has been generated by oneself, rather than by others
80	Google effect[97]	Forgetting or not attempting to remember information that can be easily found on online search engines such as Google

(*Continued*)

Table A.1 (*Continued*)

No.	Bias	Definition
81	Group attribution error[98]	Making generalized opinions about outgroup members based on narrow observations of a few of the outgroup members
82	Groupthink[99]	The tendency of groups to seek consensus and conformity, even at the cost of making bad decisions
83	Halo or horn effect[100]	Making positive (halo) or negative (horn) attributions to an object or a person based on stereotyping rather than by objective reality
84	Hard–easy effect[101]	Overestimating one's performance and success at a hard task while underestimating easy tasks
85	Health	Women prefer healthy-looking men (e.g., attractive, masculine, physically fit) as they are perceived to be more likely to invest in their family for the long term,[102] and men preferring healthy-looking women believing that they will be able to pass on their good health genes to their children[103]
86	Height	Perceiving tall men as more suitable for leadership roles
87	Hindsight[104]	Overstating one's ability to have foreseen an outcome once the outcome has already happened
88	Hostile attribution[105]	The tendency to understand uncertain information with a negative interpretation
89	Hot–cold empathy gap[106]	Having difficulty making future decisions when being influenced by instinctive bodily states in the present
90	Hot-hand and cold-hand fallacy[107]	The belief that odds of one's individual success (hot hand) or failures (cold hand) will be reproduced into the future
91	Humor effect[108]	The tendency to remember information, people, or topics if it's humorous
92	Hyperbolic discounting[109]	People's tendency to prefer short-term gains and immediate gratifications over greater future rewards
93	IKEA effect[110]	Placing a higher value on products that were partially created by oneself
94	Illicit transference[111]	Generalizing information about something or someone into the wider group of things or population
95	Illusion of asymmetric insight[112]	Believing that the knowledge one has of someone is greater than the knowledge someone else has of oneself

No.	Bias	Definition
96	Illusion of control[113]	Be convinced to have a level of control or influence over the environment
97	Illusory superiority[114]	Overestimating one's own qualities and abilities, when compared with others
98	Illusion of transparency[115]	The tendency to believe that others know one's mental state well and vice versa
99	Illusion of validity[116]	Being overconfident about one's own judgment when making interpretations and validating a particular dataset
100	Illusory correlation[117]	Misinterpreting a relationship between variables, which leads to invalid conclusions of correlations
101	Illusory truth effect[118]	Perceiving information to be true due to repeated exposure to it
102	Impact[119]	Overestimating the emotional impact that a future event will have in one's life
103	Implicit[120]	Unconsciously displaying certain attitudes and stereotyping groups
104	Information[121]	Collecting, interpreting, and reporting information incorrectly
105	In-group[122]	Favoring members of one's own group over other groups
106	Insensitivity to sample size[123]	Not considering the size of a (data) sample when reaching conclusions
107	Intelligence (IQ)	Young and physically attractive women prefer intelligent men as their long-term partners.[124] The standard psychological perception of intellect is narrowly viewed as a single type of intelligence measured by an IQ (Intelligence Quotient) test that quantifies reasoning and problem-solving ability.[125] Yet there are at least eight different types of intelligence as per *The Theory of Multiple Intelligence* developed by Harvard Professor and Psychologist, Howard Gardner in the late 1970s/early 1980s[126] that are not often considered: 1. Spatial intelligence. 2. Bodily kinesthetic intelligence. 3. Musical intelligence. 4. Linguistic intelligence. 5. Logical-mathematical intelligence. 6. Interpersonal intelligence. 7. Intrapersonal intelligence. 8. Naturalistic intelligence.[127]

(Continued)

Table A.1 (Continued)

No.	Bias	Definition
108	Interoceptive[128]	Being influenced by the sensory information sent by one's own body and considering this input when dealing with external, unrelated situations.
109	Intentionality[129]	Automatically perceiving other people's actions as intentional
110	Institutionalized[130]	The systemic (processes, procedures, practices) way that institutions create advantages for some groups while creating disadvantages for others
111	Irrational escalation or escalation of commitment[131]	Justifying irrational decisions in the present based on rational decisions taken in the past
112	Just-world hypothesis[132]	Believing that the world is just as a means to cope with inequality and injustice (i.e., "people get what they deserve")[133]
113	Lag effect[134]	Remembering information more easily if the information is repeated with longer time gaps
114	Law of the instrument[135]/Maslow's hammer/The law of the hammer/The golden hammer/Einstellung/Attitude effect	The tendency to apply the same skill or tool in many different settings, and for a multitude of purposes
115	Levels-of-processing effect[136]	Recalling information more if it's presented in a deep and meaningful way
116	Leveling and sharpening[137]	Being unable to remember the details of a particular memory
117	Less-is-better effect[138]	Preferring a less advantageous option if it's presented separately, but this preference is reversed when options are presented together
	Likability	Women face a trade-off between being liked or being competent, an issue that men do not face as they are rewarded for being assertive, while assertive women are less liked[139]
118	List-length effect[140]	Better remembering shorter versus longer lists of information
119	Loss aversion[141]	A tendency to prefer to avoid losses at the expense of potential gains
120	Maternal	When the workplace provides fewer opportunities to mothers by assuming that they are less interested in their jobs once they have kids. Women with kids are less likely to be hired, promoted, and earn a lower salary[142]

No.	Bias	Definition
121	Masculine face	Men with a dominant-looking face (i.e., a prominent chin, heavy brow ridges, and a muscular face) tend to achieve higher ranks at military academies and leadership positions
122	Masculinity	Heterosexual women prefer more masculine-looking men than average, especially women living in low-health nations.[143] Women prefer men with deep, masculine voices.[144] Masculine-looking men with attractive faces and bodies have more short-term sex partners.[145] In the English language, a masculine (he) pronoun is often used as in the case of "man, mankind," and the assumption that the gender is masculine in the absence of the correct gender (e.g., "He who has a why to live for can bear almost any how."—Nietzsche 1889) or using distinctive names such as "bitch" to describe female dogs, but using simply "dog" to describe a male dog or "son of a bitch" to offend a man's origins
123	Mere exposure effect[146]	Having a preference for things or people due to familiarity
124	Misinformation effect[147]	Having a memory changed when presented with misleading information after an event has occurred
125	Modality effect[148]	Remembering information if it's presented in a multimodal way (e.g., including visual, as well as auditory mode)
126	Money (price) illusion[149]	People's tendency to perceive money for its nominal value attributed in the past, and not adjust the same value into the present or future accounting for inflation, which presents a reduced purchasing power
127	Mood-congruent memory[150]	Remembering past events that are associated with one's mood in the present (e.g., sad, happy)
128	Moral credential effect[151]/ self-licensing	Behaving ethically for some of the time and subsequently behaving dishonestly, and believing that such behavior is offset by the previous good behavior
129	Moral luck[152]	Attributing praise or blame to someone, even if the actions and the outcomes were outside the person's control
130	Naïve cynicism[153]	Perceiving others as having more biased and self-centered motivations than oneself

(Continued)

Table A.1 (Continued)

No.	Bias	Definition
131	Naïve realism[154]	Having a self-perception of seeing the world objectively (as it is) and not considering one's misattributions and biases
132	Negativity bias or Negativity effect[155]	Paying more attention to, remembering, and attributing more truthfulness to negative events than positive events
133	Neglect of probability[156]	Ignoring probability evidence when making decisions under uncertainty
134	Next-in-line effect[157]	Having a reduced recall of events that happened before or after a performance[158]
135	Nonadaptive choice switching[159]	The tendency to not make a decision that is considered the best choice at a given time, if this choice is related to an experience of regret
136	Normalcy[160]	Believing that future events will be identical to events that happened in the past
137	Not invented here[161]	Showing a negative attitude toward things, technologies, or ideas developed outside of one's group
138	Observer-expectancy effect/Rosenthal effect[162]	The tendency for researchers to influence the participants' reactions to a survey/experiment/event with their body language, intonation, and facial expressions
139	Omission[163]	Perceiving an inaction to avoid a negative outcome is less negative than negative actions
140	Optimism[164]	Amplifying the likelihood of good events happening in one's life while diminishing the perception of the likelihood of negative events
141	Ostrich effect[165]	Avoiding information that is negative to one's finances or another area of life
142	Outcome[166]	Deciding on the present but taking information from the outcome of past events as a reference, even if past events had different variables than those found in the present
143	Outgroup homogeneity[167]	Perceiving the members of another group as more similar to each other while regarding members of one's group as more different from each other
144	Overconfidence effect[168]	Having a misleading perception of one's intelligence, and skills (e.g., overestimating one's capacity to achieve a difficult goal in a shorter period)
145	Pareidolia[169]	People's tendency to see unreal faces in inanimate objects

No.	Bias	Definition
146	Parkinson's law of triviality (bike shedding)[170]	Teams' tendency to spend more time discussing unimportant (trivial) topics while ignoring or postponing important ones
147	Part-list cuing effect[171]	Having a diminished memory for certain items on a list after receiving cues about it
148	Peak-end rule[172]	Not judging events as positive or negative by evaluating their whole duration and experience, but instead placing a greater focus on the most intense part at the end of an event
149	Performance	Making assumptions about women's and men's performances by underestimating women's, while overestimating men's. Women are generally hired based on proven past performance and men are hired based on their perceived potential. This bias forces women to accomplish more than men to demonstrate that they are equally competent as men[173]
150	Pessimism[174]	Being more prone to believe that bad things will happen compared to good things
151	Picture superiority effect[175]	Having a greater recall for pictures than for words
152	Plan continuation[176]	People's tendency to continue with a plan, even if it's no longer viable
153	Planning fallacy[177]	Underestimating the duration of a task despite knowing the duration of completing similar tasks in the past
154	Positivity effect (Socioemotional selectivity theory)[178]	The tendency for (older) adults to pay attention to and remember positive over negative experiences and information
155	Power	Women tend to prefer powerful men in high hierarchical positions because a man's social status is an indicator that he controls valuable resources that are important to offer better food, accommodation, and overall care to children[179]
156	Present[180]	Preferring payoffs that are closer to the present even when compared to greater rewards to be received in the future
157	Plant blindness[181]	The brain's tendency to group plants is due to their color similarity and static nature (compared to animals)
158	Probability matching[182]/ matching law/Herrnstein's Law	People's tendency to make choices randomly instead of following an economically beneficial behavior

(Continued)

Table A.1 (Continued)

No.	Bias	Definition
159	**Processing difficulty effect**[183]	Finding easier to recall information that takes longer to read and understand
160	**Pro-innovation**[184]	Society's fascination with innovation and its tendency to focus on rapid changes as positive, may cause other problems and thus contribute to *maladaptive planning*
161	**Projection**[185]	Believing that others think, feel, and behave like oneself
162	**Proportionality**[186]	The impulse to find extraordinary explanations for large and unusual events of great proportions (e.g., believing in conspiracy theories as it provides a *cognitive closure* to oneself)
163	**Pseudocertainty effect**[187]	People's tendency to make choices that are risk-averse when they expect positive outcomes and risk-seeking choices when trying to avoid negative results
164	**Puritanical**[188]	Implying that the cause of a negative outcome is due to someone's lack of self-control or their moral deficiency without considering if external factors would have contributed to the negative outcome
165	**Pygmalion effect**[189]	The ability of a person of authority to influence the performance of an individual
166	**Recency illusion**[190]	Believing that a word or a type of language use has been created recently,[191] when in fact it has been long established
167	**Reactance**[192]	Becoming even more attracted to think, feel, behave, or consume with a higher motivation when encountering a barrier that hinders one's freedom
168	**Reactive devaluation**[193]	The act of belittling the offer or proposal from an antagonistic party during a negotiation
169	**Regressive**[194]	Remembering high probabilities as lower than they were and lower ones as higher than they truly were, thus averaging out memories
170	**Reminiscence bump**[195]	The tendency for adults older than 40 years to remember more events that happened in their childhood from 10 years up to 30
171	**Restraint**[196]	Overestimating the level of self-control that one has in the face of visceral impulses[197]
172	**Rhyme as reason effect**[198]	The higher likelihood of people believing statements that rhyme than those that do not

No.	Bias	Definition
173	Risk compensation/Peltzman effect[199]	People's tendency to increase their risk-taking behavior once safety measures have been implemented
174	Salience[200]	Focusing on information that is more noticeable and emotionally compelling and ignoring information that is not
175	Scope neglect[201] or scope insensitivity[202]	People's frequent inability to understand the size, undervalue or ignore large problems
176	Selection[203]	When researchers select a pool of participants that is not representative of the target population
177	Selective perception[204]	Not noticing or easily forgetting information that is uncomfortable or that contradicts one's prior beliefs
178	Self-relevance effect[205]	Having a better memory for information and events that are about oneself and a diminished recall for what affects others
179	Self-serving[206]	The tendency to take credit for successes but blame failures and mishaps on external events
180	Semmelweis reflex[207]	People's tendency to not change their minds in favor of new and evidence-backed ideas
181	Serial position effect[208]	Recalling mostly the first and last words on a list and forgetting the words that are in the middle of a list
182	Sexual overperception[209]/ Sexual underperception	The perception that others are more (over) or less (under) interested in oneself as they are
183	Shared information[210]	Spending a longer period discussing information that is shared by all group members as opposed to information that is known to only a few of the group members
184	Shoulder-to-hip ratio (SHR)	Women's preference for men with a high shoulder-to-hip ratio (i.e., a V-shape torso)
185	Social comparison[211]	Disliking and competing with someone better (cognitively, physically, etc.) than oneself
186	Social cryptomnesia[212]	Disassociating the positive achievements attained by minority groups
187	Social desirability[213]	The inclination of group participants to answer survey questions, focus groups, and other discussions in a way that allows others to perceive them favorably
188	Source confusion[214]	Not recalling where certain memories came from and displaying false memories

(Continued)

Table A.1 (Continued)

No.	Bias	Definition
189	Spacing effect[215]	The propensity to learn more if information is presented with greater time lags
190	Spotlight effect[216]	The perception that one's strengths or flaws stand out more to others than they do
191	Status quo[217]	From the Latin Statū quō: "in the state in which things currently are." A preference for things to remain as they are and rejecting change
192	Stereotyping[218]	Having a prejudicial view of another group without objective evaluation of it
193	Subadditivity effect[219]	Interpreting the probability of a total to be less than the probability of each part
194	Subjective validation[220]	To consider information to be true if it has a personal meaning
195	Suffix effect[221]/dilution effect	The inability to remember items of a spoken list if the last items of such have been followed by unnecessary spoken suffixes
196	Suggestibility[222]	Having one's memory influenced by wrong information given by others, especially in emotionally charged situations[223]
197	Surrogation[224]	Being more preoccupied with metrics than the action itself, particularly in situations when a given strategy is unambiguous
198	Survivorship[225]	Taking into account a successful individual or object while not acknowledging the representation of the whole group and the reality it faces
199	Symmetry (face and body)	Facial and physical symmetry has been related to one's health signs that are valued by men and women alike[226]
200	Systematic[227]	The errors that occur in a system lead to unreliability
201	System justification[228]	People's tendency to sustain and reinforce social, economic, and political realities
202	Tachypsychia[229]	A modified perception of time in which time could speed up or slowdown in certain circumstances
203	Telescoping effect[230]	An imprecise awareness of time in which people perceive remote events as more recent (forward telescoping) while recent events are perceived as more distant in time (backward telescoping)
204	Testing effect[231]	When tests are applied during the learning phase, it enables information to be more easily recalled in long-term memory

No.	Bias	Definition
205	Time-saving[232]	Overestimating the time to be saved when increasing the speed of an action (e.g., driving)
206	Tip of the tongue phenomenon/lethologica[233]	The momentary inability to recall information from one's memory
207	Third-person effect[234]	The belief is that others (third parties) are more influenced by advertisements, the media, and persuasive messages than oneself[235]
208	Trait ascription[236]	Believing that others have more predictable characteristics (e.g., mood, personality, and behavior) than oneself[237]
209	Verbatim effect[238]	People tend to remember the summary of a long text, speech, or talk and not the details[239]
210	Virginity	The value that men place on women's virginity has declined in many countries, yet men in many cultures continue to place a greater value (than women do) on women's chastity, particularly in a long-term mate.[240] Women are aware of men's preferences for virgin-like and faithful female partners and therefore insult other female rivals by focusing on their lack of fidelity, highlighting their promiscuousness and appearance.[241] Research has shown that cross-culturally, men find unfaithfulness as the least appreciated trait in a wife[242]
211	Voice	Preference for men with manly/deep low-pitched voices or feminine high-pitched voices
212	Von Restorff effect[243]	Displaying a greater recall for items that are different in shape, color, size, or other characteristics compared to the other items on the list
213	Ultimate attribution error[244]	Perceiving a negative trait in an outgroup member as a fault in his/her/their personality while seeing a positive trait in the outgroup member as an unusual circumstance
214	Unconscious/Implicit[245]	Having an unconscious prejudice against certain groups
215	Unit[246]	People's desire to finish a perceived unit of task or object
216	Weber–Fechner law[247]	The phenomenon in which the awareness of change in a given stimulus decreases while the proportion of the stimulus increases
217	Waist-to-hip ratio (WHR)	Men's preference for women with a low waist-to-hip ratio

(Continued)

Table A.1 (Continued)

No.	Bias	Definition
218	Wealth	Wealthier men are more likely to marry at a younger age,[248] and therefore are more fertile and have more chances of reproduction[249] than their poorer male rivals. Wealthy men can select a younger and more beautiful female partner,[250] and in societies where polygamy is allowed, wealthy men also have multiple wives[251]
219	Well-traveled road effect[252]	Perceiving the journey of a familiar route as shorter than an unfamiliar route
220	Women are wonderful effect[253]	Associating more positive perceptions to women than men
221	Worse-than-average effect/Better-than-average effect[254]	Underestimating (worse-than-average) or overestimating (better-than-average) one's capabilities (physical, intellectual, financial, etc.) compared to others
222	Youth	The preference for younger women is a behavior displayed by men of most cultures, as younger women are usually perceived as healthier and able to reproduce.[255] Aging is a process that is perceived as a progressive decline of health[256] and it is generally avoided
223	Zero-risk[257]	The tendency to avoid risk completely by choosing options that seem to offer such certainty, even if better options are available
224	Zero-sum[258]	Believing that the winnings and successes of some individuals come at the expense of others, even if resources or the valuable item in question is not limited or scarce[259]
225	Zeigarnik effect[260]	Having a greater recall for incomplete tasks than complete ones

Notes

Chapter 1

1. Fink, *Creating Significant Learning Experiences*, 82–92.
2. Mack, "Hummer Drivers Get More Tickets. A Lot More."
3. Kirby, "Testosterone and the Struggle for Higher Social Status," 11–4.
4. Leander, Schaveling, and Vugt, "Basal Testosterone, Leadership and Dominance: A Field Study and Meta-Analysis," 1–8.
5. Wu, et al., "The Role of Social Status and Testosterone in Human Conspicuous Consumption," 72–79.
6. Kahle, Beatty, and Homer, *Alternative Measurement Approaches to Consumer Values: The List of Values (LOV) and Values and LifeStyle (VALS)*, 405–409.
7. Hofstede, "Value Systems in Forty Countries: Interpretation, Validation, and Consequences for Theory."
8. Darwin, *The Expression of Emotions in Man and Animals*, 5–82.
9. Saad, *The Evolutionary Basis of Consumption*, 59–121; Saad et al., "Evolutionary Psychology in the Business Sciences," 17–35.

Chapter 2

1. Fink, *Creating Significant Learning Experiences*, 82–92.
2. iMotions, "Human Behavior Research—Combined Methods for Measuring Human Behavior," 3–11.
3. Featherstone, "Talk Is Cheap: The Myth of the Focus Group."
4. NielsenIQ, "The Value of Failures in the World of SMB."
5. Coca-Cola, "New Coke: The Most Memorable Marketing Blunder Ever? The History of New Coke."
6. Burkitt, "Neuromarketing: Companies Use Neuroscience for Consumer Insights."
7. Penenberg, "NeuroFocus Uses Neuromarketing To Hack Your Brain."
8. Maslow, *A Theory of Human Motivation*, 3–19.
9. McClelland and Liberman, "The Effect of Need for Achievement on Recognition of Need-Related Words"; Murray, *Explorations in Personality*, 22–101; Pincus and Widiger, *Wiggins, Jerry S. (1931–2006)*, "The Encyclopedia of

Clinical Psychology"; Buss and Carlson, *Evolutionary Psychology—The New Science of the Mind*, 903.

10. Freud, "Aggression in Relation to Emotional Development; Normal and Pathological," 37.

11. Adler, "The Collected Clinical Works of Alfred Adler."

12. Buss, "How Can Evolutionary Psychology Successfully Explain Personality And Individual Differences?" 359–66; Buss and Penke, *Evolutionary Personality Psychology. The Handbook of Personality Psychology*; Nettle, "The Evolution of Personality Variation in Humans and Other Animals," 622–31; Nettle and Penke, "Personality: Bridging the Literature From Human Psychology and Behavioural Ecology," 4035–50; Tooby and Cosmides, "On The Universality of Human Nature and Uniqueness of the Individual: The Role of Genetics And Adaptation," 17–68; Buss, *Evolutionary Psychology: The New Science of the Mind*, 952.

13. Pinker, *The Blank Slate: The Modern Denial of Human Nature*, 102.

14. Ibid, 106.

15. Ibid.

16. Buss, "How Can Evolutionary Psychology Successfully Explain Personality and Individual Differences?" 359–66; Buss and Penke, *Evolutionary Personality Psychology: The Handbook of Personality Psychology*; Nettle, "The Evolution of Personality Variation in Humans and Other Animals," 622–31; Nettle and Penke, "Personality: Bridging The Literature From Human Psychology And Behavioural Ecology," 4035–50; Nettle, "The Evolution of Personality Variation in Humans and Other Animals." 622–31; Tooby and Cosmides, "The Past Explains the Present: Emotional Adaptations and the Structure of Ancestral Environments," 375–424; Buss, *Evolutionary Psychology: The New Science of the Mind*, 1732.

17. Plomin, et al., *Behavioral Genetics: A Primer;* Buss, *Evolutionary Psychology: The New Science of the Mind*, 952.

18. Tooby and Cosmides, "The Past Explains the Present: Emotional Adaptations and the Structure of Ancestral Environments," 375–424; Wilson, "Adaptive Genetic Variation and Human Evolutionary Psychology," 219–35; Buss, *Evolutionary Psychology: The New Science of the Mind*, 1733.

19. Saad, "Applying Evolutionary Psychology in Understanding the Representation of Women in Advertisements," 593–612.

20. Locke, *An Essay Concerning Human Understanding*.

21. Miller, *Spent—Sex, Evolution, and Consumer Behavior*, 32.

22. Branch, "Evolution Accepted by a Majority of Americans at Last."

23. Masci, "For Darwin Day, 6 Facts About the Evolution Debate."

24. "Religious Differences on the Question of Evolution," 2009, *Pew Research Center.*

25. "Views About Human Evolution by State," *Pew Research Center.*

26. Miller, et al., "Public Acceptance of Evolution in the United States," 223–38.

27. Branch, "Acceptance Level of Evolution in Twenty Countries."

28. Darwin, *On the Origin of Species by Means of Natural Selection.*

29. Confer et al., "Evolutionary Psychology: Controversies, Questions, Prospects, and Limitations," 110–26; Buss *Evolutionary Psychology: The New Science of the Mind*, 60.

30. Buss, *Evolutionary Psychology: The New Science of the Mind*, 59.

31. Ibid, 60.

32. Ibid, 61.

33. Li, Van Vugt, and Colarelli, "The Evolutionary Mismatch Hypothesis: Implications for Psychological Science," 38–44.

34. Buss, "Evolutionary Psychology: A New Paradigm for Psychological Science," 1–30; Tooby and Cosmides, "The Psychological Foundations of Culture," 19–136; Li, Van Vugt, and Colarelli, "The Evolutionary Mismatch Hypothesis: Implications for Psychological Science," 38–44.

35. Crawford, "Environments and Adaptations: Then and Now," 275–302; Tooby and Cosmides, "The Past Explains the Present: Emotional Adaptations and the Structure of Ancestral Environments," 375–424; Li, Van Vugt, and Colarelli, "The Evolutionary Mismatch Hypothesis: Implications for Psychological Science," 38–44.

36. Manus, "Evolutionary Mismatch," *Evolution, Medicine and Public Health*, 190–91.

37. Dawkins, *The Extended Phenotype*; Oxford, Freeman, and Co; Laith and Zreik, "Richard Dawkins on Constraints on Natural Selection," *Encyclopedia of Evolutionary Psychological Science*, 1–5.

38. Brown and Chia-Yun, "'Big Man'in Universalistic Perspective."

39. Courtiol et al., "Mate Choice and Human Stature: Homogamy as a Unified Framework for Understanding Mating Preferences," 2189–203; Ellis, "The Evolution of Sexual Attraction: Evaluative Mechanisms in Women," 267–88.

40. Brewer and Riley, "Sexual Dimorphism in Stature (SDS), Jealousy and Mate Retention," 1–15.

41. Stulp et al., "Does Natural Selection Favour Taller Stature Among the Tallest People on Earth?" 1–8; Enserink, "Did Natural Selection Make the Dutch

the Tallest People on the Planet? New Study Shows That Taller Men in the Netherlands Tend to Have More Children."

42. Gillis, *Too Tall, Too Small*; Stulp, Buunk and Pollet, "High and Mighty: Height Increases Authority in Professional Refereeing," 588–98; Lukaszewski et al., "The Role of Physical Formidability in Human Social Status Allocation," 385–406.

43. Gillis, *Too Tall, Too Small*; Stulp, Buunk, and Pollet, "High and Mighty: Height Increases Authority in Professional Refereeing," 588–98.

44. Murray and Schmitz, "Caveman Politics: Evolutionary Leadership Preferences and Physical Stature," 1215–35.

45. Chamorro-Premuzic, *Why Do So Many Incompetent Men Become Leaders?: (And How to Fix It)*.

46. Hill et al., 2013, "Quantifying the Strength and Form of Sexual Selection on Men's Traits," 334–41.

47. Mueller and Mazur, 1996, "Facial Dominance of We st Point Cadets as a Predictor of Later Military Rank," 823–50.

48. Krupp et al., 2013, "Psychopathy, Adaptation, and Disorder," 1–4.

49. Hare, *Without Conscience: The Disturbing World of the Psychopaths Among us*.

50. Sanz-García et al., 2021, "Prevalence of Psychopathy in the General Adult Population: A Systematic Review and Meta-Analysis," 1–12.

51. Buss, *Evolutionary Psychology: The New Science of the Mind*, 697.

52. Kiehl and Hoffman, "The Criminal Psychopath: History, Neuroscience, Treatment, And Economics," 14.

53. Hare, "The Predators Among us"; Babiak, Neumann, and Hare, "Corporate Psychopathy: Talking the Walk," 174–5.

54. Boddy, "Corporate Psychopaths, Conflict, Employee Affective We ll-Being and Counterproductive Work Behavior," 107–21.

55. Mathieu et al., 2012, "A Dark Side of Leadership: Corporate Psychopathy and Its Influence on Employee We ll-being and Job Satisfaction," 83–8; Lipman-Blumen, "Following Toxic Leaders: In Search of Posthumous Praise"; Tepper, "Consequences of Abusive Supervision," 178–90; Ashforth, "Petty Tyranny in Organizations," 755–78; Bassman, "Abuse in the Workplace: Management Remedies and Bottom Line Impact." We stport CT: Quorum Books; Einarsen, Aasland, and Skogstad, "Destructive Leadership Behavior: A Definition and Conceptual Model," 207–16.

56. Harris, Kacmar, and Zivnuska, "An Investigation of Abusive Supervision as a Predictor of Performance and the Meaning of Work as a Moderator of the Relationship," 252–63.

57. Tepper, "Consequences of Abusive Supervision," 178–90.

58. Ray and Ray, "Some Apparent Advantages of Subclinical Psychopathy," 135–42.

59. Boddy et al., "Extreme Managers, Extreme Workplaces: Capitalism, Organizations and Corporate Psychopaths," 530–51; Chiaburu, Muñoz, and Gardner, "How to Spot a Careerist Early On: Psychopathy and Exchange Ideology as Predictors of Careerism," 473–86.

60. Brooks and Fritzon, "Corporate Psychopaths Common and Can Wreak Havoc in Business, Researcher Says."

61. Patrick, Venables, and Drislane, "The Role of Fearless Dominance in Differentiating Psychopathy From Antisocial Personality Disorder: Comment on Marcus, Fulton, and Edens." 80–2.

62. Chamorro-Premuzic, "1 in 5 Business Leaders May Have Psychopathic Tendencies—Here's Why, According to a Psychology Professor."

63. Patrick, Fowles, and Krueger, "Triarchic Conceptualization of Psychopathy: Developmental Origins of Disinhibition, Boldness, and Meanness," 913–38; Patrick, "Triarchic Psychopathy Measure."

64. Hanssens and Pauwels, "Demonstrating the Value of Marketing," 173–90.

65. Lamberton and Stephen, "A Thematic Exploration of Digital, Social Media, and Mobile Marketing: Research Evolution From 2000 to 2015 and an Agenda for Future Inquiry," 146–72.

66. Estrada-Jiménez et al., "Online Advertising: Analysis of Privacy Threats and Protection Approaches," 32–51.

67. Lamberton and Stephen, "A Thematic Exploration of Digital, Social Media, and Mobile Marketing: Research Evolution From 2000 to 2015 and an Agenda for Future Inquiry," 146–72.

68. Jung, "The Influence of Perceived Ad Relevance on Social Media Advertising: An Empirical Examination of a Mediating Role of Privacy Concern," 303–09.

69. Estrada-Jiménez et al., "Online Advertising: Analysis of Privacy Threats and Protection Approaches," 32–51; Jordaan and Van Heerden, "Online Privacy-Related Predictors of Facebook Usage Intensity," 90–6.

70. Yang et al., "Applying Social Marketing Theory to Develop Retargeting and Social Networking Advertising We bsite," 1845–49.

71. Ibid.

72. Echeverri and Skålén, "Co-Creation and Co-Destruction: A Practice-Theory Based Study of Interactive Value Formation," 351–73.

73. Awad and Krishnan, "The Personalization Privacy Paradox: An Empirical Evaluation of Information Transparency and the Willingness to Be Profiled Online for Personalization," 13–28.

74. Griskevicius and Kenrick, "Fundamental Motives: How Evolutionary Needs Influence Consumer Behavior," 372–86.

75. Gilbert, "Jeff Bezos Just Sent His Annual Letter to Amazon Shareholders—Read It Here."

76. Pauwels, *It's Not the Size of the Data—It's How You Use It: Smarter Marketing With Analytics and... Dashboards.*

77. Griskevicius and Kenrick, "Fundamental Motives: How Evolutionary Needs Influence Consumer Behavior," 372–86.

78. Motoki and Sugiura, "Consumer Behavior, Hormones, and Neuroscience: Integrated Understanding of Fundamental Motives Why We Buy," 28–43.

79. Ibid.

80. Miller, *Spent: Sex, Evolution, and Consumer Behavior*, 12–32.

81. McClelland and Liberman, "The Effect of Need for Achievement on Recognition of Need-Related Words," 236–51; Murray and McAdams, "Explorations in Personality"; Pincus and Widiger, "Wiggins, Jerry S. (1931–2006)," 1–2.

82. Plackett, "Was Freud Right About Anything?"

83. Freud, "A General Introduction to Psychoanalysis," 548–49.

84. Bernays, "The Marketing of National Policies: A Study of War Propaganda," 236–44.

85. Bernays, "The Engineering of Consent," 113–20.

86. Trotter, "Herd Instinct and Its Bearing on the Psychology of Civilized Man," 227–48.

87. Wallas, "Disposition and Environment"; Wallas, "Instinct and Intelligence."

88. Lippmann, "Stereotypes as Defense."

89. Le Bon, *The Crowd: A Study of the Popular Mind.*

90. Nisbett and Wilson, "Telling More Than We can Know: Verbal Reports on Mental Processes," 231; Nisbett and Wilson, "The Halo Effect: Evidence for Unconscious Alteration of Judgments," 250.

91. Dichter, "Psychology in Market Research," 432–43.

Chapter 3

1. Fink, *Creating Significant Learning Experiences*, 82–92.

2. Descartes, *A Discourse on the Method.*

3. Damasio, *Descartes' Error: Emotion, Reason, and the Human Brain*, 205–22.

4. Ibid.

5. Descartes, *A Discourse on the Method*.

6. Damasio, *Descartes' Error: Emotion, Reason, and the Human Brain*, 205–22.

7. Damasio, *The Strange Order of Things: Life, Feeling and the Making of Cultures*, 12.

8. Descartes, *A Discourse on the Method*.

9. Jones, "Veganism: Why Are Vegan Diets on the Rise?"

10. Darwin, *The Expression of the Emotions in Man and Animals*.

11. De Waal, *Mom's Last Hug—Animal Emotions and What They Teach Us about Ourselves*.

12. Evans, "What Kind of Emotions Do Animals Feel?"

13. Huber, "Everybody's a Little Bit Sexist: A Re-Evaluation of Aristotle's and Plato's Philosophies on Women." *Department of History: Lake Forest College*.

14. Gazit, "The Fourth Generation of AI Is Here, and It's Called 'Artificial Intuition.'"

15. Mysoor, "The Science Behind Intuition and How You Can Use It to Get Ahead at Work."

16. Kotler et al., 2005. *Principles of Marketing*, 256; Griskevicius and Kenrick, "Fundamental Motives: How Evolutionary Needs Influence Consumer Behavior," 01; Buss, *Evolutionary Psychology: The New Science of the Mind*.

17. Essay, *Pascal's Pensées*, 79–80.

18. Porges, "The Polyvagal Theory: Phylogenetic Contributions to Social Behavior," 503–13; Porges, "Social Engagement and Attachment," 31–47; Porges, "The Polyvagal Perspective," 116–43.

19. Maglio and Reich, "Feeling Certain: Gut Choice, the True Self, and Attitude Certainty."

20. Pham, "The Logic of Feeling," 360–69.

21. Strohminger, Knobe, and Newman, "The True Self: A Psychological Concept Distinct From the Self," 551–60.

22. Newman, De Freitas, and Knobe, "Beliefs About the True Self Explain Asymmetries Based on Moral Judgment."

23. Quoidbach, Gilbert, and Wilson, "The End of History Illusion," 96–8; Johnson, Robinson, and Mitchell, "Inferences About the Authentic Self: When Do Actions Say More Than Mental States?" 615–30.

24. Clore, Gasper, and Garvin, "Affect as Information." 121–44; Clore and Huntsinger, "How the Object of Affect Guides Its Impact," 39–54.

25. Ajzen, "From Intentions to Actions: A Theory of Planned Behavior," 11–39; Ajzen, "The Theory of Planned Behavior," 179–211.

26. Brookes, "The Theory of Planned Behavior: Behavioral Intention."

27. Buss, *Evolutionary Psychology: The New Science of the Mind*, 132.

28. Rühli and Henneberg, "New Perspectives on Evolutionary Medicine: The Relevance of Microevolution for Human Health and Disease."

29. Grunspan et al., "Core Principles of Evolutionary Medicine," 13–23.

30. Bergstrom and Feldgarden, "The Ecology and Evolution of Antibiotic-Resistant Bacteria," 125–38.

31. Gluckman et al., "How Evolutionary Principles Improve the Understanding of Human Health and Disease," 249–63.

32. Buss, *Evolutionary Psychology: The New Science of the Mind*, 300.

33. Hendel, "Disgust: A Natural Emotional Response to Abuse."

34. Buss, *Evolutionary Psychology: The New Science of the Mind*, 300.

35. Tybur, Lieberman, and Griskevicius, "Microbes, Mating, and Morality: Individual Differences in Three Functional Domains of Disgust," 103–22.

36. Anderson and Rutherford, "Evidence of a Nesting Psychology During Human Pregnancy," 390–397.

37. Cort, King, and Stiepleman, *On the Basis of Sex*.

38. Merriam Webster, "Reason Definition & Meaning."

39. Cort, King, and Stiepleman, *On the Basis of Sex*.

40. Wang, *The Neuroscience of Everyday Life*, 1–10.

41. Ibid, 19.

42. Lorenz, "'Vergleichende Bewegungsstudien an Anatidae," 194–294; Lorenz, *Evolution and Modification of Behavior*.

43. Buss, "Evolutionary Psychology: A New Paradigm for Psychological Science," 1–30; Cosmides and Tooby, "Cognitive Adaptations for Social Exchange," 163–228.

44. Starling, *The Croonian Lectures on the Chemical Correlation of the Functions of the Body*; Tata, "One Hundred Years of Hormones," 490–96.

45. Baulieu and Kelly, "Hormones: From Molecules to Disease"; Turner, *General Endocrinology*.

46. Stanton, "The Role of Testosterone and Estrogen in Consumer Behavior and Social and Economic Decision Making: A Review," 155–63.

47. Daitzman and Zuckerman, "Disinhibitory Sensation Seeking, Personality and Gonadal Hormones," 103–10.

48. Mazur and Booth, "Testosterone and Dominance in Men," 353–63; Herrmann, McDonald, and Bozak, "A Psycho-Experimental Model for the

Investigation of Hormones as Psychotropic Agents"; Kemper, *Social Structure and Testosterone*; Klaiber et al., "Effects of Infused Testosterone on Mental Performances and Serum LH," 341–49.

49. Saad and Vongas, "The Effect of Conspicuous Consumption on Men's Testosterone Levels," 80–92.

50. Sundie et al., "Peacocks, Porsches, and Thorstein Veblen: Conspicuous Consumption as a Sexual Signaling System" 664–80.

51. Durante et al., "Ovulation, Female Competition, and Product Choice: Hormonal Influences on Consumer Behavior," 921–34.

52. Saad and Stenstrom, "Calories, Beauty, and Ovulation: The Effects of the Menstrual Cycle on Food and Appearance-Related Consumption," 102–13.

53. Griskevicius and Kenrick, "Fundamental Motives: How Evolutionary Needs Influence Consumer Behavior," 372–86.

54. Saad, "Evolutionary Consumption," 351–71.

55. Stanton, "The Role of Testosterone and Estrogen in Consumer Behavior and Social and Economic Decision Making: A Review," 155–63.

56. Stanton, "The Role of Testosterone and Estrogen in Consumer Behavior and Social and Economic Decision Making: A Review," 155–63; Durante and Griskevicius, "Evolution and Consumer Behavior," 27–32.

Chapter 4

1. Fink, *Creating Significant Learning Experiences.*

2. Brown, *Human Universals.*

3. Ibid.

4. Marx and Engels, *The Communist Manifesto.*

5. Panné et al., *The Black Book of Communism.*

6. Smithsonian National Museum of Natural History, "Survival of the Adaptable."

7. Nuwer, "Investigating the Case of the Earliest Known Murder Victim"; Knapton, "Was This the World's First Murder Victim?"

8. History.com, "Babylon"; Rattini, "Cyrus the Great"; USIDHR, "US Institute of Diplomacy and Human Rights."

9. USIDHR, "How Did Human Rights Come About?"

10. United Nations, "Universal Declarations of Human Rights"; The Danish Institute for Human Rights, "Signatories for Universal Declaration of Human Rights."

11. Freud, *Civilization and Its Discontents.*

12. Freud, *A General Introduction to Psychoanalysis*, 01.

13. Luebering, "Renaissance—European History"; Jarus and Szalay, "The Renaissance: The 'rebirth' of Science & Culture."

14. Maslow, "Dominance-Feeling, Behavior, and Status," 404–29.

15. PBS, "Thematic Window: The Civil Rights Movement."

16. Olin and Robsahm, *Modern Slavery*.

17. Singh, "The Feminist Sexual Ethics Project."

18. Niazi, "Debt Bondage Slavery in India Affects Tribal Population."

19. Merriam-Webster, "Bias Definition & Meaning."

20. Cambridge University Press, "Bias."

21. Johnson, *Strategic Instincts*; Sheffield, "Four Cognitive Biases Which Mean You Can't Trust Your Instincts."

22. Kelly, "What Is the Bandwagon Effect?"

23. American Psychological Association, "Racism, Bias, and Discrimination."

24. Martin, "Quarter Billion More People Will Fall Into Poverty in 2022."

25. Credit Suisse Research Institute, "*Global We alth Report.*"

26. Shorrock, Lluberas, and Davies, "*Global We alth Report.*"

27. Toynbee and Somervell, *A Study of History*; Van Der Dussen, *Toynbee and His Critics,* 169–93; Kemp, "Are We on the Road to Civilization Collapse?"; Spinney, "Panicking about Societal Collapse?"

28. Elliott, "History of the Environmental Movement."

29. Library Guides at UC Berkeley, "Library Guides: Non-Governmental Organizations (NGOs): The Environment"; Raj, "Top 23 Global Nonprofits Protecting the Environment."

30. *Time Magazine*, "Greta Thunberg: Time's Person of the Year 2019."

31. Haas, "9 Young Activists Who Tackled Global Issues."

32. Schinkoethe, "Activists Blocking Berlin's Roads Say They Aren't Here to Be Liked."

33. Gayle, "Just Stop Oil Activists Throw Soup at Van Gogh's Sunflowers."

34. Elkington, "25 Years Ago I Coined the Phrase 'Triple Bottom Line.' Here's Why It's Time to Rethink It"; Kraaijenbrink, "What the 3PS of the Triple Bottom Line Really Mean."

35. United Nations, "The Sustainable Development Agenda—United Nations Sustainable Development."

36. The Founder Institute, "17 Founder Institute Portfolio Companies Helping Meet the 17 UN Sustainable Development Goals."

37. Millan, "Climate Change Linked to 5 Million Deaths a Year, New Study Shows."

38. Beasley, "In the World of We alth, 9 Million People Die Every Year From Hunger."
39. Sandford, "Coronavirus: Half of Humanity on Lockdown in 90 Countries."
40. Bunn, "Report: Black People Are Still Killed by Police at a Higher Rate."
41. Rahman, "Full List of Black People Killed by Police in 2021."
42. Ibid.
43. BBC, "Marielle Franco Murder: Suspect Shot Dead by Police"; "Marielle Franco Is the First-Ever LGBTI Person to Be on the Sakharov Prize Short-list"; Londoño, "A Year After Her Killing, Marielle Franco Has Become a Rallying Cry."
44. Junte-se ao Instituto Marielle Franco, "Our Actions Guidelines."
45. Nardini et al., "Together We Rise: How Social Movements Succeed," 112–45.
46. Garza, "Black Lives Matter: A Herstory of the #Blacklivesmatter Movement by Alicia Garza."
47. Oxford Reference, "Joseph Stalin."
48. McGill University, "The Evolutionary Layers of the Human Brain."
49. Ressler, "Amygdala Activity, Fear, and Anxiety: Modulation by Stress," 1117–19.
50. Duarte, "Black Lives Matter: DO Companies Really Support the Cause?"
51. Ibid.
52. Ritson, "If 'Black Lives Matter' to Brands, Where Are Your Black Board Members?"
53. Zippia, "Chief Executive of ficer Demographics and Statistics in the US."
54. Ibid.
55. Wahba, "Only 19: The Lack of Black CEOs in the History of the Fortune 500."
56. Lowcountry Digital Library, "The Trans-Atlantic Slave Trade African Passages, Lowcountry Adaptations Lowcountry Digital History Initiative."
57. Chade, "Número de Pessoas Em Favelas Cresceu No Mundo, Mas No Brasil, CAIU, Diz Onu."
58. World Bank Group, "Population, Total."
59. Universiteit Leiden, "Michiel Van Groesen—Professor Maritime History."
60. Darwin, *On the Origin of Species by Means of Natural Selection.*
61. Griskevicius and Kenrick, "Fundamental Motives: How Evolutionary Needs Influence Consumer Behavior," 372–86.
62. Acayaba and Reis, "N° De Mortos Pela Polícia Em 2020 No Brasil Bate Recorde; 50 Cidades Concentram Mais Da Metade Dos Óbitos, Revela Anuário."

63. Globo Notícias, "Brasil Tem o Maior Número de Domésticas Do Mundo, Diz Oit."

64. Minderoo Foundation Pty., "Global Slavery Index—Regional Findings— The Americas."

65. Ibid.

66. Rodrigues, "Apenas 28,4% Dos Trabalhadores Domésticos Têm Carteira Assinada."

67. Minderoo Foundation Pty., "Global Slavery Index—Regional Findings— The Americas."

68. Lynn, "How Many Africans Were Transported to the Americas as a Result of the European Slave Trade? Has Anyone Tried to Quantify How Many Died as a Result?"

69. Olin and Robsahm, *Modern Slavery*.

70. Modern Slavery, "50 Million People Worldwide in Modern Slavery."

71. The Bank of Korea, "South Korea Population Data—2024 Forecast—1960–2022 Historical—Chart."

72. The World Bank, "Population, Total—Colombia."

73. Kahneman and Tversky, "Prospect Theory: An Analysis of Decision Under Risk," 263–92.

74. Tversky and Kahneman, "Judgment Under Uncertainty: Heuristics and Biases," 1124–131; Kahneman Slovic and Tversky, *Judgment Under Uncertainty*.

75. Kahneman, *Thinking, Fast and Slow*.

76. Ibid.

77. Griskevicius and Kenrick, "Fundamental Motives: How Evolutionary Needs Influence Consumer Behavior," 372–86.

78. Watson, "Sex Differences in Throwing: Monkeys Having a Fling," 98–9.

79. EC Europa, "Tertiary Education Statistics."

80. Belkin, "A Generation of American Men Give up on College: 'I Just Feel Lost.'."

81. Sierminska and Girshina, "Wealth and Gender in Europe," 39.

82. Madgavkar et al., "Covid-19 and Gender Equality: Countering the Regressive Effects."

83. Sierminska, "Wealth and Gender in Europe"; Scheele, *Gender Equality Index 2021*.

84. Classically Court, "A Record Number of Women Are Now Running Global 500 Businesses."

85. Bittner and Lau, "Women-Led Startups Received Just 2.3% of VC Funding in 2020."

86. Mahajan et al., "Don't Let the Pandemic Set Back Gender Equality."

87. Saraiva, "Women Could Give $20 Trillion Boost to Economic Growth by 2050."

88. McKinsey, "The Future of Women at Work Transitions in the Age of Automation," 08.

89. Ibid.

90. Klein et al., "Decisions and the Evolution of Memory: Multiple Systems, Multiple Functions," 306–29.

91. Van Dalen, De Vreese, and Albæk, "Economic News Through the Magnifying Glass: How the Media Cover Economic Boom and Bust."

92. Hester and Gibson, "The Economy and Second-Level Agenda Setting: A Time-Series Analysis of Economic News and Public Opinion About the Economy," 73–90.

93. Alexander, "Evolution of the Human Psyche," 455–513; Flinn, Geary, and Ward, "Ecological Dominance, Social Competition, and Coalitionary Arms Races: Why Humans Evolved Extraordinary Intelligence," 10–46.

94. Thompson and Aukofer, *Why We Believe in God(s): A Concise Guide to the Science of Faith.*

95. Haselton and Buss, "Error Management Theory"; Haselton and Nettle, "The Paranoid Optimist: An Integrative Evolutionary Model of Cognitive Biases," 47–66.

96. Bank of England, "Measures to Respond to the Economic Shock From Covid-19."

97. Le Bon, *The Crowd: A Study of the Popular Mind.*

98. Trujillo, Jankowitsch, and Langlois, "Beauty Is in the Ease of the Beholding: A Neurophysiological Test of the Averageness Theory of Facial Attractiveness," 1061–76.

99. Provine, Cabrera, and Nave-Blodgett, "Red, Yellow, and Super-White Sclera," 121–136; Ford and Beach, *Patterns of Sexual Behavior.*

100. Mengelkoch et al., "More Than Just a Pretty Face?: The Relationship Between Immune Function and Perceived Facial Attractiveness."

101. Newsdesk, "Attractive Women Shouldn't Include a Photo in CV."

102. Tu, Gilbert, and Bono, "Is Beauty More Than Skin Deep? Attractiveness, Power, and Nonverbal Presence in Evaluations of Hireability," 119–46.

103. Berggren, Jordahl, and Poutvaara, "The Looks of a Winner: Beauty and Electoral Success, 8–15."

104. Etcoff Stock, Haley, Vickery et al., "Cosmetics as a Feature of the Extended Human Phenotype : Modulation of the Perception of Biologically Important Facial Signals," e25656.

105. Wisner Baum Law, "Human Factors in Aviation."

106. Davis and McLeod, "Why Humans Value Sensational News: An Evolutionary Perspective," 208–16.

107. Buolamwini and Gebru, "Gender Shades: Intersectional Accuracy Disparities in Commercial Gender Classification," 77–91.

108. Bolukbasi et al., "Man Is to Computer Programmer as Woman Is to Homemaker? Debiasing Word Embeddings"; Caliskan, Bryson, and Narayana, *Semantics Derived Automatically From Language Corpora Contain Humanlike Biases.*

109. Kelly et al., "The Other-Race Effect Develops During Infancy: Evidence of Perceptual Narrowing," 1084–89.

110. Hartung, *Deceiving Down: Conjectures on the Management of Subordinate Status. Self-Deception: An Adaptive Mechanism?* 170–85.

111. World Health Organization, "Tobacco—Key Facts."

112. Reitsma et al., "Spatial, Temporal, and Demographic Patterns in Prevalence of Smoking Tobacco Use and Attributable Disease Burden in 204 Countries and Territories, 1990–2019: A Systematic Analysis from the Global Burden of Disease Study 2019," 2337–60.

113. Ibid.

114. Buss et al., "International Preferences in Selecting Mates: A Study of 37 Cultures," 5–47.

115. Sadler and Woody, "Is Who you Are Who You're Talking to? Interpersonal Style and Complementarily in Mixed-Sex Interactions," 80.

116. Vonasch et al., "Death Before Dishonor: Incurring Costs to Protect Moral Reputation," 604–13.

117. Featherstone, "Talk Is Cheap: The Myth of the Focus Group."

118. NielsenIQ, "The Value of Failures in the World of SMB."

119. Watson, "Sex Differences in Throwing: Monkeys Having a Fling," 98–9.

120. Sierminska and Girshina, "Wealth and Gender in Europe," 39; Madgavkar et al., "The Future of Women at Work Transitions in the Age of Automation," 08.

121. Saraiva, "Women Could Give $20 Trillion Boost to Economic Growth by 2050."

122. Sutherlin, "Big Take: India's Economy at Risk by Exodus of Women From Workforce."

123. Buss and Schmitt, "Sexual Strategies Theory: An Evolutionary Perspective on Human Mating," 204–32.

124. Kennon, "Mental Model: Horns Effect and Halo Effect."

125. Gillis, *Too Tall, too Small.*

126. Stulp et al., "High and Mighty: Height Increases Authority in Professional Refereeing," 588–601.

127. Lukaszewski et al., "The Role of Physical Formidability in Human Social Status Allocation," 385–406.

128. Stulp et al., "High and Mighty: Height Increases Authority in Professional Refereeing," 588–601.

129. Harrison, "Psychopaths: Charming Cheaters."

130. McCullough, "The Psychopathic CEO."

131. Heidrick and Struggles, "Where Are the Women CEOs?"

132. Klein et al., "Decisions and the Evolution of Memory: Multiple Systems, Multiple Functions," 306–29.

133. Finlay, "Credit Scoring, Response Modeling, and Insurance Rating: A Practical Guide to Forecasting Consumer Behavior."

134. Edwards, Lee, and Esposito, "Risk of Being Killed by Police use of Force in the United States by Age, Race–Ethnicity, and Sex," 16793–16798.

135. Wall, "Amazonian Tribal Warfare Sheds Light on Modern Violence, Says MU Anthropologist."

136. Fritscher, "Coping With the Fear of New Things."

137. Buss, *Evolutionary Psychology: The New Science of the Mind.*

138. Janiszewski, "Preattentive Mere Exposure Effects," 376–92.

139. Pavlovskaya, "The Fortune 100 Companies That Spend the Most on Paid Search."

140. Johnston, James, and Rathburn, "7 Companies Owned by Google (Alphabet)."

141. Swant, "The World's Most Valuable Brands."

142. Damasio, "Fundamental Feelings," 781.

143. Immordino-Yang and Damasio, "We Feel, Therefore We Learn: The Relevance of Affective and Social Neuroscience to Education," 3–10.

144. Damasio and Carvalho, "The Nature of Feelings: Evolutionary and Neurobiological Origins."

145. Ibid.

146. Olito, "How the Divorce Rate Has Changed Over the Last 150 Years."

147. Scott et al., "Reasons for Divorce and Recollections of Premarital Intervention: Implications for Improving Relationship Education," 131–45.

148. Schwarz, "Emotion, Cognition, and Decision Making," 433–40; Shevchenko and Bröder, "The Effect of Mood on Integration of Information in a Multi-Attribute Decision Task."

149. Knight, Rastegar, and Kim, "Age Differences in the Connection of Mood and Cognition: Evidence From Studies of Mood Congruent Effects," 279–302.

150. Niessner and So, "Bad News Bearers: The Negative Tilt of the Financial Press."

151. Pinker, "The Media Exaggerates Negative News. This Distortion Has Consequences."

152. Wood, "Bad News: Negative Headlines Get Much More Attention."

153. BBC, "Russia: 'Good News Day' Decimates We bsite's Readership."

154. Dijksterhuis and Aarts, "On Wildebeests and Humans: The Preferential Detection of Negative Stimuli," 14–8.

155. Soroka, Fournier, and Nir, "Cross-National Evidence of a Negativity Bias in Psychophysiological Reactions to News," 18888–92.

156. Vaish, Grossmann, and Woodward, "Not All Emotions Are Created Equal: The Negativity Bias in Social-Emotional Development," 383–403.

157. American Psychological Association, "APA Stress in America™ Survey: US at 'Lowest Point We can Remember;' Future of Nation Most Commonly Reported Source of Stress."

158. De Hoog and Verboon, "Is the News Making Us Unhappy? The Influence of Daily News Exposure on Emotional States," 157–73.

159. Kahneman, *Thinking, Fast and Slow*.

160. Murray, "System 1 and System 2: Facts and Fictions."

161. NASA, "July 20, 1969: One Giant Leap for Mankind."

162. Rapp and O'Keefe, "50 Years After the Moon Landing, Money Races Into Space,"

163. Maidenberg and Copeland, "SpaceX Shoots to $125 Billion Valuation, Shrugging off Elon Musk's Woes."

164. Drake, "Elon Musk: A Million Humans Could Live on Mars by the 2060s."

165. WHO, "Sanitation."

166. UNICEF, "7 Fast Facts About Toilets."

167. Ibid.

168. Allianz, "Allianz and Football."

169. Settimi, "The World's Highest-Paid Soccer Players 2021: Manchester United's Cristiano Ronaldo Reclaims Top Spot From PSG's Lionel Messi."

170. Ely, "Now Nurses Vote to Back Strike: Majority Say They Are in Favour of Industrial Action over No10's 'unacceptable' 3% NHS Pandemic Pay Rise."

171. Nursing Salary, Pay Scale and Bands 2021, "The UK Nursing Salary and Pay Scale Guide—2021."

172. Haselton and Buss, "Error Management Theory: A New Perspective on Biases in Cross-Sex Mind Reading," 81–91.

173. Perilloux, Easton, and Buss, "The Misperception of Sexual Interest"; Buss and Schmitt, "Sexual Strategies Theory: An Evolutionary Perspective on Human Mating," 204–32.

174. Bendixen, "Evidence of Systematic Bias in Sexual Over- and Under-Perception of Naturally Occurring Events: A Direct Replication of Haselton (2003) in a More Gender-Equal Culture."

175. World Population Review, *Gender Equality by Country 2021.*

176. Drysdale et al., "Devastatingly Pervasive: 1 in 3 Women Globally Experience Violence."

177. Senthilingam, "Sexual Harassment: How It Stands Around the Globe."

178. FBI, "2017 Crime in the United States: Rape."

179. Van Dam, "Less Than 1% of Rapes Lead to Felony Convictions. At Least 89% of Victims Face Emotional and Physical Consequences."

180. Ibid.

181. BBC, "Nirbhaya Case: Four Indian Men Executed for 2012 Delhi Bus Rape and Murder."

182. Leal, "9 Celebrities Who Have Opened up About Sexual Assault."

183. Mallon, "Gwyneth Paltrow and Angelina Jolie Both Say They We re Harassed by Harvey We instein."

184. Carlsen et al., "#MeToo Brought Down 201 Powerful Men. Nearly Half of Their Replacements Are Women."

185. Imperial War Museums, "How Europe We nt to War in 1939."

186. Lavington, "Alan Turing: Is He Really the Father of Computing?"

187. Imperial War Museums, "How Alan Turing Cracked the Enigma Code."

188. U.K. Ministry of Justice, "Royal Pardon for WW2 Code-Breaker Dr. Alan Turing."

189. Rainbow Europe, "Annual Review of the Human Rights Situation of Lesbian, Gay, Bisexual, Trans, and Intersex People in the United Kingdom."

190. Auschwitz-Birkenau State Museum, "Robert Biedroń, Nazism's Pink Hell."

191. UK Parliament, "Sexual of fences Act 1967."

192. Tatchell, "Don't Fall for the Myth That It's 50 Years Since We Decriminalized Homosexuality."

193. Drescher, "Out of DSM: Depathologizing Homosexuality," 565–75.

194. BBC, "Homosexuality: The Countries Where It Is Illegal to Be Gay"; Paletta, "ILGA World Updates State-Sponsored Homophobia Report: 'There's Progress in Times of Uncertainty.'"

195. Pew Research Center, "The Global Divide on Homosexuality—Greater Acceptance in More Secular and Affluent Countries"; Underwood, "No Scientific Basis for Gay-Specific Mental Disorders, WHO Panel Concludes."

196. Bawagan, "Scientists Explore the Evolution of Animal Homosexuality."

197. UK Parliament, "Marriage (Same Sex Couples) Act 2013."

198. Pinson, "WWII Codebreaker Alan Turing Becomes 1st gay man on a British Bank Note"; Bank of England, "The New £50 Note Unveiled."

199. Spiegelhalter, "Is 10% of the Population Really gay?"

200. Masterclass, "Tyranny of the Majority Explained."

201. Therapeutic Pathways, "How Many People Are Diagnosed With Autism in the U.S"; Center for Disease Control and Prevention, "Data & Statistics on Autism Spectrum Disorder."

202. Cannon, "Autism: The Positives—Children, Young People and Families Online Resource"; Applied Behavioral Analysis, "5 Things We Could all Stand to Learn From People With ASD."

203. Applied Behavior Analysis Programs Guide, "History's 30 Most Famous People With Autism."

204. Roosevelt et al., "Universal Declaration of Human Rights."

205. Marks, "21 Percent of CEOS Are Psychopaths. Only 21 Percent?"

206. Boddy, "Psychopathic Leadership A Case Study of a Corporate Psychopath CEO," 141–56.

207. Credit Suisse, "Global We alth Report."

208. Georgetown University, "Women Increasingly Outnumber Men at US Colleges, But Why?"

209. Kaplan, "This Women's History Month, Here's a Radical Idea: Let Women Lead. "

210. United Nations, "17 Goals."

211. Rainey, "The Age of 'Greedflation' Is Here: See How Obscene CEO-to-Worker Pay Ratios Are Right Now."

212. Mui, "Amazon CEO Andy Jassy Earned 6,474 Times the Median Amazon Employee's Salary. "

213. Morales, "10 Successful CEOs That did not get a College Degree."

214. Topping, "Campaigners Urge Bosses to Stop Asking Job Applicants for Salary History."

215. Shead, "Venture Capitalists Invested More Money Than Ever Into Start-Ups Last Year."
216. Kunthara, "Black Women Still Receive Just a Tiny Fraction of VC Funding Despite 5 yr High"; Azevedo, "Untapped Opportunity: Minority Founders Still Being Overlooked."
217. Adechi, "Why do White Men Raise More VC Dollars Than Anyone Else?"
218. Hess, "It Costs $74,570 a Year to go to Stanford-But Here's How Much Students Actually Pay."
219. Herrity, "Average Salary in the US."
220. Gramlich, "How the Attitudes of We st and East Germans Compare, 30 Years After the Fall of the Berlin Wall."
221. Weil, "The Bible Was Used to Justify Slavery"; Siliezar, "Slavery Alongside Christianity"; Buchholz, "The Countries Most Active in the Trans-Atlantic Slave Trade."
222. Leverhulme Centre for the Future of Intelligence, "Decolonising AI"; Miller, "The Movement to Decolonize AI: Centering Dignity Over Dependency."
223. Segal, "Workplace Misconduct Cost US Businesses $20 Billion in Past Year."

Chapter 5

1. Williams, "Pleiotropy, Natural Selection, and the Evolution of Senescence"; Buss, *Evolutionary Psychology: The New Science of the Mind.*
2. Fink, *Creating Significant Learning Experiences.*
3. Fink, "Taxonomy of Significant Learning Experiences."
4. Kahneman, *Thinking, Fast and Slow.*
5. Berthold, "Complete Dictionary of Scientific Biography"; Soma, "Testosterone and Aggression: Berthold, Birds and Beyond," 543–51.
6. Engelhaupt, "'Aroused' Recounts the Fascinating History of Hormones,"
7. Ibid.
8. Ibid.
9. Cunningham, "Hormone Replacement Makes Sense for Some Menopausal Women."
10. Rosen, "Questions Remain About the Benefits of Taking Testosterone."
11. Bower, "Investing on a Whiff: Chemical Spray Shows Power as Trust Booster."
12. Ibid.
13. Epstein, "Stop Calling Women Hormonal."

14. Epstein, *Get Me Out: A History of Childbirth from the Garden of Eden to the Sperm Bank.*

15. The White House, "African Americans Under the Fourteenth and Fifteenth Amendments to the American Constitution."

16. The White House, "Nineteenth Amendment of the US Constitution— Women's Right to Vote."

17. The White House, "Barack Obama: The 44th President of The United States."

18. Sky History, "Edith Wilson, America's First (Acting) Female President."

19. History.com, "Plato."

20. Todd and Scarborough, "Medicine—Surgery, Procedures and Techniques."

21. Espach, "What It Really Means When You Call a Woman 'Hysterical'"; Gilman et al., *Hysteria Beyond Freud.*

22. Espach, Ibid.

23. Bible Gateway, "Leviticus 15:19."

24. Bible Gateway, "BibleGateway—Keyword Search: Menstrual."

25. Karlsen, *The Devil in the Shape of a Woman: Witchcraft in Colonial New England*; Pruitt, "5 Notable Women Hanged in the Salem Witch Trials"; History.com Editors, "Salem Witch Trials"; Ginzburg, *The Night Battles: Witchcraft and Agrarian Cults in the Sixteenth and Seventeenth Centuries*; Roach, *The Salem Witch Trials.*

26. Bailey, "Escaping Salem: The Other Witch Hunt of 1692 (Review)," 88–91; Marshall, "Most Witches Are Women, Because Witch Hunts We re All About Persecuting the Powerless."

27. National Museums of Scotland, "James VI."

28. Sherwood, "300 Years on, Will Thousands of Women Burned as Witches Finally get Justice?"

29. Miller, "From Circe to Clinton: Why Powerful Women Are Cast as Witches."

30. Rafferty, "What Is Gerrymandering?"

31. Gorman, "Female U.S. Presidential Contenders Before Hillary Clinton in 2016"; Greenspan, "9 Things you Should Know About Victoria Woodhull."

32. Kohlberg, "Stage and Sequence: The Cognitive–Developmental Approach to Socialization," 347–480.

33. Haidt, "The Emotional Dog and Its Rational Tail: A Social Intuitionist Approach to Moral Judgment," 814–34; Haidt, "Social Intuitionists Answer Six Questions About Morality."

34. Greene et al., "An fMRI Investigation of Emotional Engagement in Moral Judgment," 2105–08.
35. Freitas and De Lima Osório, "Moral Judgment and Hormones: A Systematic Literature Review."
36. Stanton, "The Role of Testosterone and Estrogen in Consumer Behavior and Social and Economic Decision Making: A Review."
37. Williams, "Pleiotropy, Natural Selection, and the Evolution of Senescence," 398–411; Buss, *Evolutionary Psychology: The New Science of the Mind.*
38. Bidder, "Senescence," 583–85; Comfort, "Ageing. The Biology of Senescence"; Partridge, "Is Accelerated Senescence a Cost of Reproduction?" 317–20; Noodén, Guiamét, and John, "Senescence Mechanisms," 746–53.
39. Partridge, "Is Accelerated Senescence a Cost of Reproduction?" 317–20.
40. Williams, "Pleiotropy, Natural Selection, and the Evolution of Senescence," 398–411.
41. Dalton, "Evolutionary Biology: Menopause and Concomitant Dramatic Psycho-Physical and Behavioral Changes in Women."
42. Buss, *Evolutionary Psychology: The New Science of the Mind.*
43. The American College of Obstetricians and Gynaecologists, "Having a Baby After Age 35: How Aging Affects Fertility and Pregnancy."
44. British Fertility Society, "When Are Men and Women Most Fertile?"
45. Ibid.
46. Ford et al., "Increasing Paternal Age Is Associated With Delayed Conception in a Large Population of Fertile Couples: Evidence For Declining Fecundity in Older Men. The ALSPAC Study Team (Avon Longitudinal Study of Pregnancy and Childhood)," 1703–08.
47. Hassan and Killick, "Effect of Male Age on Fertility: Evidence for the Decline in Male Fertility With Increasing Age," 1520–27.
48. Williams and Nesse, "The Dawn of Darwinian Medicine," 1–22; Kruger and Nesse, "An Evolutionary Life-History Framework for Understanding Sex Differences in Human Mortality Rates," 74–97; Buss, *Evolutionary Psychology: The New Science of the Mind.*
49. Buss, *Evolutionary Psychology: The New Science of the Mind.*
50. Trivers, *Social Evolution*; Buss, Ibid.
51. Calicolabs, "Inside the Biology of Aging: How do Scientists Tackle a Planet-Wide Diagnosis?"
52. Pester, "The Longest Living Animals on Earth."
53. Bryner, "What Are Stem Cells?"

54. McGowan Institute for Regenerative Medicine, "What Is Regenerative Medicine?"

55. New York Stem Cell Science, "What Is the Difference Between Totipotent, Pluripotent, and Multipotent?"

56. Gancz and Gilboa, "Hormonal Control of Stem Cell Systems," 137–62.

57. Whitboirne, "Should you Bank Your Baby's Cord Blood?"

58. Sohn, "Human Life Span May Have an 'Absolute Limit' of 150 Years"; Pyrkov et al., "Longitudinal Analysis of Blood Markers Reveals Progressive Loss of Resilience and Predicts Human Lifespan Limit," 2765.

59. Bible Gateway, "Genesis, 9:27."

60. Kenyon et al., "Elegans Mutant That Lives Twice as Long as Wild Type," 461–64; UPMC, "UPMC Life Changing Medicine."

61. Buss, "Sex Differences in Human Mate Preferences: Evolutionary Hypotheses Tested in 37 Cultures," 1–49; Saad, "Applying Evolutionary Psychology in Understanding the Representation of Women in Advertisements," 593–612; Buss, "Conflict Between the Sexes: Strategic Interference and the Evocation of Anger and Upset," 735; Butori and Parguel, "The Impact of Visual Exposure to a Physically Attractive Other on Self-Presentation," 445–47.

62. Buss, *Evolutionary Psychology: The New Science of the Mind.*

63. Pawlowski and Dunbar, "Withholding Age as Putative Deception in Mate Search Tactics," 53–69.

64. Grammer, "Variations on a Theme: Age Dependent Mate Selection in Humans," 100–02; Buss, *Evolutionary Psychology: The New Science of the Mind.*

65. Buss, Ibid.

66. Ibid.

67. Ibid.

68. Ibid.

69. Symons, *The Evolution of Human Sexuality*; Williams, "Sex and Evolution," 3–200; Buss, *Evolutionary Psychology: The New Science of the Mind.*

70. Hill et al., "Boosting Beauty in an Economic Decline: Mating, Spending, and the Lipstick Effect," 275–91.

71. Ruffle and Shtudiner, "Are Good-Looking People More Employable?" 1760–76.

72. Jones, Russell, and Ward, "Cosmetics Alter Biologically-Based Factors of Beauty: Evidence From Facial Contrast," 210–29; Buss, *Evolutionary Psychology: The New Science of the Mind.*

73. International Society of Aesthetic Plastic Surgery (ISAPS), "2020 Statistics at a Glance. Total Procedures Performed Worldwide."

74. Ruffle and Shtudiner, "Are Good-Looking People More Employable?" 1760–76.

75. Durante et al., "Ovulation, Female Competition, and Product Choice: Hormonal Influences on Consumer Behavior," 921–34; Durante, Li, and Haselton, "Changes in Women's Choice of Dress Across the Ovulatory Cycle: Naturalistic and Laboratory Task-Based Evidence," 1451–60; Haselton et al., "Ovulatory Shifts in Human Female Ornamentation: Near Ovulation, Women Dress to Impress," 40–45; Röder, Brewer, and Fink, "Menstrual Cycle Shifts in Women's Self-Perception and Motivation: A Daily Report Method," 616–19; Saad and Stenstrom, "Calories, Beauty, and Ovulation: The Effects of the Menstrual Cycle on Food and Appearance-Related Consumption," 102–13.

76. Durante et al., "Ovulation, Female Competition, and Product Choice: Hormonal Influences on Consumer Behavior," 921–34; Durante et al., "Money, Status, and the Ovulatory Cycle," 27–39; Buss, *Evolutionary Psychology: The New Science of the Mind.*

77. Evans, Neave, and Wakelin, "Relationships Between Vocal Characteristics and Body Size and Shape in Human Males: An Evolutionary Explanation for a Deep Male Voice," 160–63; Feinberg et al., "Manipulations of Fundamental and Formant Frequencies Influence the Attractiveness of Human Male Voices," 561–68; Puts, "Mating Context and Menstrual Phase Affect Women's Preferences for Male Voice Pitch," 388–97; Grammer and Thornhill, "Human Facial Attractiveness and Sexual Selection: The Roles of Averageness and Symmetry," 233–42; Shackelford and Larsen, "Facial Asymmetry as an Indicator of Psychological, Emotional, and Physiological Distress," 456–66; Thornhill and Møller, "Developmental Stability, Disease and Medicine," 497–548; Rhodes, "The Evolutionary Psychology of Facial Beauty," 199–226; Feinberg et al., "Correlated Preferences for Men's Facial and Vocal Masculinity," 233–41; Haselton and Gangestad, "Conditional Expression of Women's Desires and Men's Mate Guarding Across The Ovulatory Cycle," 509–18; Haselton and Miller, "Women's Fertility Across the Cycle Increases the Short-Term Attractiveness of Creative Intelligence, 50–73; Gangestad, Thornhill, and Garver, "Changes in Women's Sexual Interests and Their Partner's Mate–Retention Tactics Across the Menstrual Cycle: Evidence for Shifting Conflicts of Interest," 975–82; Gangestad et al., "Women's Preferences for Male Behavioral Displays Change Across the

Menstrual Cycle," 203–07; Johnston et al., "Male Facial Attractiveness: Evidence for Hormone-Mediated Adaptive Design," 251–67; Penton-Voak, "Menstrual Cycle Alters Face Preference," 741–774; Puts, "Mating Context and Menstrual Phase Affect Women's Preferences for Male Voice Pitch," 388–97; Durante et al., "Ovulation Leads Women to Perceive Sexy Cads as Good Dads," 292.

78. Saad and Stenstrom, "Calories, Beauty, and Ovulation: The Effects of the Menstrual Cycle on Food and Appearance-Related Consumption," 102–13.

79. Schaefer et al., "Female Appearance: Facial and Bodily Attractiveness as Shape," 187–204.

80. Gray and Boothroyd, "Female Facial Appearance and Health," 66–77.

81. The Editors of Encyclopaedia Britannica, "Renin-Angiotensin System." *Encyclopedia Britannica.*

82. Buffenstein et al., "Food Intake and the Menstrual Cycle: A Retrospective Analysis, With Implications For Appetite Research," 1067–77; Saad, *The Consuming Instinct: What Juicy Burgers, Ferraris, Pornography, And Gift Giving Reveal About Human Nature.*

83. Baird et al., "Application of a Method for Estimating Day of Ovulation Using Urinary Estrogen and Progesterone Metabolites," 547–50; Puts et al., "Women's Attractiveness Changes With Estradiol and Progesterone Across the Ovulatory Cycle," 13–19.

84. Endocrine Society, "Reproductive Hormones."

85. Mccallum, "Jessica Ennis-Hill: Why I Now Train Around My Period"; Laurence, "Cycle Syncing: Everything You Need To Know."

86. The Editors of Encyclopaedia Britannica, "Renin-Angiotensin System."

87. National Health Service, "The Male Menopause."

88. Ibid.

89. Ibid.

90. Endocrine Society, "Your Health and Hormones,"

91. Mazur and Booth, "Testosterone and Dominance in Men," 353–63, Discussion 363–97; Josephs et al., "The Mismatch Effect: When Testosterone and Status Are at Odds," 999–1013; Eisenegger, Haushofer, and Fehr, "The Role of Testosterone in Social Interaction," 263–71.

92. Condon, "Palin: Obama Doesn't Have the Cojones for Immigration Reform."

93. Vasari and Christofano, "The Mutilation of Uranus. "

94. The Editors of Encyclopaedia Britannica, "Uranus."

95. The Bible, "Esther 2:14."

96. The Bible, "2:15–17."

97. Wilson, and Roehrborn, "Long-Term Consequences of Castration in Men: Lessons From the Skoptzy and the Eunuchs of the Chinese and Ottoman Courts," 4324–31.

98. Dalrymple, *City of Djinns: A Year in Delhi*; Graham-Harrison, "China's Last Eunuch Spills Sex Secrets"; Serarcangeli and Rispoli, "Human Castration: Historical Notes," 441–54.

99. Kean, "The Disappearing Spoon Podcast"; Von Deuster, "How Did The Castratos Sing? Historical Observations," 133–52 ; The Editors of Encyclopaedia Britannica, "Farinelli."

100. Tråvén, "Voicing the Third Gender–The Castrato Voice and the Stigma of Emasculation in Eighteenth-Century Society," 29.

101. The Bible, "Corinthians 14:34. "

102. Tråvén, "Voicing the Third Gender–The Castrato Voice and the Stigma of Emasculation in Eighteenth-Century Society," 29 ; De Lucca, *The Politics of Princely Entertainment: Music and Spectacle in the Lives of Lorenzo Onofrio and Maria Mancini Colonna*; Marek, *Singing: The First Art.*

103. Han and O'Mahoney, "British Colonialism and the Criminalization of Homosexuality," 268–88

104. Ofosu et al., "Same-Sex Marriage Legalization Associated With Reduced Implicit and Explicit Antigay Bias," 8846–51.

105. Selvaggi and Bellringer, "Gender Reassignment Surgery: An Overview," 274–82; Akhavan et al., "A Review of Gender Affirmation Surgery: What We Know, and What We Need to Know," 336–40; Digitale, "Better Mental Health Found Among Transgender People Who Started Hormones as Teens."

106. Mayo Clinic, "Feminizing Hormone Therapy."

107. Ibid.

108. Ibid.

109. Ibid.

110. The Associated Press, "First Openly Transgender Olympians Are Competing in Tokyo."

111. Sudai, "The Testosterone Rule-Constructing Fairness in Professional Sport," 181–93.

112. Ingle, "Trans Women Retain 12% Edge in Tests Two Years After Transitioning."

113. Meaningful Impact, "Always 'Like a Girl' Super Bowl Commercial: #Like-agirl"; Cox, "The 18 Most Creative Ad Campaigns In History"; Always, "Always #Likeagirl."

114. Buss, *Evolutionary Psychology: The New Science of the Mind*, 89–90.

115. Darwin, "The Origin of Species"; Buss, *Evolutionary Psychology: The New Science of the Mind*, 89–90.

116. Buss, *Evolutionary Psychology: The New Science of the Mind*, 273.

117. Tybur, Lieberman, and Griskevicius, "Microbes, Mating, and Morality: Individual Differences in Three Functional Domains of Disgust," 103–22; Tybur et al., "Disgust: Evolved Function and Structure," 65–84; Al-Shawaf, Lewis, and Buss, "Sex Differences in Disgust: Why Are Women More Easily Disgusted Than Men?" 149–160; Fleischman, *Women's Disgust Adaptations*; Buss, *Evolutionary Psychology: The New Science of the Mind*.

118. Lobue and Deloache, "Detecting the Snake in the Grass: Attention to Fear-Relevant Stimuli by Adults and Young Children," 284–89; Buss, *Evolutionary Psychology: The New Science of the Mind*.

119. James, *The Principles of Psychology*; Gilbert, "William James in Retrospect: 1962," 90–95; Buss, *Evolutionary Psychology: The New Science of the Mind*; Kish-Gephart, "Silenced by Fear: The Nature, Sources, and Consequences of Fear at Work," 163–93.

120. Ember, "Myths About Hunter-Gatherers," 439–48. Brown, "A Note on the Division of Labor by Sex," 1073–78.

121. Sterling, "Man the Hunter, Woman the Gatherer? The Impact of Gender Studies on Hunter-Gatherer Research (A Retrospective)"; Reyes-García et al., "Hunting Otherwise," 203–21; Venkataraman, "Women Were Successful Big Game Hunters, Challenging Beliefs About Ancient Gender Roles."

122. Reyes-García et al., "Hunting Otherwise," 203–21.

123. Venkataraman, "Women We re Successful Big Game Hunters, Challenging Beliefs About Ancient Gender Roles."

124. Noss and Hewlett, "The Contexts of Female Hunting in Central Africa," 1024–1040; Reyes-García et al., "Hunting Otherwise," 203–21; Venkataraman, "Women We re Successful Big Game Hunters, Challenging Beliefs About Ancient Gender Roles."

125. Venkataraman, "Women We re Successful Big Game Hunters, Challenging Beliefs About Ancient Gender Roles."

126. Ibid.

127. Darwin, "A Biographical Sketch of an Infant," 285–94.

128. Neuhoff, "An Adaptive Bias in the Perception of Looming Auditory Motion," 87–110; Neuhoff, Long and Worthington, "Strength and Physical Fitness Predict the Perception of Looming Sounds," 318–22; Buss, *Evolutionary Psychology: The New Science of the Mind.*

129. Gomes et al., "Beware the Serpent: The Advantage of Ecologically-Relevant Stimuli in Accessing Visual Awareness," 227–34; Marks, *Fears, Phobias, and Rituals: Panic, Anxiety, and Their Disorders*; Buss, *Evolutionary Psychology: The New Science of The Mind.*

130. De Becker, *The Gift of Fear: Survival Signals That Protect Us From Violence.*; Marks, *Fears, Phobias, and Rituals: Panic, Anxiety, and Their Disorders*; Bracha, "Freeze, Flight, Fight, Fright, Faint: Adaptationist Perspectives on the Acute Stress Response Spectrum," 679–85; Buss, *Evolutionary Psychology: The New Science of the Mind.*

131. Marks and Nesse, "Fear and Fitness: An Evolutionary Analysis of Anxiety Disorders," 155–69.

132. Marks and Nesse, Ibid; Buss, *Evolutionary Psychology: The New Science of The Mind.*

133. Edlund and Sagarin, "Sex Differences in Jealousy: A 25-Year Retrospective," 259–302; Buss, Ibid.

134. Daly, Wilson, and We ghorst, "Male Sexual Jealousy," *Ethology* 11–27; Wilson and Daly, "Sexual Rivalry and Sexual Conflict: Recurring Themes in Fatal Conflicts," 291–310; Harris, "The Evolution of Jealousy: Did Men and Women, Facing Different Selective Pressures, Evolve Different "Brands" of Jealousy? Recent Evidence Suggests Not," 62–71.

135. Khazan, "Nearly Half of All Murdered Women Are Killed by Romantic Partners"; Petrosky et al., "Racial and Ethnic Differences in Homicides of Adult Women and the Role of Intimate Partner Violence—United States," 2003–2014," 741–46.

136. Ibid.

137. Ibid.

138. Ibid.

139. Rakison, "Does Women's Greater Fear of Snakes and Spiders Originate in Infancy?" 438–44; Fetchenhauer and Buunk, "How to Explain Gender Differences in Fear of Crime: Towards an Evolutionary Approach," 95–113.

140. Buss et al., "Jealousy and the Nature of Beliefs About Infidelity: Tests of Competing Hypotheses About Sex Differences in the United States, Korea, and Japan," 125–50.

141. Andersson, *Sexual Selection*; Gould, *Wonderful Life: The Burgess Shale and the Nature of History*; Sundie, "Peacocks, Porsches, and Thorstein Veblen: Conspicuous Consumption as a Sexual Signaling System," 664.

142. Middleman and Durant, "Anabolic Steroid Use and Associated Health Risk Behaviors," 251–55; Kusev et al., "Understanding Risky Behavior: The Influence of Cognitive, Emotional and Hormonal Factors on Decision-Making Under Risk," 246–629; Haselton, *Hormonal: The Hidden Intelligence of Hormones*; Singh, "Role of Cortisol and Testosterone in Risky Decision-Making: Deciphering Male Decision-Making in the Iowa Gambling Task."

143. IIHS, "Fatality Facts 2021 Males and Females."

144. Metz, "How Age and Gender Affect Car Insurance Rates."

145. Office on Women's Health, "Premenstrual Syndrome (PMS). of fice on Women's Health"; Gudipally and Sharma, "Premenstrual Syndrome"; Higuera and Raypole, "PMS: Premenstrual Syndrome Symptoms, Treatments, and More."

146. Matsumoto and Bremner, "Breast Tenderness."

147. Yonkers, O' Brien, and Eriksson, "Premenstrual Syndrome," 1200–10.

148. Barberia, Giner, and Cortes-Gallegos, "Diurnal Variations of Plasma Testosterone in Men," 615–26.

149. Moskovic, Eisenberg, and Lipshultz, "Seasonal Fluctuations in Testosterone-Estrogen Ratio in Men From the Southwest United States," 1298–304; Kelly, "Testosterone: Why Defining a 'Normal' Level Is Hard to Do."

150. Holland and Murrell, "Can Men Get Periods?"

151. Lincoln, "The Irritable Male Syndrome," 567–76; Jantz, "Irritable Male Syndrome, It's no Laughing Matter."

152. The U.S. Department of Health and Human Services, "Health, United States, 2016"; Endocrine Society, "The Essential Guide to Your Hormones."

153. Diamond, *The Irritable Male Syndrome: Managing The Four Key Causes of Depression and Aggression*; Holland and Murrell, "Can Men Get Periods?"; CBS, "Irritable Male Syndrome."

Chapter 6

1. Fink, *Creating Significant Learning Experiences*.

2. Fink, *Taxonomy of Significant Learning Experiences*.

3. Puntmann, "How-To Guide on Biomarkers: Biomarker Definitions, Validation and Applications With Examples From Cardiovascular Disease." 538–45; Strimbu and Tavel, "What Are Biomarkers?" 463–66.

4. Mandal, "What Is a Biomarker?"; "About Biomarkers and Qualification"; Medline Plus, "Diagnostic Imaging."

5. Ziegler et al., "Personalized Medicine Using DNA Biomarkers: A Review," 1627–38; Selleck, Senthil, and Wall, "Making Meaningful Clinical Use of Biomarkers," 12; Lin et al., "Computer-Aided Biomarker Discovery for Precision Medicine: Data Resources, Models and Applications," 952–75.

6. 23andMe, "Reports Included in all Services: Ancestry Reports, Trait Reports, Health Predisposition Reports, We llness Reports, Carrier Status Reports, Pharmacogenetics Reports, Health Predisposition Reports, Blood Test Panels, 55+ Biomarkers."

7. Feldman et al., "Mother and Infant Coordinate Heart Rhythms Through Episodes of Interaction Synchrony," 569–77.

8. Ogolsky et al., "Spatial Proximity as a Behavioral Marker of Relationship Dynamics in Older Adult Couples," 3116–32.

9. Linkov, Yurkovetsky, and Lokshin, "Hormones as Biomarkers: Practical Guide to Utilizing Luminex Technologies for Biomarker Research," 129–141.

10. Buss, *Evolutionary Psychology: The New Science of the Mind,* 14

11. Ibid, 12.

12. Schaefer et al., "Female Appearance: Facial and Bodily Attractiveness as Shape," 187–205.

13. Buss, *Evolutionary Psychology: The New Science of the Mind,* 12.

14. Archer, "Testosterone and Human Aggression: An Evaluation of the Challenge Hypothesis," 319–45; Dabbs and Morris, "Testosterone, Social Class, and Antisocial Behavior in a Sample of 4,462 Men," 209–11; Mazur and Booth "Testosterone and Dominance in Men," 353–63, *discussion* 363–97.

15. Buss, *Evolutionary Psychology: The New Science of the Mind.*

16. Mazur, *Biosociology of Dominance and Deference.*

17. White, Thornhill, and Hampson, "Entrepreneurs and Evolutionary Biology: The Relationship Between Testosterone and New Venture Creation. Organization Behavior and Human Decision Processes," 21–34.

18. Burnham et al., "Men in Committed, Romantic Relationships Have Lower Testosterone," 119–22.

19. Zak et al., "Testosterone Administration Decreases Generosity in the Ultimatum Game," e8330.

20. Barrett et al., "Marriage and Motherhood Are Associated With Lower Testosterone Concentrations in Women," 72–9.

21. Baron-Cohen, "The Empathizing System," 468–92.

22. Ibid.

23. Kenrick, *Sex, Murder, and the Meaning of Life: A Psychologist Investigates How Evolution, Cognition, and Complexity Are Revolutionizing Our View of Human Nature*; Otterbring et al., "The Abercrombie & Fitch Effect: The Impact of Physical Dominance on Male Customers' Status-Signaling Consumption," 69–79.

24. Aspara and Van Den Bergh, "Naturally Designed for Masculinity vs. Femininity? Prenatal Testosterone Predicts Male Consumers' Choices of Gender-Imaged Products," 117–21.

25. Nepomuceno et al., "Testosterone at Your Fingertips: Digit Ratios (2D: 4D and rel2) as Predictors of Courtship-Related Consumption Intended to Acquire and Retain Mates," 231–44.

26. Buffenstein et al., "Food Intake and The Menstrual Cycle: A Retrospective Analysis, With Implications for Appetite Research," 1067–77; Saad and Stenstrom, "Calories, Beauty, and Ovulation: The Effects of the Menstrual Cycle on Food and Appearance-Related Consumption," 102–13.

27. Durante et al., "Ovulation, Female Competition, and Product Choice: Hormonal Influences on Consumer Behavior," 921–34; Saad and Stenstrom, "Calories, Beauty, and Ovulation: The Effects of the Menstrual Cycle on Food and Appearance-Related Consumption," 102–13.

28. Jeevanandam and Muthu, "2D:4D Ratio and Its Implications in Medicine," Cm01–Cm03; Klimek et al., "Women With a More Feminine Digit Ratio (2D:4D) Have Higher Reproductive Success," 549–53; Sitek et al., "Maternal Age and Behavior During Pregnancy Affect the 2D:4D Digit Ratio in Polish Children Aged 6–13 Years," 1286.

29. Jeevanandam, Ibid.

30. Burack, "German Efficiency: The Roots of a Stereotype."

31. Chrisafis, "French Stereotypes: They Do Not Work That Hard."

32. Sics, "British Stereotypes That We Won't Even try to Deny."

33. Abadi, "I've Been to 27 Countries, and These Are the Worst 7 Stereotypes I've Heard About Americans."

34. University of Sheffield, "How Researchers Are Challenging Complex Japanese Stereotypes."

35. Passos, Almeida-Santos, and Cordero Ramos, "Stereotypes of Brazilian Womens Hypersexuality in European Media: Data Mining," 182–200.

36. Burack, "German Efficiency: The Roots of a Stereotype."

37. Cherry, "How Othering Contributes to Discrimination and Prejudice."

38. University of Sheffield, "How Researchers Are Challenging Complex Japanese Stereotypes."

39. Interbrand, " Best Global Brands How Iconic Brands Lead Across Arenas."

40. Jeevanandam and Muthu, "2D:4D Ratio and Its Implications in Medicine." Cm01–03.

41. Archer, "Testosterone and Human Aggression: An Evaluation of the Challenge Hypothesis," 319–45; Auyeung et al., "Fetal Testosterone Predicts Sexually Differentiated Childhood Behavior in Girls and in Boys"; Udry, "Biological Limits of Gender Construction," 443–57.

42. Lutchmaya et al., "2nd to 4th Digit Ratios, Fetal Testosterone and Estradiol," 23–8; Manning et al., "The Second to Fourth Digit Ratio and Variation in the Androgen Receptor Gene," 399–405; Manning et al., "The Ratio of 2nd to 4th Digit Length: A Predictor of Sperm Numbers and Concentrations of Testosterone, Luteinizing Hormone and Oestrogen," 3000–04.

43. Ibid, 3000–004.

Chapter 7

1. Hamilton, "The Genetic Evolution of Social Behavior II," 17–52.

2. Fink, Creating Significant Learning Experiences.

3. Fink, Taxonomy of Significant Learning Experiences.

4. United States Holocaust Museum, " Life in Shadows: Hidden Children and the Holocaust."

5. Cronin, "Adaptation: A Critique of Some Current Evolutionary Thought," 19–26; Buss, Evolutionary Psychology: The New Science of the Mind.

6. Hamilton, "The Genetical Evolution of Social Behavior I and II." 1–52; Buss, Evolutionary Psychology: The New Science of the Mind.

7. Del Pozo et al., "Physical Fitness as an Indicator of Health Status and Its Relationship to Academic Performance During the Prepubertal Period," 197–204.

8. Durante and Griskevicius, "Evolution and Consumer Behavior," 27–32; Deloitte, "The Latest Research on How Emotions Sway Your Customers. And What They Expect you to do About It."

9. Buss, Evolutionary Psychology: The New Science of the Mind, 460–61.

10. Miller, Spent: Sex, Evolution, and Consumer Behavior.

11. Miller, "Aesthetic Fitness: How Sexual Selection Shaped Artistic Virtuosity as a Fitness Indicator and Aesthetic Preferences as Mate Choice Criteria," 20–25.

12. Miller, *Spent: Sex, Evolution, and Consumer Behavior*; Kenrick, Saad, and Griskevicius, "Evolutionary Consumer Psychology: Ask Not What you can do for Biology, but….," 404–09; Buss, *Evolutionary Psychology: The New Science of the Mind*, 228.

13. Miller, *Spent: Sex, Evolution, and Consumer Behavior*.

14. Ibid.

15. Griskevicius, Tybur, and Van den Bergh, "Going Green to be Seen: Status, Reputation, and Conspicuous Conservation," 392.

16. Miller, *The Mating Mind*; Miller, *Spent: Sex, Evolution, and Consumer Behavior*.

Chapter 8

1. Fink, *Creating Significant Learning Experiences*.

2. Fink, *Taxonomy of Significant Learning Experiences*.

3. Zeng, *Four Fundamental Problems for Marketing Strategy, Marketing Analytics*.

4. Mukherji, *Customer Decision-Making, Consumer Purchase Decision Process, Marketing Theory and Practice*.

5. Bouvier, "B2B Versus B2C Marketing."

6. Aspara and Van Den Bergh, "Naturally Designed for Masculinity vs. Femininity? Prenatal Testosterone Predicts Male Consumers' Choices of Gender-Imaged Products," 117–21.

7. Cohen-Bendahan, Van De Beek, and Berenbaum, "Prenatal Sex Hormone Effects on Child and Adult Sex-Typed Behavior: Methods and Findings," 353–84; Aspara and Van Den Bergh, "Naturally Designed for Masculinity vs. Femininity? Prenatal Testosterone Predicts Male Consumers' Choices of Gender-Imaged Products."

8. Eisenegger, Haushofer, and Fehr, "The Role of Testosterone in Social Interaction," 263–71.

9. Durante et al., "Ovulation, Female Competition, and Product Choice: Hormonal Influences on Consumer Behavior," 921–34.

10. Durante et al., "Ovulation Leads Women to Perceive Sexy Cads as Good Dads," 292.

11. Damasio and Damasio, "Exploring the Concept of Homeostasis and Considering Its Implications for Economics," 125–29; Mukherji, *Customer Decision-Making, Consumer Purchase Decision Process, Marketing Theory and Practice*.

Chapter 9

1. Fink, *Creating Significant Learning Experiences*.
2. Fink, *Taxonomy of Significant Learning Experiences*.
3. Harrell, "Neuromarketing: What You Need to Know."
4. Ibid.
5. Ibid.
6. Harrell, "Neuromarketing: What You Need to Know"; Farnsworth, "Using Respiration in Your Research"; Smith et al., "Respiratory Rate Measurement: A Comparison of Methods," 18–23; Wilson, "What Is Facial EMG and How Does It Work?"
7. Furr, Nel, and Zoëga, "Neuroscience Is Going to Change How Businesses Understand Their Customers."
8. Madhu, "Why Do Companies Want To Read Your Mind?" 23.

Chapter 10

1. Fink, *Creating Significant Learning Experiences*.
2. Fink, *Taxonomy of Significant Learning Experiences*.
3. Schwarz, *Feelings as Information: Informational and Motivational Functions of Affective States*; Schwarz and Clore, "Mood, Misattribution, and Judgments of Well-Being: Informative and Directive Functions of Affective States," 513.
4. Law, *Human Factors in Aviation*.
5. Makary and Daniel, "Medical Error—The Third Leading Cause of Death in the US."
6. Reeve, *Understanding Motivation and Emotion*.
7. Buss, *Evolutionary Psychology: The New Science of the Mind*, 23–4.
8. Damasio and Damasio, "Exploring the Concept of Homeostasis and Considering Its Implications for Economics," 125–29.
9. Damasio and Damasio, "Exploring the Concept of Homeostasis and Considering Its Implications for Economics."
10. Ibid.
11. Damasio et al., 2000, Immordino-Yang et al., 2009, Singer, 2015, Fox et al., 2015; Ibid, 125–29.
12. Damasio and Damasio, "Exploring the Concept of Homeostasis and Considering Its Implications for Economics."
13. Levin, *A Geography of Time: The Temporal Misadventures of a Social Psychologist*.

14. Wilson, "Homo Economicus: Meaning, Overview, and Criticisms."

15. Smith, *An Inquiry Into the Nature and Causes of the We alth of Nations,* 32.

16. Plutchik and Kellerman, *Theories of Emotion.*

17. Ekman, *Are There Basic Emotions?* 550.

18. Smith, T. W. 2016. *The Book of Human Emotions.* We lcome Collection.

19. Plutchik and Kellerman, *Theories of Emotion.*

20. Ekman, *Are There Basic Emotions?* 550.

21. André et al., *Humane—Human-Machine Interaction Network on Emotion.*

22. Strack, Martin, and Stepper, "Inhibiting and Facilitating Conditions of the Human Smile: A Non-Obtrusive Test of the Facial Feedback Hypothesis," 768.

23. Darwin, "General Principles of Expression," 61–8; Ekman, "Universals and Cultural Differences in the Judgments of Facial Expressions of Emotion," 712.

24. McDuff et al., "AFFDEX SDK: A Cross-Platform Real-Time Multi-Face Expression Recognition Toolkit."

25. The Open University, "How FMRI Works"; Heeger and Ress, "What Does fMRI Tell Us About Neuronal Activity?" 142–51; Karmarkar, Yoon, and Plassmann, "Marketers Should Pay Attention to fMRI."

26. Vlemincx, et al., "Respiratory Variability and Sighing: A Psychophysiological Reset Model," 24–32; Grassmann et al., "Respiratory Changes in Response to Cognitive Load: A Systematic Review"; Young et al., "State of Science: Mental Workload in Ergonomics." 1–17; Bach et al., "A Linear Model for Event-Related Respiration Responses," 147–55.

27. Meijer et al., "Memory Detection With the Concealed Information Test: A Meta-Analysis of Skin Conductance, Respiration, Heart Rate, and P300 Data," 879–904.

28. Kim, Steinhoff, and Palmatier, "An Emerging Theory of Loyalty Program Dynamics," 71–95.

29. Capgemini, "Loyalty Deciphered—How Emotions Drive Genuine Engagement."

Chapter 11

1. Fink, *Creating Significant Learning Experiences.*

2. Fink, *Taxonomy of Significant Learning Experiences.*

3. Jager, *Modeling Consumer Behavior.*

4. Moulettes, "The Absence of Women's Voices in Hofstede's Cultural Consequences: A Postcolonial Reading," 443–55.

5. MacKenzie, Meyer, and Noble, "How Retailers Can Keep up With
Consumers."

6. Griskevicius and Kenrick, "Fundamental Motives: How Evolutionary
Needs Influence Consumer Behavior," 372–86.

7. Williams, "Pleiotropy, Natural Selection, and the Evolution of Senescence,"
398–411.

8. Nesse and Williams, *Why We get Sick*; Buss, *Evolutionary Psychology: The
New Science of the Mind*, 242–43.

9. Buss, *Evolutionary Psychology: The New Science of the Mind, 243*.

10. Griskevicius and Kenrick, "Fundamental Motives: How Evolutionary
Needs Influence Consumer Behavior." 372–86.

11. Buss, *Evolutionary Psychology: The New Science of the Mind*.

12. Ibid.

13. Karremans, Frankenhuis, and Arons, "Blind Men Prefer a Low Waist-to-
Hip Ratio," 182–86; Ibid.

14. Mangold, Danna, and Dodd, *Girl, Interrupted*.

15. Harron, *American Psycho*.

16. Night Shyamalan, *Split*.

17. Royal College of Psychiatrists, "Mental Health of Children and Young People in England, 2023—Wave 4 Follow up to the 2017 Survey of ficial Statistics, Survey."

18. National Institute of Mental Health, "Prevalence of Personality Disorders
in Adults."

19. Griskevicius and Kenrick, "Fundamental Motives: How Evolutionary
Needs Influence Consumer Behavior," 372–86.

20. Maslow, "A Theory of Human Motivation," 370–96.

21. Griskevicius and Kenrick, "Fundamental Motives: How Evolutionary
Needs Influence Consumer Behavior," 372–86.

22. Durante et al., "Ovulation, Female Competition, and Product Choice:
Hormonal Influences on Consumer Behavior," 921–34; Durante, Li,
and Haselton, "Changes in Women's Choice of Dress Across the Ovula-
tory Cycle: Naturalistic and Laboratory Task-Based Evidence," 1451–60;
Haselton et al., "Ovulatory Shifts in Human Female Ornamentation: Near
Ovulation, Women Dress to Impress," 40–5; Roder, Brewer, and Fink,
"Menstrual Cycle Shifts in Women's Self-Perception and Motivation: A
Daily Report Method. Personality and Individual Differences," 616–19;

Saad and Stenstrom, "Calories, Beauty, and Ovulation: The Effects of the Menstrual Cycle on Food and Appearance-Related Consumption," 102–13.

23. Durante et al., "Money, Status, and the Ovulatory Cycle," 27–39.

24. Buss, *The Evolution of Desire: Strategies of Human Mating*; Kruger, Fisher, and Jobling, "Proper and Dark Heroes as Dads and Cads: Alternative Mating Strategies in British Romantic Literature," 305–17; Rhodes, Simmons, and Peters, "Attractiveness and Sexual Behavior: Does Attractiveness Enhance Mating Success?" 186–201; Durante et al., "Ovulation Leads Women to Perceive Sexy Cads as Good Dads," 292.

25. Miller and Maner, "Scent of a Woman: Men's Testosterone Responses to Olfactory Ovulation Cues," 276–83.

26. Archer, "Testosterone and Human Aggression: An Evaluation of the Challenge Hypothesis," 319–45.

27. Ibid; Dabbs and Morris, "Testosterone, Social Class, and Antisocial Behavior in a Sample of 4,462 Men," 209–11; Mazur and Booth, "Testosterone and Dominance in Men," 353–63.

28. McIntyre et al., "Romantic Involvement of ten Reduces Men's Testosterone Levels—but not Always: The Moderating Effects of Extra-Pair Sexual Interest," 642–51.

29. Roney, "Effects of Visual Exposure to the Opposite Sex: Cognitive Aspects of Mate Attraction in Human Males," 393–404; Griskevicius et al., "Blatant Benevolence and Conspicuous Consumption: When Romantic Motives Elicit Strategic Costly Signals," 85.

30. Saad and Vongas, "The Effect of Conspicuous Consumption on Men's Testosterone Levels," 80–92.

31. Otterbring et al., "The Abercrombie & Fitch effect: The Impact of Physical Dominance on Male Customers' Status-Signaling Consumption," 69–79.

32. Virgin and Sapolsky, "Styles of Male Social Behavior and Their Endocrine Correlates Among Low-Ranking Baboons," 25–39; Booth et al., "Testosterone and Social Behavior," 167–91.

33. Motoki and Sugiura, "Consumer Behavior, Hormones, and Neuroscience: Integrated Understanding of Fundamental Motives Why We buy," 28–43.

34. Griskevicius and Kenrick, "Fundamental Motives: How Evolutionary Needs Influence Consumer Behavior."

35. Wilson, G. D. 1983, "Finger-Length as an Index of Assertiveness in Women," 111–12.

36. Manning et al., "The Ratio of 2nd to 4th Digit Length: A Predictor of Sperm Numbers and Concentrations of Testosterone, Luteinizing Hormone and Oestrogen," 3000–04.

37. Zheng and Cohn, "Developmental Basis of Sexually Dimorphic Digit Ratios," 16289–16294; Jeevanandam and Muthu, "2D:4D Ratio and Its Implications in Medicine," Cm01–03.

38. Bailey and Hurd, "Finger Length Ratio (2D:4D) Correlates With Physical Aggression in Men but not in Women," 215–22.

39. Ibid.

40. Aspara and Van Den Bergh, "Naturally Designed for Masculinity vs. Femininity? Prenatal Testosterone Predicts Male Consumers' Choices of Gender-Imaged Products," 117–21.

41. Ibid.

42. Moskowitz et al., "Fetal Exposure to Androgens, as Indicated by Digit Ratios (2D:4D), Increases Men's Agreeableness With Women," 97–101.

43. Sorokowski et al., "The Second to Fourth Digit Ratio and Age at First Marriage in Semi-Nomadic People From Namibia," 703–10.

44. Wlodarski, Manning, and Dunbar, "Stay or Stray? Evidence for Alternative Mating Strategy Phenotypes in Both Men and Women."

45. Ibid.

46. Manning and Hill, "Digit Ratio (2D: 4D) and Sprinting Speed in Boys," 210–13.

47. Bogaert and Skorska, "A Short Review of Biological Research on the Development of Sexual Orientation."

48. Lippa, "Are 2D: 4D Finger-Length Ratios Related to Sexual Orientation? Yes for Men, no for women," 179.

49. Stenstrom et al., "Testosterone and Domain-Specific Risk: Digit Ratios (2D:4D and rel2) as Predictors of Recreational, Financial, and Social Risk-Taking Behaviors," 412–16.

50. Manning and Fink, "Digit Ratio, Nicotine and Alcohol Intake and National Rates of Smoking and Alcohol Consumption," 344–48.

51. Bönte et al., "Digit Ratio (2D:4D) Predicts Self-Reported Measures of General Competitiveness, but not Behavior in Economic Experiments."

52. Fink, Manning, and Neave, "The 2nd–4th Digit Ratio (2D:4D) and Neck Circumference: Implications for Risk Factors in Coronary Heart Disease," 711–14.

53. Lu et al., "Second to Fourth Digit Ratio (2D:4D) and Coronary Heart Disease," 417–20.

54. Walsh, "Index Finger Length Prostate Cancer Clue."

55. Choi, "Second to Fourth Digit Ratio: A Predictor of Adult Penile Length," 710–14.

56. Gilbert, "Jeff Bezos Just Sent His Annual Letter to Amazon Shareholders"; Martin, "Jeff Bezos Steps Down as Amazon CEO Today—but How Much Power Is He Really Giving up?"

57. Macrotrends, "Amazon Revenue 2010–2023."

58. Schneider and Hall, "Why Most Product Launches Fail."

59. Ibid.

60. Schneider and Associates, "Sentient Decision Science."

61. Strategy Analytics, "Half the World Owns a Smartphone"; Business Wire, "Strategy Analytics: Half the World Owns a Smartphone"; United Nations, "World Population Day."

62. Chen, "Apple Registers Trademark for 'There's an App for That'"; Schippers, "App Fatigue"; Benes, "Most Apps get Deleted Within a Week of Last Use"; Ceci, "Number of Apps Available in Leading app Stores Q3 2022."

63. Schneider and Hall, "Why Most Product Launches Fail," 21–3.

64. Vitti, *Womancode: Perfect Your Cycle, Amplify Your Fertility, Supercharge Your Sex Drive and Become a Power Source*; Bhuvaneswari, Rabindran, and Bharadwaj, "Prevalence of Premenstrual Syndrome and Its Impact on Quality of Life Among Selected College Students in Puducherry," 17–9; Laurence and Whitfield, "Cycle Syncing: Everything You Need to Know."

65. Encyclopedia Britannica, "Roe v. Wade."

66. Garamvolgyi, "Why US women Are Deleting Their Period Tracking Apps."

67. McCallum, "Jessica Ennis-Hill: Why I now Train Around my Period"; Lowe, "Jessica Ennis-Hill's New App Will Completely Change Your Approach to Fitness—and Periods."

68. Hildebrandt et al., "The Effects of Ovarian Hormones and Emotional Eating on Changes in We ight Preoccupation Across the Menstrual Cycle," 477–86; Franklin et al., "Influence of Menstrual Cycle Phase on Neural and Craving Responses to Appetitive Smoking Cues in Naturally Cycling Females," 390–97; Andersen, "6 Weird Period Symptoms You've Never Heard of Before."

69. Song, Hur, and Kim, "Brand Trust and Affect in the Luxury Brand–Customer Relationship," 331–38; Lassoued and Hobbs, "Consumer Confidence in Credence Attributes: The Role of Brand Trust," 99–107; Huang et al., "Brand Image and Customer Loyalty: Transmitting Roles of Cognitive and Affective Brand Trust," 1–12.

70. Peper and Dahl, "The Teenage Brain:Surging Hormones—Brain-Behavior Interactions During Puberty," 134–39.

71. Freeman et al., "Symptoms in the Menopausal Transition: Hormone and Behavioral Correlates," 127–36.

72. Chaudhuri and Holbrook, "The Chain of Effects From Brand Trust and Brand Affect to Brand Performance: The Role of Brand Loyalty," 81–93; Fournier, "Consumers and Their Brands: Developing Relationship Theory in Consumer Research," 343–73; Song, Hur, and Kim, "Brand Trust and Affect in the Luxury Brand–Customer Relationship," 03.

73. O'Shaughnessy, *Explaining Buyer Behavior: Central Concepts and Philosophy of Science Issues.*

74. Moorman, "Market-Level Effects of Information: Competitive Responses and Consumer Dynamics," 82–98; Koller, "Risk As a Determinant of Trust," 265–76.

75. Chaudhuri and Holbrook, "The Chain of Effects From Brand Trust and Brand Affect to Brand Performance: The Role of Brand Loyalty," 81–93; Song, Hur, and Kim, "Brand Trust and Affect in the Luxury Brand–Customer Relationship," 331–38.

76. Dickerson and Kemeny, "Acute Stressors and Cortisol Responses: A Theoretical Integration and Synthesis of Laboratory Research," 355; Kusev et al., "Understanding Risky Behavior: The Influence of Cognitive, Emotional and Hormonal Factors on Decision-Making Under Risk."

77. Dickerson and Kemeny, "Acute Stressors and Cortisol Responses: A Theoretical Integration and Synthesis of Laboratory Research," 355; Kusev et al., "Understanding Risky Behavior: The Influence of Cognitive, Emotional and Hormonal Factors on Decision-Making Under Risk."

78. Lovallo and Thomas, "Stress Hormones in Psychophysiological Research: Emotional, Behavioral, and Cognitive Implications," 342–67; Sapolsky, Romero, and Munck, "How Do Glucocorticoids Influence Stress Responses? Integrating Permissive, Suppressive, Stimulatory, and Preparative Actions," 55–89; Kusev et al., "Understanding Risky Behavior: The Influence of Cognitive, Emotional and Hormonal Factors on Decision-Making Under Risk."

79. Carver and Scheier, "Stress, Coping, and Self-Regulatory Processes"; Kusev et al., "Understanding Risky Behavior: The Influence of Cognitive, Emotional and Hormonal Factors on Decision-Making Under Risk."

80. Mazur and Booth, "Testosterone and Dominance in Men," 353–63; Josephs, "The Mismatch Effect: When Testosterone and Status Are at Odds," 999; Eisenegger, Haushofer, and Fehr, "The Role of Testosterone in Social Interaction," 263–71.

81. Mazur and Booth, "Testosterone and Dominance in Men," 353–63; Josephs et al., "The Mismatch Effect: When Testosterone and Status Are at Odds," 999; Eisenegger, Haushofer, and Fehr, "The Role of Testosterone in Social Interaction," 263–71; Bergland, "Cortisol and Oxytocin Hardwire Fear-Based Memories."

82. Zak, Kurzban, and Matzner, "The Neurobiology oTrust," 224–27; Kosfeld et al., "Oxytocin Increases Trust in Humans," 673–676; Kusev et al., "Understanding Risky Behavior: The Influence of Cognitive, Emotional and Hormonal Factors on Decision-Making Under Risk."

83. Durante et al., "Ovulation, Female Competition, and Product Choice: Hormonal Influences on Consumer Behavior," 921–34.

84. Francis et al., "Naturally Occurring Differences in Maternal Care Are Associated With the Expression of Oxytocin and Vasopressin (V1a) Receptors: Gender Differences," 349–53; Durante et al., "Ovulation, Female Competition, and Product Choice: Hormonal Influences on Consumer Behavior," 921–34.

85. Dixon et al., "Eye-Tracking of Men's Preferences for Waist-to-Hip Ratio and Breast Size of Women," 43–50; Schaefer Female Appearance: Facial and Bodily Attractiveness as Shape," 187–205; Buss, *Evolutionary Psychology: The New Science of the Mind*, 125, 351.

86. Hoffman, "Estrogen and Women's Emotions."

87. Fisher, "Female Intrasexual Competition Decreases Female Facial Attractiveness," S283–5.

88. Fisher, *Evolutionary Psychology: The New Science of the Mind*, 23–4.

89. Buffenstein et al., "Food Intake and the Menstrual Cycle: A Retrospective Analysis, With Implications for Appetite Research," 1067–77; Saad and Stenstrom, "Calories, Beauty, and Ovulation: The Effects of the Menstrual Cycle on Food and Appearance-Related Consumption," 102–13.

90. Durante, Li, and Haselton, "Changes in Women's Choice of Dress Across the Ovulatory Cycle: Naturalistic and Laboratory Task-Based Evidence," 1451–60.

91. Nepomuceno, De Aguiar Pastore, and Stenstrom, "Prenatal Hormones (2D:4D), Intrasexual Competition, and Materialism in Women," 239–48.

92. Zilioli and Watson, "Testosterone Across Successive Competitions: Evidence for a 'Winner Effect' in Humans?" 1–9.

93. Hirsch, *Social Limits to Growth*; Saad and Vongas, "The Effect of Conspicuous Consumption on Men's Testosterone Levels," 80–92.

94. Saad and Vongas, "The Effect of Conspicuous Consumption on Men's Testosterone Levels," 80–92.

95. Wang and Griskevicius, "Conspicuous Consumption, Relationships, and Rivals: Women's Luxury Products as Signals to Other Women," 834–54.

96. Cristol, "What Is Dopamine?"; Eske, "What Are the Differences Between Serotonin and Dopamine?"

97. Cristol, Ibid.

98. Burhan and Moradzadeh, "Neurotransmitter Dopamine (DA) and Its Role in the Development of Social Media Addiction," 1–2.

99. Schultz, "Predictive Reward Signal of Dopamine Neurons," 1–27.

100. Burdine et al., *The Future of Luxury New Luxury Consumer Values*.

101. Akre et al., "Smart Digital Marketing of Financial Services to Millennial Generation Using Emerging Technological Tools and Buyer Persona," 20–21; Stoychev, "Digital and Social Media Marketing Strategy," 98–120; Mclachlan, "How to Create a Buyer Persona (Free Buyer/Audience Persona Template)."

102. Samuel, "Psychographics Are Just as Important for Marketers as Demographics"; An et al., "Customer Segmentation Using Online Platforms: Isolating Behavioral and Demographic Segments for Persona Creation Via Aggregated User Data," 54; Needle, "How to Create Detailed Buyer Personas for Your Business"; Buyer Persona Institute, "Buyer Persona Research"; Revella, "Meet Our Example Buyer Persona"; American Marketing Association, 2022; Semrush, How to Create a Buyer Persona to Boost Your Marketing.

103. Griskevicius, Tybur, and Van Den Bergh, "Going Green to Be Seen: Status, Reputation, and Conspicuous Conservation," 392–404.

104. Durante et al., "Spending on Daughters Versus Sons in Economic Recessions," 435–57.

105. Seales, "Let's Save Maya Angelou From Fake Quotes."

106. Schwarz, and Clore, "Mood, Misattribution, and Judgments of Well-Being: Informative and Directive Functions of Affective States," 513; Wyer et al., "The Role of Syllogistic Reasoning in Inferences Based Upon New and Old Information," 221–74; Pham, "The Logic of Feeling," 360–69.

107. Fishbein and Middlestadt, "Noncognitive Effects on Attitude Formation and Change: Fact or Artifact?" 181–202; Pham, "The Logic of Feeling," 360–69.

108. Kapferer and Bastien, *The Luxury Strategy: Break The Rules of Marketing to Build Luxury Brands*.

109. World Prison Brief, "Prison Population Total."

110. United Nations, "Global Study on Homicide"; Shaw, "Why Are We not Outraged That Prisons Are Filled With Men?".

111. Dabbs et al., "Testosterone, Crime, and Misbehavior Among 692 Male Prison Inmates," 627–33.

112. National Geographic, "Testosterone Factor, Explorer; DW Documentary, "Testosterone—New Discoveries About the Male Hormone."

113. Barr, "Gillette Tackles Toxic Masculinity in New Advert for #Metoo Era"; King, "Gillette Responds to Controversial Advert Challenging Toxic Masculinity."

114. Petter, "Gillette Sales Unchanged After Controversial Advert About Toxic Masculinity"; Vizard, "Gillette Brand Takes a Hit as '#Metoo' Ad Backfires"; Khatoon and Rehman, "Negative Emotions in Consumer Brand Relationship: A Review and Future Research Agenda," 719–49.

115. Saad and Vongas, "The Effect of Conspicuous Consumption on Men's Testosterone Levels," 80–92.

116. Otterbring et al., "The Abercrombie & Fitch Effect: The Impact of Physical Dominance on Male Customers' Status-Signaling Consumption," 69–79.

117. Farrelly et al., "The Effects of Being in a "New Relationship" on Levels of Testosterone in Men"; Buss, *Evolutionary Psychology: The New Science of the Mind*, 360, 360–84.

118. Burnham, "Men in Committed, Romantic Relationships Have Lower Testosterone," 119–22; Gray et al., "Human Male Pair Bonding and Testosterone," 119–31; Buss, *Evolutionary Psychology: The New Science of the Mind*, 385.

119. Buss, *Evolutionary Psychology: The New Science of the Mind*, 608.

120. ZIPPIA, "Casino Games Dealer Demographics and Statistics in the US."

121. Ronay and Von Hippel, "The Presence of an Attractive Woman Elevates Testosterone and Physical Risk-Taking in Young Men," 57–64; Buss, *Evolutionary Psychology: The New Science of the Mind*, 385.

122. Dabbs et al., "Salivary Testosterone Measurements in Behavioral Studies," 177–183; Booth et al., "Testosterone and Social Behavior," 167–91.

Chapter 12

1. The University of Queensland, "Corpus Callosum"; National Institute of Neurological Disorder and Stroke, "Brain Basics: Know Your Brain"; Johns Hopkins Medicine, "Brain Anatomy and How the Brain Works"; Anderson, "Brainstem: What to Know"; Basinger and Hogg, *Neuroanatomy, Brainstem*; Sukel, "Beyond Emotion: Understanding the Amygdala's Role in Memory"; Cleveland Clinic, "Pituitary Gland"; Barrow Neurological Institute, "About

the Pituitary Gland"; Cleveland Clinic, "Hypothalamus"; Seladi-Schulman, "Hypothalamus Overview"; Schiller, "The Cerebral Ventricles: From Soul to Sink," 1158–62; Scelsi et al., "The Lateral Ventricles: A Detailed Review of Anatomy, Development, and Anatomic Variations," 566–72; Shahid, "Corpus Callosum"; The University of Queensland, "Corpus Callosum"; Healthline Editorial Team, "Fourth Ventricle"; Torrico and Munakomi, *Neuroanatomy, Thalamus*; Gummadavelli and Blumenfeld, "Thalamus"; Leopold, "Everything you Need to Know About the Cerebellum"; Khasawneh, Garling, and Harris, "Cerebrospinal Fluid Circulation: What do We Know and How do We Know It?" 14–8.

Appendix

1. Action Bias, *BehavioralEconomics*.
2. Cherry, "Actor-Observer Bias in Social Psychology."
3. Adams et al., "People Systematically Overlook Subtractive Changes," 258–61.
4. Lean In, "50 Ways to Fight Bias: An Introduction to the Common Biases Women Experience."
5. Fields, "Motion, Identity and the Bias Toward Agency," 8.
6. Barclay, "Altruism as a Courtship Display: Some Effects of Third-party Generosity on Audience Perceptions," 123–35; Phillips, Barnard, Ferguson, and Reade, "Do Humans Prefer Altruistic Mates? Testing a Link Between Sexual Selection and Altruism Towards Non-relatives," 555–72.
7. Griskevicius et al., "Blatant Benevolence and Conspicuous Consumption: When Romantic Motives Elicit Strategic Costly Signals," 85.
8. Griskevicius et al., "Blatant Benevolence and Conspicuous Consumption: When Romantic Motives Elicit Strategic Costly Signals," 85; Miller, *Spent: Sex, Evolution, and Consumer Behavior*.
9. The Decision Lab, "Why do We Prefer Options We Know?"
10. Vipond, "Anchoring Bias."
11. Hunter, "Company Familiarity Moderates Anti-corporate Bias and Jurors' Compensatory Award Amounts."
12. Holland and Hart LLP and Broda-Bah, "Understand Anti-Corporate Bias: the Extent of the Bias and the Effect of Familiarity."
13. Boslaugh, "Anthropocentrism,"
14. Epley, Waytz, and Cacioppo, "On Seeing Human: a Three-factor theory of Anthropomorphism." 864–86.

15. Cherry, "What Is Attentional Bias?"

16. Buss, 2019. *Evolutionary Psychology: the New Science of the Mind*, 243–44, 360.

17. Ibid.

18. Psychology Wiki, "Attribute Substitution."

19. Ballinger, "Authority Bias."

20. Databrics Inc., "Automation Bias,"

21. Shatz, "The Availability Cascade: How Information Spreads on a Large Scale."

22. Perry, "The Cognitive Biases Caused by the Availability Heuristic."

23. Swire-Thompson, DeGutis, and Lazer, "Searching for the Backfire Effect: Measurement and Design Considerations," 286–99.

24. Perry, "The Cognitive Biases Caused by the Availability Heuristic."

25. Chen, "What Is Base Rate Fallacy and Its Impact?"

26. Recruiting Times, "Attractive Women Shouldn't Include Photo in CV, Research Finds"; Tu, Gilbert, and Bono, "Is Beauty More Than Skin Deep? Attractiveness, Power, and Nonverbal Presence in Evaluations of hireability," 119–46.

27. Berggren, Jordahl, and Poutvaara, "The Looks of a Winner: Beauty and Electoral Success," 8–15.

28. Etcoff, *Survival of the Prettiest: the Science of Beauty*.

29. Shatz, "Belief Bias: When People Rely on Beliefs Rather Than Logic,"

30. Shatz, "The Benjamin Franklin Effect: Build Rapport by Asking for Favors."

31. Bobbitt, "Berkson's Bias: Definition + Examples."

32. Taft College, "Bias: Blind Spot Bias."

33. Monks, "Bizarreness Effect: the Behavioural Bias Series."

34. Econowmics, "The Cheerleader Effect,"

35. Conversion Uplift, "Choice-Supportive Bias."

36. Kapri "Clustering Illusion: Clusters Lie in the Eye of the Beholder!"

37. George and Pandey, "We Know the Yin-But Where Is the Yang? Toward a Balanced Approach on Common Source Bias in Public Administration Scholarship," 245–70.

38. Pamuk, "Compassion Fade."

39. Lifton, "Beyond Psychic Numbing: a Call to Awareness," 619–29.

40. Casad, and Luebering, "Confirmation Bias,"

41. *DBpedia*, "Congruence Bias."

42. fs.blog, "Mental Model: Bias from Conjunction Fallacy,"

43. Pompian, "Conservatism Bias," 63–71.

44. Leising, "The Consistency Bias in Judgments of One's Own Interpersonal Behavior: Two Possible Sources," 137–43.

45. PsychOutWhat Is Context Effect? [Definition and Example]—Understanding Cognitive Biases.

46. Shatz,"The Contrast Effect: When Comparison Enhances Differences."

47. Kiryttopoulou, "Overcoming the Courtesy Bias in Constituent Feedback."

48. Wong, Stephen, and Keeble, "The Own-Race Bias for Face Recognition in a Multiracial Society," 208.

49. APA Dictionary of Psychology, "Cryptomnesia."

50. "The Curse of Knowledge: How It Impacts You, and What to Do About It."

51. "Why Do We Think the Past Is Better Than the Future?"

52. "Why Do We Feel More Strongly About one Option After a Third One Is Added?"

53. "By the Power of Default."

54. Gyekye and Salminen, "The Self-defensive Attribution Hypothesis in the Work Environment: Co-workers' Perspectives," 157–68.

55. Rohleder, "Othering,"1306–08

56. "No.16 of 36 the Denomination Effect,"

57. Curtis, Aunger, and Rabie, "Evidence That Disgust Evolved to Protect From Risk of Disease," S131–33; Oaten, Stevenson, and Case," Disgust as a Disease-avoidance Mechanism," 303.

58. Fleischman, "Women's Disgust Adaptations," 277–96

59. Al-Shawaf, Lewis, and Buss, "Sex Differences in Disgust: Why Are Women More Easily Disgusted than Men?" 149–60; Buss, *Evolutionary Psychology: the New Science of the Mind,* 191–93.

60. BehavioralEconomics.com, "Disposition Effect,"

61. Hsee and Zhang, "Distinction Bias: Misprediction and Mischoice Due to Joint Evaluation." 680–95.

62. Lean In, "50 Ways to Fight Bias: An Introduction to the Common Biases Women Experience."

63. Mueller and Mazur, "Facial Dominance of We st Point Cadets as a Predictor of Later Military Rank," 823–50.

64. Rhodes, Simmons, and Peters, "Attractiveness and Sexual Behavior: Does Attractiveness Enhance Mating Success?" 186–201.

65. Hill, Hunt, Welling et al, "Quantifying the Strength and Form of Sexual Selection on Men's Traits," 334–41.

66. Hennighausen, Hudders, Lange, and Fink, "What If the Rival Drives a Porsche? Luxury Car Spending as a Costly Signal in Male Intrasexual Competition"

67. Buss, "The Evolution of Human Intrasexual Competition: Tactics of Mate Attraction," 616–28; Schmitt and Buss, "Strategic Self-promotion and Competitor Derogation: Sex and Context Effects on the Perceived Effectiveness of Mate Attraction Tactics," 1185.

68. Dawson, and Johnson, "Dread Aversion and Economic Preferences".

69. Duignan, "Dunning-Kruger effect,"

70. Müller, Witteman, Spijker et al. "All's Bad That Ends Bad: there Is a Peak-End Memory Bias in Anxiety," 1272.

71. Kahneman, Fredrickson, Schreiber et al, "When More Pain Is Preferred to Less: Adding a Better End," 401–05.

72. Effectiviology, "The Egocentric Bias: Why It's Hard to See Things from a Different Perspective."

73. Quoidbach, Gilbert, and Wilson, "The End of History Illusion," 96–8.

74. BehavioralEconomics.com, "Endowment Effect."

75. Kahneman, Knetsch, and Thaler, "Experimental Tests of the Endowment Effect and the Coase Theorem," 1325–48; List, and Mason, "Are CEOs Expected Utility Maximizers?" 114–23; Marzilli Ericso, and Fuster, "The Endowment Effect," 555–79.

76. Williams, et al., "P-640—The Power of Expectation Bias."

77. CRO-tool.com, "Extrinsic Incentives Bias."

78. Buss, *Evolutionary Psychology: the New Science of the Mind*, 376.

79. Ibid, 351.

80. Ibid, 394.

81. Skowronski, Walker, Henderson et al., "Chapter Three—The Fading Affect Bias: Its History, Its Implications, and Its Future," 163–218.

82. Nickerson, "False Consensus Effect: Definition And Examples."

83. Cherry, "How False Memories Are Formed in Your Brain."

84. "False Uniqueness Bias."

85. De Becker, and Stechschulte, *The gift of fear;* Marks, "The Development of Normal Fear: a Review," 667–97; Marks and Nesse, "Fear and Fitness: An Evolutionary Analysis of Anxiety Disorders," 247–61.

86. Rakison, "Does Women's Greater Fear of Snakes and Spiders Originate in Infancy? Evolution and Human Behavior," 30, 438–44.

87. Buss, 234–35.

88. The Decision Lab, "Why do We Believe Our Horoscopes?"

89. Haring et al., "FFAB-the Form Function Attribution Bias in Human-Robot Interaction," 843–51.

90. Tversky and Kahneman, "The Framing of Decisions and the Psychology of Choice," 453–58.

91. Rich, "What Is the Baader-Meinhof Phenomenon?"

92. Healy, "The Fundamental Attribution Error: What it Is and How to Avoid It."

93. Cherry, "Functional Fixedness as a Cognitive Bias."

94. Kenton, "Gambler's Fallacy: Overview and Examples."

95. Cornell Law School, "Gender Bias."

96. Bertsch et al., "The Generation Effect: a Meta-analytic Review," 201–10.

97. Peshin, "What Is the "Google" Effect?"

98. Mackie and Allison, "Group Attribution Errors and the Illusion of Group Attitude Change," 460–80.

99. Psychology Today, "Groupthink."

100. Sachdev, "What Is the Halo Effect?"

101. Bordley, Licalzi, and Tibiletti," A Target-Based Foundation for the "Hard-Easy Effect" Bias."

102. Buss, *Evolutionary Psychology: the New Science of the Mind,* 325–26.

103. Ibid, 342.

104. Inman. "Hindsight Bias."

105. Wang, et al, "Hostile Attribution Bias Mediates the Relationship Between Structural Variations in the Left Middle Frontal Gyrus and Trait Angry Rumination," 9.

106. The BE Hub, "(Hot-Cold) Empathy gap."

107. Chen, "Hot Hand: What It Is, How It Works, Evidence."

108. Gerlach, "Humor Effect: the Benefits of Using Humor."

109. Hart, "Hyperbolic Discounting: How to Use This Psychological Bias to Sell More."

110. Norton, Mochon, and Ariely, "The IKEA Effect: When Labor Leads to Love," 453–60.

111. MathsGee, "What Is Illicit Transference Bias?"

112. Holland, "How We ll Do You Really Know your Acquaintances? the Illusion of Asymmetric Insight,"

113. Pompian, "Illusion of Control Bias," 99–106.

114. Hoorens, "Self-enhancement and Superiority Biases in Social Comparison." 113–39.

115. Gilovich, Savitsky, and Medvec, "The Illusion of Transparency: Biased Assessments of Others' Ability to Read One's Emotional States," 332–46.

116. Einhorn and Hogarth, "Confidence in Judgment: Persistence of the Illusion of Validity," 395.

117. Hamilton and Rose, "Illusory Correlation and the Maintenance of Stereotypic Beliefs," 832.

118. Newman, Jalbert, Schwarz et al, "Truthiness, the Illusory Truth Effect, and the Role of Need for Cognition," 78.

119. Dean, "Impact Bias: Why We Overestimate Our Emotional Reactions."

120. Greenwald and Hamilton Krieger, "Implicit Bias: Scientific Foundations," 945–67.

121. Catalog of Bias Collaboration, "Information Bias."

122. Everett, Faber, and Crockett, "Preferences and Beliefs in Ingroup Favoritism," 9.

123. Hamill, Wilson, and Nisbett, "Insensitivity to Sample Bias: Generalizing From Atypical Cases," 578–89.

124. Pawlowski, Bogusław, and Dunbar, "Withholding Age as Aputative Deception in Mate Search Tactics," 53–69; Waynforth, and Dunbar," Conditional Mate Choice Strategies in Humans: Evidence From ' Lonely Hearts' Advertisements," 755–80; De Sousa Campos, Otta, and De Oliveira Siqueira, "Sex Differences in Mate Selection Strategies: Content Analyses and Responses to Personal Advertisements in Brazil," 395–406; Oda, "Sexually Dimorphic Mate Preference in Japan," 191–206; Regan, "Minimum Mate Selection Standards as a Function of Perceived Mate Value, Relationship Context, and Gender," 53–73; Buss, *Evolutionary psychology: The New Science of the Mind,* 315, 342.

125. Wilson, "What Your IQ Score Doesn't Tell You."

126. Mehta, "A Harvard Psychologist Says Humans Have 8 Types of Intelligence. Which Ones do you Score the Highest in?"

127. Gardner, *Frames of Mind: The theory of Multiple Intelligences.*

128. Petersen, "Interoception and Symptom Reporting: Disentangling Accuracy and Bias," 6.

129. Moore and Pope, "The Intentionality Bias and Schizotypy," 2218–24.

130. Lucas, "Institutionalized Bias."

131. Fandom Lifestyle Community, "Irrational Escalation."

132. Wenzel, Schindler, and Reinhard, "General Belief in a Just World Is Positively Associated With Dishonest Behavior."

133. Effectiviology, "The Just-World Hypothesis: Believing That Everyone Gets What they Deserve."

134. The Decision Lab, "Lag Effect."

135. The Decision Lab, "Law of the Instrument."

136. Ragland et al., "Levels-of-Processing Effect on Word Recognition in Schizophrenia," 1154–61.

137. The Decision Lab, "Leveling and Sharpening."

138. The BE Hub, "Less-Is-Better Effect."

139. Lean In, "50 Ways to Fight Bias: An Introduction to the Common Biases Women Experience."

140. Kinnell and Dennis, "The List Length Effect in Recognition Memory: An Analysis of Potential Confounds," 348–63.

141. Kahneman, Knetsch, and Thaler, "Anomalies: the Endowment Effect, Loss Aversion, and Status Quo Bias," 193–206.

142. Lean In, "50 Ways to Fight Bias: An Introduction to the Common Biases Women Experience."

143. Buss, *Evolutionary Psychology: the New Science of the Mind*, 295–96.

144. Ibid, 295.

145. Ibid, 461.

146. Nickerson, "Mere Exposure Effect in Psychology: Biases and Heuristics."

147. Cherry, What Is the Misinformation Effect?

148. Low, "Modality Effect on Learning."

149. CFI Team, "What Is Money Illusion?"

150. Barry, Naus, and Rehm, "Depression and Implicit Memory: Understanding Mood Congruent Memory Bias," 387–414.

151. Brown et al., "Moral Credentialing and the Rationalization of Misconduct," 1–12.

152. Nelkin, Zalta, and Nodelman, "Moral Luck."

153. Kruger and Gilovich, "'Naive Cynicism'" in Everyday Theories of Responsibility Assessment: On Biased Assumptions of Bias," 743.

154. López-Rodríguez et al., "Awareness of the Psychological Bias of Naïve Realism can Increase Acceptance of Cultural Differences," 888–900.

155. Cherry, "What Is the Negativity Bias?"

156. Parker, "Neglect of Probability Bias," 245–50.

157. Oxford Reference, *Next-in-Line Effect*.

158. Kuehn, "What Was That? I Can't Remember What You Said, I Was Next-in-Line."

159. Marcatto, Cosulich, and Ferrante, "Once Bitten, Twice Shy: Experienced Regret and Non-Adaptive Choice Switching," E1035.

160. Johnson and Murray, "What a Crisis Teaches Us About Innovation."

161. Antons and Piller, "Opening the Black Box of 'Not Invented Here': Attitudes, Decision Biases, and Behavioral Consequences," 193–217.

162. APA Dictionary of Psychology, "Experimenter Expectancy Effect,"

163. Baron and Ritov, "Omission Bias, Individual Differences, and Normality," 74–85.

164. Mudditt, "How 'Optimism Bias' Shapes Our Decisions and Futures."

165. Karlsson, Loewenstein, and Seppi, "The Ostrich Effect: Selective Attention to Information," 95–115.

166. Brownback and Kuhn, "Understanding Outcome Bias," 342–60.

167. Rubin and Badea, "Why do People Perceive Ingroup Homogeneity on Ingroup Traits and Outgroup Homogeneity on Outgroup Traits?" 31–42.

168. Dunning et al., "The Overconfidence Effect in Social Prediction," 568.

169. Wardle et al., "Illusory Faces Are More Likely to Be Perceived as Male Than Female," E2117413119.

170. Mcfedries, "Agile Words [Technically Speaking]," 21.

171. Xing, Niu, and Liu, "The Part-List Cuing Effect in Working Memory: The Influence of Task Presentation Mode," 219.

172. The BE Hub, "Peak-End Rule."

173. Lean In, "50 Ways to Fight Bias: An Introduction to the Common Biases Women Experience."

174. Hammad et al., "Optimism Bias, Pessimism Bias, Magical Beliefs, and Conspiracy theory Beliefs Related to COVID-19 Among the Jordanian Population," 1661–71.

175. Ensor, Bancroft, and Hockley, "Listening to the Picture-Superiority Effect," 134–53.

176. APA Dictionary of Psychology, "Plan-Continuation Bias."

177. Buehler, Griffin, and Peetz, "Chapter One—the Planning Fallacy: Cognitive, Motivational, and Social Origins," 1–62.

178. Barber et al., "Thinking About a Limited Future Enhances the Positivity of Younger and Older Adults' Recall: Support for Socioemotional Selectivity theory," 869–82.

179. Buss, *Evolutionary Psychology: the New Science of the Mind*, 280–81.

180. The BE Hub, "Present Bias."

181. Ro, "Why 'Plant Blindness' Matters—and What you can do About It."

182. Lo, Marlowe, and Zhang, "To Maximize or Randomize? An Experimental Study of Probability Matching in Financial Decision Making," E0252540.

183. Crible and Pickering, "Compensating for Processing Difficulty in Discourse: Effect of Parallelism in Contrastive Relations," 862–79.

184. Ferreira et al., "Maladaptive Planning and the Pro-Innovation Bias: Considering the Case of Automated Vehicles," 41.

185. Cherry, "What Is the Projection Bias?"

186. Douglas, Sutton, and Cichocka, "Belief in Conspiracy theories: Looking Beyond Gullibility," 61–76.

187. Fandom Lifestyle Community," Pseudocertainty Effect."

188. Kokkoris and Stavrova, "The Dark Side of Self-Control."

189. Collins, "Pygmalion Effect," 1206.

190. Blawatt, "Marconomics: Future Direction for Research," 267–84.

191. Macmillan Education, "Welcome to Macmillan Education Customer Support."

192. Clee and Wicklund, "Consumer Behavior and Psychological Reactance," 389–405.

193. Cheung and Li, "Special Forms of Bias: Endowment Effect and Reactive Devaluation," 83–118.

194. Psychout, What Is Regressive Bias?

195. Zimprich and Wolf, "Leveling up the Analysis of the Reminiscence Bump in Autobiographical Memory: A New Approach Based on Multilevel Multinomial Models," 1178–93.

196. Nordgren, Van Harreveld, and Van Der Pligt, "The Restraint Bias: How the Illusion of Self-Restraint Promotes Impulsive Behavior," 1523–28.

197. The Decision Lab, "Restraint Bias."

198. Effectiviology, "The Rhyme-as-Reason Effect: Why Rhyming Makes Messages More Persuasive."

199. Trogen and Caplan, "Risk Compensation and COVID-19 Vaccines," 858–859.

200. The Decision Lab, "Salience Bias."

201. Kahneman, "Evaluation by Moments, Past and Future," 708; Dickert et al., "Scope Insensitivity: the Limits of Intuitive Valuation of Human Lives in Public Policy," 248–55.

202. Lopes and Kipperberg, "Diagnosing Insensitivity to Scope in Contingent Valuation," 191–216.

203. Farnsworth, "What Is Selection Bias? (And How to Defeat It)."

204. Walsh, "Selectivity and Selective Perception: An Investigation of Managers' Belief Structures and Information Processing," 873–96.

205. He, Han, and Shi, "Self-Reference Effect Induced by Self-Cues Presented During Retrieval."

206. Herndon, "What Is a Self-Serving Bias and What Are Some Examples of It?"

207. Gupta et al., "Semmelweis Reflex: An Age-Old Prejudice," E119–25.

208. Mcleod, "Serial Position Effect (Glanzer And Cunitz, 1966)."

209. Haselton, "The Sexual Overperception Bias: Evidence of a Systematic Bias in Men From a Survey of Naturally Occurring Events," 34–47.

210. Ting and Xiaomin, "Shared Information Bias in Group Decision-Making: Based on Hidden Profile Paradigm," 132–42.

211. Garcia, Song, and Tesser, "Tainted Recommendations: the Social Comparison Bias," 97–101.

212. Eichhorn, "Social Cryptomnesia—An Argument for Change."

213. Krumpal, "Determinants of Social Desirability Bias in Sensitive Surveys: a Literature Review," 2025–47.

214. Takarangi et al., "Source Confusion Influences the Effectiveness of the Autobiographical IAT," 1232–8.

215. Slone and Sandhofer, "Consider the Category: the Effect of Spacing Depends on Individual Learning Histories," 34–49.

216. Raypole, "Always Feeling Self-Conscious? Here's Why You Shouldn't, According to Science."

217. Cherry, "How the Status Quo Bias Affects our Decisions."

218. Nova Scotia Health Authority, "What Is Bias and Stereotyping?"

219. Mulford and Dawes, "Subadditivity in Memory for Personal Events," 47–51.

220. Forer, "The Fallacy of Personal Validation: a Classroom Demonstration of Gullibility," 118–121; Psychology Concepts, Cognition. Subjective Validation.

221. Morton, Crowder, and Prussin, "Experiments With the Stimulus Suffix Effect," 169–90.

222. Wells and Bradfield, "Good, you Identified the Suspect: Feedback to Eyewitnesses Distorts their Reports of the Witnessing Experience," 360.

223. Dean, "Suggestibility of Memory in Psychology: Definition and Examples."

224. Harris and Tayler, "Don't Let Metrics Undermine Your Business."

225. Miller, "How 'Survivorship Bias' can Cause you to Make Mistakes."

226. Grammer and Thornhill, "Human (Homo Sapiens) Facial Attractiveness and Sexual Selection: the Role of Symmetry and Averageness," 233; Shackelford and Larsen, "Facial Asymmetry as an Indicator of Psychological,

Emotional, and Physiological Distress," 456; Gangestad and Thornhill, "The Evolutionary Psychology of Extrapair Sex: the Role of Fluctuating Asymmetry," 69–88; Møller and Thornhill, "Bilateral Symmetry and Sexual Selection: a Meta-Analysis," 174–92; Buss, *Evolutionary Psychology: the New Science of the Mind*, 294.

227. Psychology Wiki, "Systematic Bias."

228. Jost and Van Der Toorn, "System Justification theory," 313–43.

229. Tachypsychia, "APA Dictionary of Psychology."

230. Johnson and Schultz, "Forward Telescoping Bias in Reported Age of Onset: An Example From Cigarette Smoking," 119–29.

231. Schwieren, Barenberg, and Dutke, "The Testing Effect in the Psychology Classroom: a Meta-Analytic Perspective," 179–96.

232. Svenson, "Decisions Among Time Saving Options: When Intuition Is Strong and Wrong," 501–09.

233. Dean, "Tip-of-the-Tongue Phenomenon or Lethologica."

234. Gunther and Mundy, "Biased Optimism and the Third-Person Effect," 58–67.

235. Dean, "Third-Person Effect theory: the Media Only Influences Others."

236. Hampson, "Trait Ascription and Depth of Acquaintance: the Preference for Traits in Personality Descriptions And Its Relation to Target Familiarity," 398–411.

237. Psychology Wiki, "Trait Ascription Bias."

238. Poppenk, "Why Is the Meaning of a Sentence Better Remembered Than Its Form? An Fmri Study on the Role of Novelty-Encoding Processes," 909–18.

239. Effectiviology, "The Verbatim Effect: People Remember Gist Better Than Details."

240. Chang et al., "Chinese Mate Preferences: Cultural Evolution and Continuity Across a Quarter of a Century," 678–83; Souza, Conroy-Beam, and Buss, "Mate Preferences in Brazil: Evolved Desires and Cultural Evolution Over Three Decades," 45–49; Buss, *Evolutionary Psychology: the New Science of the Mind*, 370.

241. Buss, *Evolutionary Psychology: The New Science of the Mind*, 358.

242. Betzig, "Causes of Conjugal Dissolution: a Cross-Cultural Study," 654–76; Buss, "Conflict Between the Sexes: Strategic Interference and the Evocation of Anger and Upset," 735–47; Buss, *Evolutionary Psychology: the New Science of the Mind*, 372.

243. Encyclopedia Britannica, "Von Restorff Effect."

244. Hewstone, "The 'Ultimate Attribution Error'? a Review of the Literature on Intergroup Causal Attribution," 311–35.

245. University of California, "Unconscious Bias Training."

246. Geier, Rozin, and Doros, "Unit Bias: a New Heuristic That Helps Explain the Effect of Portion Size on Food Intake," 521–25.

247. the Editors of Encyclopaedia Britannica, "Weber's Law."

248. Nettle and Pollet, "Natural Selection on Male We alth in Humans," 658–66.

249. Buss, *Evolutionary Psychology: the New Science of the Mind*, 148.

250. Ibid, 381.

251. Buss, *Evolutionary Psychology: the New Science of the Mind*, 318; Mulder, "Kipsigis Women's Preferences for Wealthy Men: Evidence for Female Choice in Mammals?" 255–64.

252. Ibid.

253. Krys et al., "Catching up With Wonderful Women: the Women-Are-Wonderful Effect Is Smaller in More Gender Egalitarian Societies," 21–6.

254. Whillans, Jordan, and Chen, "The Upside to Feeling Worse Than Average (WTA): a Conceptual Framework to Understand When, How, and for Whom WTA Beliefs Have Long-Term Benefits," 642.

255. Buss, "Sex Differences in Human Mate Preferences: Evolutionary Hypotheses Testing in 37 Cultures," 1–49; Saad, "Applying Evolutionary Psychology in Understanding the Representation of Women in Advertisements," 593–612; Buss, *Evolutionary Psychology: the New Science of the Mind*, 242–43.

256. Williams, "Pleiotropy, Natural Selection, and the Evolution of Senescence," 398–411.

257. The Decision Lab, "Zero Risk Bias."

258. Meegan, "Zero-Sum Bias: Perceived Competition Despite Unlimited Resources," 191.

259. Shatz, "The Zero-Sum Bias: When People Think That Everything Is a Competition."

260. Nickerson, "Zeigarnik Effect Examples in Psychology."

References

23andMe. 2022. "Reports Included in All Services: Ancestry Reports, Trait Reports, Health Predisposition Reports, Wellness Reports, Carrier Status Reports, Pharmacogenetics Reports, Health Predisposition Reports, Blood Test Panels, 55+ Biomarkers."

Abadi, M. 2018. "I've Been to 27 Countries, and These Are the Worst 7 Stereotypes I've Heard About Americans." Business Insider.

Acayaba, C., and T. Reis. 2021. "No De Mortos Pela Polícia Em 2020 No Brasil Bate Recorde; 50 Cidades Concentram Mais Da Metade Dos Óbitos, Revela Anuário." G1 Globo.

Adams, G.S., B.A. Converse, A.H. Hales, L.E. Klotz. 2021. "People Systematically Overlook Subtractive Changes." Nature 592: 258–61.

Adcock Solutions. 2022. "No.16 of 36 the Denomination Effect."

Adechi, J.P. 2020. "Why do White Men Raise More VC Dollars Than Anyone Else?" Techstars.

Adler, A. 1924. The Collected Clinical Works of Alfred Adler: Talent & Occupation, Crime and Revolution, Philosophy of Living.

Ajzen, I. 1985. "From Intentions to Actions: A Theory of Planned Behavior." Action Control: 11–39.

Ajzen, I. 1991. "The Theory of Planned Behavior." Organizational Behavior and Human Decision Processes 50 (2): 179–11.

Akre, V., A. Rajan, J. Ahamed, A. Al Amri, and S. Al Daisi. 2019. "Smart Digital Marketing of Financial Services to Millennial Generation Using Emerging Technological Tools and Buyer Persona." 2019 Sixth HCT Information Technology Trends (ITT), 20–1; Stoychev, I. 2020. "Digital and Social Media Marketing Strategy." In Digital and Social Media Marketing, 98–120. Routledge; McLachlan, S. 2021. "How to Create a Buyer Persona (Free Buyer/Audience Persona Template)." Hotsuite.

Al-Shawaf, L., D.M.G. Lewis, and D. Buss. 2017. "Sex Differences in Disgust: Why Are Women More Easily Disgusted Than Men?" Emotion review 10 (2):149–60; Buss, D. 2019. Evolutionary Psychology: The New Science of the Mind, 191–93. Oxfordshire: Routledge.

Alexander, R.D. 1989. "Evolution of the Human Psyche". In The Human Revolution: Behavioral and Biological Perspectives on the Origins of Modern Humans, 455–513, edited by P. Mellars, and C. Stringer. Princeton. New Jersey, NJ: Princeton University Press; Flinn M.V., D.C. Geary, and C.V. Ward. 2005. "Ecological Dominance, Social Competition, and Coalitionary

Arms Races: Why Humans Evolved Extraordinary Intelligence." Evolution and Human Behavior 26: 10–46.

Allianz. 2022. "Allianz and Football." Allianz.com.

American Marketing Association. 2022. "Meet Our Example Buyer Persona." www.ama.org/toolkits/buyer-persona-template/.

American Psychological Association. 2017. "APA Stress in America™ Survey: US at 'Lowest Point we can Remember' Future of Nation Most Commonly Reported Source of Stress."

American Psychological Association. 2022. "Racism, Bias, and Discrimination." APA.Org.

Anderson, M.V., and M.D. Rutherford. 2013. "Evidence of a Nesting Psychology During Human Pregnancy." Evolution and Human Behavior 34 (6): 390–97.

Andersson, M. 1994. Sexual Selection, 72 vols. Princeton University Press; Gould, S.J. 1989. Wonderful Life: The Burgess Shale and the Nature of History. WW Norton & Company; Sundie, J.M., D.T. Kenrick, V. Griskevicius, J.M. Tybur, K.D. Vohs, and D.J. Beal. 2011. "Peacocks, Porsches, and Thorstein Veblen: Conspicuous Consumption as a Sexual Signaling System." Journal of Personality and Social Psychology 100 (4): 664.

André, E., J. Kim, M. Rehm, and T. Vogt. 2004. Humane—Human-Machine Interaction Network on Emotion.

Antons, D., and F.T. Piller. 2015. "Opening the Black Box of "Not Invented Here": Attitudes, Decision Biases, and Behavioral Consequences." Academy of Management Perspectives 29 (2): 193–217.

APA Dictionary of Psychology. .n.d. "Cryptomnesia." American Psychological Association.

APA Dictionary of Psychology. n.d. "Experimenter Expectancy Effect."

APA Dictionary of Psychology. n.d. "Plan-Continuation Bias." American Psychological Association.

Applied Behavior Analysis Programs Guide. 2022. "History's 30 Most Famous People With Autism."

Archer, J. 2006. "Testosterone and Human Aggression: An Evaluation of the Challenge Hypothesis." Neuroscience & Biobehavioral Reviews 30 (3): 319–45; Dabbs, J.M., and R. Morris. 1990. "Testosterone, Social Class, and Antisocial Behavior in a Sample of 4,462 Men." Psychological Science 1 (3): 209–11; Mazur, A., and A. Booth. 1998. "Testosterone and Dominance in Men." Behavioral and Brain Sciences 21 (3): 353–63; Discussion 363–97.

Ibid, 319–45; Auyeung, B., S. Baron-Cohen, E. Ashwin, R. Knickmeyer, K. Taylor, G. Hackett, and M. Hines. 2009. "Fetal Testosterone Predicts Sexually Differentiated Childhood Behavior in Girls and in Boys." Psychological Science 20 (2): 144–48; Udry, J.R. 2000. "Biological Limits of Gender Construction." American Sociological Review 65 (3): 443–57.

Aspara, J., and B.V.D. Bergh. 2014. "Naturally Designed for Masculinity vs. Femininity? Prenatal Testosterone Predicts Male Consumers' Choices of Gender-Imaged Products." International Journal of Research in Marketing 31 (1): 117–21.

Auschwitz-Birkenau State Museum. 2022. "Robert Biedroń, Nazism's Pink Hell." Auschwitz.org.

Awad, N.F., and M.S. Krishnan. 2006. "The Personalization Privacy Paradox: An Empirical Evaluation of Information Transparency and the Willingness to Be Profiled Online for Personalization." MIS Quarterly: 13–28. Bailey, A.A., and P.L. Hurd. 2005. "Finger Length Ratio (2D:4D) Correlates With Physical Aggression in Men but not in Women." Biological Psychology 68 (3): 215–22.

Bailey, M. 2008. "Escaping Salem: The Other Witch Hunt of 1692 (Review)." Magic, Ritual, and Witchcraft 3: 88–91; Marshall, B. 2019. "Most Witches Are Women, Because Witch Hunts Were All About Persecuting the Powerless." The Conversation UK.

Baird, D.D., D.R. McConnaughey, C.R. Weinberg, P.L. Musey, D.C. Collins, J.S. Kesner, E.A. Knecht, et al. 1995. "Application of a Method for Estimating Day of Ovulation Using Urinary Estrogen and Progesterone Metabolites." Epidemiology 6 (5): 547–50; Puts, D.A., D.H. Bailey, R.R.A. Cárdenas, R.P. Burriss, L.M. Welling, J.R. Wheatley, and K. Dawood. 2013. "Women's Attractiveness Changes With Estradiol and Progesterone Across the Ovulatory Cycle." Hormones and Behavior 63 (1):13–9.

Ballinger, J. "Authority Bias." Thebchavioursagency.

Bank of England. 2020. "Bank of England Measures to Respond to the Economic Shock From Covid-19."

Barber, S.J., P.C. Opitz, B. Martins, M. Sakaki, and M. Mather. 2016. "Thinking About a Limited Future Enhances the Positivity of Younger and Older Adults' Recall: Support for Socioemotional Selectivity Theory." Memory & Cognition 44 (6): 869–82.

Barberia, J.M., J. Giner, and V. Cortes-Gallegos. 1973. "Diurnal Variations of Plasma Testosterone in Men." Steroids 22 (5): 615–26.

Barclay, P. 2010. "Altruism as a Courtship Display: Some Effects of Third-party Generosity on Audience Perceptions." British Journal of Psychology 101 (1): 123–135; Phillips, T., C. Barnard, E. Ferguson, and T. Reader. 2008. "Do Humans Prefer Altruistic Mates? Testing a Link Between Sexual Selection and Altruism Towards Non-Relatives." British Journal of Psychology 99 (4): 555–72.

Baron-Cohen, S. 2005. "The Empathizing System." Origins of the Social Mind: Evolutionary Psychology and Child Development: 468–492.

Baron, J., and I. Ritov. 2004. "Omission Bias, Individual Differences, and Normality." Organizational Behavior and Human Decision Processes 94 (2): 74–85.

Barr, S. 2019. "Gillette Tackles Toxic Masculinity in New Advert for #MeToo era." Independent; King, M.P. 2019. "Gillette Responds to Controversial Advert Challenging Toxic Masculinity." Forbes.

Barrett, E.S., V. Tran, S. Thurston, G. Jasienska, A.S. Furberg, P.T. Ellison, and I. Thune. 2013. "Marriage and Motherhood Are Associated With Lower Testosterone Concentrations in Women." Hormones and Behavior 63 (1): 72–9.

Barry, E.S., M.J. Naus, and L.P. Rehm. 2004. "Depression and Implicit Memory: Understanding Mood Congruent Memory Bias." Cognitive Therapy and Research 28: 387–414.

Baulieu, E.E., and P. Kelly. 1990. "Hormones: From Molecules to Disease"; Turner, C.D. 1948. General Endocrinology.

Baum Hedlund Law. 2021. Human Factors in Aviation.

Bawagan, J. 2019. "Scientists Explore the Evolution of Animal Homosexuality." Imperial News.

BBC.n.d. "Nirbhaya Case: Four Indian Men Executed for 2012 Delhi Bus Rape and Murder." BBC News.

BBC. 2014. "Russia: 'Good News Day' Decimates Website's Readership." BBC News.

BBC. 2019. "Marielle Franco Murder: Suspect Shot Dead by Police." BBC News; Reintke, T. n.d. "Marielle Franco Is the First-Ever LGBTI Person to Be on the Sakharov Prize Shortlist." https://lgbti-ep.eu/2019/10/10/marielle-franco-is-the-first-ever-lgbti-person-to-be-on-the-sakharov-prize-shortlist/#:~:text=Marielle%20Franco%20and%20Jean%20Wyllys,come%20from%20the%20LGBTI%20community.; Londoño, E. 2019. "A Year After her Killing, Marielle Franco Has Become a Rallying Cry in a Polarized Brazil." The New York Times.

BBC. 2023. "Homosexuality: The Countries Where It Is Illegal to Be Gay." BBC News; Paletta, D. 2020. "ILGA World Updates State-Sponsored Homophobia Report: 'There's Progress in Times of Uncertainty." ILGA.

Beasley, D. 2021. "In the World of Wealth, 9 Million People Die Every Year From Hunger, WFP Chief Tells Food System Summit: World Food Programme." UN World Food Programme; Becker, D.G. 1997. The Gift of Fear: Survival Signals That Protect Us From Violence. Boston: Little, Brown and Company; Marks, I.M. 1987. Fears, Phobias, and Rituals: Panic, Anxiety, and Their Disorders. Oxford University Press, USA; Bracha, H.S. 2004. "Freeze, Flight, Fight, Fright, Faint: Adaptationist Perspectives on the Acute Stress Response Spectrum." CNS Spectrums 9 (9): 679–85; Buss, D. 2019. Evolutionary Psychology: The New Science of the Mind. Oxfordshire: Routledge.

Becker, D.G., and T. Stechschulte. 1997. The Gift of Fear. New York, NY: Dell Publishing; Marks, I. 1987. "The Development of Normal Fear: A Review." Journal of Child Psychology and Psychiatry 28 (5): 667–97; Marks, I.M., and R.M. Nesse. 1994. "Fear and Fitness: An Evolutionary Analysis of Anxiety Disorders." Ethology and Sociobiology 15: 247–61.

BehavioralEconomics. n.d. "Action Bias."

Belkin, D. 2021. "A Generation of American Men Give up on College: 'I Just Feel Lost.'" The Wall Street Journal.

Bendixen, M. 2014. "Evidence of Systematic Bias in Sexual Over- and Under-Perception of Naturally Occurring Events: A Direct Replication of Haselton (2003) in a More Gender-Equal Culture." Evolutionary Psychology.

Berggren, N., H. Jordahl, and P. Poutvaara. 2010. "The Looks of a Winner: Beauty and Electoral Success." Journal of Public Economics 94 (1–2): 8–15.

Bergland, C. 2015. "Cortisol and Oxytocin Hardwire Fear-Based Memories."

Bergstrom, C.T., and M. Feldgarden. 2007. "The Ecology and Evolution of Antibiotic-Resistant Bacteria." Evolution in Health and Disease: 125–38.

Bernays, E.L. 1942. "The Marketing of National Policies: A Study of War Propaganda." Journal of Marketing 6 (3): 236–44.

Bernays, E.L. 1947. "The Engineering of Consent." The Annals of the American Academy of Political and Social Science 250 (1): 113–20.

Berthold, A.A. 2023. "Complete Dictionary of Scientific Biography." Encyclopedia.com; Soma, K.K. 2006. "Testosterone and Aggression: Berthold, Birds and Beyond." Journal of Neuroendocrinology 18 (7): 543–51.

Bertsch, S., B.J. Pesta, R. Wiscott, and M.A. McDaniel. 2007. "The Generation Effect: A Meta–Analytic Review." Memory & Cognition 35 (2): 201–10.

Betzig, L. 1989. "Causes of Conjugal Dissolution: A Cross-Cultural Study." Current Anthropology 30 (5): 654–76; Buss, D. 1989. "Conflict Between the Sexes: Strategic Interference and the Evocation of Anger and Upset." Journal of Personality and Social Psychology 56: 735–47; Daly and Wilson. 1998. Evolutionary Psychology: The New Science of the Mind, 372. Oxfordshire: Routledge.

Bible Gateway. n.d. "BibleGateway—Keyword Search: Menstrual." Biblegateway. com.

Bible Gateway. n.d. "Genesis, 9:27."

Bible Gateway. n.d. "Leviticus 15:19." Biblegateway.com.

Bidder, G.P. 1932. "Senescence." British Medical Journal 2 (3742): 583–5; Comfort, A. 1964. "Ageing: The Biology of Senescence"; Partridge, L. 1987. "Is Accelerated Senescence a Cost of Reproduction?" Functional Ecology 1 (4): 317–20; Noodén, L.D., J.J. Guiamét, and I. John. 1997. "Senescence Mechanisms." Physiologia Plantarum 101 (4): 746–53.

Bittner, A., and B. Lau. 2021. "Women-Led Startups Received Just 2.3% of VC Funding in 2020." Harvard Business Review.

Blawatt, K.R. 2016. "Marconomics: Future Direction for Research." In Marconomics, 267–84. Emerald Group Publishing Limited.

Bobbitt, Z. 2021. "Berkson's Bias: Definition + Examples." Statology.

Boddy, C., D. Miles, C. Sanyal, and M. Hartog. 2015. "Extreme Managers, Extreme Workplaces: Capitalism, Organizations and Corporate Psychopaths." Organization 22 (4): 530–51; Chiaburu, D.S., G.J. Muñoz, and R.G. Gardner. 2013. "How to Spot a Careerist Early on: Psychopathy and Exchange Ideology as Predictors of Careerism." Journal of Business Ethics 118 (3): 473–86.

Boddy, C.R. 2014. "Corporate Psychopaths, Conflict, Employee Affective well-Being and Counterproductive Work Behavior." Journal of Business Ethics 121: 107–21.

Boddy, C.R. 2017. "Psychopathic Leadership a Case Study of a Corporate Psychopath CEO." Journal of Business Ethics 145: 141–56.

Bogaert, A.F., and M.N. Skorska. 2020. "A Short Review of Biological Research on the Development of Sexual Orientation." Hormones and Behavior 119.

Bolukbasi, T., K.W. Chang, J. Zou, V. Saligrama, and A. Kalai. 2016. "Man Is to Computer Programmer as Woman Is to Homemaker? Debiasing Word Embeddings." Computer Science, Computation and Language; Caliskan, A., J.J. Bryson, and A. Narayana. 2016. "Semantics Derived Automatically From Language Corpora Contain Human-Like Biases." https://www.science.org/doi/10.1126/science.aal4230.

Bon, G.L. 1914. The Crowd: A Study of the Popular Mind. London: The Gresham Press.

Bönte, W., V.D. Procher, D. Urbig, and M. Voracek. 2017. "Digit Ratio (2D:4D) Predicts Self-Reported Measures of General Competitiveness, but not Behavior in Economic Experiments." Frontiers in Behavioral Neuroscience 11.

Bordley, R., M. Licalzi, and L. Tibiletti. 2017. "A Target-Based Foundation for the 'Hard-Easy Effect' Bias." Cham.

Boslaugh, S.E. 2016. "Anthropocentrism." Encyclopedia Britannica.

Bouvier K. 2021. "B2B Versus B2C Marketing." Bouvier Kelly.

Bower, B. 2005. "Investing on a Whiff: Chemical Spray Shows Power as Trust Booster." Science News.

Branch, G. 2020. "Acceptance Level of Evolution in Twenty Countries." National Center for Science.

Branch, G. 2021. "Evolution Accepted by a Majority of Americans at Last."National Center for Science Education.

Brewer, G., and C. Riley. 2010. "Sexual Dimorphism in Stature (SDS), Jealousy and Mate Retention." Evolutionary Psychology 8 (4): 1–15.

British Fertility Society. 2022. "When Are Men and Women Most Fertile?" British Fertility Society.

Brookes, E. 2023. "The Theory of Planned Behavior: Behavioral Intention." Simply Psychology.

Brooks, N., and K. Fritzon. 2016. "Corporate Psychopaths Common and Can Wreak Havoc in Business, Researcher Says." Australian Psychological Society.

Brown, D.G. 1991. Human Universals. New York, NY: McGraw-Hill.

Brown, E., and Y. Chia-Yun. 1993. "'Big Man' in Universalistic Perspective." Unpublished Manuscript. Santa Barbara. CA: University of California, Santa Barbara.

Brown, J.K. 1970. "A Note on the Division of Labor by Sex." American Anthropologist 72 (5): 1073–78; Bryner, J. 2019. "What Are Stem Cells?" Live Science.

Brown, R.P., M. Tamborski, X. Wang, C.D. Barnes, M.D. Mumford, S. Connelly, and L.D. Devenport. 2011. "Moral Credentialing and the Rationalization of Misconduct." Ethics Behavior 21 (1): 1–12.

Brownback, A., and M.A. Kuhn. 2019. "Understanding Outcome Bias." Games and Economic Behavior 117: 342–60.

Buehler, R., D. Griffin, and J. Peetz. 2010. "Chapter One—The Planning Fallacy: Cognitive, Motivational, and Social Origins." In Advances in Experimental Social Psychology, edited by M.P. Zanna, and J.M. Olson, 1–62. Academic Press.

Buffenstein, R., S.D. Poppitt, R.M. McDevitt, and A.M. Prentice. 1995. "Food Intake and the Menstrual Cycle: A Retrospective Analysis, With Implications for Appetite Research." Physiology and Behavior 58 (6):1067–77; Saad, G., and E. Stenstrom. 2012. "Calories, Beauty, and Ovulation: The Effects of the Menstrual Cycle on Food and Appearance-Related Consumption." Journal of Consumer Psychology 22 (1):102–13.

Buffenstein, R., S.D. Poppitt, R.M. McDevitt, and A.M. Prentice. 1995. "Food Intake and the Menstrual Cycle: A Retrospective Analysis, With Implications for Appetite Research." Physiology and Behavior 58 (6):1067–77; Saad, G. 2011. The Consuming Instinct: What Juicy Burgers, Ferraris, Pornography, and Gift Giving Reveal About Human Nature. Prometheus Books.

Bunn, C. 2022. "Report: Black People Are Still Killed by Police at a Higher Rate Than Other Groups." NBCNews.Com.

Buolamwini, J., and T. Gebru. 2018. "Gender Shades: Intersectional Accuracy Disparities in Commercial Gender Classification." Proceedings of the 1st Conference on Fairness, Accountability and Transparency in Proceedings of Machine Learning Research 81: 77–91.

Burack, C. 2021. "German Efficiency: The Roots of a Stereotype." DW.com.

Burdine, B., W. Cho, K. Levis, L. Marx, C. Moran, A. Navia, M. Talabucon, et al. 2015. "The Future of Luxury New Luxury Consumer Values." Fashion Institute of Technology State University of New York.

Burhan, R., and J. Moradzadeh. 2020. "Neurotransmitter Dopamine (DA) and Its Role in the Development of Social Media Addiction." Journal of Neurology & Neurophysiology 11 (7): 1–2.

Burkitt, L. 2009. "Neuromarketing: Companies Use Neuroscience for Consumer Insights." Forbes.

Burnham, T.C., J.F. Chapman., P.B. Gray, M.H. McIntyre, S.F. Lipson, and P.T. Ellison. 2003. "Men in Committed, Romantic Relationships Have Lower Testosterone." Hormones and Behavior 44 (2):119–22.

Ibid; Gray, P.B., J.F. Chapman, T.C. Burnham, M.H. McIntyre, S.F. Lipson, and P.T. Ellison. 2004. "Human Male Pair Bonding and Testosterone." Human Nature 15: 119–31; Buss, D. 2019. Evolutionary Psychology: The New Science of the Mind, 385. Oxfordshire: Routledge.

Buss, D. 1988. "The Evolution of Human Intrasexual Competition: Tactics of Mate Attraction." Journal of Personality and Social Psychology 54: 616–28; Schmitt, D.P., and D. Buss. 1996. "Strategic Self-promotion and Competitor Derogation: Sex and Context Effects on the Perceived Effectiveness of Mate Attraction Tactics." Journal of Personality and Social Psychology 70 (6): 1185.

Buss, D. 1989. "Sex Differences in Human Mate Preferences: Evolutionary Hypotheses Tested in 37 Cultures." Behavioral and Brain Sciences 12 (1): 1–49; Saad, G. 2004. "Applying Evolutionary Psychology in Understanding the Representation of Women in Advertisements." Psychology & Marketing 21 (8): 593–612; Buss, D. 1989. "Conflict Between the Sexes: Strategic Interference and the Evocation of Anger and Upset." Journal of Personality and Social Psychology 56 (5): 735; Butori, R., and B. Parguel. 2014. "The Impact of Visual Exposure to a Physically Attractive Other on Self-Presentation." International Journal of Research in Marketing 31 (4): 445–7.

Ibid, 1–49; Saad, G. 2004. Applying Evolutionary Psychology in Understanding the Representation of Women in Advertisements." Psychology & Marketing 21 (8): 593–612; Nesse, and Williams. 1994. Evolutionary Psychology: The New Science of the Mind, 242–3. Oxfordshire: Routledge.

Buss, D. 1995. "Evolutionary Psychology: A New Paradigm for Psychological Science." Psychological Inquiry 6 (1): 1–30; Cosmides, L., and J. Tooby. 1992. "Cognitive Adaptations for Social Exchange." The Adapted Mind: Evolutionary Psychology and the Generation of Culture 163: 163–228.

Buss, D. 1995. "Evolutionary Psychology: A New Paradigm for Psychological Science." Psychological Inquiry 6 (1): 1–30; Tooby, J. and L. Cosmides. 1992. "The Psychological Foundations of Culture." The Adapted Mind: Evolutionary Psychology and the Generation of Culture 19: 19–136; Li, N.P., M. Van Vugt and S.M. Colarelli. 2017. "The Evolutionary Mismatch Hypothesis: Implications for Psychological Science." Current Directions in Psychological Science 27 (1): 38–44.

Buss, D. 2003. The Evolution of Desire: Strategies of Human Mating (Revised Edition). New York, NY : Free Press; Kruger, D.J., M. Fisher, and I. Jobling. 2003. "Proper and Dark Heroes as Dads and Cads: Alternative Mating Strategies in British Romantic Literature." Human Nature 14: 305–17; Rhodes, G., L.W. Simmons, and M. Peters. "Attractiveness and Sexual Behavior: Does Attractiveness Enhance Mating Success?" Evolution and Human Behavior 26 (2): 186–201; Durante, K.M., V. Griskevicius, J.A. Simpson, S.M. Cantú, and N.P. Li. 2012. "Ovulation Leads Women to Perceive Sexy Cads as Good Dads." Journal of Personality and Social Psychology 103 (2): 292.

Buss, D. 2009. "How Can Evolutionary Psychology Successfully Explain Personality and Individual Differences?" Perspectives on Psychological Science 4: 359–66; Buss, D., and L. Penke. 2014. "Evolutionary Personality Psychology." In The Handbook of Personality Psychology. Washington: APA Press; Nettle, D. 2006. "The Evolution of Personality Variation in Humans and Other Animals." American Psychologist 61: 622–31; Nettle, D., and L. Penke. 2010. "Personality: Bridging The Literature From Human Psychology and Behavioural Ecology." Philosophical Transactions of the Royal Society B 365: 4035–4050; Tooby, J., and L. Cosmides. 1990. "On the Universality of Human Nature and Uniqueness of the Individual: The Role of Genetics and Adaptation." Journal of Personality 58 (1): 17–68; Buss, D. 2019. Evolutionary Psychology: The New Science of the Mind, 6th ed, 952. New York, NY: Routledge Taylor Francis Group.

Ibid, 359–66; Buss, D., and L. Penke. 2014. Evolutionary Personality Psychology: The Handbook of Personality Psychology. Washington: APA Press; Nettle, D. 2006. "The Evolution of Personality Variation in Humans and Other Animals." American Psychologist 61 (6): 622–31; Nettle, D., and L. Penke. 2010. "Personality: Bridging The Literature From Human Psychology and Behavioural Ecology." Philosophical Transactions of the Royal Society B 365: 4035–50; Nettle, D. 2006. "The Evolution of Personality Variation in Humans and Other Animals." American Psychologist 61 (6): 622–31; Tooby, J., and L. Cosmides. 1990. "The Past Explains the Present: Emotional Adaptations and the Structure of Ancestral Environments." Ethology and Sociobiology 11 (4–5): 375–424; Buss, D. 2019. Evolutionary Psychology: The New Science of the Mind. 6th ed, 1732. New York, NY: Routledge Taylor Francis Group.

Buss, D. 2015. Evolutionary Psychology: The New Science of the Mind. New York, NY: Taylor and Francis.

Ibid, 89–90.

Ibid, 273.

Ibid, 14.

Ibid, 12.

Ibid, 460–61.

Buss, D. 2019. Evolutionary Psychology: The New Science of the Mind. Oxfordshire: Routledge.

Ibid, 952.

Ibid, 1732.

Ibid, 1733.

Ibid, 61.

Ibid, 59.

Ibid, 60.

Ibid, 697.

Ibid, 132.

Ibid, 300.

Ibid, 228.

Ibid, 23–4.

Ibid, 242–3.

Ibid, 243.

Ibid, 125, 321.

Ibid, 360, 384–84.

Ibid, 608.

Ibid, 385.

Ibid, 56, 243–4, 360.

Ibid, 191–3.

Ibid, 351.

Ibid, 394.

Ibid, 325–6.

Ibid, 342.

Ibid, 315–42.

Ibid, 295–6.

Ibid, 295.

Ibid, 461.

Ibid, 280–1.

Ibid, 294.

ibid, 358.

Ibid, 372.

Ibid, 381.

Ibid, 318.

Buss, D., and Schmitt, D.P. 1993. "Sexual Strategies Theory: An Evolutionary Perspective on Human Mating". Psychological Review100: 204–232.

Buss, D., M. Shackelford, L.A. Kirkpatrick, J.C. Choe, H.K. Lim, M. Hasegawa, T. Hasegawa, and K. Bennett. 1999. "Jealousy and the Nature of Beliefs

About Infidelity: Tests of Competing Hypotheses About Sex Differences in the United States, Korea, and Japan." Personal relationships 6 (1):125–150.

Buss, D., and N.R. Carlson. 2019. Evolutionary Psychology—The New Science of the Mind, 903, Oxfordshire: Routledge.

Buss, D.M., M. Abbott, A. Angleitner, A. Asherian, A. Biaggio, A. Blanco-Villasenor, M. Bruchon-Schweitzer, et al. 1990. "International Preferences in Selecting Mates: A Study of 37 Cultures." Journal of Cross-Cultural Psychology 21 (1):5–47.

Buss, David. 2019. Evolutionary Psychology: The New Science of the Mind. Oxfordshire: Routledge.

Calicolabs. 2022. "Inside the Biology of Aging: How do Scientists Tackle a Planet-Wide Diagnosis?" Calicolabs.

Cambridge University Press. 2022. "Bias." Cambridge Dictionary.

Cannon, H. 2018. "Autism: The Positives—Children, Young People and Families Online Resource." Berkshire Healthcare; Applied Behavioral Analysis. 2022. "5 Things we Could all Stand to Learn From People With ASD." Wiley University Services.

Capgemini. 2017. "Loyalty Deciphered. How Emotions Drive Genuine Engagement."

Carlsen, A., M. Salam, C.C. Miller, D. Lu, A. Ngu, J.K. Patel, and Z. Wichter. 2018. "#MeToo Brought Down 201 Powerful Men. Nearly Half of Their Replacements Are Women." The New York Times.

Carver, C.S., and M.F. Scheier. 1999. "Stress, Coping, and Self-Regulatory Processes"; Kusev, P., H. Purser, R. Heilman, A.J. Cooke, P. VanSchaik, V. Baranova, et al. 2017. "Understanding Risky Behavior: The Influence of Cognitive, Emotional and Hormonal Factors on Decision-making Under Risk." Frontiers in Psychology 8.

Casad, B.J., and J.E. Luebering. "Confirmation Bias." Encyclopedia Britannica.

Catalog of Bias Collaboration. 2019. "Information Bias." Sackett Catalog of Biases.

Center for Advanced Hindsight. 2018. "By the Power of Default."

CFI Team. n.d. "What Is Money Illusion?" CFI.

Chade, J. 2020. "Número de Pessoas Em Favelas Cresceu No Mundo, Mas No Brasil, CAIU, Diz Onu." Notícias.

Chamorro-Premuzic, T. 2019. "1 in 5 Business Leaders may Have Psychopathic Tendencies—Here's Why, According to a Psychology Professor." CNBC.

Chamorro-Premuzic, T. 2019. Why do so Many Incompetent Men Become Leaders?: (And How to Fix It). Boston: Harvard Business Review Press.

Chang, L., Y. Wang, T.K. Shackelford, and D. Buss. 2011. "Chinese Mate Preferences: Cultural Evolution and Continuity Across a Quarter of a Century." Personality and Individual Differences 50 (5): 678–83; Souza, A.

L., D. Conroy-Beam, and D.M. Buss. 2016. "Mate Preferences in Brazil: Evolved Desires and Cultural Evolution Over Three Decades." Personality and Individual Differences 95: 45–9; Buss. 2014. Evolutionary Psychology: The New Science of the Mind, 370. Oxfordshire: Routledge.

Chaudhuri, A., and M.B. Holbrook. 2001. "The Chain of Effects From Brand Trust and Brand Affect to Brand Performance: The Role of Brand Loyalty." Journal of Marketing 65 (2): 81–93; Fournier, S. 1998. "Consumers and Their Brands: Developing Relationship Theory in Consumer Research." Journal of Consumer Research 24 (4): 343–73; Song, Y., W.M. Hur, and M. Kim. 2012. "Brand Trust and Affect in the Luxury Brand-Customer Relationship." Social Behavior and Personality: An International Journal 40 (2): 03.

Ibid, 81–93; Song, Y., W.M. Hur, and M. Kim. 2012. "Brand Trust and Affect in the Luxury Brand-Customer Relationship." Social Behavior and Personality: An International Journal 40 (2): 331–8.

Chen, B.X. 2010. "Apple Registers Trademark for 'There's an app for That'." WIRED; Schippers, B. 2016. "App Fatigue." TechCrunch; Benes, R. 2018. "Most Apps Get Deleted Within a Week of Last Use." Emarketer; Ceci, L. 2023. "Number of Apps Available in Leading app Stores Q3 2022." Statista.

Chen, J. 2021. "What Is Base Rate Fallacy and Its Impact?" Investopedia.

Chen, J. 2022. "Hot Hand: What It Is, How It Works, Evidence." Investopedia.

Cherry, K. n.d. "What Is Attentional Bias?" verywellmind.com.

Cherry, K. 2017. "What Is the Projection Bias?" ExplorePsychology.com.

Cherry, K. 2020. "Functional Fixedness as a Cognitive Bias." verywellmind.com.

Cherry, K. 2020. "How Othering Contributes to Discrimination and Prejudice." VeryWellMind.

Cherry, K. 2023. "Actor-Observer Bias in Social Psychology." Verywellmind.

Cherry, K. 2023. "How False Memories Are Formed in Your Brain." verywellmind. com.

Cherry, K. 2023. "How the Status Quo Bias Affects Our Decisions." verywellmind. com.

Cherry, K. 2023. "What Is the Negativity Bias?" verywellmind.com.

Cherry, K. 2023. What Is the Misinformation Effect? verywellmind.

Cheung, S., and K. Li. 2022. "Special Forms of Bias: Endowment Effect and Reactive Devaluation." In Construction Dispute Research Expanded, 83–118.

Choi, I.H., K.H. Kim, H. Jung, S.J. Yoon, S.W. Kim, and T.B. Kim. 2011. "Second to Fourth Digit Ratio: A Predictor of Adult Penile Length." Asian Journal of Andrology 13 (5): 710–4.

Chrisafis, A. 2011. "French Stereotypes: They do not Work That Hard." The Guardian.

Classically Court. 2021. "A Record Number of Women Are Now Running Global 500 Businesses." CNBC.

Clee, M.A., R.A. Wicklund. 1980. "Consumer Behavior and Psychological Reactance." Journal of Consumer Research 6(4): 389–405.

Clore, G.L., K. Gasper, and E. Garvin. 2001. "Affect as Information." Handbook of Affect and Social Cognition, 121–144; Clore, G. L., and J.R. Huntsinger. 2009. "How the Object of Affect Guides Its Impact." Emotion Review 1 (1): 39–54.

Coca-Cola. 2023. "New Coke: The Most Memorable Marketing Blunder Ever? The History of New Coke." CocaCola.com.

Cohen-Bendahan, C.C., C.V.D. Beek, and S.A. Berenbaum. 2005. "Prenatal Sex Hormone Effects on Child and Adult Sex-Typed Behavior: Methods and Findings." Neuroscience and Biobehavioral Reviews 29 (2): 353–384; Aspara, J., and B.V.D. Bergh. 2014. "Naturally Nesigned for Masculinity vs. Femininity? Prenatal Testosterone Predicts Male Consumers' Choices of Gender-Imaged Products." International Journal of Research in Marketing 31 (1).

Collins, K.C. 2011. "Pygmalion Effect." In Encyclopedia of Child Behavior and Development, edited by S. Goldstein, and J.A. Naglieri, 1206. Boston, MA: Springer US.

Condon, S. 2010. "Palin: Obama Doesn't Have the Cojones for Immigration Reform."

Confer, J.C., J.E. Easton, D.S. Fleischman, C. Goetz, D.M. Lewis, C. Perilloux, and D.M. Buss. 2010. "Evolutionary Psychology: Controversies, Questions, Prospects, and Limitations." American Psychologist 65: 110–26; Buss, D. 2019. Evolutionary Psychology: The New Science of the Mind, 6th ed, 60. New York, NY: Routledge Taylor Francis Group.

Conversion Uplift. n.d. "Choice-Supportive Bias."

Cornell Law School. "Gender Bias." Legal Information Institute-Cornell Law School.

Cort, R.W., J. King, and D. Stiepleman. 2018. "On the Basis of Sex." Directed by Mimi Leder. United States: Focus Features.

Courtiol, A., M. Raymond, B. Godelle, and J.M. Ferdy. 2010. "Mate Choice and Human Stature: Homogamy as a Unified Framework for Understanding Mating Preferences." Evolution 64 (8): 2189–203; Ellis, B.J. 1992. "The Evolution of Sexual Attraction: Evaluative Mechanisms in Women." The Adapted Mind: Evolutionary Psychology and the Generation of Culture: 267–88.

Crawford, C. 1998. "Environments and Adaptations: Then and Now." In Handbook of Evolutionary Psychology: Ideas, Issues, and Applications, 275–302; Tooby, J. and L. Cosmides. 1990. "The Past Explains the Present:

Emotional Adaptations and the Structure of Ancestral Environments." Ethology and Sociobiology 11 (4–5): 375–424; Li, N.P., M. Van Vugt, and S.M. Colarelli. 2017. "The Evolutionary Mismatch Hypothesis: Implications for Psychological Science." Current Directions in Psychological Science 27 (1): 38–44.

Credit Suisse Research Institute. 2022. "Global Wealth Report." Credit Suisse.

Credit Suisse. 2022. "Global Wealth Report." Credit Suisse Research Institute.

Crible, L., and M.J. Pickering. 2020. "Compensating for Processing Difficulty in Discourse: Effect of Parallelism in Contrastive Relations." Discourse Processes 57 (10): 862–79.

Cristol, H. 2023. "What Is Dopamine?"

Ibid; Eske, J. 2022. "What Are the Differences Between Serotonin and Dopamine?" Medical News Today.

CRO-tool.com. n.d. "Extrinsic Incentives Bias."

Cronin, H. 2005. "Adaptation: A Critique of Some Current Evolutionary Thought." The Quarterly Review of Biology 80 (1): 19–26; Buss, D. 2019. Evolutionary Psychology: The New Science of the Mind. Oxfordshire: Routledge.

Cunningham, A. 2018. "Hormone Replacement Makes Sense for Some Menopausal Women." Science News.

Curtis, V., R. Aunger, and T. Rabie. 2004. "Evidence That Disgust Evolved to Protect From Risk of Disease." Proceedings of the Royal Society of London. Series B: Biological Sciences 271 (4): S131–3; Oaten, M., R.J. Stevenson, and T.I. Case. 2009. "Disgust as a Disease-Avoidance Mechanism." Psychological Bulletin 135 (2): 303.

Dabbs Jr, J.M., and R. Morris. 1990. "Testosterone, Social Class, and Antisocial Behavior in a Sample of 4,462 Men." Psychological Science 1 (3): 209–11; Mazur, A., and A. Booth. 1998. "Testosterone and Dominance in Men." Behavioral and Brain Sciences 21 (3): 353–63.

Dabbs, J.M., T.S. Carr, R.L. Frady, and J.K. Riad. 1995. "Testosterone, Crime, and Misbehavior Among 692 Male Prison Inmates." Personality and Individual Differences 18 (5): 627–33.

Dabbs, J.R., M. James, et al. 1993. "Salivary Testosterone Measurements in Behavioral Studies." Annals of the New York Academy of Sciences 694 (1): 177–183; Booth, A., D.A. Granger, A. Mazur, and K.T. Kivlighan. 2006. "Testosterone and Social Behavior." Social Forces 85 (1): 167–91.

Daitzman, R., and M. Zuckerman. 1980. "Disinhibitory Sensation Seeking, Personality and Gonadal Hormones." Personality and Individual Differences 1 (2): 103–10.

Dalen, A.V, C.D. Vreese, and E. Albæk. 2015. "Economic News Through the Magnifying Glass: How the Media Cover Economic Boom and Bust."

Journalism Studies.

Dalrymple, W. 2003. City of Djinns: A Year in Delhi. Penguin; Graham-Harrison, E. 2009. "China's Last Eunuch Spills Sex Secrets." Reuters; Serarcangeli, C., and G. Rispoli. 2001. "Human Castration: Historical Notes." Medicina nei secoli 13 (2): 441–54.

Dalton, D. 2021. "Evolutionary Biology: Menopause and Concomitant Dramatic Psycho-Physical and Behavioral Changes in Women." SSRN.

Daly, M., M. Wilson, and S.J. Weghorst. 1982. "Male Sexual Jealousy." Ethology and Sociobiology 3 (1): 11–27; Wilson, M., and D. Daly. 1998. "Sexual Rivalry and Sexual Conflict:Recurring Themes in Fatal Conflicts." Theoretical Criminology 2 (3): 291–310; Harris, C.R. 2004. "The Evolution of Jealousy: Did Men and Women, Facing Different Selective Pressures, Evolve Different "Brands" of Jealousy? Recent Evidence Suggests Not." American Scientist 92 (1): 62–71.

Dam, A.V. 2018. "Less Than 1% of Rapes Lead to Felony Convictions. At Least 89% of Victims Face Emotional and Physical Consequences." Washington Post.

Damasio, A.R., T.J. Grabowski, A. Bechara, H. Damasio, L.L.B Ponto, J. Parvizi, et al. 2000. "Subcortical and Cortical Brain Activity During the Feeling of Self-Generated Emotions." Nature Neuroscience 3 (10): 1049–1056. https://www.nature.com/articles/nn1000_1049.

Damasio, A. 2001. "Fundamental Feelings." Nature 413 (6858): 781–781.

Damasio, A., and G.B. Carvalho. 2013. "The Nature of Feelings: Evolutionary and Neurobiological Origins." Nature Reviews Neuroscience 14 (2).

Damasio, A., and H. Damasio. 2015. "Exploring the Concept of Homeostasis and Considering Its Implications for Economics." Journal of Economic Behavior and Organization 1269(B).

Ibid, 125–129.

Ibid; Mukherji, P. 2017, 2018. Customer Decision-Making, Consumer Purchase Decision Process, Marketing Theory and Practice. King's College London.

Damasio, A.R. 1994. "Testing the Somatic Marker Hypothesis." In Descartes'Error: Emotion, Reason, and the Human Brain, 205–22. New York, NY: Penguin.

Damasio, A.R. 2021. The Strange Order of Things: Life, Feeling and the Making of Cultures, 12. Robinson. (Kindle version).

Darwin, C. 1859. On the Origin of Species by Means of Natural Selection. New York, NY: Appleton and Company.

Ibid; Buss, D. 2015. Evolutionary Psychology: The New Science of the Mind, 89–90. New York, NY: Taylor and Francis.

Darwin, C. 1872. "General Principles of Expression." In Literature and Philosophy in Nineteenth Century British Culture, 61–68. Routledge; Ekman, P., W.V. Friesen, M. O'sullivan, A. Chan, I. Diacoyanni-Tarlatzis,

K. Heider , and A. Tzavaras. 1987. "Universals and Cultural Differences in the Judgments of Facial Expressions of Emotion." Journal of Personality and Social Psychology 53 (4): 712.

Darwin, C. 1872. The Expression of the Emotions in Man and Animals. London: John Murray.

Ibid, 5–82.

Darwin, C.R. 1877. "A Biographical Sketch of an Infant Mind." A Quarterly Review of Psychology and Philosophy 2 (7): 285–94.

Davis, H., and S.L. Mcleod. 2003. "Why Humans Value Sensational News: An Evolutionary Perspective." Evolution and Human Behavior 24 (3): 208–16.

Dawkins, R. 1982. The Extended Phenotype. Oxford: W.H. Freeman and Co; Laith, L., and K. Zreik. 2017. "Richard Dawkins on Constraints on Natural Selection." Encyclopedia of Evolutionary Psychological Science,1–5.

Dawson, C., and S.G.B. Johnson. 2021. "Dread Aversion and Economic Preferences." University of Bath.

DBpedia. n.d. "Congruence Bias."

De Waal, F. 2021. Mom's Last Hug—Animal Emotions and What They Teach us About Ourselves.

Dean, J. 2021. "Impact Bias: Why we Overestimate our Emotional Reactions." Spring.Co.Uk.

Dean, J. 2023a. "Suggestibility of Memory in Psychology: Definition and Examples." Spring.Co.Uk.

Dean, J. 2023b. "Third-Person Effect Theory: The Media Only Influences Others." Spring.Co.Uk.

Dean, J. 2023c. "Tip-of-the-Tongue Phenomenon or Lethologica." Spring. Co.Uk.

Descartes, R. 1637. A Discourse on the Method.

Diamond, J. 2004. The Irritable Male Syndrome: Managing the Four Key Causes of Depressionand Aggression. Germany: Holtzbrinck Publishers; Holland, K., and D. Murrell, MD. 2018. "Can Men Get Periods?" Healthline; CBS. 2014. "Irritable Male Syndrome." Youtube.

Dichter, E. 1947. "Psychology in Market Research." Harvard Business Review.

Dickerson, S.S., and M.E. Kemeny. 2004. "Acute Stressors and Cortisol Responses: A Theoretical Integration and Synthesis of Laboratory Research." Psychological Bulletin 130 (3): 355; Kusev, P., H. Purser, R. Heilman, A.J. Cooke, P. Van Schaik, V. Baranova, et al. 2017. "Understanding Risky Behavior: The Influence of Cognitive, Emotional and Hormonal Factors on Decision-Making Under Risk." Frontiers in Psychology 8.

Dijksterhuis, A., and H. Aarts. 2003. "On Wildebeests and Humans: The Preferential Detection of Negative Stimuli." Psychological Science 14 (1): 14–8.

Dixon, B.J., G.M. Grimshaw, W.L. Linklater, and A.F. Dixon. 2011. "Eye-Tracking of Men's Preferences for Waist-to-Hip Ratio and Breast Size of Women." Archives of Sexual Behavior 40: 43–50; Schaefer, K., B. Fink, K. Grammer, P. Mitteroecker, P. Gunz, and F.L. Bookstein. 2006. "Female Appearance: Facial and Bodily Attractiveness as Shape." Psychology Science 48: 187–205; Buss, D. 2019. Evolutionary Psychology: The New Science of the Mind. 125, 351. Oxfordshire: Routledge.

Douglas, K.M, R.M. Sutton, and A. Cichocka. 2019. "Belief in Conspiracy Theories: Looking Beyond Gullibility." The Social Psychology of Gullibility 61–76. Routledge.

Drake, N. 2016. "Elon Musk: A Million Humans Could Live on Mars by the 2060s." Science.

Drescher J. 2015. "Out of DSM: Depathologizing Homosexuality." Behavioral Sciences 5(4): 565–75. Basel, Switzerland.

Drysdale, C., L. Keenan, and M.S. Aponte. 2021. "Devastatingly Pervasive: 1 in 3 Women Globally Experience Violence." World Health Organization.

Duarte, F. 2020. "Black Lives Matter: Do Companies Really Support the Cause?" BBC Work Life.

Duignan, B. "Dunning-Kruger Effect." Encyclopedia Britannica.

Dunning, D., D.W. Griffin, J.D. Milojkovic, and L. Ross. 1990. "The Overconfidence Effect in Social Prediction." Journal of Personality and Social Psychology 58 (4): 568.

Durante, K.M., and V. Griskevicius. 2016. "Evolution and Consumer Behavior." Current Opinion in Psychology 10: 27–32; Deloitte. 2019. "The Latest Research on how Emotions Sway Your Customers. and What They Expect you to do About It." Deloitte Digital.

Durante, K.M., N.P. Li, and M.G. Haselton. 2008. "Changes in Women's Choice of Dress Across the Ovulatory Cycle: Naturalistic and Laboratory Task-Based Evidence." Personality and Social Psychology Bulletin 34 (11): 1451–60.

Durante, K.M., V. Griskevicius, J.A. Simpson, S.A. Cantu, and N.P. Li. 2012. "Ovulation Leads Women to Perceive Sexy Cads as Good Dads." Journal of Personality and Social Psychology 103 (2): 292.

Durante, K.M., V. Griskevicius, J.P. Redden, and A.E. White. 2015. "Spending on Daughters Versus Sons in Economic Recessions." Journal of Consumer Research 42 (3): 435–457.

Durante, K.M., V. Griskevicius, S.E. Hill, C. Perilloux, and N.P. Li. 2010. "Ovulation, Female Competition, and Product Choice: Hormonal Influences on Consumer Behavior." Journal of Consumer Research 37 (6): 921–34; Durante, K M., N.P. Li, and M.G. Haselton. 2008. "Changes in Women's Choice of Dress Across the Ovulatory Cycle: Naturalistic and Laboratory Task-Based Evidence." Personality and Social Psychology Bulletin 34 (11).

1451–60; Haselton, M.G., M. Mortezaie, E.G. Pillsworth, A. Bleske-Rechek, and D.A. Frederick. 2007. "Ovulatory Shifts in Human Female Ornamentation: Near Ovulation, Women Dress to Impress." Hormones and Behavior 51 (1): 40–45; Röder, S., G. Brewer, and B. Fink. 2009. "Menstrual Cycle Shifts in Women's Self-Perception and Motivation: A Daily Report Method." Personality and Individual Differences 47 (6): 616–19; Saad, G, and E. Stenstrom. 2012. "Calories, Beauty, and Ovulation: The Effects of the Menstrual Cycle on Food and Appearance–Related Consumption." Journal of Consumer Psychology 22 (1): 102–13.

Durante, K.M., V. Griskevicius, S.E. Hill, C. Perilloux, and N.P. Li. 2010. "Ovulation, Female Competition, and Product Choice: Hormonal Influences on Consumer Behavior." Journal of Consumer Research 37 (6): 921–34; Durante, K.M., V. Griskevicius, S.M. Cantú, J.A. Simpson. 2014. "Money, Status, and the Ovulatory Cycle." Journal of Marketing Research 51 (1): 27–39; Buss, D. 2019. Evolutionary Psychology: The New Science of the Mind. Oxfordshire: Routledge.

Durante, K.M., V. Griskevicius, S.E. Hill, C. Perilloux, and N.P. Li. 2011. "Ovulation, Female Competition, and Product Choice: Hormonal Influences on Consumer Behavior." Journal of Consumer Research 37 (6): 921–34.

Ibid; Durante, K.M., N.P. Li, and M.G. Haselton. 2008. "Changes in Women's Choice of Dress Across the Ovulatory Cycle: Naturalistic and Laboratory Task-Based Evidence." Personality and Social Psychology Bulletin 34 (11): 1451–1460; Haselton, M.G., M. Mortezaie, E.G. Pillsworth, A. Bleske-Rechek, and D.A. Frederick. 2007. "Ovulatory Shifts in Human Female Ornamentation: Near Ovulation, Women Dress to Impress." Hormones and Behavior 51 (1): 40–45; Roder, S., G. Brewer, and B. Fink. 2009. "Menstrual Cycle Shifts in Women's Self-Perception and Motivation: A Daily Report Method." Personality and Individual Differences 47, 616–19; Saad, G., and E. Stenstrom. 2012. "Calories, Beauty, and Ovulation: The Effects of the Menstrual Cycle on Food and Appearance-Related Consumption." Journal of Consumer Psychology 22 (1): 102–13.

Durante, K.M., V. Griskevicius, S.M. Cantu, and J.A. Simpson. 2014. "Money, Status, and the Ovulatory Cycle." Journal of Marketing Research 51 (1): 27–39.

EC Europa. 2018. "Tertiary Education Statistics." Eurostat—Statistics Explained.

Echeverri, P., and P. Skålén. 2011. "Co-Creation and Co-Destruction: A Practice-Theory Based Study of Interactive Value Formation." Marketing Theory 11 (3): 351–73.

Econowmics. n.d. "The Cheerleader Effect."

Edlund, J.E., and B.J. Sagarin. 2017. "Sex Differences in Jealousy: A 25-Year Retrospective." In Advances in Experimental Social Psychology, 259–302;

Buss, D. 2019. Evolutionary Psychology: The New Science of the Mind. Oxfordshire: Routledge.

Edwards, F., H. Lee, and M. Esposito. 2019. "Risk of Being Killed by Police use of Force in the United States by Age, Race-Ethnicity, and Sex." Proceedings of the National Academy of Sciences 116 (34): 16793–8.

Effectiviology. n.d. "The Egocentric Bias: Why It's Hard to see Things From a Different Perspective."

Effectiviology. n.d. "The Just-World Hypothesis: Believing That Everyone Gets What They Deserve."

Effectiviology. n.d. "The Rhyme-as-Reason Effect: Why Rhyming Makes Messages More Persuasive."

Effectiviology. n.d. "The Verbatim Effect: People Remember Gist Better Than Details."

Eichhorn, C. 2020. "Social Cryptomnesia—An Argument for Change." V—Das Studimagazin.

Einhorn, H.J., and R.M. Hogarth. 1978. "Confidence in Judgment: Persistence of the Illusion of Validity." Psychological Review 85 (5): 395.

Eisenegger, C., J. Haushofer, and E. Fehr. 2011. "The Role of Testosterone in Social Interaction." Trends in Cognitive Sciences 15 (6): 263–71.

Ekman, P. 1992. "Are There Basic Emotions?" 550.

Elkington, J. 2018. "25 Years ago I Coined the Phrase 'Triple Bottom Line.' Here's Why It's Time to Rethink It." Harvard Business Review; Kraaijenbrink, J. 2019. "What the 3PS of the Triple Bottom Line Really Mean." Forbes.

Elliott, L. 2022. "History of the Environmental Movement." Encyclopædia Britannica.

Ely, J. 2021. "Now Nurses Vote to Back Strike: Majority say They Are in Favour of Industrial Action Over No10's 'Unacceptable' 3% NHS Pandemic pay Rise." Daily Mail Online.

Ember, C.R. 1978. "Myths About Hunter-Gatherers." Ethnology 17 (4): 439–48.

Encyclopedia Britannica. 2022. "Roe V. Wade."

Encyclopedia Britannica. n.d. "Von Restorff Effect."

Endocrine Society. n.d. "Your Health and Hormones."

Engelhaupt, E. 2018. 'Aroused' Recounts the Fascinating History of Hormones. (Epstein, R. H. 2018. Aroused: The History of Hormones and How They Control Just About Everything).

Ensor, T.M., T.D. Bancroft, and W.E. Hockley. 2019. "Listening to the Picture-Superiority Effect." Journal of Experimental Psychology 66 (2): 134–53.

Epley, N., A. Waytz, and J.T. Cacioppo. 2007. "On Seeing Human: A Three-Factor Theory of Anthropomorphism." Psychological Review 114 (4): 864–86.

Epstein, R.H. 2011. Get Me Out: A History of Childbirth From the Garden of Eden to the Sperm Bank. W.W. Norton

Epstein, R.H. 2018. "Stop Calling Women Hormonal." Sunday Opinion.

Espach, A. 2017. "What It Really Means When you call a Woman 'Hysterical.'" Vogue; Gilman, S.L., H. King, R. Porter, G.S. Rousseau and E. Showalter. 1993. "Hysteria Beyond Freud." Univ of California Press.

Essay. 1958 (Originally Published in 1669). Pascal's Pensées, 79–80. New York, NY.

Estrada-Jiménez, J., J. Parra-Arnau, A. Rodríguez-Hoyos, and J. Forné. 2017. "Online Advertising: Analysis of Privacy Threats and Protection Approaches." Computer Communications 100: 32–51.

Ibid; Jordaan, Y., and G. Van Heerden. 2017. "Online Privacy-Related Predictors of Facebook Usage Intensity." Computers in Human Behavior 70: 90–6.

Etcoff, N. 2011. Survival of the Prettiest: The Science of Beauty. Anchor.

Etcoff, N.L., S. Stock, L.E. Haley, S.A. Vickeryand, and D.M. House. 2011. "Cosmetics as a Feature of the Extended Human Phenotype: Modulation of the Perception of Biologically Important Facial Signals." Plos One 6 (10): E25656.

Evans, K. 2019. "What Kind of Emotions do Animals Feel?" The Greater Good Science Center at the University of California, Berkeley.

Evans, S., N. Neave, and D. Wakelin. 2006. "Relationships Between Vocal Characteristics and Body Size and Shape in Human Males: An Evolutionary Explanation for a Deep Male Voice." Biological Psychology 72 (2):160–3; Feinberg, D.R., B.C. Jones, A.C. Little, D.M. Burt, and D.I. Perrett. 2005. "Manipulations of Fundamental and Formant Frequencies Influence the Attractiveness of Human Male Voices." Animal Behavior 69 (3): 561–8; D.A. Puts. 2005. "Mating Context and Menstrual Phase Affect Women's Preferences for Male Voice Pitch." Evolution and Human Behavior 26 (5): 388–97; Grammer, K., and R. Thornhill. 1994. "Human Facial Attractiveness and Sexual Selection: The Roles of Averageness and Symmetry." Journal of Comparative Psychology 108 (3): 233–42; Shackelford, T.K., and R.J. Larsen. 1997. "Facial Asymmetry as an Indicator of Psychological, Emotional, and Physiological Distress." Journal of Personality and Social Psychology 72 (2): 456–66; Thornhill, R, and A.P. Møller. 1997. "Developmental Stability, Disease and Medicine." Biological Reviews 72 (4): 497–548; Rhodes, G. 2006. "The Evolutionary Psychology of Facial Beauty." Annual Review of Psychology 57: 199–226; Feinberg, D.R., L.M. Debruine, L.M., Jones, B.C., and Little, A.C. 2008. "Correlated Preferences for Men's Facial and Vocal Masculinity." Evolution and Human Behavior 29 (4): 233–41; Haselton, M.G., and S. Gangestad. 2006. "Conditional Expression of Women's

Desires and Men's Mate Guarding Across the Ovulatory Cycle." Hormones and Behavior 49 (4): 509–518; Haselton, M.G., and G.F. Miller. 2006. "Women's Fertility Across the Cycle Increases the Short-Term Attractiveness of Creative Intelligence." Human Nature 17 (1): 50–73; Gangestad, S.W., R. Thornhill, and C.E. Garver. 2002. "Changes in Women's Sexual Interests and Their Partner's Mate-Retention Tactics Across the Menstrual Cycle: Evidence for Shifting Conflicts of Interest." Proceedings of the Royal Society of London. Series B: Biological Sciences 269 (1494): 975–82; Gangestad, S.W., J.A. Simpson, A.J. Cousins, C.E. Garver-Apgar, and P.E. Christensen. 2004. "Women's Preferences for Male Behavioral Displays Change Across the Menstrual Cycle." Psychological Science 15 (3): 203–07; Johnston, V.S., R. Hagel, M. Franklin, B. Fink, and K. Grammer. 2001. "Male Facial Attractiveness: Evidence for Hormone-Mediated Adaptive Design." Evolution and Human Behavior 22 (4): 251–67; Penton-Voak, I.S., D.I. Perrett, D.L. Castles, T. Kobayashi, D.M. Burt, L.K. Murray, and R. Minamisawa. 1999. "Menstrual Cycle Alters Face Preference." Nature 399 (6738): 741–74; Puts, D.A. 2005. "Mating Context and Menstrual Phase Affect Women's Preferences for Male Voice Pitch." Evolution and Human Behavior 26 (5): 388–97; Durante, K.M., V. Griskevicius, J.A. Simpson, S.M. Cantú, and N.P. Li. 2012. "Ovulation Leads Women to Perceive Sexy Cads as Good Dads." Journal of Personality and Social Psychology 103 (2): 292.

Everett, J.A.C., N.S. Faber, and M. Crockett. 2015. "Preferences and Beliefs in Ingroup Favoritism." Frontiers in Behavioral Neuroscience 9.

Fandom Lifestyle Community. n.d. "Irrational Escalation." Psychology Wiki.

Fandom Lifestyle Community. n.d. "Pseudocertainty Effect." Psychology Wiki.

Farnsworth, B. 2020. "What Is Selection Bias? (And How to Defeat It)." Imotions.Com.

Farrelly, D., R. Owens, H.R. Elliott, H.R. Walden, and M.A. Wetherell. 2015. "The Effects of Being in a "New Relationship" on Levels of Testosterone in Men." Evolutionary Psychology 13 (1). https://journals.sagepub.com/doi/full/10.1177/147470491501300116; Buss, D. 2019. Evolutionary Psychology: The New Science of the Mind 360: 154, 384–84. Oxfordshire: Routledge.

FBI. 2017. "2017 Crime in the United States: Rape."

Featherstone, L. 2018. "Talk Is Cheap: The Myth of the Focus Group." The Guardian.

Feldman, R., R. Magori-Cohen, G. Galili, M. Singer, and Y. Louzoun. 2011. "Mother and Infant Coordinate Heart Rhythms Through Episodes of Interaction Synchrony." Infant Behavior and Development 34 (4): 569–77.

Ferreira, A., K.C. Von Schönfeld, W. Tan, and E. Papa. 2020. "Maladaptive Planning and the Pro-Innovation Bias: Considering the Case of Automated Vehicles." Urban Science 4 (3): 41.

Fields, C. 2014. "Motion, Identity and the Bias Toward Agency." Frontiers in Human Neuroscience 8.

Fink, B., J.T. Manning, and N. Neave. 2006. "The 2nd-4th Digit Ratio (2D:4D) and Neck Circumference: Implications for Risk Factors in Coronary Heart Disease." International Journal of Obesity 30 (4): 711–14.

Fink, D. 2003. "Taxonomy of Significant Learning Experiences."

Fink, D. 2013. Creating Significant Learning Experiences. Jossey-Bass.

Ibid, 82–92.

Finlay, S. 2012. Credit Scoring, Response Modeling, and Insurance Rating: Apractical Guide to Forecasting Consumer Behavior. Springer.

Fishbein, M., and S. Middlestadt. 1995. "Noncognitive Effects on Attitude Formation and Change: Fact or Artifact?" Journal of Consumer Psychology 4(2): 181–202; Pham, M. T. 2004. "The Logic of Feeling." Journal of Consumer Psychology 14 (4): 360–69.

Fisher, M. 2004. "Female Intrasexual Competition Decreases Female Facial Attractiveness." Proceedings of The Royal Society of London, B, 271: S283–S285.

Fleischman, D.S. 2018. "Women's Disgust Adaptations." In Evolutionary Perspectives on Human Sexual Psychology and Behavior. 277–96. New York, NY: Springer, 2014.

Fonseca Del Pozo, F.J., J.V. Alonso, M.V. Álvarez, S. Orr, and F.J.L. Cantarero. 2017. "Physical Fitness as an Indicator of Health Status and Its Relationship to Academic Performance During the Prepubertal Period." Health Promotion Perspectives 7 (4): 197–204.

Ford, W.C., K. North, H. Taylor, A. Farrow, M.G. Hull, and J. Golding. 2000. "Increasing Paternal Age Is Associated With Delayed Conception in a Large Population of Fertile Couples: Evidence for Declining Fecundity in Older Men. The ALSPAC Study Team (Avon Longitudinal Study of Pregnancy and Childhood)." Human Reproduction 15 (8): 1703–8.

Forer, B.R. 1949. "The Fallacy of Personal Validation: A Classroom Demonstration of Gullibility." Journal of Abnormal Psychology 44: 118–21; Psychology Concepts. 2020. "Cognition Subjective Validation."

Fox, G.R., J. Kaplan, H. Damasio, and A. Damasio. "Neural Correlates of Gratitude." Frontiers in Psychology 6: 151058. https://www.frontiersin.org/journals/psychology/articles/10.3389/fpsyg.2015.01491/full?source=post_page.

Francis, D.D., L.J. Young, M.J. Meaney, and T.R. Insel. 2002. "Naturally Occurring Differences in Maternal Care Are Associated With the Expression of Oxytocin and Vasopressin (V1a) Receptors: Gender Differences." Journal of Neuroendocrinology 14 (5): 349–53; Durante, K,M., V. Griskevicius, S.E. Hill, C. Perilloux, and N.P. Li. 2011. "Ovulation, Female Competition, and

Product Choice: Hormonal Influences on Consumer Behavior." Journal of Consumer Research 37 (6): 921–34.

Freeman, E.W., M.D. Sammel, H. Lin, C.R. Gracia, and S. Kapoor. 2008. "Symptoms in the Menopausal Transition: Hormone and Behavioral Correlates." Obstetrics & Gynecology 111 (1): 127–136.

Freitas, C.C.M.D, and F.D.L. Osório. 2022. "Moral Judgment and Hormones: A Systematic Literature Review." PLOS ONE 17 (4).

Freud, A. 1947. "Aggression in Relation to Emotional Development: Normal and Pathological." Royal Society of Medicine. Section of Psychiatry, 37.

Freud, S. 1920. "A General Introduction to Psychoanalysis." The Journal of Nervous and Mental Disease 52 (6): 548–49.

Freud, S. 1920. A General Introduction to Psychoanalysis, 01. New York, NY: Horace Liveright, Inc.

Freud, S. 1930. Civilization and Its Discontents.

Fritscher, L. 2022. "Coping With the Fear of New Things." Very Well Mind.

Fs.Blog. "Mental Model: Bias From Conjunction Fallacy." Farnam Street Media Inc.

Furr, N., K. Nel, and R.T. Zoega. 2019. "Neuroscience Is Going to Change how Businesses Understand Their Customers." Harvard Business Review.

Gancz, D., and L. Gilboa. 2013. "Hormonal Control of Stem Cell Systems." Annual Review of Cell and Developmental Biology 29: 137–62.

Garamvolgyi, F. 2022. "Why US Women Are Deleting Their Period Tracking Apps." The Guardian.

Garcia, S.M., H. Song, and A. Tesser. 2010. "Tainted Recommendations: The Social Comparison Bias." Organizational Behavior and Human Decision Processes 113 (2): 97–101.

Gardner, H.E. 2011. Frames of Mind: The Theory of Multiple Intelligences. Basic Books.

Garza, A. 2022. "Black Lives Matter: A Herstory of the #Blacklivesmatter Movement by Alicia Garza." School of Medicine Anti-Racist Coalition: Stanford University.

Gayle, D. 2022. "Just Stop oil Activists Throw Soup at Van Gogh's Sunflowers." The Guardian.

Gazit, M. 2020. "The Fourth Generation of AI Is Here, and It's Called 'Artificial Intuition.'" TNW—Financial Times.

Geier, A.B., P. Rozin, and G. Doros. 2006. "Unit Bias: A New Heuristic That Helps Explain the Effect of Portion Size on Food Intake." Psychological Science 17 (6): 521–25.

George, B., and S.K. Pandey. 2017. "We Know the Yin-but Where Is the Yang? Toward a Balanced Approach on Common Source Bias in Public Administration Scholarship." Review of Public Personnel Administration 37 (2): 245–70.

Georgetown University. 2021. "Women Increasingly Outnumber Men at US Colleges, but Why?" Georgetown University.

Gerlach, A. 2021. "Humor Effect: The Benefits of Using Humor." Neurofied.

Gilbert, B. 2019. "Jeff Bezos Just Sent his Annual Letter to Amazon Shareholders—Read It Here." Business Insider Nederland.

Ibid; Martin, A. 2021. "Jeff Bezos Steps Down as Amazon CEO Today—but how much Power Is he Really Giving up?" Sky News.

Gillis, J.S. 1982. Too Tall, Too Small. Champaign, Ill.: Institute For Personality and Ability Testing; Stulp, G., A.P. Buunk and T.V. Pollet. 2012. "High and Mighty: Height Increases Authority in Professional Refereeing." Evolutionary Psychology 10(3): 588–598; Lukaszewski, A.W., Z.L. Simmons, C. Anderson, and J.R. Roney. 2016. "The Role of Physical Formidability in Human Social Status Allocation." Journal of Personality and Social Psychology 110 (3): 385–406.

Gillis, J.S. 1982. Too Tall, Too Small. Champaign, Ill.: Institute for Personality and Ability Testing.

Gilovich, T., K. Savitsky, and V.H. Medvec. 1998. "The Illusion of Transparency: Biased Assessments of Others' Ability to Read one's Emotional States." Journal of Personality and Social Psychology 75 (2): 332–46.

Globo Notícias. 2013. "Brasil Tem O Maior Número De Domésticas Do Mundo, Diz Oit." G1 Globo.

Gluckman, P.D., F.M. Low, T. Buklijas., M.A. Hanson., and A.S. Beedle. 2011. "How Evolutionary Principles Improve the Understanding of Human Health and Disease." Evolutionary Applications 4 (2): 249–63.

Gomes, N., S. Silva, F. Silva. and S.C. Soares. 2017. "Beware the Serpent: The Advantage of Ecologically-Relevant Stimuli in Accessing Visual Awareness." Evolution and Human Behavior 38 (2): 227–34; Marks, I.M. 1987. Fears, Phobias, and Rituals: Panic, Anxiety, and Their Disorders. Oxford University Press, USA; Buss, D. 2019. Evolutionary Psychology: The New Science of the Mind. Oxfordshire: Routledge.

Gorman, M. 2016. "Female U.S. Presidential Contenders Before Hillary Clinton in 2016." Newsweek; Greenspan, J. 2013. "9 Things You Should Know About Victoria Woodhull." History.Com.

Gramlich, J. 2019. "How the Attitudes of West and East Germans Compare, 30 Years After the Fall of the Berlin Wall." Pew Research Center.

Grammer, K. 1992. "Variations on a Theme: Age Dependent Mate Selection in Humans." Behavioral and Brain Sciences 15 (1): 100–102; Buss, D. 2019. Evolutionary Psychology: The New Science of the Mind. Oxfordshire: Routledge.

Grammer, K., and R. Thornhill. 1994. "Human (Homo Sapiens) Facial Attractiveness and Sexual Selection: The Role of Symmetry and Averageness." Journal of Comparative Psychology 108 (3): 233; Shackelford, T.K., and R.J.

Larsen. 1997. "Facial Asymmetry as an Indicator of Psychological, Emotional, and Physiological Distress." Journal of Personality and Social Psychology 72 (2): 456; Gangestad, S.W., and R. Thornhill. 1997. "The Evolutionary Psychology of Extrapair Sex: The Role of Fluctuating Asymmetry." Evolution and Human Behavior 18 (2): 69–88; Møller, A.P., and R. Thornhill. 1998. "Bilateral Symmetry and Sexual Selection: A Meta-Analysis." The American Naturalist 151 (2): 174–92; Buss, D. 2019. Evolutionary Psychology: The New Science of the Mind, 294. Oxfordshire: Routledge.

Gray, A.W., and L.G. Boothroyd. 2012. "Female Facial Appearance and Health." Evolutionary Psychology 10 (1) 66–77.

Greene, J.D., R.B. Sommerville, L. Nystrom, J.M. Darley, and J.D. Cohen. 2001. "An Fmri Investigation of Emotional Engagement in Moral Judgment." Science 293 (5537): 2105–08.

Greenwald, A.G., and L.H. Krieger. 2006. "Implicit Bias: Scientific Foundations." California Law Review 94 (4): 945–67.

Griskevicius, V, and D.T. Kenrick. 2013. "Fundamental Motives: How Evolutionary Needs Influence Consumer Behavior." Journal of Consumer Psychology 23 (3): 372–86.

Griskevicius, V., J.M. Tybur, and B. Van Den Bergh. 2010. "Going Green to Be Seen: Status, Reputation, and Conspicuous Conservation." Journal of Personality and Social Psychology 98 (3): 392–404.

Ibid, 392.

Griskevicius, V., J.M. Tybur, J.M. Sundie, R.B. Cialdini, G.F. Miller, and D.T. Kenrick. 2007. "Blatant Benevolence and Conspicuous Consumption: When Romantic Motives Elicit Strategic Costly Signals." Journal of Personality and Social Psychology 93 (1): 85.

Grunspan, D.Z, R.M. Nesse, E. Barnes, and S.E. Brownell. 2017. "Core Principles of Evolutionary Medicine." Evolution, Medicine, and Public Health (1): 13–23.

Gunther, A.C., and P. Mundy. 1993. "Biased Optimism and the Third-Person Effect." Journalism Quarterly 70 (1): 58–67.

Gupta, V.K., C. Saini, M. Oberoi, G. Kalra, and I. Nasir Md. 2020. "Semmelweis Reflex: An age-old Prejudice." World Neurosurgery 136: E119–25.

Gyekye, S.A., and S. Salminen. 2006. "The Self-Defensive Attribution Hypothesis in the Work Environment: Co-Workers' Perspectives." Safety Science 44 (2): 157–68.

Haas, B. 2022. "9 Young Activists who Tackled Global Issues." Dw.Com.

Haidt, J. 2001. "The Emotional dog and Its Rational Tail: A Social Intuitionist Approach to Moral Judgment." Psychological Review 108 (4): 814–34; Haidt, J., and F. Bjorklund. 2007. "Social Intuitionists Answer Six Questions About Morality." Moral Psychology.

Hamill, R., T. Wilson, and R. Nisbett. 1980. "Insensitivity to Sample Bias: Generalizing From Atypical Cases." Journal of Personality and Social Psychology 39: 578–89.

Hamilton, D.L., and T.L. Rose. 1980. "Illusory Correlation and the Maintenance of Stereotypic Beliefs." Journal of Personality and Social Psychology 39 (5): 832.

Hamilton, W.D. 1964. "The Genetic Evolution of Social Behavior II." Journal of Theoretical Biology 7 (1): 17–52.

Hamilton, W.D. 1964. "The Genetical Evolution of Social Behavior I and II." Journal of Theoretical Biology 7: 1–52; Buss, D. 2019. Evolutionary Psychology: The New Science of the Mind. Oxfordshire: Routledge.

Hammad, A.M., R. Hamed, W. Al-Qerem, A. Bandar, and F.S. Hall. 2021. "Optimism Bias, Pessimism Bias, Magical Beliefs, and Conspiracy Theory Beliefs Related to COVID-19 Among the Jordanian Population." American Journal of Tropical Medicine and Hygiene 104 (5): 1661–71.

Hampson, S.E. 1983. "Trait Ascription and Depth of Acquaintance: The Preference for Traits in Personality Descriptions and Its Relation to Target Familiarity." Journal of Research in Personality 17 (4): 398–411.

Han, E., and J. O'Mahoney. 2014. "British Colonialism and the Criminalization of Homosexuality." Cambridge Review of International Affairs 27 (2): 268–88.

Hanssens, D.M., and K.H. Pauwels. 2016. "Demonstrating the Value of Marketing." Journal of Marketing 80 (6): 173–90.

Hare, R.D. 1999. Without Conscience: The Disturbing World of the Psychopaths Among us. Guilford Press.

Hare, R.D. 2002. "The Predators Among us." Keynote Address. Canadian Police Association Annual General Meeting, St. John's, Newfoundland and Labrador; Babiak, P., C.S. Neumann, and R.D. Hare. 2010. "Corporate Psychopathy: Talking the Walk." Behavioral Sciences and the Law 28 (2): 174–5.

Haring, K.S., K. Watanabe, M. Velonaki, C.C. Tossell, and V. Finomore. 2018. "FFAB-The Form Function Attribution Bias in Human-Robot Interaction." IEEE Transactions on Cognitive and Developmental Systems 10 (4): 843–51.

Harrell, E. 2019. "Neuromarketing: What you Need to Know." Harvard Business Review.

Ibid; Farnsworth, B. 2020. "Using Respiration in Your Research." Imotions; Smith, I., J. Mackay, N. Fahrid, and D. Krucheck. 2011. "Respiratory Rate Measurement: A Comparison of Methods." British Journal of Healthcare Assistants 5 (1): 18–23; Wilson, J. 2018. "What Is Facial EMG and how Does It Work?" Imotions.

Harris, K.J., K.M. Kacmar, and S. Zivnuska. 2007. "An Investigation of Abusive Supervision as a Predictor of Performance and the Meaning of Work as a Moderator of the Relationship." The Leadership Quarterly 18 (3): 252–63.

Harris, M., and B. Tayler. 2019. "Don't Let Metrics Undermine Your Business." Harvard Business Review.

Harrison, D. 2020. "Psychopaths: Charming Cheaters." Iflow Psychology.

Harron, M. 2000. American Psycho. Lions Gate Films.

Hart, M. 2021. "Hyperbolic Discounting: How To Use This Psychological Bias To Sell More." Hubspot.Com.

Hartung, J. 1987. "Deceiving Down: Conjectures on the Management of Subordinate Status. Self-Deception: An Adaptive Mechanism?" In Self-deception: An Adaptive Mechanism?" edited by J. Lockart, and D.L. Paulhus, 170–185. Englewood Cliffs,New Jersey, NJ: Prentice-Hall.

Haselton, M. G. 2003. "The Sexual Overperception Bias: Evidence of a Systematic Bias in Men From a Survey of Naturally Occurring Events." Journal of Research in Personality 37 (1): 34–47.

Haselton, M.G., and M. Buss. 2000. "Error Management Theory: A New Perspective on Biases in Cross-Sex Mind Reading." Journal of Personality and Social Psychology 78: 81–91.

Ibid, 81–91; Haselton, M.G., and D. Nettle. 2006. "The Paranoid Optimist: An Integrative Evolutionary Model of Cognitive Biases." Personality and Social Psychology Review 10: 47–66.

Hassan, M.A., and S.R. Killick. 2003. "Effect of Male Age on Fertility: Evidence for the Decline in Male Fertility With Increasing Age." Fertility and Sterility 79 (3): 1520–7.

He, L., W. Han, and Z. Shi . 2021. "Self-Reference Effect Induced by Self-Cues Presented During Retrieval." Frontiers in Psychology 12.

Healy, P. 2017. "The Fundamental Attribution Error: What It Is and How to Avoid It." Harvard Business School.

Heidrick and Struggles. 2022. "Where Are The Women Ceos?" Heidrick and Struggles International, Inc.

Hendel, H.J. 2020. "Disgust: A Natural Emotional Response to Abuse." NAMI. National Alliance on Mental Illness.

Hennighausen, C., L. Hudders, B.P. Lange, and H. Fink. 2016. "What If the Rival Drives a Porsche? Luxury Car Spending as a Costly Signal in Male Intrasexual Competition." Evolutionary Psychology 14 (4).

Herndon, J. 2018. "What Is a Self-Serving Bias and What Are Some Examples of It?" Healthline.

Herrity, J. 2023. "Average Salary in the US." Indeed.

Hess, A.J. 2019. "It Costs $74,570 a Year to go to Stanford-but Here's how Much Students Actually Pay." CNBC.

Hester, J.B., and R. Gibson. 2003. "The Economy and Second-Level Agenda Setting: A Time-Series Analysis of Economic News and Public Opinion About the Economy." Journalism and Mass Communication Quarterly 80 (1): 73–90.

Hewstone, M. 1990. "The 'Ultimate Attribution Error'? a Review of the Literature on Intergroup Causal Attribution." European Journal of Social Psychology 20 (4): 311–35.

Hildebrandt, B.A., S.E. Racine, P.K. Keel, S.A. Burt, M. Neale, S. Boker, C.L. Sisk, et al. 2015. "The Effects of Ovarian Hormones and Emotional Eating on Changes in Weight Preoccupation Across the Menstrual Cycle." International Journal of Eating Disorders 48 (5): 477–86; Franklin, T.R., K. Jagannathan, R.R. Wetherill, B. Johnson, S. Kelly, J. Langguth, J. Mumma, et al. 2015. "Influence of Menstrual Cycle Phase on Neural and Craving Responses to Appetitive Smoking Cues in Naturally Cycling Females." Nicotine & Tobacco Research 17 (4): 390–97; Andersen, C.H. 2018. "6 Weird Period Symptoms You've Never Heard of Before."

Hill, A.K., J. Hunt, L.L.M. Welling, R.A. Cárdenas, M.A. Rotella, J.R. Wheatley, et al. 2013. Quantifying the Strength and Form of Sexual Selection on Men's Traits." Evolution and Human Behavior 34(5): 334–41.

Hill, S.E., C.D. Rodeheffer, V. Griskevicis, K. Durante, and A.E. White. 2012. "Boosting Beauty in an Economic Decline: Mating, Spending, and the Lipstick Effect."Journal of Personality and Social Psychology 103 (2): 275–291.

Hirsch, F. 1976. Social Limits to Growth. Harvard University Press; Saad, G., and J.G. Vongas. 2009. "The Effect of Conspicuous Consumption on Men's Testosterone Levels." Organizational Behavior and Human Decision Processes 110 (2): 80–92.

History.com. 2009. "Plato."

History.com. 2018 "Babylon: Hanging Gardens & Tower of Babel."

Hoffman, M. 2022. "Estrogen and Women's Emotions." Webmd.

Hofstede, G. 1979. "Value Systems in Forty Countries: Interpretation, Validation, and Consequences for Theory." Cross-Cultural Contributions to Psychology, edited by L.H. Eckensberger, W.J. Lonner, and Y.H. Poortinga, pp. 398–407. https://link.springer.com/article/10.1007/BF00881307.

Holland and Hart LLP, and K. Broda-Bahm. 2019. "Understand Anti-Corporate Bias: The Extent of the Bias and the Effect of Familiarity." JD Supra.

Holland, E. 2017. "How Well Do You Really Know Your Acquaintances? The Illusion of Asymmetric Insight." Cogblog—A Cognitive Psychology Blog.

Holland, K., and D.M.D. Murrell. 2018. "Can Men Get Periods?" Healthline.

Hoog, N.D., and P. Verboon. 2019. "Is the News Making us Unhappy? The Influence of Daily News Exposure on Emotional States." British Journal of

Psychology 111 (2): 157–73.

Hoorens, V. 1993. "Self-Enhancement and Superiority Biases in Social Comparison." European Review of Social Psychology 4 (1): 113–39.

Hsee, C.K., and J. Zhang. 2004. "Distinction Bias: Misprediction and Mischoice due to Joint Evaluation." Journal of Personality and Social Psychology 86 (5): 680–95.

Huber, K. 2015. "Everybody's a Little Bit Sexist: A Re-Evaluation of Aristotle's and Plato's Philosophies on Women." Department of History: Lake Forest College.

Hunter, K.D. 2018. "Company Familiarity Moderates Anti-Corporate Bias and Jurors' Compensatory Award Amounts." Fielding Graduate University Theses, Pro Quest.

IIHS. 2022. "Fatality Facts 2021 Males and Females." Insurance Institute for Highway Safety.

Immordino-Yang, M.H., and A. Damasio. 2007. "We Feel, Therefore We Learn: The Relevance of Affective and Social Neuroscience to Education." Mind, Brain, and Education 1 (1): 3–10.

Imotions. 2019. Human Behavior Research—Combined Methods for Measuring Human Behavior, 3–11.

Imperial War Museums. 2022. "How Alan Turing Cracked the Enigma Code." Imperial War Museums.

Imperial War Museums. 2022. "How Europe Went to War in 1939."

Ingle, S. 2020. "Trans Women Retain 12% Edge in Tests two Years After Transitioning." The Guardian.

Inman, M. 2023. "Hindsight Bias." Encyclopedia Britannica.

Interbrand. 2022. "Best Global Brands How Iconic Brands Lead Across Arenas."

International Society of Aesthetic Plastic Surgery (ISAPS). "2020 Statistics at a Glance. Total Procedures Performed Worldwide."

IResearchNet. 2016. "False Uniqueness Bias."

Jager, W. 2000. "Modeling Consumer Behavior." [Thesis Fully Internal (DIV), University of Groningen]. S.N.

James, W. 1890. The Principles of Psychology. 1 vol. New York, NY: Henry Holt and Co; Gilbert, J. 1962. "William James in Retrospect: 1962." Journal of Humanistic Psychology 2 (1): 90–95; Buss, D. 2019. Evolutionary Psychology: The New Science of the Mind. Oxfordshire: Routledge; Kish-Gephart, J.J., J.R. Detert, L.K. Treviño, and A. Edmondson. 2009. "Silenced by Fear: The Nature, Sources, and Consequences of Fear at Work." Research in Organizational Behavior 29: 163–93.

Janiszewski, C. 1993. "Preattentive Mere Exposure Effects." Journal of Consumer Research 20 (3): 376–92.

Jeevanandam, S., and P.K. Muthu. 2016. "2D:4D Ratio and Its Implications in Medicine." *Journal of Clinical and Diagnostic Research for Doctors* 10 (12): Cm01–3.

Ibid, Cm01–3; Klimek, M., A. Galbarczyk, I. Nenko, and G. Jasienska. 2016. "Women With a More Feminine Digit Ratio (2D:4D) Have Higher Reproductive Success." *American Journal of Biological Anthropology* 160 (3): 549–53; Sitek, A., I. Rosset, M. Kobus, P. Pruszkowska-Przybylska, and E. Żądzińska. 2022. "Maternal Age and Behavior During Pregnancy Affect the 2D:4D Digit Ratio in Polish Children Aged 6–13 Years." *Biology* 11 (9): 1286.

Johnson, D.D. 2022. *Strategic Instincts: The Adaptive Advantages of Cognitive Biases in International Politics*. Princeton: Princeton University Press; Sheffield, H. 2015. "Four Cognitive Biases Which Mean You Can't Trust Your Instincts." *The Independent*.

Johnson, E., and F. Murray. 2020. "What a Crisis Teaches us About Innovation." *MIT Sloan Management Review* 62 (2).

Johnson, E.O., and L. Schultz. 2005. "Forward Telescoping Bias in Reported Age of Onset: An Example From Cigarette Smoking." *International Journal of Methods in Psychiatric Research* 14 (3): 119–29.

Johnston, M., M. James, and P. Rathburn. 2022. "7 Companies Owned by Google (Alphabet)." *Investopedia*.

Jones, A.L, R. Russell, and R. Ward. 2015. "Cosmetics Alter Biologically-Based Factors of Beauty: Evidence From Facial Contrast." *Evolutionary Psychology* 13 (1): 210–29; Buss, D. 2019. *Evolutionary Psychology: The New Science of the Mind*. Oxfordshire: Routledge.

Jones, L. 2020. "Veganism: Why Are Vegan Diets on the Rise?" *BBC News*.

Jost, J.T, and J. van der Toorn. 2012. "System Justification Theory." *Handbook of Theories of Social Psychology* 2: 313–43.

Jung, A. 2017. "The Influence of Perceived ad Relevance on Social Media Advertising: An Empirical Examination of a Mediating Role of Privacy Concern." *Computers in Human Behavior* 70: 303–9.

Junte–Se Ao Instituto Marielle Franco. 2023. "Our Actions Guidelines." *Junte-Se Ao Instituto Marielle Franco*.

Kahle, L.R., S.E. Beatty, and P. Homer. 1986. "Alternative Measurement Approaches to Consumer Values: The List of Values (LOV) and Values and Lifestyle (VALS)." Journal of Consumer Research: Journal of Consumer Research: 405–09. https://psycnet.apa.org/record/1987-17567-001. https://psycnet.apa.org/record/1987-17567-001.

Kahneman, D. 2011. *Thinking, Fast and Slow*. Macmillan.

Kahneman, D. 2011. *Thinking, Fast and Slow*. New York, NY: Farrar, Straus and Giroux.

Kahneman, D., and A. Tversky. 1979. "Prospect Theory: An Analysis of Decision Under Risk." *Econometrica* 47 (2): 263–92.

Kahneman, D., B.L. Fredrickson, C.A. Schreiber, and D.A. Redelmeier. 1993. "When More Pain Is Preferred to Less: Adding a Better End." *Psychological Science* 4 (6): 401–05.

Kahneman, D., J.L. Knetsch, and R.H. Thaler. 1990. "Experimental Tests of the Endowment Effect and the Coase Theorem." *Journal of Political Economy* 98(6): 1325–48; List, J. A., and C.F. Mason. 2011. "Are Ceos Expected Utility Maximizers?" *Journal of Econometrics* 162 (1): 114–23; Ericson, K.M.M., and A. Fuster. 2014. "The Endowment Effect." *Annual Review of Economics* 6 (1): 555–79.

Kahneman, D., J.L. Knetsch, and R.H. Thaler. 1991. "Anomalies: The Endowment Effect, Loss Aversion, and Status Quo Bias." *Journal of Economic Perspectives* 5 (1): 193–206.

Kahneman, D. 2000. "Evaluation by Moments, Past and Future". In *Choices, Values and Frames*, edited by D. Kahneman, A. Tversky, 708; Dickert, S., D. Västfjäll, J. Kleber, P. Slovic. 2015. "Scope Insensitivity: The Limits of Intuitive Valuation of Human Lives in Public Policy." *Journal of Applied Research in Memory and Cognition* 4 (3): 248–55.

Kapferer, J.N., and V. Bastien. 2012. *The Luxury Strategy: Break the Rules of Marketing to Build Luxury Brands*.

Kaplan, L. 2022. "This Women's History Month, Here's a Radical Idea: Let Women Lead." *Fortune*.

Kapri, B. "Clustering Illusion: Clusters lie in the Eye of the Beholder!" *Absolutdata*.

Karlsen, C.F. 1998. *The Devil in the Shape of a Woman: Witchcraft in Colonial New England*. W.W. Norton and Company; Pruitt, S. 2018. "5 Notable Women Hanged in the Salem Witch Trials." *History.com*; History.com Editors. 2011. "Salem Witch Trials." *History.com*; Ginzburg, C. 1996. *The Night Battles: Witchcraft and Agrarian Cults in the Sixteenth and Seventeenth Centuries*. Routledge and Kegan P; Roach, M.K. 2002. *The Salem Witch Trials*. Boulder: Taylor Trade Publishing.

Karlsson, N., G. Loewenstein, and D. Seppi. 2009. "The Ostrich Effect: Selective Attention to Information." *Journal of Risk and Uncertainty* 38: 95–115.

Karremans, J.C., W.E. Frankenhuis, and S. Arons. 2010. "Blind Men Prefer a Low Waist-to-Hip Ratio." *Evolution and Human Behavior* 31: 182–6; Buss, D. 2019. *Evolutionary Psychology: The New Science of the Mind*. Oxfordshire: Routledge.

Kean, S. 2021. "The Disappearing Spoon Podcast." *The Disappearing Spoon Podcast*; Von Deuster, C. 2006. "How Did the Castratos Sing? Historical Observations." *Wurzbg Medizinhist Mitt* 25: 133–52; The Editors of Encyclopaedia Britannica. 2023. "Farinelli."

Kelly, R.C. 2022. "What Is the Bandwagon Effect? Why People Follow the Crowd." *Investopedia*.

Kelly. D.J., P.C. Quinn, A.M. Slater, K. Lee, L. Ge, and O. Pascalis. 2007. "The Other-Race Effect Develops During Infancy: Evidence of Perceptual Narrowing." *Psychological Science* 18 (12): 1084–9.

Kennon, J. 2011. "Mental Model: Horns Effect and Halo Effect." *Joshua Kennon*.

Kenrick, D.T. 2011. *Sex, Murder, and the Meaning of Life: A Psychologist Investigates How Evolution, Cognition, and Complexity Are Revolutionizing Our View of Human Nature.* Basic Books; Otterbring, T., C. Ringler, N.J. Sirianni, and A. Gustafsson. 2018. "The Abercrombie & Fitch Effect: The Impact of Physical Dominance on Male Customers' Status-Signaling Consumption." *Journal of Marketing Research* 55 (1): 69–79.

Kenton, W. 2023. "Gambler's Fallacy: Overview and Examples." *Investopedia*.

Kenyon, C., J. Chang, E. Gensch, A. Rudner, and R. Tabtiang. 1993. "A C. Elegans Mutant That Lives Twice as Long as Wild Type." *Nature* 366 (6454): 461–64; UPMC. 2021. "UPMC Life Changing Medicine." *UPMC Life Changing Medicine*.

Khazan, O. 2017. "Nearly Half of All Murdered Women Are Killed by Romantic Partners." *The Atlantic*; Petrosky, E., J.M. Blair, C.J. Betz, K.A. Fowler, S.P. Jackand, and B.H. Lyons.

2017. "Racial and Ethnic Differences in Homicides of Adult Women and the Role of Intimate Partner Violence—United States, 2003–2014." *CDC Morbidity and Mortality Weekly Report* 66 (28): 741–46.

Kiehl, K.A., and M.B. Hoffman. 2011. "The Criminal Psychopath: History, Neuroscience, Treatment, and Economics." *Jurimetrics* 51: 14.

Kim, J.J., L. Steinhoff, and R.W. Palmatier. 2021. "An Emerging Theory of Loyalty Program Dynamics." *Journal of the Academy of Marketing Science* 49 (1): 71–95.

Kinnell, A., and S. Dennis. 2011. "The List Length Effect in Recognition Memory: An Analysis of Potential Confounds." *Memory and Cognition* 39: 348–63.

Kirby, R. 2014. "Testosterone and the Struggle for Higher Social Status." *Trends in Urology and Men's Health*: 11–4.

Kiryttopoulou, N. 2013. "Overcoming the Courtesy Bias in Constituent Feedback." *Feedback Labs*.

Klein, S., L. Cosmides, J. Tooby, and S. Chance. 2002. "Decisions and the Evolution of Memory: Multiple Systems, Multiple Functions." *Psychological Review* 109: 306–29.

Knight, B.G., S. Rastegar, and S. Kim. 2016. "Age Differences in the Connection of Mood and Cognition: Evidence From Studies of Mood Congruent Effects." In *Handbook of the Psychology of Aging*, 279–302. Academic Press.

Kohlberg, L. 1969. "Stage and Sequence: The Cognitive-Developmental Approach to Socialization." In *Handbook of Socialization Theory and Research*, edited by D.A. Goslin, 347–480.

Kokkoris, M.D., and O. Stavrova. 2020. "The Dark Side of Self-Control." *Harvard Business Review.*

Kotler, P., V. Wong, J. Saunders, and G. Armstrong. 2005. *Principles of Marketing*, 4th ed. Harlow: Pearson Education Limited, 256; Griskevicius, V., and D.T. Kenrick. 2013. "Fundamental Motives: How Evolutionary Needs Influence Consumer Behavior." *Journal of Consumer Psychology* 23 (3): 01; Buss, D. 2019. *Evolutionary Psychology: The New Science of the Mind*, 6th ed. New York, NY: Routledge Taylor Francis Group.

Kruger, J., and T. Gilovich. 1999. "Naive Cynicism" in Everyday Theories of Responsibility Assessment: On Biased Assumptions of Bias." *Journal of Personality and Social Psychology* 76 (5): 743.

Krumpal, I. 2013. "Determinants of Social Desirability Bias in Sensitive Surveys: A Literature Review." *Quality & Q Daniel Kahneman; Amos Tversky Quantity* 47 (4): 2025–47.

Krupp, D.B., L.A. Sewall, M.L. Lalumière, C. Sheriff, and G. Harris. 2013. "Psychopathy, Adaptation, and Disorder." *Frontiers in Psychology* 4 (139):1–4.

Krys, K., C.A. Capaldi, W.V. Tilburg, O.V. Lipp, M.H. Bond, C.M. Vauclair, L. Manickam, et al. 2018. "Catching up With Wonderful Women: The Women-Are-Wonderful Effect Is Smaller in More Gender Egalitarian Societies." *International Journal of Psychology* 53(1): 21–26.

Kuehn, E. 2017. "What Was That? I Can't Remember What You Said, I Was Next-In-Line." *CogBlog—A Cognitive Psychology Blog.*

Kunthara, S. 2021. "Black Women Still Receive Just a Tiny Fraction of VC Funding Despite 5 yr High." *Crunchbase;* Azevedo, M.A. 2019. "Untapped Opportunity: Minority Founders Still Being Overlooked." Crunchbase.

Lamberton, C., and A.T. Stephen. 2016. "A Thematic Exploration of Digital, Social Media, and Mobile Marketing: Research Evolution From 2000 to 2015 and an Agenda for Future Inquiry." *Journal of Marketing* 80 (6): 146–72.

Lavington, Prof. S. 2012. "Alan Turing: Is He Really the Father of Computing?" *BBC News.*

Leal, S. 2016. "9 Celebrities Who Have Opened up About Sexual Assault." *Marie Claire Magazine.*

Lean In. n.d. "50 Ways to Fight Bias: An Introduction to the Common Biases Women Experience."

Leander, V.D.M., J. Schaveling, and M.V. Vugt. 2016. "Basal Testosterone, Leadership and Dominance: A Field Study and Meta-Analysis." *Psychoneuroendocrinology, Elsevier Science*: 1–8.

Leising, D. 2011. "The Consistency Bias in Judgments of One's Own Interpersonal Behavior: Two Possible Sources." *Journal of Individual Differences* 32 (3): 137–43.

Leverhulme Centre for the Future of Intelligence. 2022. "Decolonising AI"; Miller, K. 2022. "The Movement to Decolonize AI: Centering Dignity Over Dependency." *Stanford University.*

Levin, R. 1997. *A Geography of Time: The Temporal Misadventures of a Social Psychologist.* New York, NY: Basic.

Li, N.P., M.V. Vugt, and S.M. Colarelli. 2017. "The Evolutionary Mismatch Hypothesis: Implications for Psychological Science." *Current Directions in Psychological Science* 27 (1): 38–44.

Library Guides at UC Berkeley. 2022. "Library Guides: Non-Governmental Organizations (NGOs): The Environment"; Raj. 2022. "Top 23 Global Nonprofits Protecting the Environment." *Nonprofit Blog.*

Lifton, R.J. 1982. "Beyond Psychic Numbing: A Call to Awareness." *American Journal of Orthopsychiatry* 52 (4): 619–629.

Lincoln, G.A. 2002. "The Irritable Male Syndrome." *Reproduction, Fertility and Development* 13 (7–8); 567–76. https://pubmed.ncbi.nlm.nih.gov/11999307/; Jantz, G. MD. 2012. "Irritable Male syndrome, It's No Laughing Matter." *Huffpost.*

Linkov, F., Z. Yurkovetsky, and A Lokshin. 2009. "Hormones as Biomarkers: Practical Guide to Utilizing Luminex Technologies for Biomarker Research." *Tumor Biomarker Discovery: Methods and Protocols*: 129–41.

Lippa, R.A. 2003. "Are 2D: 4D Finger-length Ratios Related to Sexual Orientation? Yes for Men, no for Women." *Journal of Personality and Social Psychology* 85 (1): 179.

Lippmann, W. 1922. *Stereotypes as Defense.*

Lo, A.W., K.P. Marlowe, and R. Zhang. 2021. "To Maximize or Randomize? An Experimental Study of Probability Matching in Financial Decision Making." *PLOS ONE* 16 (8): e0252540.

LoBue, V., and J.S. DeLoache. 2008. "Detecting the Snake in the Grass: Attention to Fear-Relevant Stimuli by Adults and Young Children." *Psychological Science* 19 (3): 284–289; Buss, D. 2019. *Evolutionary Psychology: The New Science of the Mind.* New York, NY: Taylor and Francis.

Locke, J. 1689. *An Essay Concerning Human Understanding.* Raleigh: Generic NL Freebook Publisher.

Lopes, A.F., and G. Kipperberg. 2020. "Diagnosing Insensitivity to Scope in Contingent Valuation." *Environmental and Resource Economics* 77 (1): 191–216.

López-Rodríguez, L., E. Halperin, A. Vázquez, I. Cuadrado, M. Navas, and A. Gómez. 2022. "Awareness of the Psychological Bias of Naïve Realism Can

Increase Acceptance of Cultural Differences." *Personality and Social Psychology Bulletin* 48 (6): 888–900.

Lorenz, K.Z. 1941. "'Vergleichende Bewegungsstudien an Anatidae'" *Journal of Ornithology* 89: 194–294; Lorenz, K. 1965. *Evolution and Modification of Behavior*. Chicago: The University of Chicago Press.

Lovallo, W.R., and T.L. Thomas. 2000. "Stress Hormones in Psychophysiological Research: Emotional, Behavioral, and Cognitive Implications." In *Handbook of Psychophysiology*, 2nd ed., edited by J.T. Cacioppo, L.G. Tassinary, and G.G. Berntson, 342–67. Cambridge University Press; Sapolsky, R.M., L.M. Romero, and A.U. Munck. 2000. "How Do Glucocorticoids Influence Stress Responses? Integrating Permissive, Suppressive, Stimulatory, and Preparative Actions." *Endocrine Reviews* 21: 55–89; Kusev, P., H. Purser, R. Heilman, A.J. Cooke, P.V. Schaik, V. Baranova, et al. 2017. "Understanding Risky Behavior: The Influence of Cognitive, Emotional and Hormonal Factors on Decision-Making Under Risk." *Frontiers in Psychology* 8.

Low, R. 2012. "Modality Effect on Learning." In *Encyclopedia of the Sciences of Learning*, edited by N.M. Seel.

Low. 1991. *Evolutionary Psychology: The New Science of the Mind.* 148. Oxfordshire: Routledge.

Lowcountry Digital Library. 2021. "The Trans-Atlantic Slave Trade African Passages, Lowcountry Adaptations Lowcountry Digital History Initiative." *Lcdl Library*.

Lu, H., Z. Ma, J. Zhao, and Z. Huo. 2015. "Second to Fourth Digit Ratio (2D:4D) and Coronary Heart Disease." *Early Human Development* 91 (7): 417–20.

Lucas, J.W. 2016. "Institutionalized Bias." *Encyclopedia Britannica*.

Lucca, V.D. 2020. *The Politics of Princely Entertainment: Music and Spectacle in the Lives of Lorenzo Onofrio and Maria Mancini Colonna*. Oxford University Press, USA; Marek, D.H. 2006. *Singing: The First Art*. Lanham, MD: Scarecrow Press.

Luebering, J.E. 2021. "Renaissance—European History." *Encyclopædia Britannica*; Jarus, O., and J. Szalay. 2022. "The Renaissance: The 'Rebirth' of Science & Culture." *LiveScience*.

Lukaszewski, A.W., Z.L. Simmons,C. Anderson, and J.R. Roney. 2016. "The Role of Physical Formidability in Human Social Status Allocation." *Journal of Personality and Social Psychology* 110 (3): 385–406.

Lutchmaya, S., S. Baron-Cohen, P. Raggatt, R. Knickmeyer, and J.T. Manning. 2004. "2nd to 4th Digit Ratios, Fetal Testosterone and Estradiol." *Early Human Development* 77 (1): 23–28; Manning, J.T, P.E. Bundred, D.J. Newton, and B.F. Flanagan. 2003. "The Second to Fourth Digit Ratio and Variation in the Androgen Receptor Gene." *Evolution and Human Behavior*

24 (6): 399–405; Manning, J.T., D. Scutt, J. Wilson, and D.I. Lewis-Jones. 1998. "The Ratio of 2nd to 4th Digit Length: A Predictor of Sperm Numbers and Concentrations of Testosterone, Luteinizing Hormone and Oestrogen." *Human Reproduction* 13 (11): 3000–04.

Lynn, M. 2011. "How Many Africans Were Transported to the Americas as a Result of the European Slave Trade? Has Anyone Tried to Quantify How Many Died as a Result?" *The Guardian.*

Mack, B. 2009. "Hummer Drivers Get More Tickets. A Lot More." *Wired, Online.*

MacKenzie, I., C. Meyer, and S. Noble. 2013. "How Retailers Can Keep up With Consumers."

Mackie, D.M., and S.T. Allison. 1987. "Group Attribution Errors and the Illusion of Group Attitude Change." *Journal of Experimental Social Psychology* 23 (6): 460–80.

Macmillan Education. n.d. "Welcome to Macmillan Education Customer Support."

Macrotrends. 2023. "Amazon Revenue 2010–2023." *AMZN.*

Madgavkar, A., O. White, M. Krishnan, D. Mahajan, and X. Azcue. 2020. "Covid-19 and Gender Equality: Countering the Regressive Effects." *McKinsey & Company.*

Madhu, V. 2021. "Perspectives 2021. Why Do Companies Want to Read Your Mind?" *Capgemini,* 23.

Maglio, S.J., and T. Reich. 2019. "Feeling Certain: Gut Choice, the True Self, and Attitude Certainty." *Emotion* 19 (5).

Mahajan, D., O. White, A. Madgavkar, and M. Krishnan. 2020. "Don't Let the Pandemic Set Back Gender Equality." *McKinsey & Company.*

Maidenberg, M., and R. Copeland. 2022. "SpaceX Shoots to $125 Billion Valuation, Shrugging off Elon Musk's Woes." *The Wall Street Journal.*

Makary, M.A., and D.M. 2016. "Medical Error—The Third Leading Cause of Death in the U.S." *BMJ.*

Mallon, M. 2017. "Gwyneth Paltrow and Angelina Jolie Both Say They Were Harassed by Harvey Weinstein." *Glamour.*

Mandal, A.M. D. 2019. "What Is a Biomarker?" Newsmedical.net; FDA. 2021. "About Biomarkers and Qualification." FDA.gov; Medline Plus. 2016. "Diagnostic Imaging." *Medlineplus.*

Mangold, J., M. Danna, and N. Dodd. 1999. *Girl, Interrupted.* USA.

Manning, J. T., D. Scutt, J. Wilson, and D.I. Lewis-Jones. 1998. "The Ratio of 2nd to 4th Digit Length: A Predictor of Sperm Numbers and Concentrations of Testosterone, Luteinizing Hormone, and Oestrogen." *Human Reproduction* 13 (11): 3000–04.

Manning, J.T., and B. Fink. 2011. "Digit Ratio, Nicotine and Alcohol Intake, and National Rates of Smoking and Alcohol Consumption." *Personality and Individual Differences* 50 (3): 344–48.

Manning, J.T., and M.R. Hill. 2009. "Digit Ratio (2D:4D) and Sprinting Speed in Boys." American Journal of Human Biology: The Official Journal of the Human Biology Association 21 (2): 210–3.

Manus, M.B. 2018. "Evolutionary Mismatch." *Evolution, Medicine and Public Health* 2018 (1): 190–91.

Marcatto, F., A. Cosulich, and D. Ferrante. 2015. "Once Bitten, Twice Shy: Experienced Regret and Non-Adaptive Choice Switching." *PeerJ* 3: e1035.

Marks, G. 2016. "21 Percent of CEOs Are Psychopaths. Only 21 Percent?" *Washington Post.*

Marks, I.M., and R.M. Nesse. 2013. "Fear and Fitness: An Evolutionary Analysis of Anxiety Disorders." In *Fear and Anxiety*, 155–69.

Martin, E. 2022. "Quarter Billion More People Will Fall Into Poverty in 2022." *Time.*

Marx, K., and F. Engels. 1848. *The Communist Manifesto.* New York, NY: Monthly Review Press. Reprint, Gutenberg.org.

Masci, D. 2019. "For Darwin Day, 6 Facts About the Evolution Debate." *Pew Research Center.*

Maslow, A.H. 1937. "Dominance-Feeling, Behavior, and Status." *Psychological Review* 44 (5): 404–29.

Maslow, A.H. 1943. "A Theory of Human Motivation." 3–19.

Maslow, A.H. 1943. "A Theory of Human Motivation." *Psychological Review* 50: 370–96.

Masterclass. 2022. "Tyranny of the Majority Explained."

Mathieu, C., C.S. Neumann, R.D. Hare, and P. Babiak. 2012. "A Dark Side of Leadership: Corporate Psychopathy and Its Influence on Employee Well-Being and Job Satisfaction." *Personality and Individual Differences* 59: 83–8; Lipman-Blumen, J. 2008. "Following Toxic Leaders: In Search of Posthumous Praise"; Tepper, B.J. 2000. "Consequences of Abusive Supervision." *The Academy of Management Journal* 43 (2): 178–90; Hforth, B. 1994. "Petty Tyranny in Organizations." *Human Relations* 47: 755–78; Bassman, E.S. 1992. *Abuse in the Workplace: Management Remedies and Bottom Line Impact.* Westport, CT: Quorum Books; Einarsen, S., M.S. Aasland, and A. Skogstad. 2007. "Destructive Leadership Behavior: A Definition and Conceptual Model." *The Leadership Quarterly* 18 (3): 207–16.

MathsGee. 2022. "What Is Illicit Transference Bias?"

Matsumoto, A.M., and W. J. Bremner. 2016. "Breast Tenderness." *ScienceDirect.*

Mayo Clinic. 2022. "Feminizing Hormone Therapy." *Mayo Clinic.*

Mazur, A. 2005. *Biosociology of Dominance and Deference.* Lanham: Rowman & Littlefield.

Mazur, A., and A. Booth. 1998. "Testosterone and Dominance in Men." *Behavioral and Brain Sciences* 21 (3): 353–63; *discussion* 363–97. https://pubmed.ncbi.nlm.nih.gov/10097017/; Josephs, R.A., J.G. Sellers, M.L. Newman, and P.H. Mehta. 2006. "The Mismatch Effect: When Testosterone and Status Are at Odds." *Journal of Personality and Social Psychology* 90 (6): 999–1013; Eisenegger, C, C. Haushofer, and E. Fehr. 2011. "The Role of Testosterone in Social Interaction." *Trends in Cognitive Sciences* 15 (6): 263–71.

Ibid, 353–63; Herrmann, W., R. McDonald, and M. Bozak. 1976. "A Psycho-Experimental Model for the Investigation of Hormones as Psychotropic Agents." In *The Psychotropic Effects of Hormones,* edited by T. Itil, G. Laudahn, and W.S. Herrmann; T.D. Kemper. 1990. *Social Structure and Testosterone.* Rutgers University Press; Klaiber, L., D. Broverman, W. Vogel, G. Abraham, and F. Cone. 1971. "Effects of Infused Testosterone on Mental Performances and Serum LH." *Journal of Clinical Endocrinology* 32: 341–49.

Mazur, A., and A. Booth. 1998. "Testosterone and Dominance in Men." *Behavioral and Brain Sciences* 21 (3): 353–63; Josephs, R.A., J. Guinn Sellers, M.L. Newman, and P.H. Mehta. 2006. "The Mismatch Effect: When Testosterone and Status Are at Odds." *Journal of Personality and Social Psychology* 90 (6): 999; Eisenegger, C., J. Haushofer, and E. Fehr. 2011. "The Role of Testosterone in Social Interaction." *Trends in Cognitive Sciences* 15 (6): 263–71.

McCallum, S. 2022. "Jessica Ennis-Hill: Why I Now Train Around My Period." *BBC*; Laurence, E. 2023. "Cycle Syncing: Everything You Need to Know." *Forbes.*

McCallum, S. 2022. "Jessica Ennis-Hill: Why I Now Train Around My Period." *BBC*; Lowe, A. 2021. "Jessica Ennis-Hill's New App Will Completely Change Your Approach to Fitness—And Periods."

McClelland, D.C., and A.L. Liberman. 1949. "The Effect of Need for Achievement on Recognition of Need-Related Words." *Journal of Personality* 18 (2): 236–51; Murray, H.A., and D.P. McAdams. 2007. "Explorations in Personality"; Pincus, A.L., and T.A. Widiger. 2014. "J.S. Wiggins. (1931–2006)." *The Encyclopedia of Clinical Psychology* 1–2.

McCullough, J. 2019. "The Psychopathic CEO." *Forbes.*

McDuff, D., A. Mahmoud, M. Mavadati, M. Amr, J. Turcot, and R.E. Kaliouby. 2016. "AFFDEX SDK: A Cross-Platform Real-Time Multi-Face Expression Recognition to Olkit." *Proceedings of the 2016 CHI Conference Extended Abstracts on Human Factors in Computing Systems.* San Jose, California, USA.

Mcfedries, P. 2017. "Agile Words [Technically Speaking]." *IEEE Spectrum.* 54 (6): 21.

McGill University. "The Evolutionary Layers of the Human Brain." 2021. *The Brain From top to Bottom.*

McGowan Institute for Regenerative Medicine. 2022. "What Is Regenerative Medicine?" *McGowan Institute for Regenerative Medicine.*

McIntyre, M.H., S.W. Gangestad,, P.B. Gray, ,J.F. Chapman, T.C. Burnham,, M.T. O'Rourke, and R. Thornhill. 2006. "Romantic Involvement Often Reduces Men's Testosterone Levels—But Not Always: The Moderating Effects of Extra-Pair Sexual Interest." *Journal of Personality and Social Psychology* 91: 642–51.

Mckinsey. 2019. "The Future of Women at Work Transitions in the Age of Automation."

Ibid, 08.

Mcleod, S. 2023. "Serial Position Effect (Glanzer and Cunitz, 1966)." *SimplyPsychology.*

Meaningful Impact. 2016. Always 'Like a Girl' Super Bowl Commercial: #LikeAGirl. *YouTube*; Kolowich C.L. 2023. "The 18 Most Creative Ad Campaigns in History." *HubSpot.com*; Always. 2022. "Always #LikeAGirl." *Always.com.*

Meegan, D.V. 2010. "Zero-Sum Bias: Perceived Competition Despite Unlimited Resources." *Frontiers in Psychology* 1: 191.

Mehta, K. 2021. "A Harvard Psychologist Says Humans Have 8 Types of Intelligence. Which Ones Do You Score the Highest in?" *CNBC.com.*

Meijer, E.H., N.K. Selle, L. Elber, and G. Ben-Shakhar. 2014. "Memory Detection With the Concealed Information Test: A Meta-Analysis of Skin Conductance, Respiration, Heart Rate, and P300 Data." *Psychophysiology* 51 (9): 879–904.

Mengelkoch, S., J. Gassen, M.L. Prokosch, G.W. Boehm, S.E. Hill. 2022. "More Than Just a Pretty Face? The Relationship Between Immune Function and Perceived Facial Attractiveness." *Proceedings of the Royal Society B* 289 (1969).

Merriam-Webster. 2020. "Reason Definition & Meaning".

Merriam-Webster. 2021. "Bias Definition & Meaning."

Metz, J. 2023. "How Age and Gender Affect Car Insurance Rates." *Forbes.*

Middleman, A.B., and R. DuRant. 1996. "Anabolic Steroid Use and Associated Health Risk Behaviors." *Sports Medicine* 21: 251–55; Kusev, P., H. Purser, R. Heilman, A.J. Cooke, P.V. Schaik, V. Baranova, R. Martin, and P. Ayton. 2017. "Understanding Risky Behavior: The Influence of Cognitive, Emotional and Hormonal Factors on Decision-Making Under Risk." *Frontiers in Psychology* 8: 246–629; Haselton, M.G. 2019. *Hormonal: The Hidden Intelligence of Hormones.* Boston, MA: Little, Brown Spark; Singh, V. 2021. "Role of Cortisol and Testosterone in Risky Decision-Making: Deciphering Male Decision-Making in the Iowa Gambling Task." *Frontiers in Neuroscience* 15.

Millan, L. 2021. "Climate Change Linked to 5 Million Deaths a Year, New Study Shows." *Bloomberg.Com.*

Miller, B. 2020. "How 'Survivorship Bias' Can Cause You to Make Mistakes." *BBC*.

Miller, G. 2000. *The Mating Mind.* New York, NY: Doubleday; Miller, G. 2009. *Spent: Sex, Evolution, and Consumer Behavior.* Penguin.

Miller, G. 2001. "Aesthetic Fitness: How Sexual Selection Shaped Artistic Virtuosity as a Fitness Indicator and Aesthetic Preferences as Mate Choice Criteria." *Bulletin of Psychology and the Arts* 2 (1): 20–5.

Miller, G. 2009. **"Essay."** In Spent: Sex, Evolution, and Consumer Behavior. Penguin.

Miller, G. 2009. Spent: Sex, Evolution, and Consumer Behavior. Penguin.

Ibid, 12–12.

Ibid; Kenrick, D.T., G. Saad, and V. Griskevicius. 2013. "Evolutionary Consumer Psychology: Ask Not What You Can Do for Biology, but……." Journal of Consumer Psychology 23 (3): 404–09; Buss, D. 2019. Evolutionary Psychology: The New Science of the Mind, 228. Oxfordshire: Routledge.

Miller, J.D., E.C. Scott, M.S. Ackerman, B. Laspra, G. Branch, C. Polino, nd J.S. Huffaker. 2021. "Public Acceptance of Evolution in the United States. 1985–2020." *Public Understanding of Science* 31 (2): 223–38.

Miller, S.L., and J.K. Maner. 2010. "Scent of A Woman: Men's Testosterone Responses to Olfactory Ovulation Cues." *Psychological Science* 21 (2): 276–83.

Minderoo Foundation Pty. 2018. "Global Slavery Index —Regional Findings— The Americas." *Walk Free.*

Mack, B. 2009. "Hummer Drivers Get More Tickets. A Lot More." *Wired.*

Modern Slavery: 50 Million People Worldwide in Modern Slavery. 2022. "50 Million People Worldwide in Modern Slavery."

Monks, P. 2018. "Bizarreness Effect: The Behavioural Bias Series." *The Behaviours Agency.*

Moore, J.W., and A. Pope. 2014. "The Intentionality Bias and Schizotypy." *Quarterly Journal of Experimental Psychology (Hove)* 67 (11): 2218–24.

Moorman, C. 1998. "Market-Level Effects of Information: Competitive Responses and Consumer Dynamics." *Journal of Marketing Research* 35 (1): 82–98; Koller, M. 1988. "Risk as a Determinant of Trust." *Basic and Applied Social Psychology* 9 (4): 265–76.

Morales, A. 2021. "10 Successful CEOs That Did Not get a College Degree." *StartUp Mindset.*

Morton, J., R.G. Crowder, and H.A. Prussin. 1971. "Experiments With the Stimulus Suffix Effect." *Journal of Experimental Psychology* 91(1): 169–90.

Moskovic, D.J., M.L. Eisenberg, and L.I. Lipshultz. 2012. "Seasonal Fluctuations in Testosterone-Estrogen Ratio in Men From the Southwest United States." *Journal of Andrology* 33 (6): 1298–304; Kelly, D. 2019. "Testosterone: Why Defining a 'Normal' Level Is Hard to Do." *The Conversation.*

Moskowitz, D.S., R. Sutton, D.C. Zuroff, and S.N. Young. 2015. "Fetal Exposure to Androgens, as Indicated by Digit Ratios (2D:4D), Increases Men's Agreeableness With Women." *Personality and Individual Differences* 75: 97–101.

Motoki, K., and M. Sugiura. 2017. "Consumer Behavior, Hormones, and Neuroscience: Integrated Understanding of Fundamental Motives Why We Buy." *Psychologia* 60 (1): 28–43.

Moulettes, A. 2007. "The Absence of Women's Voices in Hofstede's Cultural Consequences: A Postcolonial Reading." *Women in Management Review* 22 (6): 443–55.

Mudditt, J. 2021. "How 'Optimism Bias' Shapes Our Decisions and Futures." *BBC.*

Mueller, U., and A. Mazur. 1996. "Facial Dominance of West Point Cadets as a Predictor of Later Military Rank." *Social Forces* 74 (3): 823–850.

Mui, C. 2022. "Amazon CEO Andy Jassy Earned 6,474 Times the Median Amazon Employee's Salary." *YahooFinance.*

Mukherji, P. 2017, 2018. *Customer Decision-Making, Consumer Purchase Decision Process, Marketing Theory and Practice.* King's College London.

Mulford, M., and R.M. Dawes. 1999. "Subadditivity in Memory for Personal Events." *Psychological Science* 10 (1): 47–51.

Müller, U.W.D., C.L.M. Witteman, J. Spijker, and G.W. Alpers. 2019. "All's Bad That Ends Bad: There Is a Peak-End Memory Bias in Anxiety." *Frontiers in Psychology* 10: 1272.

Murray, B. 2019. "System 1 and System 2: Facts and Fictions." *iMotions.*

Murray, G.R., and J.D. Schmitz. 2011. "Caveman Politics: Evolutionary Leadership Preferences and Physical Stature." *Social Science Quarterly* 92 (5): 1215–35.

Mysoor, A. 2017. "The Science Behind Intuition and How You Can Use It to Get Ahead at Work." *Forbes.*

Nardini, G., T. Rank-Christman, M.G. Bublitz, S.N. Cross, and L.A. Peracchio. 2021. "Together We Rise: How Social Movements Succeed." *Journal of Consumer Psychology* 31 (1): 112–45.

NASA. 2019. "July 20, 1969: One Giant Leap for Mankind." *NASA.*

National Geographic. 2008. "Testosterone Factor, Explorer." *YouTube*; DW Documentary. 2019. "Testosterone—New Discoveries About the Male Hormone." *DW Documentary.*

National Health Service. 2019. "The Male Menopause." *National Health Service.*

National Institute of Mental Health. 2021. "Prevalence of Personality Disorders in Adults." *USA.*

National Museums of Scotland. 2022. "James VI."

Nelkin, D.K., E.N. Zalta, and U. Nodelman, eds. 2023. "Moral Luck." *The Stanford Encyclopedia of Philosophy.*

Nepomuceno, M.V., C.M. De Aguiar Pastore, and E. Stenstrom. 2021. "Prenatal Hormones (2D:4D), Intrasexual Competition, and Materialism in Women." *Psychology & Marketing* 38 (2): 239–48.

Nepomuceno, M.V., G. Saad, G. Stenstrom, Z. Mendenhall, and F. Iglesias. 2016. "Testosterone at Your Fingertips: Digit Ratios (2D:4D and rel2) as Predictors of Courtship-Related Consumption Intended to Acquire and Retain Mates." *Journal of Consumer Psychology* 26 (2): 231–44.

Nesse, R.M., and G.C. Williams. 1994. *Why We get Sick*. New York, NY: Times Books Random House; Buss, D. 2019. *Evolutionary Psychology: The New Science of the Mind*, 242–3. Oxfordshire: Routledge.

Nettle, D., and T.V. Pollet. 2007. "Natural Selection on Male Wealth in Humans." *The American Naturalist* 172 (5): 658–66.

Neuhoff, J.G. 2001. "An Adaptive Bias in the Perception of Looming Auditory Motion." *Ecological Psychology* 13 (2): 87–110; Neuhoff, J.G., K.L. Long, and R.C. Worthington. 2012. "Strength and Physical Fitness Predict the Perception of Looming Sounds." *Evolution and Human Behavior* 33 (4): 318–22; Buss, D. 2019. *Evolutionary Psychology: The New Science of the Mind*. Oxfordshire: Routledge.

New York Stem Cell Science. 2022. "What Is the Difference Between Totipotent, Pluripotent, and Multipotent?" *New York Stem Cell Science*.

Newman, E.J., M.C. Jalbert, N. Schwarz, and D.P. Ly. 2020. "Truthiness, the Illusory Truth Effect, and the Role of Need for Cognition." *Consciousness and Cognition* 78.

Newman, G.E., J.D. Freitas, and J. Knobe. 2014. "Beliefs About the True Self Explain Asymmetries Based on Moral Judgment." *Cognitive Science* 39 (1).

Newsdesk. 2015. "Attractive Women Shouldn't Include a Photo in CV Research Finds." *Newsdesk*.

Niazi, S. 2021. "Debt Bondage Slavery in India Affects Tribal Population." *Anadolu Ajansı*.

Nickerson, C. 2023. "False Consensus Effect: Definition and Examples." *SimplyPsychology*.

Nickerson, C. 2023. "Mere Exposure Effect in Psychology: Biases and Heuristics." *SimplyPsychology*.

Nickerson, C. 2023. "Zeigarnik Effect Examples in Psychology." *SimplyPsychology*.

NielsenIQ. 2022. "The Value of Failures in the World of SMB." *Nielsen*.

Niessner, M., and E.C. So. 2018. "Bad News Bearers: The Negative Tilt of the Financial Press."

Nisbett, R.E., and T.D. Wilson. 1977. "*Telling More Than We Can Know: Verbal Reports on Mental Processes.*" *Psychological Review* 84 (3): 231; Nisbett, R.E., and T.D. Wilson. 1977. "The Halo Effect: Evidence for Unconscious Alteration of Judgments". *Journal of Personality and Social Psychology* 35 (4): 250.

Nordgren, L.F., F.V. Harreveld, and J.V.D. Pligt. 2009. "The Restraint Bias: How the Illusion of Self-Restraint Promotes Impulsive Behavior." *Psychological Science* 20 (12): 1523–8.

Norton, M.I, D. Mochon, and D. Ariely. 2012. "The IKEA Effect: When Labor Leads to Love." *Journal of Consumer Psychology* 22 (3): 453–60.

Noss, A.J., and B.S. Hewlett. 2001. "The Contexts of Female Hunting in Central Africa." *American Anthropologist* 103 (4):1024–40; Reyes-García, V., I. Díaz-Reviriego, R. Duda, A. Fernández-Llamazares, and S. Gallois. 2020. "Hunting Otherwise". *Human Nature* 31 (3): 203–21; Venkataraman, V. 2021. "Women Were Successful Big Game Hunters, Challenging Beliefs About Ancient Gender Roles." *University of Calgary.*

Nova Scotia Health Authority. n.d."What Is Bias and Stereotyping?"

Nursing Salary, Pay Scale and Bands. 2021. "The UK Nursing Salary and Pay Scale Guide — 2021." *Nurses.co.uk.*

Nuwer, R.L. 2015. "Investigating the Case of the Earliest Known Murder Victim." *Smithsonian.Com*; Knapton, S. 2015. "Was This the World's First Murder Victim?" *The Telegraph.*

O'Shaughnessy, J. 1992. *Explaining Buyer Behavior: Central Concepts and Philosophy of Science Issues.* Oxford University Press.

Office on Women's Health. 2021. "Premenstrual Syndrome (PMS). Office on Women's Health." *Office on Women's Health*; Gudipally, P.R., and G.K. Sharma. 2023. "Premenstrual Syndrome." *National Library of Medicine*; Higuera, V., and C. Raypole. 2022. "PMS: Premenstrual Syndrome Symptoms, Treatments, and More." *Healthline.*

Ofosu, E.K., M.K. Chambers, J.M. Chen, and E. Hehman. 2019. "Same-Sex Marriage Legalization Associated With Reduced Implicit and Explicit Antigay Bias." *Proceedings of the National Academy of Sciences* 116 (18): 8846–51.

Ogolsky, B.G., S.T. Mejia, A. Chronopoulou, K. Dobson, C.R. Maniotes, T.M. Rice, Y. Hu, et al. 2022. "Spatial Proximity as a Behavioral Marker of Relationship Dynamics in Older Adult Couples." *Journal of Social and Personal Relationships* 39 (10):3116–32.

Olin, M., and T. Robsahm. 2009. *Modern Slavery.* Directed by Tina Davis and Thomas Robsahm.

Olito, F. 2019. "How the Divorce Rate Has Changed Over the Last 150 Years." *Insider.*

Otterbring, T., C. Ringler, N.J. Sirianni, and A. Gustafsson. 2018. "The Abercrombie & Fitch Effect: The Impact of Physical Dominance on Male Customers' Status-Signaling Consumption." *Journal of Marketing Research* 55 (1): 69–79.

Oxford Reference. n.d. "Next-In-Line Effect." *Oxford University Press.*

Oxford Reference. 2021. "Joseph Stalin."

Pamuk, O. n.d. "Compassion Fade." *Econowmics*.

Panné, J.L., A. Paczkowski, K. Bartosek, J.L. Margolin, and S. Courtois. 1999. *The Black Book of Communism: Crimes, Terror, Repression*. Translated by Kramer, M., and J. Murphy. Cambridge, MA: Harvard University Press.

Parker, R. 2021. "Neglect of Probability Bias." In *Decision Making in Emergency Medicine: Biases, Errors and Solutions*, edited by M. Raz, and P. Pouryahya, 245–50. Singapore: Springer.

Partridge, L. 1987. "Is Accelerated Senescence a Cost of Reproduction?" *Functional Ecology* 1 (4): 317–20.

Passos, T.S., M.A. Almeida-Santos, and N.C. Ramos. 2022. "Stereotypes of Brazilian Womens Hypersexuality in European Media: Data Mining." *Cadernos de Gênero e Tecnologia* 15 (45): 182–200.

Patrick, C.J., D.C. Fowles and R.F. Krueger. 2009. "Triarchic Conceptualization of Psychopathy: Developmental Origins of Disinhibition, Boldness, and Meanness." *Development and Psychopathology* 21 (3): 913–38; Patrick, C.J. 2010. "Triarchic Psychopathy Measure." *Triarchic Psychopathy Measure*.

Patrick, C.J., N.C. Venables, and L.E. Drislane. 2013. "The Role of Fearless Dominance in Differentiating Psychopathy From Antisocial Personality Disorder: Comment on Marcus, Fulton, and Edens." *Personality Disorders: Theory, Research, and Treatment* 4 (1): 80–2.

Pauwels, K. 2014. *It's Not the Size of the Data — It's How You Use It: Smarter Marketing With Analytics and... Dashboards. Amazon*. S.l.: Amacom.

Pavlovskaya, E. 2021. "The Fortune 100 Companies That Spend the Most on Paid Search." *SEM Rush*.

Pawlowski, B., and R.I.M. Dunbar. 1999. "Withholding Age as Putative Deception in Mate Search Tactics." *Evolution and Human Behavior* 20 (1): 53–69.

PBS. 2022. "Thematic Window: The Civil Rights Movement." *Public Broadcasting Service*.

Penenberg, A.L. 2011. "NeuroFocus Uses Neuromarketing to Hack Your Brain". *Fast Company*.

Peper, J.S., and R.E. Dahl. 2013. "The Teenage Brain:Surging Hormones—Brain-Behavior Interactions During Puberty." *Current Directions in Psychological Science* 22 (2): 134–9.

Perilloux, C., J.A. Easton, and D.M. Buss. 2012. "The Misperception of Sexual Interest." *Psychological Science* 23 (2); Buss D.M., D.P. Schmitt. 1993. "Sexual Strategies Theory: An Evolutionary Perspective on Human Mating." *Psychological Review* 100: 204–232.

Perry, E. 2021. "The Cognitive Biases Caused by the Availability Heuristic." *BetterUp*.

Perusse. 1993. Cited: Buss, D. 2019. *Evolutionary Psychology: The New Science of the Mind*. 318. Oxfordshire: Routledge; Mulder, M.B. 1990. "Kipsigis

Women's Preferences for Wealthy Men: Evidence for Female Choice in Mammals?" *Behavioral Ecology and Sociobiology* 27: 255–264.

Peshin, A. 2018. "What Is the "Google" Effect?" *Science ABC.*

Pester, P. 2021. "The Longest Living Animals on Earth." *Live Science.*

Petersen, S., K.V. Staeyen, C. Vögele, A. Von Leupoldt, and O.V.D. Bergh. 2015. "Interoception and Symptom Reporting: Disentangling Accuracy and Bias." *Frontiers in Psychology* 6.

Petter, O. 2019. "Gillette Sales Unchanged After Controversial Advert About Toxic Masculinity." *Independent*; Vizard, S. 2019. "Gillette Brand Takes a Hit as '#MeToo' ad Backfires." *Marketing Week*; Khatoon, S., and V. Rehman. 2021. "Negative Emotions in Consumer Brand Relationship: A Review and Future Research Agenda." *International Journal of Consumer Studies* 45 (4): 719–49.

Pew Research Center. 2009. "Religious Differees on the Question of Evolution."

Pew Research Center. 2013. "The Global Divide on Homosexuality — Greater Acceptance in More Secular and Affluent Countries." *Pew Research Center's Global Attitudes Project*; Underwood, E. 2014. "No Scientific Basis for Gay-Specific Mental Disorders, WHO Panel Concludes." *Science.org.*

Pew Research Center. 2014. "Views About Human Evolution by State."

Pham, T.M. 2004. "The Logic of Feeling." *Journal of Consumer Psychology* 14 (4): 360–69.

Pincus, A.L., and T.A. Widiger. 2015. "Wiggins, Jerry S. (1931–2006)." January 23. https://doi.org/10.1002/9781118625392wbecp402.

Pinker, S. 2016. The Blank Slate: The Modern Denial of Human Nature, New York, NY: Penguin Books.

Ibid, 102.

Ibid, 106.

Pinker, S. 2018. "The Media Exaggerates Negative News. This Distortion Has Consequences". *The Guardian.*

Pinson, S. 2021. "WWII Codebreaker Alan Turing Becomes 1st Gay Man on a British Bank Note." *NBCNews.com*; Bank of England. 2020 "The New £50 Note Unveiled."

Plackett, B. 2020. "Was Freud Right About Anything?" *LiveScience.*

Plomin, R., J.C. DeFries ,G.C. McClearn, and P. McGuffin. 2008. *Behavioral Genetics: A Primer*, 5th ed. New York, NY: Worth. Buss, D. 2019. *Evolutionary Psychology: The New Science of the Mind*, 6th ed, 952. New York, NY: Routledge Taylor Francis Group.

Plutchik, R., and H. Kellerman. 1980. "Wheel of Emotions (Illustration)." *Emotion: Theory, Research and Experience 1, Theories of Emotion.*

Pompian, M., ed. 2012. "Conservatism Bias." In *Behavioral Finance and Wealth Management*, 63–71.

Pompian, M. ed. 2012. "Illusion of Control Bias." In *Behavioral Finance and Wealth Management*, 99–106.

Poppenk, J., G. Walia, A.R. McIntosh, M.F. Joanisse, D. Klein, and S. Köhler. 2008. "Why Is the Meaning of a Sentence Better Remembered Than Its Form? an fMRI Study on the Role of Novelty-Encoding Processes." *Hippocampus* 18 (9): 909–18.

Porges, S.W. 2003. "The Polyvagal Theory: Phylogenetic Contributions to Social Behavior." *Physiology Behavior* 79 (3): 503–13; Porges, S.W. 2003a. "Social Engagement and Attachment." *Annals of the New York Academy of Sciences* 1008 (1): 31–47; Porges, S.W. 2007. "The Polyvagal Perspective." *Biological Psychology* 74 (2): 116–43.

Provine, R.R., M.O. Cabrera, and J. Nave-Blodgett. 2013. "Red, Yellow, and Super-White Sclera". *Human Nature* 24 (2): 126–36; Ford, C.S., and F.A. Beach. 1951. *Patterns of Sexual Behavior.* New York, NY: Harper & Row.

Psychology Today. n.d. "Groupthink."

Psychology Wiki. n.d. "Attribute Substitution."

Psychology Wiki. n.d. "Systematic Bias."

Psychology Wiki. n.d. "Trait Ascription Bias."

PsychOut. 2020. "What Is Context Effect? [Definition and Example] — Understanding Cognitive Biases." *YouTube.*

Puntmann, V.O. 2009. "How-To Guide on Biomarkers: Biomarker Definitions, Validation and Applications With Examples From Cardiovascular disease." *Postgraduate Medical Journal* 85 (1008): 538–45; Strimbu, K., and J.A. Tavel. 2010. "What Are Biomarkers?" *Current Opinion in HIV and AIDS* 5 (6): 463–6.

Quoidbach, J., D.T. Gilbert, and T.D. Wilson. 2013. "The End of History Illusion." *Science* 339 (6115): 96–98; Johnson, J.T., M.D. Robinson, and E.B. Mitchell. 2004. "Inferences About the Authentic Self: When Do Actions Say More Than Mental States?" *Journal of Personality and Social Psychology* 87 (5): 615–30.

Quoidbach, J., D.T. Gilbert, and T.D. Wilson. 2013. "The End of History Illusion." *Science* 339 (6115): 96–8.

Rafferty, J. P. 2017. "What Is Gerrymandering?" *Encyclopedia Britannica.*

Ragland, J.D., S.T. Moelter, C. McGrath, S.K. Hill, R.E. Gur, and W.B. Bilker. 2003. "Levels-Of-Processing Effect on Word Recognition in Schizophrenia." *Biological Psychiatry* 54 (11): 1154–61.

Rahman, K. 2021. "Full List of Black People Killed by Police in 2021." *Newsweek.*

Rainbow Europe. 2023. "Annual Review of the Human Rights Situation of Lesbian, Gay, Bisexual, Trans, and Intersex People in the United Kingdom."

Rainey, C. 2022. "The Age of 'Greedflation' Is Here: See How Obscene CEO-To-Worker Pay Ratios Are Right Now." *Fast Company.*

Rakison, D. H. 2009. Does Women's Greater Fear of Snakes and Spiders Originate in Infancy? Evolution and Human Behavior 30: 438–44.

Ibid Fetchenhauer, D., and B.P. Buunk. 2005. "How to Explain Gender Differences in Fear of Crime: Towards an Evolutionary Approach." *Sexualities, Evolution & Gender* 7 (2): 95–113.

Rapp, N., and B. O'Keefe 2019. "50 Years After the Moon Landing, Money Races Into Space." *Fortune.*

Rattini, K.B. 2021. "Cyrus the Great: History's Most Merciful Conqueror?" *Culture. National Geographic*; USIDHR. 2021. "US Institute of Diplomacy and Human Rights."

Ray, J.J., and J.A. Ray. 1981. "Some Apparent Advantages of Subclinical Psychopathy." *The Journal of Social Psychology* 117 (1): 135–42.

Raypole, C. 2020. "Always Feeling Self-Conscious? Here's Why You Shouldn't, According to Science." *Healthline.*

Recruiting Times. 2015. "Attractive Women Shouldn't Include Photo in CV, Research Finds"; Tu, M. H., E.K. Gilbert, and J.E. Bono. 2022. "Is Beauty More Than Skin Deep? Attractiveness, Power, and Nonverbal Presence in Evaluations of Hireability." *Personnel Psychology* 75 (1): 119–46.

Reeve, J. 2015. *Understanding Motivation and Emotion*, 6th ed. Hoboken, New Jersey, NJ: John Wiley & Sons, Inc.

Reitsma, M.B., P.J. Kendrick, E. Ababneh, C. Abbafati, M. Abbasi-Kangevari, A. Abdoli, A. Abedi, et al. 2021. "Spatial, Temporal, and Demographic Patterns in Prevalence of Smoking Tobacco Use and Attributable Disease Burden in 204 Countries and Territories, 1990–2019: A Systematic Analysis From the Global Burden of Disease Study 2019." *The Lancet* 397 (10292): 2337–60.

Ressler, K. J. 2010. "Amygdala Activity, Fear, and Anxiety: Modulation by Stress." *Biological Psychiatry* 67 (12): 1117–9.

Reyes-García, V., I. Díaz-Reviriego, R. Duda, A. Fernández-Llamazares, and S. Gallois. 2020. "Hunting Otherwise". *Human Nature* 31 (3): 203–21.

Rhodes, G., L.W. Simmons, and M. Peters. 2005. "Attractiveness and Sexual Behavior: Does Attractiveness Enhance Mating Success?" *Evolution and Human Behavior* 26 (2): 186–201.

Rich, A. 2020. "What Is the Baader-Meinhof Phenomenon?" *Macquarie University.*

Ritson, M. 2020. "If 'Black Lives Matter' to Brands, Where Are Your Black Board Members?" *Marketing Week.*

Ro, C. 2022. "Why 'Plant blindness' Matters—and What You Can Do About It." *BBC.*

Rodrigues, M. 2019. "Apenas 28,4% Dos Trabalhadores Domésticos Têm Carteira Assinada." *R7.Com.*

Rohleder, P.2014. "Othering." In *Encyclopedia of Critical Psychology*, edited by T. Teo, 1306–08. New York, NY: Springer New York.

Ronay, R., and W.V. Hippel. 2010. "The Presence of an Attractive Woman Elevates Testosterone and Physical Risk-Taking in Young Men." *Social Psychological and Personality Science* 1 (1): 57–64; Buss, D. 2019. *Evolutionary Psychology: The New Science of the Mind*, 385. Oxfordshire: Routledge.

Roney, J.R. 2003. "Effects of Visual Exposure to the Opposite Sex: Cognitive Aspects of Mate Attraction in Human Males." *Personality and Social Psychology Bulletin*, 29: 393–404; Griskevicius, V., J.M. Tybur, J.M. Sundie, R.B. Cialdini, G.F. Miller, and D.T. Kenrick. 2007. "Blatant Benevolence and Conspicuous Consumption: When Romantic Motives Elicit Strategic Costly Signals." *Journal of Personality and Social Psychology* 93 (1): 85.

Roosevelt, E., P.C. Chang, C. Malik, W. Hodgson, H. Cruz, R. Cassin, A. Bogomolov, et al. 1948. "Universal Declaration of Human Rights." *United Nations*.

Rosen, M. 2017. "Questions Remain About the Benefits of Taking Testosterone." *Science News*.

Royal College of Psychiatrists. 2023. "Mental Health of Children and Young People in England, 2023-Wave 4 Follow up to the 2017 Survey Official Statistics, Survey." *National Health Service. England.*

Rubin, M., and C. Badea. 2007. "Why Do People Perceive Ingroup Homogeneity on Ingroup Traits and Outgroup Homogeneity on Outgroup Traits?" *Personality and Social Psychology Bulletin* 33 (1): 31–42.

Ruffle, B.J., and Z. Shtudiner. 2015. "Are Good-Looking People More Employable?" *Management Science* 61 (8): 1760–76.

Rühli, F.J., and M. Henneberg. 2013. "New Perspectives on Evolutionary Medicine: The Relevance of Microevolution for Human Health and Disease." *BMC Medicine* 11 (1).

Saad, G. 2004. "Applying Evolutionary Psychology in Understanding the Representation of Women in Advertisements." *Psychology & Marketing, Wiley InterScience* 21 (8): 593–612.

Saad, G. 2007. The Evolutionary Basis of Consumption, 59–121; Saad, G., V. Griskevicious, J.M. Ackermanm, B.V.D. Bergh, and Y.J. Li. 2011. "Evolutionary Psychology in the Business Sciences." *Fundamental Motives and Business Decisions*. 17–35.

Saad, G. 2013. "Evolutionary Consumption." *Journal of Consumer Psychology* 23 (3): 351–71.

Saad, G, and E. Stenstrom. 2012. "Calories, Beauty, and Ovulation: The Effects of the Menstrual Cycle on Food and Appearance-Related Consumption." *Journal of Consumer Psychology* 22 (1):102–13.

Saad, G, and J.G. Vongas. 2009. "The Effect of Conspicuous Consumption on Men's Testosterone Levels." *Organizational Behavior and Human Decision Processes* 110 (2): 80–92.

Sachdev, P. 2022. "What Is the Halo Effect?" *WebMD.*

Sadler, P., and E. Woody 2003. "Is Who You Are Who You're Talking to ? Interpersonal Style and Complementarily in Mixed-Sex Interactions." *Journal of Personality and Social Psychology* 84 (1): 80.

Samuel, A. 2016. "Psychographics Are Just as Important for Marketers as Demographics"; An, J., H. Kwak, S.G. Jung, J. Salminen, and B.J. Jansen. 2018. "Customer Segmentation Using Online Platforms: Isolating Behavioral and Demographic Segments for Persona Creation Via Aggregated User Data." *Social Network Analysis and Mining* 8 (1): 54; Needle, F. 2015. "How to Create Detailed Buyer Personas for Your Business"; Buyer Persona Institute. 2022. Buyer Persona Research; Revella, Adele. 2017. "Meet Our Example Buyer Persona"; American Marketing Association, 2022; Semrush. 2020. "How to Create a Buyer Persona to Boost Your Marketing." *YouTube.*

Sandford, A. 2020. "Coronavirus: Half of Humanity on Lockdown in 90 Countries." *Euronews.*

Sanz–García, A., C. Gesteira, J. Sanz, and M.P. García–Vera. 2021. "Prevalence of Psychopathy in the General Adult Population: A Systematic Review and Meta–Analysis." *Frontiers in Psychology* 12: 1–12.

Saraiva, C. 2021. "Women Could Give $20 Trillion Boost to Economic Growth by 2050." *Bloomberg.Com.*

Schaefer, K., B. Fink, K. Grammer, P. Mitteroecker, P. Gunz, and F. L. Bookstein. 2006. "Female Appearance: Facial and Bodily Attractiveness as Shape." *Psychology Science* 48 (2): 187–204.

Schaefer, K., B. Fink, K. Grammer, P. Mitteroecker, P. Gunz, and F.L. Bookstein. 2006. "Female Appearance: Facial and Bodily Attractiveness as Shape." *Psychology Science* 48: 187–205.

Schinkoethe, L. 2022. "Activists Blocking Berlin's Roads Say They Aren't Here to Be Liked." *Euronews.*

Schneider and Associates. 2018. *Sentient Decision Science,* 19.

Schneider, J., and J. Hall. 2011. "Why Most Product Launches Fail." *Harvard Business Review.*

Ibid, 21–3.

Schultz, W. 1998. "Predictive Reward Signal of Dopamine Neurons." *Journal of Neurophysiology* 80 (1): 1–27.

Schwarz, N. 1990. *Feelings as Information: Informational and Motivational Functions of Affective States.* The Guilford Press; Schwarz, N., and G.L. Clore. 1983. "Mood, Misattribution, and Judgments of Well-Being: Informative and Directive Functions of Affective States." *Journal of Personality and Social Psychology* 45 (3): 513.

Schwarz, N. 2000. "Emotion, Cognition, and Decision Making." *Cognition & Emotion* 14 (4): 433–40; Shevchenko, Y., and A. Bröder. 2018. "The Effect of Mood on Integration of Information in a Multi-Attribute Decision Task." *Acta Psychologica (Amst).*

Schwarz, N., and G.L. Clore. 1983. "Mood, Misattribution, and Judgments of Well-being: Informative and Directive Functions of Affective States." *Journal of Personality and Social Psychology* 45 (3): 513; Wyer R.S., Jr, D.E. Carlston, and J. Hartwick. 1979. "The Role of Syllogistic Reasoning in Inferences Based Upon New and Old Information." *Robert S. Wyer, Jr., and Donald E. Carlston, Social Cognition, Inference, and Attribution (Hillsdale, NJ: Erlbaum)*: 221–74; Pham, M.T. 2004. "The Logic of Feeling." *Journal of Consumer Psychology* 14 (4): 360–69.

Schwieren, J., J. Barenberg, and S. Dutke. 2017. "The Testing Effect in the Psychology Classroom: A Meta-Analytic Perspective." *Psychology Learning and Teaching* 16 (2): 179–96.

Scott, S.B., G.K. Rhoades, S.M. Stanley, E.S. Allen, and H.J. Markman. 2013. "Reasons for Divorce and Recollections of Premarital Intervention: Implications for Improving Relationship Education." *Couple and Family Psychology: Research and Practice* 2 (2): 131–45.

Seales, R. 2017. "Let's Save Maya Angelou From Fake Quotes." *BBC.*

Segal, E. 2021. "Workplace Misconduct Cost US Businesses $20 Billion in Past Year." *Forbes.*

Selvaggi, G., and J. Bellringer. 2011. "Gender Reassignment Surgery: An Overview." *Nature Reviews Urology* 8 (5): 274–82; Akhavan, A.A., S. Sandhu, I. Ndem, and A.A. Ogunleye. 2021. "A Review of Gender Affirmation Surgery: What We Know, and What We Need to Know." *Surgery* 170 (1): 336–40; Digitale, E. 2022. "Better Mental Health Found Among Transgender People Who Started Hormones as Teens." *StanfordMedicine.*

Senthilingam, M. 2017. "Sexual Harassment: How It Stands Around the Globe." *CNN.*

Settimi, C. 2021. "The World's Highest-Paid Soccer Players 2021: Manchester United's Cristiano Ronaldo Reclaims Top Spot From PSG's Lionel Messi." *Forbes.*

Shatz, I. n.d. "Belief Bias: When People Rely on Beliefs Rather Than Logic." *Effectiviology.*

Shatz, I. n.d. "The Availability Cascade: How Information Spreads on a Large Scale." *Effectiviology.*

Shatz, I. n.d. "The Benjamin Franklin Effect: Build Rapport by Asking for Favors." *Effectiviology.*

Shatz, I. n.d. "The Contrast Effect: When Comparison Enhances Differences." *Effectiviology.*

Shatz, I. n.d."The Zero-Sum Bias: When People Think That Everything Is a Competition." *Effectiviology*.

Shead, S. 2022. "Venture Capitalists Invested More Money Than Ever Into Start-Ups Last Year." *CNBC*.

Sherwood, H. 2020. "300 Years on, Will Thousands of Women Burned as Witches Finally Get Justice?" *The Guardian*.

Shorrock, A., R. Lluberas, and J. Davies. 2022. "Global Wealth Report." *Credit Suisse*.

Shyamalan, M.N. 2016. *Split*. Universal Pictures.

Sics, A. 2023. "British Stereotypes That We Won't Even try to Deny." *CultureTrip*.

Sierminska, E. 2017. "Wealth and Gender in Europe." *OP Europa, European Commission, Directorate-General for Justice and Consumers*; Scheele, C. 2021. Publication. *Gender Equality Index 2021. European Institute for Gender Equality*.

Sierminska, E., and A. Girshina. 2017. "Wealth and Gender in Europe." 39. *Publications Office of the EU. European Commission — Directorate-General for Justice*; Madgavkar, A., J. Manyika, M. Krishnan, K. Ellingrud, L. Yee, J. Woetzel, M. Chui, V. Hunt, et al. 2019. "The Future of Women at Work Transitions in the Age of Automation." 08. *Mckinsey*.

Singh, M. 2022. "The Feminist Sexual Ethics Project." *Bonded Labor | The Feminist Sexual Ethics Project | Brandeis University*.

Skowronski, J.J., W.R. Walker, D.X. Henderson, and G.D. Bond. 2014. "Chapter Three—The Fading Affect Bias: Its History, Its Implications, and Its Future," In *Advances in Experimental Social Psychology*, edited by J.M. Olson, and M.P. Zanna. 163–218. Academic Press.

Sky History. n.d."Edith Wilson, America's First (Acting) Female President." *Sky History*.

Slone, L.K., and C.M. Sandhofer. 2017. "Consider the Category: The Effect of Spacing Depends on Individual Learning Histories." *Journal of Experimental Child Psychology* 159: 34–49.

Smith, A. 1776. An Inquiry Into the Nature and Causes of the Wealth of Nations. 1st ed. Edited by W. Strahan and T. Cadell. London: W. Strahan and T. Cadell.

Smith, T.W. 2016. *The Book of Human Emotions*. Welcome Collection.

Smithsonian National Museum of Natural History. 2022. "Survival of the Adaptable."

Sohn, R. 2021. "Human Life Span May Have an 'Absolute Limit' of 150 Years." *Live Science*; Pyrkov, T.V., K. Avchaciov, E. Andrei, L.I. Tarkhov, G.A.V. Menshikov, and P.O. Fedichev. 2021. "Longitudinal Analysis of Blood Markers Reveals Progressive Loss of Resilience and Predicts Human Lifespan Limit." *Nature Communications* 12 (1): 2765.

Song, Y., W.M. Hur, and M. Kim. 2012. "Brand Trust and Affect in the Luxury Brand-Customer Relationship." *Social Behavior and Personality: An International Journal* 40 (2): 331–8; Lassoued, R., and J.E. Hobbs. 2015. "Consumer Confidence in Credence Attributes: The Role of Brand Trust." *Food Policy* 52: 99–107; Huang, L., M. Wang, Z. Chen, B. Deng, and W. Huang. 2020. "Brand Image and Customer Loyalty: Transmitting Roles of Cognitive and Affective Brand Trust." *Social Behavior and Personality: An International Journal* 48 (5): 1–12.

Soroka, S., P. Fournier, and L. Nir. 2019. "Cross–National Evidence of a Negativity Bias in Psychophysiological Reactions to News." *Proceedings of the National Academy of Sciences* 116 (38): 18888–92.

Sorokowski, P., A. Sorokowska, D. Danel, M.L. Mberira, and L. Pokrywka. 2012. "The Second to Fourth Digit Ratio and Age at First Marriage in Semi-Nomadic People From Namibia." *Archives of Sexual Behavior* 41 (3): 703–10.

Spiegelhalter, D. 2015. "Is 10% of the Population Really Gay?" *The Guardian*.

Stanton, S. J. 2016a. "The Role of Testosterone and Estrogen in Consumer Behavior and Social and Economic Decision Making: A Review." *Hormones and Behavior* 92: 155–63.

Ibid; Durante, K. M., and Griskevicius, V. 2016. "Evolution and Consumer Behavior." *Current Opinion in Psychology* 10: 27–32.

Stanton, S.J. 2017. "The Role of Testosterone and Estrogen in Consumer Behavior and Social and Economic Decision Making: A Review." *Hormones and Behavior*.

Starling, E.H. 1905. "The Croonian Lectures on the Chemical Correlation of the Functions of the Body." *Delivered Before the Royal College of Physics of London:Women's Printing Society*; Tata, J.R. 2005. "One Hundred Years of Hormones." *EMBO Reports* 6 (6): 490–96.

Stenstrom, E., G. Saad, M.V. Nepomuceno, and Z. Mendenhall. 2011. "Testosterone and Domain-specific Risk: Digit Ratios (2D:4D and rel2) as Predictors of Recreational, Financial, and Social Risk-taking Behaviors." *Personality and Individual Differences* 51 (4): 412–16.

Sterling, K. 2014. "Man the Hunter, Woman the Gatherer? The Impact of Gender Studies on Hunter-Gatherer Research (A Retrospective)." In *The Oxford Handbook of the Archaeology and Anthropology of Hunter-Gatherers*, edited by, V. Cummings, P. Jordan, and M. Zvelebil. Oxford University Press; Reyes-García, V., I. Díaz–Reviriego, R. Duda, A. Fernández-Llamazares, and S. Gallois. 2020. "Hunting Otherwise". *Human Nature* 31 (3): 203–221; Venkataraman, V. 2021. "Women were Successful Big Game Hunters, Challenging Beliefs about Ancient Gender Roles." *University of Calgary.*

Strack, F., L.L. Martin, and S. Stepper. 1988. "Inhibiting and Facilitating Conditions of the Human Smile: A Non-Obtrusive Test of the Facial

Feedback Hypothesis." *Journal of Personality and Social Psychology* 54 (5): 768.

Strategy Analytics. 2021. "Half the World Owns a Smartphone"; Business Wire. 2021. "Strategy Analytics: Half the World Owns a Smartphone"; United Nations. 2023. "World Population Day."

Strohminger, N., J. Knobe and G. Newman. 2017. "The True Self: A Psychological Concept Distinct From the Self." *Perspectives on Psychological Science* 12 (4): 551–60.

Stulp, G., A.P. Buunk, S. Verhulst, and T.V. Pollet. 2012. "High and Mighty: Height Increases Authority in Professional Refereeing." *Evolutionary Psychology* 10 (3): 588–601.

Stulp, G., L. Barret, F.C. Tropf and M. Mills. 2015. "Does Natural Selection Favour Taller Stature among the Tallest People on Earth?" *The Royal Society— Biological Sciences* 282 (1806): 1–8; Enserink, M. 2015. "Did Natural Selection Make the Dutch the Tallest People on the Planet? New Study Shows that Taller Men in the Netherlands Tend to Have More Children." *Science. American as sociation for the Advancement of Science.*

Sudai, M. 2017. "The Testosterone Rule-Constructing Fairness in Professional Sport." *Journal of Law and the Biosciences* 4 (1): 181–193.

Sundie, J. M., D.T. Kenrick, V. Griskevicius, J.M. Tybur, K.D. Vohs, and D.J. Beal. 2011. "Peacocks, Porsches, and Thorstein Veblen: Conspicuous Consumption as a Sexual Signaling System." *Journal of Personality and Social Psychology* 100 (4): 664–80.

Sutherlin, M. 2022. "Big Take: India's Economy at Risk by Exodus of Women From Workforce." *Bloomberg.Com.*

Svenson, O. 2008. "Decisions Among Time Saving Options: When Intuition Is Strong and Wrong." *Acta Psychologica* 127 (2): 501–509.

Swant, M. 2020. "The World's Most Valuable Brands." *Forbes.*

Swire-Thompson B, J. DeGutis, D. Lazer. 2020. "Searching for The Backfire Effect: Measurement and Design Considerations." *Journal of Applied Research in Memory and Cognition.* 9 (3): 286–299.

Symons, D. 1979. *The Evolution of Human Sexuality.* New York, NY: Oxford University Press; Williams, G.C. 1975. "Sex and Evolution." *Monogr Popul Biol* (8): 3–200; Buss, D. 2019. *Evolutionary Psychology: The New Science of the Mind.* Oxfordshire: Routledge.

Tachypsychia. n.d. "APA Dictionary of Psychology."

Takarangi, M.K.T., D. Strange, A.E. Shortland, and H.E. James. 2013. "Source Confusion Influences the Effectiveness of The Autobiographical IAT." *Psychonomic Bulletin & Review* 20 (6): 1232–38.

Tatchell, P. 2017. "Don't Fall for the Myth That It's 50 Years since We Decriminalized Homosexuality." *The Guardian.*

Tepper, B.J. 2000. "Consequences of Abusive Supervision." *The Academy of Management Journal* 43 (2): 178–190.

The American College of Obstetricians and Gynaecologists. 2022. "Having a Baby After Age 35: How Aging Affects Fertility and Pregnancy."

The Associated Press. 2021. "First Openly Transgender Olympians Are Competing in to kyo." *NBCNews.*

The Bank of Korea. 2022. "South Korea Population Data—2024 Forecast—1960–2022 Historical—Chart." *Trading Economics—The Bank of Korea.*

The BE Hub. 2023. "Disposition Effect." BehavioralEconomics.com.

The BE Hub. 2023. "Endowment Effect." BehavioralEconomics.com.

The BE Hub. 2023 "Less-Is-Better Effect." BehavioralEconomics.com.

The BE Hub. 2023. "Peak-end Rule." BehavioralEconomics.com.

The BE Hub. 2023. "Present Bias." BehavioralEconomics.com.

The Bible. "2:15–17." *BibleHub.*

The Bible. "Corinthians 14:34." *Bible Hub.*

The Bible. "Esther 2:14." *BibleHub.*

The Decision Lab. n.d. "Why do We Prefer Options We Know?"

The Decision Lab. 2021a. "Lag Effect."

The Decision Lab. 2021b. "Law of the Instrument."

The Decision Lab. 2021c. "Leveling and Sharpening."

The Decision Lab. 2021d. "Restraint Bias."

The Decision Lab. 2021e. "Salience Bias."

The Decision Lab. 2021f. "Why do We Believe Our Horoscopes?"

The Decision Lab. 2021g. "Why do We Feel More Strongly About one Option After a Third one Is Added?"

The Decision Lab. 2021h. "Why do We Think the Past Is Better Than the Future?"

The Decision Lab. 2021i. "Zero Risk Bias."

The Editors of Encyclopaedia Britannica. n.d. "Renin-Angiotensin System." *Encyclopedia Britannica.*

The Editors of Encyclopaedia Britannica. n.d. "Uranus." *Encyclopedia Britannica.*

The Editors of Encyclopaedia Britannica. n.d. "Weber's law." *Encyclopedia Britannica.*

The Founder Institute. 2023. "17 Founder Institute Portfolio Companies Helping Meet the 17 UN Sustainable Development Goals."

The Open University. 2022. "How FMRI Works"; Heeger, D.J., and D. Ress. 2002. "What Does fMRI Tell Us About Neuronal Activity?" *Nature Reviews Neuroscience* 3 (2): 142–151; Karmarkar, U.R., C. Yoon, and H. Plassmann. 2015. "Marketers Should Pay Attention to fMRI."

The U.S. Department of Health and Human Services. 2016. "Health, United States, 2016"; Endocrine Society. 2022. "The Essential Guide to Your Hormones." *Endocrine.org.*

The University of Queensland. "Corpus Callosum"; National Institute of Neurological Disorder and Stroke. "Brain Basics: Know Your Brain"; Johns Hopkins Medicine. "Brain Anatomy and How the Brain Works"; Anderson, A. 2022. "Brainstem: What to Know." *WebMD;* Basinger, H., and J.P. Hogg. 2022. "*Neuroanatomy, Brainstem."* StatPearls Publishing; Sukel. 2018. "Beyond Emotion: Understanding the Amygdala's Role in Memory." *Dana Foundation. "News & Insights"*; Cleveland Clinic. "Pituitary Gland"; Barrow Neurological Institute. "About the Pituitary Gland"; Cleveland Clinic. "Hypothalamus"; Seladi-Schulman, J. 2022. "Hypothalamus Overview." Healthline; Schiller, F. 1997. "The Cerebral Ventricles: From Soul to Sink." *Archives of Neurology* 54 (9): 1158–1162; Scelsi, C. L., T.A. Rahim, J.A. Morris, G.J. Kramer, B.C. Gilbert and S.E. Forseen. 2020. "The Lateral Ventricles: A Detailed Review of Anatomy, Development, and Anatomic Variations." *AJNR American Journal of Neuroradiology* 41 (4): 566–572; Shahid, S. 2022. "Corpus Callosum." *Ken Hub;* The University of Queensland. "Corpus Callosum"; Healthline Editorial Team. 2018. "Fourth Ventricle." *Healthline*; to rrico, T. J, and S. Munakomi. 2019. "*Neuroanatomy, Thalamus."* In: Gummadavelli, A., and Blumenfeld, H. StatPearls "Thalamus"; Leopold, C. 2023. "Everything You Need to Know About the Cerebellum." *Medical News to day*; Khasawneh, A.H., R.J. Garling, and C.A. Harris. 2018. "Cerebrospinal Fluid Circulation: What Do We Know and How do We Know It?" *Brain Circulation* 4 (1): 14–18.

The White House.n.d. "African Americans Under the Fourteenth and Fifteenth Amendments to the American Constitution." *whitehouse.gov.*

The White House. n.d. "Nineteenth Amendment of the US Constitution—Women's Right to Vote." *whitehouse.gov.*

The World Bank. 2021. "Population, to tal – Colombia." *World Bank Open Data.*

Therapeutic Pathways. 2021. "How Many People Are Diagnosed with Autism in the U.S." *Therapeutic Pathways;* Center For Disease Control and Prevention. 2022. "Data & Statistics on Autism Spectrum Disorder." *Centers for Disease Control and Prevention.*

Thompson, J.A., and C. Aukofer. 2011. *Why We Believe in God(s): A Concise Guide to the Science of Faith.* Charlottesville, VA: Pitchstone Pub.

Time Magazine. 2023. "Greta Thunberg: Time's Person of the Year 2019." *Time.*

Ting, C., and S. Xiaomin. 2016. "Shared Information Bias in Group Decision-Making: Based on Hidden Profile Paradigm." *Advances in Psychological Science* 24 (1): 132–142.

Todd, J.W, and H. Scarborough. 2022. "Medicine – Surgery, Procedures and Techniques." *Britannica.*

Tooby, J., and L. Cosmides. 1990. "The Past Explains the Present: Emotional Adaptations and the Structure of Ancestral Environments." *Ethology and Sociobiology* 11 (4–5): 375–424; Wilson, D.S. 1994. "Adaptive Genetic

Variation and Human Evolutionary Psychology." *Ethology and Sociobiology* 15(4): 219–235; Buss, D. 2019. *Evolutionary Psychology: The New Science of the Mind.*1733. 6th ed. New York. NY: Routledge Taylor Francis Group.

Topping, A. 2021. "Campaigners Urge Bosses to Stop as king Job Applicants for Salary History." *The Guardian.*

Toynbee, A.J., and D.C. Somervell. 1987. *A Study of History Vol. 2.* Oxford: Oxford University Press; Dussen, J.V.D. 2016. "Toynbee and His Critics." *Studies on Collingwood, History and Civilization:*169–93; Kemp, L. 2019. "Are We on the Road to Civilization Collapse?" *BBC Future*; Spinney, L. 2020. "Panicking About Societal Collapse? Plunder the Bookshelves." *Nature News.*

Tråvén, M. 2016. "Voicing the Third Gender-The Castrato Voice and the Stigma of Emasculation in Eighteenth-century Society." Études Épistémè. Revue de littérature et de civilisation (XVIe-XVIIIe siècles) 29.

Trivers, R. 1985. *Social Evolution.* Menlo Park, CA: Benjamin; Cummings; Buss, D. 2019. *Evolutionary Psychology: The New Science of the Mind.* Oxfordshire: Routledge.

Trogen, B., and A. Caplan. 2021. "Risk Compensation and COVID-19 Vaccines." *Annals of Internal Medicine* 174 (6): 858–859.

Trotter, W. 1908. "Herd Instinct and Its Bearing on the Psychology of Civilized Man." *The Sociological Review* 1 (3): 227–248. Trujillo, L.T., J.M. Jankowitsch, and J.H. Langlois. 2014. "Beauty Is in the Ease of the Beholding: A Neurophysiological Test of the Averageness Theory of Facial Attractiveness." *Cognitive, Affective, & Behavioral Neuroscience* 14: 1061–1076.

Tu, M.H., E.K. Gilbert, and J.E. Bono. 2022. "Is Beauty More than Skin Deep? Attractiveness, Power, and Nonverbal Presence in Evaluations of Hireability." *Personnel Psychology* 75 (1):119–146.

Tversky, A., and D. Kahneman. 1974. "Judgment Under Uncertainty: Heuristics and Biases." *Science* 185(4157): 1124–31; Kahneman, D., P. Slovic and A. Tversky. 1982. "Judgment Under Uncertainty." *Cambridge University Press.*

Tversky, A., and D. Kahneman. 1981. "The Framing of Decisions and the Psychology of Choice." *Science* 211 (4481): 453–458.

Tybur, J. M., D. Lieberman, and V. Griskevicius. 2009. "Microbes, Mating, and Morality: Individual Differences in Three Functional Domains of Disgust." *Journal of Personality and Social Psychology* 97 (1): 103–122.

Tybur, J.M., D. Lieberman, R. Kurzban, and P. DeScioli. 2013. "Disgust: Evolved Function and Structure." *Psychological Review* 120 (1): 65–84; Al-Shawaf, L., D.M.G. Lewis, and D. Buss. 2018. "Sex Differences in Disgust: Why Are Women More Easily Disgusted Than Men?" *Emotion Review* 10 (2):149–160; Fleischman, D.S. 2014. "Women's Disgust Adaptations." Springer; Buss, D. 2019. *Evolutionary Psychology: The New Science of the Mind.* New York, NY: Taylor and Francis.

U.K. Ministry of Justice. "Royal Pardon for WW2 Code-Breaker Dr. Alan Turing." *GOV.UK.*

UK Parliament. 2023. "Marriage (Same Sex Couples) Act 2013." *UK Parliament.*

UK Parliament. 2023. "Sexual Offences Act 1967." *UK Parliament.*

UNICEF. 2018. "7 Fast Facts About to ilets." *UNICEF.*

United Nations. n.d. "17 Goals." *Department of Economic and Social Affairs.*

United Nations. 1948. "Universal Declarations of Human Rights." *UN.Org*; The Danish Institute For Human Rights. 2021. "Signatories for Universal Declaration of Human Rights." *SDG.Humanrights.*

United Nations. 2019. "Global Study on Homicide"; Shaw, J. 2019. "Why Are We Not Outraged That Prisons Are Filled With Men?"

United Nations. 2022. "The Sustainable Development Agenda–United Nations Sustainable Development."

United States Holocaust Museum. 2022. "Life in Shadows: Hidden Children and the Holocaust."

Universiteit Leiden. 2022. "Michiel Van Groesen—Professor Maritime History." *Leiden University.*

University of California. n.d. "Unconscious Bias Training." *University of California.*

University of Sheffield. n.d. "How Researchers Are Challenging Complex Japanese Stereotypes."

UserTesting. 2019. "The Curse of Knowledge: How It Impacts you, and What to Do About It."

USIDHR. 2021. "How Did Human Rights Come about? A Brief History Overtime." *US Institute of Diplomacy and Human Rights.*

Vaish, A., T. Grossmann, and A. Woodward. 2008. "Not All Emotions Are Created Equal: The Negativity Bias in Social-Emotional Development." *Psychological Bulletin* 134 (3): 383–403.

Vasari, G., and G. Christofano. 1555. "The Mutilation of Uranus." *Useum.org.*

Venkataraman, V. 2021. "Women were Successful Big Game Hunters, Challenging Beliefs about Ancient Gender Roles." *University of Calgary.*

Vipond, T. "Anchoring Bias." *CFI.*

Virgin J.C.E., and R.M. Sapolsky. 1997. "Styles of Male Social Behavior and Their Endocrine Correlates Among Low-Ranking Baboons." *American Journal of Primatology* 42 (1): 25–39; Booth, A., D.A. Granger, A. Mazur, and K.T. Kivlighan. 2006. "Testosterone and Social Behavior." *Social forces* 85 (1): 167–191.

Vitti, A. 2014. *Womancode: Perfect Your Cycle, Amplify Your Fertility, Supercharge Your Sex Drive and Become a Power Source*: HarperOne; Bhuvaneswari, K., P. Rabindran, and B. Bharadwaj. 2019. "Prevalence of Premenstrual Syndrome and Its Impact on Quality of Life Among Selected College Students in Puducherry." *The National Medical Journal of India* 32 (1): 17–9; Laurence,

E., and J. Whitfield. 2022. "Cycle Syncing: Everything You Need to Know." *Forbes*.

Vlemincx, E., J.L. Abelson, P.M. Lehrer, P.W. Davenport, I.V.Diest, and O.V.D. Bergh. 2013. "Respiratory Variability and Sighing: A Psychophysiological Reset Model." *Biological Psychology* 93 (1): 24–32; Grassmann, M., E. Vlemincx, A.V. Leupoldt, J.M. Mittelstädt, and O.V.D. Bergh. 2016. "Respiratory Changes in Response to Cognitive Load: A Systematic Review." *Neural Plasticity*; Young, M.S., K. Brookhuis, C.D. Wickens, and P.A. Hancock. 2015. "State of Science: Mental Workload in Ergonomics." *Ergonomics* 58 (1): 1–17; Bach, D.R., S. Gerster, A. Tzovara, and G. Castegnetti. 2016. "A Linear Model for Event-Related Respiration Responses." *Journal of Neuroscience Methods* 270: 147–155.

Vonasch, A.J., T. Reynolds, B.M. Winegard, and R.F. Baumeister. 2017. "Death Before Dishonor: Incurring Costs to Protect Moral Reputation". *Social Psychological and Personality Science* 9 (5): 604–613.

Wahba, P. 2021. "Only 19: The Lack of Black CEOS in the History of the Fortune 500." *Fortune*.

Wall, T. 2012. "Amazonian Tribal Warfare Sheds Light on Modern Violence, Says MU Anthropologist." *MU News Bureau*.

Wallas, G. 1914. "Disposition andEnvironment"; Wallas, G. 1914. "Instinct and Intelligence."

Walsh, F. 2010. "Index Finger Length Prostate Cancer Clue." *BBC*.

Walsh, J.P. 1988. "Selectivity and Selective Perception: an Investigation of Managers' Belief Structures and Information Processing." *Academy of Management Journal* 31 (4): 873–896.

Wang, S. 2010. "The Brain Is an Ever-Changing Biological Organ." Essay. In *The Neuroscience of Everyday Life*. 19. The Great Courses. Chantilly, Virginia: The Teaching Company.

Wang, Y., and V. Griskevicius. 2014. "Conspicuous Consumption, Relationships, and Rivals: Women's Luxury Products as Signals to Other Women." *Journal of Consumer Research* 40 (5): 834–854.

Wang, Y., W. Zhu, M. Xiao, Q. Zhang, Y. Zhao, H. Zhang, 2018. "Hostile Attribution Bias Mediates the Relationship Between Structural Variations in the Left Middle Frontal Gyrus and Trait Angry Rumination." *Frontiers in Psychology* 9.

Wardle, S.G., S. Paranjape, J. Taubert, and C.I. Baker. 2022. "Illusory Faces Are More Likely to be Perceived as Male than Female." *Proceedings of the National Academy of Sciences* 119 (5): e2117413119.

Watson, N.V. 2001. "Sex Differences in Throwing: Monkeys having a Fling." *Trends in Cognitive Science* 5: 98–99.

Wells, G. L, and A.L. Bradfield. 1998. Good, You Identified the Suspect: Feedback to Eyewitnesses Distorts their Reports of the Witnessing Experience." *Journal of Applied Psychology* 83 (3): 360.

Wenzel, K., S. Schindler, and M.A. Reinhard. 2017. "General Belief in a Just World Is Positively as sociated with Dishonest Behavior." *Frontiers in Psychology* 8.

Whillans, A. V., A.H. Jordan, and F.S. Chen. 2020. "The Upside to Feeling Worse Than Average (WTA): A Conceptual Framework to Understand When, How, and for Whom WTA Beliefs Have Long-Term Benefits." *Front Psychol* 11: 642.

Whitboirne, K. 2023. "Should You Bank You r Baby's Cord Blood?" *Webmd.com.*

White, R. E., S. Thornhill, and E. Hampson. 2006. "Entrepreneurs and Evolutionary Biology: The Relationship Between Testosterone and New Venture Creation." *Organization Behavior and Human Decision Processes* 100: 21–34.

WHO. 2023. "Sanitation."

Williams, G.C. 1957. "Pleiotropy, Natural Selection, and The Evolution of Senescence." *Evolution* 11: 398–411; Buss, D. 2015. *Evolutionary Psychology: The New Science of the Mind*, 5th ed. Psychology Press.

Williams, G.C., and R.M. Nesse. 1991. "The Dawn of Darwinian Medicine." *The Quarterly Review of Biology* 66 (1): 1–22; Kruger, D.J., and R.M. Nesse. 2006. "An Evolutionary Life-History Framework for Understanding Sex Differences in Human Mortality Rates." *Human Nature* 17 (1): 74–97

Williams, J. B., D. Popp, K.A. Kobak, and M.J. Detke. 2012. "P–640 – The Power of Expectation Bias." *European Psychiatry* 27: 1.

Wilson, G.D. 1983. "Finger-length as an Index of as sertiveness in Women." *Personality and Individual Differences* 4 (1): 111–112.

Wilson, J. 2014. "What You r IQ Score Doesn't Tell You." *CNN Health.*

Wilson, J.D., and Roehrborn, C. 1999. "Long-Term Consequences of Castration in Men: Lessons From the Skoptzy and the Eunuchs of the Chinese and Ottoman Courts." *The Journal of Clinical Endocrinology and Metabolism* 84 (12): 4324–4331.

Wilson, R.C. 2023. "Homo Economicus: Meaning, Overview, and Criticisms." *Investopedia.*

Wisner Baum Law. 2021 "Human Factors in Aviation."

Wlodarski, R., J. Manning, and R.I.M. Dunbar. 2015. "Stay or Stray? Evidence for Alternative Mating Strategy Phenotypes in Both Men and Women." *Biology Letters* 11 (2).

Wong, H.K., I.D. Stephen, and D.R.T. Keeble. 2020. "The Own-Race Bias for Face Recognition in a Multiracial Society." *Frontiers in Psychology* 11: 208.

Wood, S.P. 2014. "Bad News: Negative Headlines Get Much More Attention."*Adweek.*

World Bank Group. 2022. "Population, to tal."

World Health Organization. 2023. "Tobacco-Key Facts."

World Population Review. 2021. "Gender Equality by Country 2021."

World Prison Brief. 2018. "Prison Population to tal."

Wu, Y., C. Eisenegger, N. Sivanathan, M.J. Crockett and L. Clark. 2017. "The Role of Social Status and Testosterone in Human Conspicuous Consumption." *Psychoneuroendocrinology. Elsevier.*72–79.

Xing, M., Z. Niu, and T. Liu. 2021. "The Part-list Cuing Effect in Working Memory: The Influence of Task Presentation Mode." *Acta Psychologica* 219.

Immordino-Yang, M.H., A. McColl, H. Damasio, and A. Damasio. 2009. "Neural Correlates of Admiration and Compassion." Proceedings of the National Academy of Sciences 106 (19): 8021–8026. https://doi. org/10.1073/pnas.0810363106.

Yang, K.C., C.H. Huang, C. Yang, and C.W. Tsai. 2015. "Applying Social Marketing Theory to Develop Retargeting and Social Networking Advertising Website." *2015 IEEE International Conference on Industrial Engineering and Engineering Management (IEEM)*, December: 1845–49.

Yonkers, K.A., P.M. O' Brien, S., and Eriksson, E. 2008. "Premenstrual Syndrome." *The Lancet* 371 (9619): 1200–1210.

Zak, P.J., R. Kurzban, and W.T. Matzner. 2004. "The Neurobiology of Trust." *Annals of the New York Academy of Sciences* 1032 (1): 224227; Kosfeld, M., M. Heinrichs, P.J. Zak, U. Fischbacher, and E. Fehr. 2005. "Oxytocin Increases Trust in Humans." *Nature* 435 (7042): 673–676; Kusev, P., H. Purser, R. Heilman, A.J. Cooke, P.V. Schaik, V. Baranova, et al. 2017. "Understanding Risky Behavior: The Influence of Cognitive, Emotional and Hormonal Factors on Decision-making Under Risk." *Frontiers in Psychology* 8.

Zak, P.J., R. Kurzban, S. Ahmadi, R.S. Swerdloff, Park, J., Efremidze, L., Redwine, K., Morgan, K., and Matzner, W. 2009. "Testosterone Administration Decreases Generosity in the Ultimatum Game." *PLOS ONE* 4 (12): e8330; Saad, G., and E. Stenstrom. 2012. "Calories, Beauty, and Ovulation: The Effects of the Menstrual Cycle on Food and Appearance-Related Consumption." *Journal of Consumer Psychology 22* (1): 102–13.

Zauzmer W.J. 2019. "The Bible Was Used to Justify Slavery." *The Washington Post*; Siliezar, J. 2019. "Slavery Alongside Christianity." *The Harvard Gazette*; Buchholz, K. 2019. "The Countries Most Active in the Trans-Atlantic Slave Trade." *Statista.*

Zeng, M. 2018. *Four Fundamental Problems for Marketing Strategy, Marketing Analytics.* King's College London.

Zheng, Z., and M.J. Cohn. 2011. "Developmental Basis of Sexually Dimorphic Digit Ratios." *Proceedings of the National Academy of Sciences* 108 (39): 16289–16294; Jeevanandam, S., and P.K. Muthu. 2016. "2D:4D Ratio and Its Implications in Medicine." *Journal of Clinical and Diagnostic Research* 10 (12): Cm01–cm03.

Ziegler, A., A. Koch, K. Krockenberger and A. Großhennig. 2012. "Personalized Medicine Using DNA Biomarkers: AReview." *Human Genetics* 131 (10): 1627–1638; Selleck, M.J., M. Senthil, and N.R. Wall. 2017. "Making Meaningful Clinical Use of Biomarkers." *Biomark Insights 12*; Lin, Y., F. Qian, L. Shen, F. Chen, J. Chen and B. Shen. 2019. "Computer-Aided Biomarker Discovery for Precision Medicine: Data Resources, Models and Applications." *Briefings in Bioinformatics* 20 (3): 952–975.

Zilioli, S., and N.V. Watson. 2014. "Testosterone Across Successive Competitions: Evidence for a 'Winner Effect' in Humans?" *Psychoneuroendocrinology* 47: 1–9.

Zimprich, D., and T. Wolf. 2018. "Leveling up the Analysis of the Reminiscence Bump in Autobiographical Memory: A New Approach Based on Multilevel Multinomial Models." *Memory and Cognition* 46 (7): 1178–1193.

ZIPPIA. 2019. "Casino Games Dealer Demographics and Statistics in the US."

Zippia. 2023. "Chief Executive Officer Demographics and Statistics in the US."

About the Author

Dr. Gill Merrill's PhD research is focused on consumer neuroscience decision making, and evolutionary psychology. She began her career in marketing, holding senior positions across Europe, North America, and South America. With over two decades of experience in senior positions, she has managed large teams and multimillion budgets in both start-ups and established companies.

Dr. Merrill's primary research interests include decision making, consumer behavior, business innovation, and brand creation. She has made significant contributions to the field through her research on the effects of hormones and biomarkers on consumer decision making, measured by advanced biosensors. Her work aims to advance the novel field of evolutionary marketing.

In addition to her professional achievements, Dr. Merrill lectures on marketing, consumer behavior, business strategy, entrepreneurship, and change management. She has inspired many students with her engaging teaching style and deep knowledge of the subject matter.

Her publications have been recognized for her contributions to the field. Her research bridges the gap between theoretical knowledge and practical application, providing valuable insights for businesses looking to innovate, become more equitable, and thrive in a competitive landscape.

She enjoys extensive cross-cultural research collaborations. Her passion for understanding human motivations and behaviors has driven her lifelong dedication to the study of human decision making. In her spare time, she enjoys sailing, golf, cooking, watching documentaries, and traveling.

Index

www.ingramcontent.com/pod-product-compliance
Lightning Source LLC
Chambersburg PA
CBHW061135220326
41599CB00025B/4235